Real World .NET Applications

BUDI KURNIAWAN

Apress™

Real World .NET Applications

Copyright ©2003 by Budi Kurniawan

ISBN (pbk): 1-59059-082-1

Printed and bound in the United States of America 12345678910

Trademarked names may appear in this book. Rather than use a trademark symbol with every occurrence of a trademarked name, we use the names only in an editorial fashion and to the benefit of the trademark owner, with no intention of infringement of the trademark.

Technical Reviewer: Alwi Wijaya

Editorial Directors: Dan Appleman, Gary Cornell, Simon Hayes, Martin Streicher, Karen Watterson, John Zukowski

Assistant Publisher: Grace Wong

Project Managers: Sofia Marchant, Laura Cheu

Copy Editor: Kim Wimpsett

Compositor: Diana Van Winkle, Van Winkle Design Group

Artists: Kurt Krames, Cara Brunk

Indexer: Valerie Perry

Cover Designer: Kurt Krames

Production Manager: Kari Brooks

Manufacturing Manager: Tom Debolski

Distributed to the book trade in the United States by Springer-Verlag New York, Inc., 175 Fifth Avenue, New York, NY, 10010 and outside the United States by Springer-Verlag GmbH & Co. KG, Tiergartenstr. 17, 69112 Heidelberg, Germany.

In the United States, phone 1-800-SPRINGER, email orders@springer-ny.com, or visit http://www.springer-ny.com.

Outside the United States, fax +49 6221 345229, email orders@springer.de, or visit http://www.springer.de.

For information on translations, please contact Apress directly at 2560 9th Street, Suite 219, Berkeley, CA 94710. Phone 510-549-5930, fax: 510-549-5939, email info@apress.com, or visit http://www.apress.com.

The information in this book is distributed on an "as is" basis, without warranty. Although every precaution has been taken in the preparation of this work, neither the author nor Apress shall have any liability to any person or entity with respect to any loss or damage caused or alleged to be caused directly or indirectly by the information contained in this work.

The source code for this book is available to readers at http://www.apress.com in the Downloads section. You will need to answer questions pertaining to this book in order to successfully download the code.

Contents at a Glance

Contents

About the Author

Budi Kurniawan is an IT consultant specializing in Internet and object-oriented programming, and he has taught both Java and Microsoft technologies. He is the author of *Internet Programming with Visual Basic* (Apress) and *Java for the Web with Servlets, JSP, and EJB* (New Riders), and he has published articles in more than ten publications.

Budi comes from a solid programming background, developing applications for small to multinational companies and selling software used by major organization such as Commerce One (NASDAQ: CMRC), Saudi Business Machine Ltd (www.sbm.com.sa), and Baxter Healthcare Corporation (www.baxter.com).

Budi has a Masters by Research degree in Electrical Engineering from Sydney University, Australia, and co-owns the Web site hosting company Monofrog (www.monofrog.com).

Acknowledgments

Many people contributed to the production of this book. Without them, this book would be much worse. Paul Karjo, a brilliant programmer, did the preliminary work of the applications in Chapters 3 and 5. I would like to thank him for his creativity and help. Maria Francisco, a graphic designer in Bali, created the images for Chapter 3. Thanks!

Alwi Wijaya, the technical editor for this book, not only reviewed all chapters and applications, but I also consulted him on technical problems many times. Liron Shapira tested all the applications and provided valuable feedback. A million thanks to Alwi and Liron.

I would also like to thank the other production members at Apress for their invaluable support: Sofia Marchant and Laura Cheu (project managers), Kari Brooks (production editor), Kim Wimpsett (copy editor), Dan Appleman (editorial director), and all the other folks who worked hard to make the publication of this book possible. Thank you.

Introduction

Welcome to *Real World .NET Applications*. This book presents six "real" medium-sized software projects that contain about 1,500 lines of code each—not simply toy applications that have little or no use. Each application matches (or is close to) commercial software. But the main purpose of the applications is to teach how to design and develop .NET applications. As such, each chapter gives the reader enough background information of the technologies used in the application. All chapters give sample code that explains the techniques before discussing the application. However, for reading convenience, the text is concise. Also, not surprisingly, you will see several popular design patterns that you may have used in other projects. I have tested all applications developed for this book with the .NET Framework versions 1.0 and 1.1.

Each chapter has the following general structure:

- An introduction to supporting theories/technologies to give you enough background knowledge to understand the application

- A simple application that illustrates relevant techniques and technologies

- A class diagram containing the project's classes and their relationships

- A detailed description of the types (classes, interfaces, and structures) used in the project

- A detailed description of each member of the types used in the project

Overview of Each Chapter

The following sections give an overview of each chapter.

Chapter 1: Creating a Custom Control: StyledTextArea

This chapter teaches you how to create Windows controls by extending the `System.Windows.Forms.Control` class, and it teaches you several aspects of Windows custom control programming. This chapter covers the following topics:

- Using Windows controls in general

- Drawing a control's Graphical User Interface (GUI)

- Capturing key presses

- Using delegates

- Creating custom events

- Understanding the Observer design pattern

- Understanding the Model-View-Controller (MVC) paradigm

- Creating carets

- Using the `System.Threading.Thread` class

Chapter 2: Building an XML Document Editor

This chapter discusses a Multiple Document Interface (MDI) application that can be used to edit Extensible Markup Language (XML) documents. This chapter covers the following topics:

- Introducing a brief theory of XML

- XML programming in the .NET Framework

- Understanding the Singleton design pattern

- Printing in the .NET Framework

- Using the XMLViewer component

Chapter 3: Writing Games

This chapter explains the theory of games in general and how to write the game Doggie (a Pac-Man clone). This chapter covers the following topics:

- Working with threads

- Creating a news ticker application

- Using a timer

- Understanding game theory

Chapter 4: Creating a UML Class Diagram Editor

This chapter teaches how to write a Unified Modeling Language (UML) class diagram editor to draw and edit class diagrams. This chapter covers the following topics:

- Basic and advanced drawing in the .NET Framework

- Creating a vector-based drawing application

- Understanding object serialization

- Understanding the Memento design pattern

- Introducing a brief theory of UML

Chapter 5: Developing an FTP Client Application

This chapter explains how to use sockets in a File Transfer Protocol (FTP) client application. This chapter covers the following topics:

- Networking with the .NET Framework in general

- Using sockets

- Using FTP

Chapter 6: Building an Online Store

This chapter explains ASP.NET and ADO.NET in general and uses them and other related technologies to develop an online store. This chapter covers the following topics:

- Using ASP.NET

- Using ADO.NET

- Using Web controls

- Configuring security

- Managing session state

Code Listings

You can download the code listings for all source files from the author's Web site at www.brainysoftware.com or from the Downloads section of the Apress Web site at www.apress.com. The zip file contains six directories, one for each chapter. Each directory has four subdirectories:

- The Project directory, which contains the source files for the application

- The Other directory, which contains the source files that are not part of the project

- The VSNET2002 directory, which contains the source files for use with Visual Studio .NET 2002

- The VSNET2003 directory, which contains the source files for use with Visual Studio .NET

CHAPTER 1

Creating a Custom Control: StyledTextArea

FOR WRITING WINDOWS applications, the .NET Framework class library provides the System.Windows.Forms namespace that contains, among others, classes that represent controls to use on your form. Most of these controls derive from the Control class; they range from the simple Label control to the sophisticated TreeView control and from the Button control that has a very simple graphical user interface (GUI) to the MonthCalendar control whose GUI is rich and complex.

For many, or maybe most, Windows applications, these standard controls are sufficient. They are ready to use and come with documented class members. However, numerous software projects require customized controls that you cannot find in the System.Windows.Forms namespace. These requirements could be purely technical or they could be for artistic purposes. For example, a project's specification might require using a control that can display the hierarchical structure of the elements in an Extensible Markup Language (XML) document, given the name of the XML file. Or, the client might demand that all buttons be round. An XML viewer control such as the one mentioned or a round button is unfortunately not available in any namespace in the .NET Framework class library.

Unavailability of certain controls in a software project specification does not mean the software cannot be delivered. It is just that it takes more time and effort to create such controls. However, understanding what is practically possible and what is technically impossible is vital before you start any coding.

This chapter shows how to create your own Windows control. The control you will develop in this chapter is called StyledTextArea. It is a control that can receive user input. It is much more complex than the TextBox control; it is comparable to the RichTextBox control. I came to realize that people would need a different kind of text area control when I could not find these important features in the RichTextBox control:

- An event that triggers when the user changes line or changes column. Having this kind of event enables you to display the position of the caret, just like in Microsoft Word or the Visual Studio .NET Integrated Development Environment (IDE).

- The ability to keep selected text highlighted after the control loses focus.

- The ability to display certain keywords in different colors automatically.

- Properties to change the text color, the selected text color, and the caret color.

- A section in the control that displays the line numbers.

- The feature to adjust how fast the caret flashes on and off.

NOTE *A* caret *is the blinking vertical line that indicates the character insertion point in a text-based control.*

However, the main objective of this project is not to write a replacement for the RichTextBox control. Rather, its purpose is to introduce the techniques for writing custom controls—not only text input controls but any kind of Windows control. For those needing this kind of control, you can use the code as the starting point.

In this project, I explain the complete process of developing a custom control. As such, I build everything from scratch and refrain from incorporating other existing controls. For example, the application includes two System.Windows.Forms.ScrollBar controls for providing the scrolling feature, rather than putting everything in a System.Windows.Forms.Panel control and using its AutoScroll property, which it inherits from System.Windows.Forms.ScrollableControl.

NOTE *Some techniques discussed in this chapter are useful not only for writing custom controls. Techniques such as capturing key presses and raising events help when programming Windows applications in general.*

The `StyledTextArea` control is similar to the text area in Notepad. At more than 1,500 lines of code, the project might look intimidating at first. However, if you follow along with this chapter, you will find that it is easy to write a Windows control thanks to the .NET Framework's full support of object-oriented programming features.

Overview of the Chapter

This chapter starts by discussing introductory topics you need to understand to write custom controls. It then provides the steps to create the application in the section "Implementing the Project."

More specifically, the following are the main sections in this chapter:

"Using the `Control` and `UserControl` Classes": This section describes the two members of the `System.Windows.Forms` namespace that you extend when writing a custom control. This section provides you with a general description of the two controls.

"Drawing the Graphical User Interface": This section explains how to draw the GUI part of a custom control. You will develop the `RoundButton` control, a simple button with a circular shape.

"Capturing Key Presses": This section looks at the different types of keys on a computer keyboard and discusses what happens when the user presses a key. It then explains how to capture a user key press and how your application can respond to a key press.

"Creating Events with Delegates and the Observer Design Pattern": This section explains how events work, discusses the Observer design pattern, and illustrates how to write a custom event in step-by-step instructions.

"Understanding the Model-View-Controller (MVC) Paradigm": This section explains the MVC paradigm used in many GUI controls. The `StyledTextArea` control is based on this model; therefore, understanding MVC is crucial.

"Implementing the Project": This section thoroughly explains the `StyledTextArea` control. It starts from the specification and the class diagram and then continues with a detailed discussion of each class and its members. At the end of this section, the "Using the StyledTextArea Control" subsection presents an application that uses this custom control.

Using the Control and UserControl Classes

You can find information about the Control and UserControl classes of the System.Windows.Forms namespace in the Reference/Class Library section of the .NET Framework Software Development Kit (SDK) documentation. You should be familiar with these two classes before you start coding your Windows custom control. You should, for example, know what methods and properties are available so that you do not end up writing your own while you could have used the existing ones. This section addresses some important points about the Control and UserControl classes.

The Control class is the central member of the System.Windows.Forms namespace. It is the direct or indirect parent class of Windows controls. The Form class, for example, also derives from the Control class. The Control class has properties, methods, and events that make programming Windows controls easy.

For starters, the Control class has more than 70 properties. There are properties that deal with its appearance and dimension (BackColor, ForeColor, Font, Visible, Width, Size, Location, Left, Top, Dock), properties to manage other controls as child controls (HasChildren, Controls), a property that enables the control to reference its container (Parent), and so on.

It also has useful methods you use in child classes, such as Focus, Hide, Dispose, GetNextControl, and Show. Additionally, it has useful methods that you only use when creating your own controls by extending the Control class, such as Invalidate, Update, ProcessDialogKey, ProcessDialogChar, and so on.

Last but not least, there are events that trigger automatically when an action is carried out upon that control: Click, DoubleClick, MouseOver, MouseDown, MouseUp, Resize, and so on. The Paint event triggers whenever the control needs to be repainted.

NOTE *In the .NET Framework class library, events in a class are triggered by the OnXXX methods in that class. For example, the OnClick method raises the Click event. The OnPaint method triggers the Paint event, and so on. You can override these OnXXX methods to change their behaviors in subclasses. You will learn about this more in the "Creating Events with Delegates and the Observer Design Pattern" section. For now, you will override the OnPaint method of the Control class to provide a GUI for your control.*

The UserControl class derives directly from the Control class and provides several additional members. You will extend this class in the StyledTextArea control. When extending the Control or UserControl classes, you are responsible for providing and managing your own GUI. This brings us to the next topic, managing the GUI.

TIP *When creating a custom Windows control, you do not always extend the* Control *or* UserControl *class directly. In many circumstances, you may want to extend other control classes. For instance, to create a text box that accepts numbers only, it is easier to extend the* TextBox *class. Also, even when you extend the* Control *or* UserControl *class, you still can incorporate other controls in your custom control.*

Drawing the Graphical User Interface

As previously mentioned, you need to draw your own user interface when you create a custom control by inheriting the Control or UserControl class. Not only are you responsible for drawing the GUI the first time the control is displayed, you must also repaint it when the control is resized, when the control is restored after being minimized, and whenever the GUI needs to repainted. The way to do this is by overriding the OnPaint method in your class:

```
Protected Overrides Sub OnPaint(ByVal e As PaintEventArgs)
  . . .
End Sub
```

The OnPaint method is automatically called when the control needs to be repainted. This method receives a System.Windows.Forms.PaintEventArgs object from which you can obtain a reference to the System.Drawing.Graphics object of the control. Use this Graphics object to draw your GUI.

Listing 1-1 shows how easy it is to use the OnPaint method to draw your GUI. It shows the code for a simple custom control called RoundButton, which is a round button that has all the properties, methods, and events of the Control class. However, it has its own GUI, which is a circle with some text. Even though the class only has 14 lines, it functions as a proper control. For instance, you can capture the Click event so that you can have some code execute when a user clicks it.

Listing 1-1. A Simple Custom Control That Paints Its Own GUI

```
Imports System.Windows.Forms
Imports System.Drawing

Public Class RoundButton : Inherits UserControl
  Protected Overrides Sub OnPaint(ByVal e As PaintEventArgs)
    Dim graphics As Graphics = e.Graphics
    Dim pen As New Pen(Color.BlueViolet)
    Dim area As New Rectangle(0, 0, 90, 90)
    graphics.DrawEllipse(pen, area)
    ' draw the value of the Text property
    Dim font As New Font("Times New Roman", 10)
    Dim brush As Brush = New SolidBrush(Color.Black)
    graphics.DrawString(Me.Text, font, brush, 10, 35)
  End Sub
End Class
```

The RoundButton class extends the UserControl class and overrides its OnPaint method. In this method, you first obtain the Graphics object from the PaintEventArgs object. You then create a System.Drawing.Pen object and a System.Drawing.Rectangle object and pass them to the DrawEllipse method of the Graphics class. The result from calling the DrawEllipse method is a circle.

The second part of the OnPaint method in Listing 1-1 uses the DrawString method of the Graphics class to print the value of the Text property of this control.

NOTE *To compile the code in Listing 1-1, use the following command from the directory in which the* listing-01.01.vb *file resides:*

```
vbc /t:library /r:System.dll,System.Windows.Forms.dll,
System.Drawing.dll listing-01.01.vb /out:RoundButton.dll
```

(all on one line). The outcome of the compilation is a DLL file named RoundButton.dll.

After you compile the class, you can put it on a form just like you would a normal control. For example, Listing 1-2 shows a form that includes a RoundButton control.

Listing 1-2. Using the RoundButton *Control*

```
Imports System
Public Class MyForm : Inherits System.Windows.Forms.Form
  Private myButton As New RoundButton()
  Public Sub New()
    myButton.Location = New System.Drawing.Point(24, 24)
    myButton.Size = New System.Drawing.Size(100, 100)
    myButton.Text = "Show Magic"
    Me.Controls.Add(myButton)
    Me.Text = "Demonstrating Round Button"
  End Sub

  <STAThread()> Shared Sub Main()
    System.Windows.Forms.Application.Run(New MyForm())
  End Sub

End Class
```

To compile this form, from the directory where the .vb file resides, type the following:

```
vbc /t:winexe /r:System.dll,System.Windows.Forms.dll,System.Drawing.dll, ⤹
RoundButton.dll listing-01.02.vb
```

You can then double-click the resulting .exe file. Figure 1-1 shows the control in a form.

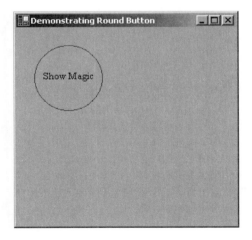

Figure 1-1. The RoundButton *control*

Although the OnPaint method is useful for painting the whole GUI, in many occasions you need to modify only some part of the GUI. Redrawing the whole lot will be a waste of resource and processor cycles if all you need, for instance, is to update a character in a document. And, repainting parts that have not changed can also cause flickers. To selectively repaint part of the Graphics object's area, you invalidate the area in the Graphics object of your control and force the control to repaint the area. For this purpose, you use the Invalidate and Update methods.

The Invalidate method invalidates a specific area of the control and causes a paint message to be sent to the control. This method has six overloads. One of these overloads accepts a Rectangle representing the area to be invalidated. Another overload accepts no argument, which will cause the whole area of the control to be invalidated.

After calling the Invalidate method, you need to call the Update method to repaint the invalidated area. The Update method will cause the OnPaint method to be called, but only the invalidated area is redrawn.

Capturing Key Presses

Capturing key presses is an important Windows programming task. The keys in a computer keyboard are differentiated into several categories. The first category includes the keys that correspond to characters, including alphanumeric and punctuation marks. The second category includes the function keys: F1 to F12. In the last category are control keys: the Control key, the alternate key, the arrow keys, and others. Processing the complete set of keys not only requires you to detect the keying of each individual key but also the combination of several keys.

When the user presses a key in the first category, three events of the control trigger. The three key events occur in the following order:

1. KeyDown occurs when the user starts pressing the key—in other words, when the key is down.

2. KeyPress occurs when a key is pressed, after the KeyDown event triggers.

3. KeyUp occurs when the user releases the key.

The easiest way to capture keyboard input from the user is to use a control's KeyPress event. The event handler for this event receives a System.Windows.Forms.KeyPressEventArgs object containing two properties:

- Handled is a Boolean indicating whether the key has been handled.

- KeyChar is a read-only property from which the corresponding character of the pressed key can be obtained.

Because the KeyChar property gives you the character of the key being pressed, displaying the character, for example, is very straightforward. However, some keys do not have visual representation and are not for display. The backspace key, for instance, normally acts as a text-based control to delete the character to the left of the caret and move the caret back by one character. Also, the carriage-return character terminates a line and does not display. For these nonvisual characters, you can simply convert the character into an integer and compare the integer with the ASCII value of the character:

```
Dim c As Char = e.KeyChar        ' e is a System.Windows.Forms.KeyPressEventArgs
Dim convertedChar As Integer = Convert.ToInt32(c)
```

The backspace key will have an integer value of 8, and the carriage-return key will have an integer of 13. However, rather than trying to remember these values, you can conveniently use the System.Windows.Forms.Keys enumeration members. For instance, Keys.Back represents the backspace key, and Keys.Return represents the Enter key. See the .NET Framework class library documentation for a list of values of the Keys enumeration.

For example, Listing 1-3 does different things based on a user's key input. It detects the key pressed by comparing the integer value of the character with a value in the Keys enumeration.

Listing 1-3. Detecting Key Presses

```
Dim c As Char = e.KeyChar        ' e is a System.Windows.Forms.KeyPressEventArgs
Dim convertedChar As Integer = Convert.ToInt32(c)
Select Case convertedChar
  Case Keys.Back    'backspace
    ' backspace, do something here
  Case Keys.Return ' return key
    ' Enter was pressed, do something
  Case Keys.Escape 'Escape
    ' Escape key, do something
  Case Else
    ' do something
End Select
```

However, there are problems with using the Control class's KeyPress event alone. For example, the KeyChar property of KeyPressEventArgs has the same value when either the backspace or Ctrl+H is pressed. Therefore, you cannot distinguish the backspace key and Ctrl+H using the KeyPress event alone. Also, function keys, control keys, and arrow keys do not raise the KeyPress event. Function keys generate the KeyDown event, and arrow keys only trigger the KeyUp event. However, KeyUp only triggers when the user releases the key.

 NOTE *It is interesting that pressing arrow keys triggers the* Control *class's* KeyUp *event but not its* KeyDown *event. More interesting is the fact that the* Form *class's* KeyDown *event triggers when a user presses an arrow key. The* Form *class extends* ContainerControl, *which derives from* ScrollableControl. *The* ScrollableControl *class is a direct child class of the* Control *class. The .NET Framework documentation does not say that the* MouseDown *event is overridden in* ContainerControl, ScrollableControl, *or* Form. *Therefore, the behavior of the* KeyDown *event should be the same in both the* Control *class and the* Form *class. A bug in the implementation of the class library could be the cause of the difference. Or, it could also be because the documentation is not up-to-date. Therefore, in the* StyledTextArea *control, I avoid using the* KeyDown *event. Instead, I resort to the* ProcessDialogKey *method of the* Control *class.*

When you need to capture noncharacter keys (control keys and function keys) when a user is pressing the key, you have to use the ProcessDialogKey method. The ProcessDialogKey method in the Control class is called automatically when a key or a combination of keys on the keyboard is pressed. Unlike the KeyPress event, ProcessDialogKey can capture any key, including the Control key, Tab, and arrow keys. However, it does not give you the character associated with the key; it only tells you which key is being pressed. For example, pressing the A key informs you that the A key has been pressed, but it does not tell you if it is the capital A or small a. There is a way to check the character case, but this requires longer code. For a simpler solution, you can use ProcessDialogKey in conjunction with the KeyPress event. The KeyPress event is invoked after the ProcessDialogKey method is called. Therefore, you can use a flag to tell the KeyPress event handler whether it needs to handle a key press. The ProcessDialogKey method controls the flag. If the key press is a combination of control keys and a character key, the ProcessDialogKey will handle it and reset the flag. On the other hand, if the key pressed is a character key, the ProcessDialogKey will set the flag and let the KeyPress event handler take care of the key press.

When overriding the ProcessDialogKey method, you should return True when the key was handled and False otherwise. Normally, when your ProcessDialogKey method does not process the key, you call the `ProcessDialogKey` method of the base class and return whatever value was returned by the base class's `ProcessDialogKey` method.

The `ProcessDialogKey` method receives one of the `Keys` enumeration values as its argument. The `Keys` enumeration allows a bitwise combination of its values.

The argument sent to the `ProcessDialogKey` method depends on the key(s) being pressed. For instance, if the user pressed the A key, the method will receive `Keys.A`; if the user pressed `Ctrl+S`, the value sent is the bitwise combination of the Control key and the S key. The down arrow sends `Keys.Down`, the up arrow sends `Keys.Up`, and the right and left arrows send `Keys.Right` and `Keys.Left` (respectively). The F1 key sends `Keys.F1`, and Alt+F4 sends the bitwise combination of `Keys.Alt` and `Keys.F4`. When a user presses the Shift key, the method receives `Keys.Shift`, enabling you to detect whether the user is sending an uppercase or lowercase character.

Creating Events with Delegates and the Observer Design Pattern

Anyone doing Windows programming must have done some event handling in one or another way: capturing the double-click of some button, handling the click of a menu item, reacting to the mouse moving over a label, and so forth. But, what about creating your own event in your own control and letting others capture that event? In this section, you will learn how to use the Observer design pattern to raise and handle events for your .NET control and learn how to pass event argument data.

An *event* is a message sent by an object to notify other object(s) of the occurrence of an action. The action could be caused by user interaction, such as a mouse click, or it could be triggered by some other program logic. The object that raises the event is the *event sender*, and the object that receives the event notification is the *event receiver*. The event receiver has a method that executes automatically in response to the event.

The .NET Framework supports easy event-driven Windows programming. It is so easy that often the programmer does not need to know how events work in the underlying .NET technology. All you have to remember is this: If you are interested in receiving an event from a Windows control, you provide an *event* handler and register the event handler with the event source. This is called eve*nt wiring*. In Visual Basic .NET (VB .NET), you need to write the following syntax, normally in the class constructor of your form:

```
AddHandler eventSource.someEvent, AddressOf someMethod
```

For instance, if you want to handle the Click event of a button named button1, and you want the private button1_Clicked method to execute when the Click event occurs, you write the following:

```
AddHandler button1.Click, AddressOf button1_Clicked
```

Then, you must also provide the implementation of button1_Clicked in your class as follows:

```
Private Sub button1_Clicked(sender As Object sender, e As EventArgs)
    ' code to be executed when the Click event occurs
End Sub
```

The method does not have to be private, but it must accept two arguments: an object of type Object and a System.EventArgs object.

Alternatively, declare a control with the WithEvents keyword, omit the AddHandler statement, and assign an event handler to handle an event by using the keyword Handles followed by the event source. In the previous example, this would be the following.

```
Friend WithEvents button1 As TextBox
Private Sub button1_Clicked(sender As Object sender, e As EventArgs) Handles↵
button1.Click
    ' code to be executed when the Click event occurs
End Sub
```

So, consuming events is a piece of cake (and I am sure you have been doing it all the time). Now, let's look at creating your own custom event that other programmers can use. Before doing this, however, you should first learn about the Observer pattern in object-oriented programming.

Introducing the Observer Pattern

There are two key objects in the Observer pattern: the subject and the observer. The *subject* represents the data and may have one or many observers. These *observers* register their interest in the subject and listen for notification from the subject of a state change inside the subject. This pattern is also known as *dependents* or *publish-subscribe*. Figure 1-2 shows the UML class diagram of the Observer pattern.

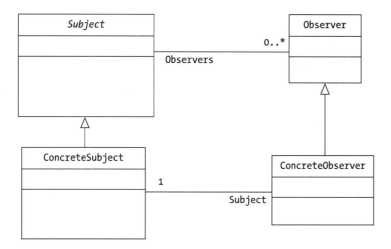

Figure 1-2. The Observer pattern class diagram

As an example, Listing 1-4 shows a form that has a TextBox control named myTextBox.

Listing 1-4. The Observer Design Pattern at Work

```
Imports System
Public Class Form1 : Inherits System.Windows.Forms.Form
  Friend WithEvents myTextBox As System.Windows.Forms.TextBox
  Public Sub New()
    myTextBox = New System.Windows.Forms.TextBox()
    myTextBox.Location = New System.Drawing.Point(24, 24)
    myTextBox.Size = New System.Drawing.Size(248, 20)
    AddHandler myTextBox.TextChanged, AddressOf myTextBox_TextChanged
    Me.Controls.Add(myTextBox)
  End Sub

  Private Sub myTextBox_TextChanged(ByVal sender As System.Object, _
    ByVal e As System.EventArgs)
    Me.Text = myTextBox.Text
  End Sub

  <STAThread()> Shared Sub Main()
    System.Windows.Forms.Application.Run(New Form1())
  End Sub

End Class
```

NOTE *To compile the code in Listing 1-4, use the following command from the directory in which the* listing-01.03.vb *file resides:* vbc /t:winexe /r:System.dll,System.Windows.Forms.dll, System.Drawing.dll listing-01.03.vb *(all on one line).*

Note that you declare the TextBox with the WithEvents keyword. Note also that an AddHandler statement is present in the class's constructor to wire the TextChanged event of myTextBox with the myTextBox_TextChanged event handler. As a result, every time the TextChanged event occurs in the TextBox control, the myTextBox_TextChanged event handler is invoked. This in turn updates the text in the form's title bar. Figure 1-3 shows this form.

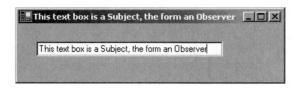

Figure 1-3. A form (observer) listening to a TextBox *(subject)*

This example demonstrates the Observer design pattern in action. The TextBox control behaves as the subject. It contains data, which is the text entered by the user. An observer, which is the form Form1, is interested in the changes in the TextBox control. It registers its interest using the AddHandler statement:

```
AddHandler myTextBox.TextChanged, AddressOf myTextBox_TextChanged
```

Every time the TextBox control changes, the TextBox control notifies the form. This notification materializes in the invocation of the myTextBox_TextChanged event handler.

According to "The Gang of Four" (Erich Gamma, Richard Helm, Ralph Johnson, and John Vlissides) in their book *Design Pattern: Elements of Reusable Object-Oriented Software* (Addison-Wesley, 1995), you can apply the Observer pattern in the following situations:

- When an abstraction has two aspects, one dependent on the other. Encapsulating these aspects in separate objects lets you vary and reuse them independently.

- When a change to one object requires changing others, and you do not know how many objects need to be changed.

- When an object should be able to notify other objects without making assumptions about what these objects are. In other words, you do not want these objects to be tightly coupled.

The Observer pattern is useful because it introduces abstract coupling to the subject. The subject does not need to know the details of its observers. However, there is a potential disadvantage of repeated notification to the observers when there is a series of incremental changes to the subject. This can sometimes complicate application programming. This consequence also arises in the StyledTextArea control development when a series of characters need to be pasted from the Clipboard in the Paste method of the StyledTextArea class. This problem, and how you get around it, should become apparent when you study the project carefully.

In event communication in the .NET Framework, the event sender class does not know which object or method will receive the events it raises. In the case of Listing 1-4, the TextBox does not know who will be listening to its state change. What is needed is an intermediary (or pointer-like mechanism) between the source and the receiver. The .NET Framework defines a special type called *delegate* that provides the capability of a function pointer.

A delegate is a class that can hold a reference to a method. Unlike other classes, a delegate class has a signature, and it can hold references only to methods that match its signature. A delegate is thus equivalent to a type-safe function pointer or a callback.

The "Understanding the Model-View-Controller Paradigm" section describes how to use delegates to communicate an event from an object to another object. But first, the next section puts the theory into practice by providing a control that has two custom events.

Writing a Custom Event Step-by-Step

Suppose you want to write a custom event called MyEvent for your custom control named MyControl, which extends System.Windows.Forms.UserControl. You need to follow these steps:

1. Declare a delegate with the public access modifier. For this example, call this delegate MyEventHandler. It has two arguments: an Object called sender and MyEventArgs called e. You will look at MyEventArgs in step 2. Note that you must declare the delegate outside your Control class:

   ```
   Public Delegate Sub MyEventHandler(ByVal sender As Object, _
     ByVal e As MyEventArgs)
   Public Class MyControl: Inherits UserControl

     . . .

   End Class
   ```

2. MyEventArgs in step 1 is the object that contains the data, which can be passed from the event sender (MyControl) to the event receiver. MyEventArgs must extend the System.EventArgs class. Therefore, you now have the following code:

   ```
   Public Class MyEventArgs: Inherits EventArgs

     . . .

   End Class
   Public Delegate Sub MyEventHandler(ByVal sender As Object, _
     ByVal e As MyEventArgs)
   Public Class MyControl: Inherits UserControl

     . . .

   End Class
   ```

   You still need to write some implementation inside MyEventArgs class; however, you will learn about it when you write your own custom control.

3. In your Control class, declare an event called MyEvent:

   ```
   Public Class MyEventArgs: Inherits EventArgs

     . . .

   End Class
   Public Delegate Sub MyEventHandler(ByVal sender As Object, _
     ByVal e As MyEventArgs)
   Public Class MyControl: Inherits UserControl
     Public Event MyEvent As MyEventHandler

     . . .

   End Class
   ```

4. In your Control class, declare a protected virtual method called On plus
    the name of the event. Because the event in this example is MyEvent, the
    method is OnMyEvent. Note that OnMyEvent has one argument of type
    MyEventArgs. Inside this method you raise the event. In VB .NET, you raise
    an event by using the RaiseEvent statement. To the event, you pass two
    arguments: the sender (the control MyControl) and the MyEventArgs object
    passed to the method:

```
Public Class MyEventArgs: Inherits EventArgs

  . . .

End Class
Public Delegate Sub MyEventHandler(ByVal sender As Object, _
  ByVal e As MyEventArgs)
Public Class MyControl: Inherits UserControl
  Public Event MyEvent As MyEventHandler
  Protected Overridable Sub OnMyEvent(ByVal e As MyEventArgs)
    RaiseEvent MyEvent (Me, e)
  End Sub

  . . .

End Class
```

5. Finally, call OnMyEvent from somewhere in the MyControl class. How you do
    this depends on what should cause the event to occur. This will become
    clear when you see the StyledTextArea control in the next section.

Afterward, users of your control can consume the MyEvent event in your
control by wiring the event to an event handler in their form, as shown at the
beginning of this section.

Understanding the Model-View-Controller Paradigm

The StyledTextArea control conforms to the Model-View-Controller (MVC) design
pattern. This section therefore starts with an overview of this design pattern,
including its objectives.

The MVC pattern was the central concept behind the Smalltalk-80 user
interface. At that time the term *pattern* had not been used. Instead, it was called
the *MVC paradigm*.

NOTE *You can find a paper on the MVC paradigm by Steve Burbeck, "Applications Programming in Smalltalk-80: How to Use Model-View-Controller (MVC)," at* `http://st-www.cs.uiuc.edu/users/smarch/st-docs/mvc.html`.

The MVC pattern consists of three kinds of main classes: Model, View, and Controller. The Model represents the application object or data. The View displays the model, and the Controller takes care of the user interface interaction with the user input. Prior to the MVC pattern, these three parts existed in one class, making the application inflexible and difficult to reuse. Figure 1-4 shows the MVC pattern component.

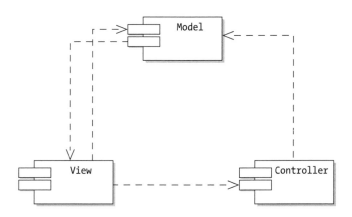

Figure 1-4. The MVC pattern

The MVC pattern loosens the coupling between views and models. The model simply encapsulates the application object. It does not know anything about the view. The view, on the other hand, is the visual representation of the model and depends on the model. The view has a reference to the instance of the model and so does the controller.

To understand the MVC pattern better, consider a Microsoft Excel spreadsheet in which the data can be represented using a pie chart, a line diagram, and so on. The pie chart and the line diagram are the views displaying the same piece of data. The controller gives commands to both the model and the view according to the user input. For example, in a text area component, when the user types a character, the controller invokes a method in the model to update the data and send a command to the view to update the visual representation accordingly.

In the passive model, the model does not do anything other than take care of the data. In another variant of the MVC pattern, however, an Observer pattern often exists between the model and the view. When some state in the model changes, the model notifies the view of the change. The view in turn can update itself so that the change is reflected.

Unlike the relationship between the model and the view, the view and the controller have a more intimate relationship. A view is normally passed a reference to the controller object and can access some of the variables in the controller.

In an application, often there is only one view for each MVC triad. However, it is not uncommon to have multiple views for the same model. The StyledTextArea component you are building, for instance, employs two views. You will see the architecture in the following section.

NOTE *I base this* StyledTextArea *control on the MVC pattern to promote code reuse and to increase flexibility. In addition, separating the code into smaller classes makes the code more manageable. However, the MVC pattern does not come without a "side effect." It does make it harder for the user of the component to use it. Instead of having to deal with one class, now there are three main classes: the* Model, *the* View, *and the* Controller. *To minimize this side effect, you hide the* Model *and* View *classes from the user. The user only sees one class:* StyledTextArea, *which is the controller in the component.*

Implementing the Project

Now that you have enough background knowledge for writing a custom control, you can start by learning about the StyledTextArea control's specification. I first describe the specification of the StyledTextArea control so that you know exactly what to expect. Then, I present the class diagram and detail all the classes and structures that make up the control.

The StyledTextArea control is a text area, similar to the RichTextBox control, with the following features:

- Each character occupies the same width and height.

- Each line can have an unlimited number of characters.

- A blinking caret indicates the character insertion point. The column and line numbers of the text area specify the insertion point. Both column and line numbers are 1-based. Therefore, the character on the second line and at the first column is at position (1, 2).

- The user can press the arrow keys to move the caret in any of the four directions, effectively moving the insertion point. Pressing the left arrow key when the caret is on the first column moves the caret to the last column of the previous line, if any. Pressing the right arrow key when the caret is on the last column moves the caret to the first column of the next line. Pressing the down arrow key moves the caret to the next line of the same column. If the next line has fewer characters than the column number, the caret moves to the right of the last character of the next line. By the same token, pressing the up arrow key moves the caret to the previous line of the same column. If the previous line has fewer characters than the column number, the caret moves to the right of the last character of the previous line.

- The user can press the backspace key to delete the character to the left of the caret. If the caret is on the first column of a line, the caret moves to the last character of the previous line and concatenates the previous line with the line that the caret is on before the backspace key is pressed. All the lines after the caret location will then move up by one line.

- The user can press the Delete key to delete the character to the right of the caret. All the remaining characters in the same line will then shift one character to the left. If the user presses the Delete key when the caret is on the last column of a line, the next line joins the current line, and all the lines next to it move up by one line.

- The text area ignores the pressing of a character or a combination of characters that it cannot display. For example, pressing Ctrl+A does not have any effect.

- The `StyledTextArea` component has a vertical scrollbar as well as a horizontal scrollbar to scroll the text area.

- The `StyledTextArea` component raises the `ColumnChanged` event when the caret is moved to another column and raises the `LineChanged` event when the caret moves to another line.

- The user can select part of the text on the text area by dragging the mouse over the text.

- The user can cut and copy selected text into the Clipboard programmatically.

- The user can paste the contents of the Clipboard into the text area as long as the content is in text format. The text area, for example, cannot paste an image.

Figure 1-5 shows the StyledTextArea component in a form.

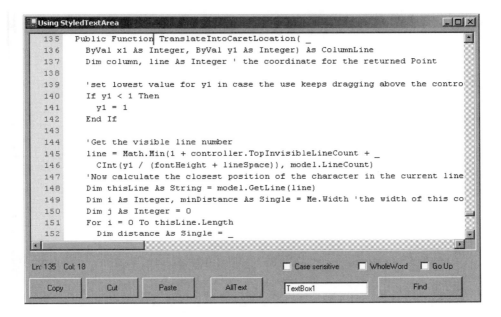

Figure 1-5. The StyledTextArea *component*

Viewing the Class Diagram

Figure 1-6 shows the class diagram for the StyledTextArea component.

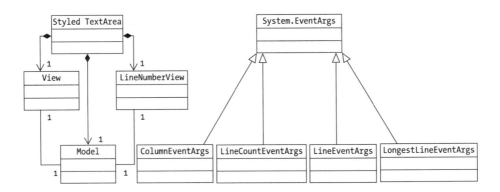

Figure 1-6. The StyledTextArea *class diagram*

The StyledTextArea component implements a MVC pattern with two views. It has the following main classes:

- Model represents the model of the component.

- View represents the screen to display the data of the model.

- LineNumberView is another view visualizing the line numbers of the model.

- StyledTextArea is the controller.

NOTE *All the classes comprising the* StyledTextArea *control are part of the default namespace. You can find all the classes in the* SytledTextArea.vb *file in the project's directory.*

Instances of the Model, View, and LineNumberView classes are created when the StyledTextArea class is constructed. The following InitializeComponent method of the StyledTextArea class describes the interrelationships between the four main objects:

```
model = New Model()
view = New View(model)
' Me is the StyledTextArea object,
' so we are passing the controller to the view
view.controller = Me
lineNumberView = New LineNumberView(model)
lineNumberView.controller = Me  ' pass the controller to the lineNumberView
```

Both the controller (StyledTextArea) and the two views (View and LineNumberView) receive the same instance of the Model class. In addition, both views also get the reference to the controller.

NOTE *In addition to the four main classes, there are also supporting small types: the* ColumnLine *structure, some delegates, and some event argument classes. I first discuss these supporting classes because they are much simpler, and then I talk about the four main classes. Each type has a section of its own.*

Using the ColumnLine Structure

The column number and the line number on which the character lies denote the character's location. The ColumnLine structure represents this column-line coordinate. This structure is similar to the System.Drawing.Point structure. However, the Point structure normally represents a location in a drawing area and is in pixels.

The ColumnLine structure is as follows:

```
Public Structure ColumnLine
  Public Column As Integer
  Public Line As Integer
  Public Sub New(ByVal column As Integer, ByVal line As Integer)
    Me.Column = column
    Me.Line = line
  End Sub
End Structure
```

The ColumnLine structure has two public integers that represent a column and a line, respectively.

By making ColumnLine a structure rather than a class, ColumnLine will automatically inherit the System.ValueType class and not the System.Object class. The System.ValueType class's Equals method supports value equality, which is inherited by the ColumnLine structure. Therefore, if cl1 and cl2 reference two different ColumnLine objects and both cl1 and cl2 have the same column and line values, cl1.Equals(cl2) and cl2.Equals(cl1) will return True.

On the other hand, the Equals method in the System.Object class only supports reference equality. The two object references a and b are only equal if they reference the same instance.

If you use a class and not a structure, you have to override the Equals method, as shown in Listing 1-5.

Listing 1-5. Overriding Equals

```
Public Overloads Overrides Function Equals(ByVal obj As Object) As Boolean
    If obj Is Nothing Then
      Return False
    End If
    If TypeOf obj Is ColumnLine Then
      Dim cl As ColumnLine = CType(obj, ColumnLine)
      If cl.Column = Column And cl.Line = Line Then
        Return True
      Else
        Return False
      End If
    Else
      Return False
    End If
End Function
```

Declaring the Delegates

The Model class can raise two events: when the number of lines changes and when the number of characters of the longest line changes. In addition, the StyledTextArea class can raise two events: when the caret moves to another column and when the caret moves to another line. For these four events, you declare the four delegates as in Listing 1-6.

Listing 1-6. Declaring the Delegates

```
Public Delegate Sub ColumnEventHandler(ByVal sender As Object, _
  ByVal e As ColumnEventArgs)

Public Delegate Sub LineEventHandler(ByVal sender As Object, _
  ByVal e As LineEventArgs)

Public Delegate Sub LineCountEventHandler(ByVal sender As Object, _
  ByVal e As LineCountEventArgs)

Public Delegate Sub LongestLineEventHandler(ByVal sender As Object, _
  ByVal e As LongestLineEventArgs)
```

I give you more details on these delegates when discussing the Model and StyledTextArea classes.

Using the Event Arguments Classes

Each of the four events that can be raised from within the Model class and the StyledTextArea class passes different data. The data is encapsulated by the following four classes that all inherit the System.EventArgs class: ColumnEventArgs, LineEventArgs, LineCountEventArgs, and LongestLineEventArgs.

ColumnEventArgs

Listing 1-7 shows the ColumnEventArgs class.

Listing 1-7. ColumnEventArgs

```
Public Class ColumnEventArgs : Inherits EventArgs
  Private oldColumnField, newColumnField As Integer

  Public Sub New(ByVal oldColumn As Integer, ByVal newColumn As Integer)
    oldColumnField = oldColumn
    newColumnField = newColumn
  End Sub

  Public ReadOnly Property OldColumn() As Integer
    Get
      Return oldColumnField
    End Get
  End Property

  Public ReadOnly Property NewColumn() As Integer
    Get
      Return newColumnField
    End Get
  End Property
End Class
```

You construct a ColumnEventArgs object by passing two integers to its constructor: the value for the old column and the value for the new column. An event receiver can then obtain these two values from the OldColumn and NewColumn properties.

LineEventArgs

Listing 1-8 shows the LineEventArgs class.

Listing 1-8. LineEventArgs

```
Public Class LineEventArgs : Inherits EventArgs
  Private oldLineField, newLineField As Integer

  Public Sub New(ByVal oldLine As Integer, ByVal newLine As Integer)
    oldLineField = oldLine
    newLineField = newLine
  End Sub

  Public ReadOnly Property OldLine() As Integer
    Get
      Return oldLineField
    End Get
  End Property

  Public ReadOnly Property NewLine() As Integer
    Get
      Return newLineField
    End Get
  End Property
End Class
```

You construct a LineEventArgs object by passing two integers to its constructor: the value for the old line and the value for the new line. An event receiver can then obtain these two values from the OldLine and NewLine properties.

LineCountEventArgs

Listing 1-9 shows the LineCountEventArgs class.

Listing 1-9. LineCountEventArgs

```
Public Class LineCountEventArgs : Inherits EventArgs
  Private lineCountField As Integer ' the current line count
```

```
  Public Sub New(ByVal lineCount As Integer)
    lineCountField = lineCount
  End Sub

  Public ReadOnly Property LineCount() As Integer
    Get
      Return lineCountField
    End Get
  End Property
End Class
```

You can instantiate a LineCountEventArgs object by passing an integer to its constructor: the new line count. An event receiver can then obtain this value from the LineCount property.

LongestLineEventArgs

Listing 1-10 shows the LongestLineEventArgs class.

Listing 1-10. LongestLineEventArgs

```
Public Class LongestLineEventArgs : Inherits EventArgs
  Private charCountField As Integer

  Public Sub New(ByVal charCount As Integer)
    charCountField = charCount
  End Sub

  Public ReadOnly Property LongestLineCharCount() As Integer
    Get
      Return charCountField
    End Get
  End Property
End Class
```

You instantiate a LongestLineEventArgs object by passing an integer to its constructor: the new longest line character count. An event receiver can then obtain this value from the LongestLineCharCount property.

Understanding the Model Class

The data in the Model class is a collection of characters entered by the user. These
characters are grouped into strings. The first string comprises all characters from
the first character to the character before the first carriage-return character. The
character after the carriage-return character is the first character of the second
string, and this string spans until the character just before the second carriage-
return character, and so on. The last string's element starts from the character
after the last carriage-return character to the last character the user entered.

Consider the following set of characters in which \n represents a carriage-
return character. The user of the StyledTextArea component has input this series
of characters:

```
The speaker was\nthe well-known\nAnna Pavlovna Scherer
```

These characters will be grouped into three strings. The first string will have
the value of The speaker was, the second will have the value of the well-known,
and the third will have the value of Anna Pavlovna Scherer. Note that the carriage-
return characters are not part of the string objects.

In the StyledTextArea component, the public class Model represents the model:

```
Public Class Model
. . .
End Class
```

The data holder in the Model class is a System.Collections.ArrayList named
list. Each member of the ArrayList is a String object. The ArrayList appears in the
declaration section of the Model class:

```
Private list As New ArrayList(1024)
```

In this example, you declare and instantiate list in the same line by passing
the number of initial members to its constructor. The choice of 1,024 is arbitrary,
and the ArrayList will grow automatically when the number of members exceeds
1,024. In theory, list can contain an unlimited number of lines.

The Model class has another field: longestLineCharCountField, which holds the
value for the LongestLineCharCount property:

```
Private longestLineCharCountField As Integer
```

Constructing the Model Object

When instantiated, the Model object will add an empty string as its first member. The behavior of Model is that it will have at least one member. When all characters in the ArrayList are deleted, the first empty string will remain.

You add an empty string in the Model class's constructor:

```
Public Sub New()
  list.Add("")
End Sub
```

The Model class provides different public properties and methods for the view and controller to flexibly access its data. In addition, the Model class can raise four events. The following sections describe the properties, methods, and events.

Understanding the Model Class's Properties

The Model class has three public properties: CharCount, LineCount, and LongestLineCharCount.

CharCount

The CharCount read-only property returns the number of characters in the Model class (see Listing 1-11). Bear in mind that the Model instance does not store carriage-return characters; therefore they are not counted.

Listing 1-11. CharCount

```
Public ReadOnly Property CharCount() As Integer
  ' the total of lengths of all lines, therefore newline is not counted
  Get
    Dim i, total As Integer
    For i = 0 To LineCount - 1
      total = total + list.Item(i).ToString().Length
    Next i
    Return total
  End Get
End Property
```

The number of characters is calculated every time the CharCount property is called. The return value is the total number of characters in all the strings in the ArrayList.

LineCount

The LineCount read-only property returns the number of lines in the Model object—in other words, the number of members of the ArrayList named list. The implementation of this property is as follows:

```
Public ReadOnly Property LineCount() As Integer
  Get
    Return list.Count
  End Get
End Property
```

LongestLineCharCount

The LongestLineCharCount read-only property returns the number of characters in the longest string (see Listing 1-12). This is useful because the controller (the StyledTextArea class) uses a horizontal scrollbar whose maximum and value change dynamically according to the number of characters in the longest string.

Listing 1-12. LongestLineCharCount

```
Public ReadOnly Property LongestLineCharCount() As Integer
  Get
    Dim lineCount As Integer = list.Count
    If lineCount = 0 Then
      Return 0
    Else
      Dim i, max As Integer
      For i = 0 To lineCount - 1
        Dim thisLineCharCount As Integer = CType(list.Item(i), String).Length
        If thisLineCharCount > max Then
          max = thisLineCharCount
        End If
      Next
      Return max
    End If
  End Get
End Property
```

The getter of the `LongestLineCharCount` property works by checking the length of each string in the `ArrayList`.

Understanding the Model Class's Methods

The `Model` class has several methods you can use to manipulate the data in the `Model` object.

DeleteChar

The `DeleteChar` method deletes a character from the location indicated by the `ColumnLine` structure (see Listing 1-13). If the longest line's character count changes because of the deletion, this method raises the `LongestLineCharCountChanged` event.

Listing 1-13. `DeleteChar`

```
Public Sub DeleteChar(ByVal deleteLocation As ColumnLine)
    Dim oldLongestLineCharCount As Integer = LongestLineCharCount
    list.Item(deleteLocation.Line - 1) = _
      GetLine(deleteLocation.Line).Remove(deleteLocation.Column - 1, 1)
    Dim newLongestLineCharCount As Integer = LongestLineCharCount
    If oldLongestLineCharCount <> newLongestLineCharCount Then
      OnLongestLineCharCountChanged(New _
        LongestLineEventArgs(newLongestLineCharCount))
    End If
  End Sub
```

You delete characters by assigning a new string to a specified item of the `ArrayList` named `list`. The new string is an old string whose character at the specified column has been removed using the `Remove` method of the `String` class. The `GetLine` method obtains the specified line from which a character needs to be removed:

```
list.Item(deleteLocation.Line - 1) = _
    GetLine(deleteLocation.Line).Remove(deleteLocation.Column - 1, 1)
```

Before and after the deletion, the LongestLineCharCount property is called and its value is stored in oldLongestLineCharCount and newLongestLineCharCount (respectively):

```
Dim oldLongestLineCharCount As Integer = LongestLineCharCount

    .

    .

    .

Dim newLongestLineCharCount As Integer = LongestLineCharCount
```

If newLongestLineCharCount and oldLongestLineCharCount are different after the character deletion, the LongestLineCharCountChanged method is called, which in turns raises the LongestLineCharCountChanged event:

```
If oldLongestLineCharCount <> newLongestLineCharCount Then
  OnLongestLineCharCountChanged(New _
    LongestLineEventArgs(newLongestLineCharCount))
End If
```

GetLine

The GetLine method returns the line at the specified line number. Line numbers are 1-based—in other words, the first line is line number 1. This method throws an ArgumentOutOfRangeException if the specified line is a negative number or greater than the number of members in the ArrayList named list.

The implementation of the GetLine method is as follows:

```
Public Function GetLine(ByVal lineNo As Integer) As String 'lineNo is 1-based
  If lineNo > 0 And lineNo <= list.Count Then
    Return CType(list.Item(lineNo - 1), String)
  Else
    Throw New ArgumentOutOfRangeException()
  End If
End Function
```

InsertChar

The InsertChar method inserts a character at the specified ColumnLine (see Listing 1-14). If the longest line's character count changes because of the insertion, this method raises the LongestLineCharCountChanged event.

Listing 1-14. InsertChar

```
Public Sub InsertChar(ByVal c As Char, ByVal insertLocation As ColumnLine)
   Dim oldLongestLineCharCount As Integer = LongestLineCharCount
   Dim oldLine As String = list.Item(insertLocation.Line - 1).ToString()
   Dim newLine As String = _
     oldLine.Insert(insertLocation.Column - 1, c.ToString())
   list.Item(insertLocation.Line - 1) = newLine
   Dim newLongestLineCharCount As Integer = LongestLineCharCount
   If oldLongestLineCharCount <> newLongestLineCharCount Then
     OnLongestLineCharCountChanged(New _
       LongestLineEventArgs(newLongestLineCharCount))
   End If
End Sub
```

You insert a character into a string using the Insert method of the String class
at the specified index. You obtain the string into which a character is inserted
using the Item property of the ArrayList class:

```
Dim oldLine As String = list.Item(insertLocation.Line - 1).ToString()
Dim newLine As String = _
  oldLine.Insert(insertLocation.Column - 1, c.ToString())
```

The new line then replaces the old line:

```
list.Item(insertLocation.Line - 1) = newLine
```

Before and after the insertion, the LongestLineCharCount property is called
and its value is stored in oldLongestLineCharCount and newLongestLineCharCount
(respectively):

```
Dim oldLongestLineCharCount As Integer = LongestLineCharCount
  .
  .
  .
Dim newLongestLineCharCount As Integer = LongestLineCharCount
```

If newLongestLineCharCount and oldLongestLineCharCount are different after the character insertion, the LongestLineCharCountChanged method is called, which in turns raises the LongestLineCharCountChanged event:

```
If oldLongestLineCharCount <> newLongestLineCharCount Then
   OnLongestLineCharCountChanged(New _
     LongestLineEventArgs(newLongestLineCharCount))
End If
```

InsertData

The InsertData method inserts a string at the specified ColumnLine (see Listing 1-15). The string can contain carriage-return and line-feed characters after the string is separated into multiple shorter strings at every occurrence of a carriage-return character. Line-feed characters, if they exist, will be removed prior to insertion. The method can raise the LongestLineCharCountChanged event as well as the LineCountChanged event.

The Paste method of the StyledTextArea class calls this method, which returns the new location of the insertion point that will be used by the StyledTextArea object to move the caret.

Listing 1-15. InsertData

```
Public Function InsertData(ByVal data As String, _
  ByVal insertLocation As ColumnLine) As ColumnLine

    'delete vbLf character
    data = data.Replace(Microsoft.VisualBasic.Constants.vbLf.ToString(), "")

    Dim initialLongestLineCharCount As Integer = LongestLineCharCount
    Dim x As Integer = insertLocation.Column
    Dim y As Integer = insertLocation.Line

    Dim returnInserted As Boolean
    ' data may contain carriage return character
    Dim thisLine As String = GetLine(y)
    Dim head As String = thisLine.Substring(0, x - 1)
    Dim tail As String = thisLine.Substring(x - 1)
    list.RemoveAt(y - 1)
    Dim startIndex As Integer
    Do While (startIndex >= 0)
```

```
  Dim endIndex As Integer = _
    data.IndexOf(Microsoft.VisualBasic.Constants.vbCr, startIndex)
  Dim line As String
  If endIndex = -1 Then
    line = data.Substring(startIndex)
    'don't use SetLine bec it can raise event
    Dim newLine As String = head & line & tail
    list.Insert(y - 1, newLine)
    x = head.Length + line.Length + 1
    startIndex = endIndex
  Else
    line = data.Substring(startIndex, endIndex - startIndex)
    list.Insert(y - 1, head & line)
    returnInserted = True
    y = y + 1
    x = 1
    head = ""
    startIndex = endIndex + 1 'without carriage return
  End If

Loop

Dim currentCharCount As Integer = LongestLineCharCount
If initialLongestLineCharCount <> currentCharCount Then
  OnLongestLineCharCountChanged(New LongestLineEventArgs(currentCharCount))
End If
If returnInserted Then
  OnLineCountChanged(New LineCountEventArgs(LineCount))
End If
Return New ColumnLine(x, y)
End Function
```

The InsertData method first removes any line-feed character using the Replace method of the String class:

```
data = data.Replace(Microsoft.VisualBasic.Constants.vbLf.ToString(), "")
```

It then retrieves the number of characters of the longest line prior to insertion:

```
Dim initialLongestLineCharCount As Integer = LongestLineCharCount
```

The `Boolean` `returnInserted` acts as a flag to indicate the presence of a carriage-return character in the `String` argument data:

```
Dim returnInserted As Boolean
```

It then obtains the line into which `data` will be inserted. The substring before the insertion point and the substring after the insertion point are also stored into `head` and `tail`:

```
Dim thisLine As String = GetLine(y)
Dim head As String = thisLine.Substring(0, x - 1)
Dim tail As String = thisLine.Substring(x - 1)
```

The method then deletes the line into which `data` will be inserted:

```
list.RemoveAt(y - 1)
```

The `String` argument data is then divided into smaller strings in which a carriage-return character denotes the end of a string. Each resulting string is then inserted into the `ArrayList` named `list`:

```
Dim startIndex As Integer
Do While (startIndex >= 0)
  Dim endIndex As Integer = _
    data.IndexOf(Microsoft.VisualBasic.Constants.vbCr, startIndex)
  Dim line As String
  If endIndex = -1 Then
    ' last line
    line = data.Substring(startIndex)
    'don't use SetLine bec it can raise event
    Dim newLine As String = head & line & tail
    list.Insert(y - 1, newLine)
    x = head.Length + line.Length + 1
    startIndex = endIndex
  Else
    line = data.Substring(startIndex, endIndex - startIndex)
    list.Insert(y - 1, head & line)
    returnInserted = True
    y = y + 1
    x = 1
    head = ""
    startIndex = endIndex + 1 'without carriage return
  End If

Loop
```

Note that the `returnInserted` flag will be `True` if there is a carriage-return character in the data.

The method then checks if the longest line's character count has changed. If so, it raises `LongestLineCharCountChanged` by calling the `OnLongesLineCharCountChanged` method:

```
Dim currentCharCount As Integer = LongestLineCharCount
If initialLongestLineCharCount <> currentCharCount Then
  OnLongestLineCharCountChanged(New LongestLineEventArgs(currentCharCount))
End If
```

It also checks if the number of lines has changed by checking the `returnInserted` Boolean. If it has, it raises the `LineCountChanged` event by calling the `OnLineCountChanged` method:

```
If returnInserted Then
  OnLineCountChanged(New LineCountEventArgs(LineCount))
End If
```

Finally, it returns a new `ColumnLine` object representing the insertion point after the data insertion:

```
Return New ColumnLine(x, y)
```

InsertLine

The `InsertLine` method inserts a line at the specified line number. It raises the `LineCountChanged` event and can raise the `LongestLineCharCountChanged` event:

```
Public Sub InsertLine(ByVal lineNo As Integer, ByVal line As String)
  If lineNo > 0 And lineNo <= list.Count + 1 Then
    Dim oldLongestLineCharCount As Integer = LongestLineCharCount
    list.Insert(lineNo - 1, line)
    OnLineCountChanged(New LineCountEventArgs(LineCount))
    Dim newLongestLineCharCount As Integer = LongestLineCharCount
    If oldLongestLineCharCount <> newLongestLineCharCount Then
      OnLongestLineCharCountChanged(New _
        LongestLineEventArgs(newLongestLineCharCount))
    End If
  End If
End Sub
```

Note that the `LongestLineCharCount` property is called before and after the line is inserted. If the property value is different after the insertion, the `LongestLineCharCountChanged` event is raised by calling the `OnLongestLineCharCountChanged` method.

OnColumnChanged

`OnColumnChanged` is a protected method used internally to raise the `ColumnChanged` event:

```
Protected Overridable Sub OnColumnChanged(ByVal e As ColumnEventArgs)
   RaiseEvent ColumnChanged(Me, e)
End Sub
```

OnLineChanged

`OnLineChanged` is a protected method used internally to raise the `LineChanged` event:

```
Protected Overridable Sub OnLineChanged(ByVal e As LineEventArgs)
   RaiseEvent LineChanged(Me, e)
End Sub
```

OnLineCountChanged

`OnLineCountChanged` is a protected method used internally to raise the `LineCountChanged` event:

```
Protected Overridable Sub OnLineCountChanged(ByVal e As LineCountEventArgs)
   RaiseEvent LineCountChanged(Me, e)
End Sub
```

OnLongestLineCharCountChanged

`OnLongestLineCharCountChanged` is a protected method used internally to raise the `LongestLineCharCount` event:

```
Protected Overridable Sub OnLongestLineCharCountChanged( _
   ByVal e As LongestLineEventArgs)
   RaiseEvent LongestLineCharCountChanged(Me, e)
End Sub
```

RemoveLine

RemoveLine removes a line at the specified line number. This method accepts a second argument that is a Boolean. A value of False for this argument will prevent any event to be raised from inside this method. Otherwise, it raises the LineCountChanged event and can raise the LongestLineCharCount event. Its implementation is as follows:

```
Public Sub RemoveLine(ByVal lineNo As Integer, ByVal triggerEvent As Boolean)
  If lineNo > 0 And lineNo <= list.Count Then
    Dim oldLongestLineCharCount As Integer = LongestLineCharCount
    list.RemoveAt(lineNo - 1)
    If triggerEvent Then
      Dim newLongestLineCharCount As Integer = LongestLineCharCount
      If oldLongestLineCharCount <> newLongestLineCharCount Then
        OnLongestLineCharCountChanged(New _
          LongestLineEventArgs(newLongestLineCharCount))
      End If
      OnLineCountChanged(New LineCountEventArgs(LineCount))
    End If
  End If
End Sub
```

SetLine

SetLine changes the line at the specified line number with the specified string. It can raise the LongestLineCharCountChanged event. Its implementation is as follows:

```
Public Sub SetLine(ByVal lineNo As Integer, ByVal line As String)
  Dim oldLongestLineCharCount As Integer = LongestLineCharCount
  If (lineNo > 0 And lineNo <= list.Count) Then
    list.Item(lineNo - 1) = line
  End If
  Dim newLongestLineCharCount As Integer = LongestLineCharCount
  If oldLongestLineCharCount <> newLongestLineCharCount Then
    OnLongestLineCharCountChanged(New _
      LongestLineEventArgs(newLongestLineCharCount))
  End If
End Sub
```

Understanding the Model Class's Events

The Model class contains several events.

LineCountChanged

LineCountChanged raises when the number of lines—in other words, the number of members of the ArrayList list—changes. Its signature is as follows:

```
Public Event LineCountChanged As LineCountEventHandler
```

LongestLineCharCountChanged

LongestLineCharCountChanged raises when the number of characters of the longest line changes:

```
Public Event LongestLineCharCountChanged As LongestLineEventHandler
```

Understanding the View Class

The View class represents a screen that displays the data (the collection of string lines) in the Model object. As such, the View must reference the instance of the Model object. In addition, the View has a reference to the controller object so that it can communicate with the controller the way it should display the data. For example, the controller has the variable named TopInvisibleLineCount, which contains the number of lines that should be skipped because the user has scrolled down the screen. When displaying the data, the view needs to know the value of TopInvisibleLineCount so that it can display the correct data.

You declare these object references as follows:

```
Public controller As StyledTextArea
Public model As model
```

There is also a variable named LeftInvisibleCharCount, which contains the number of invisible characters to the left of the screen:

```
Public LeftInvisibleCharCount As Integer
```

The value of `LeftInvisibleCharCount` changes when the user continues typing after the caret reaches the rightmost character space of the screen. To make what is being typed visible, the screen must scroll to the left. The value of `LeftInvisibleCharCount` also changes when the user moves the horizontal scrollbar of the controller.

> **NOTE** `LeftInvisibleCharCount` *is actually similar to the controller's* `TopInvisibleLineCount`. *However, although* `LeftInvisibleCharCount` *exists inside the* `View` *class,* `TopInvisibleLineCount` *resides in the controller. The latter has to be in the controller because this value is also needed by the second view,* `LineNumberView`. *By keeping* `TopInvisibleLineCount` *in the controller, both views do not have to know each other. On the other hand, only the* `View` *class uses* `LeftInvisibleCharCount`. *The* `LineNumberView` *class does not need it.*

The declaration part of the `View` class also contains variables that define how each character should be displayed. For example, `lineSpace` defines the number of pixels that should separate two lines:

```
Public lineSpace As Integer = 2   ' number of pixels between 2 lines
```

Also, `fontFace` determines the font type used to draw characters, and the `characterWidth` value represents the number of pixels occupied by the width of every character:

```
Public fontFace As String = "Courier New"
Public characterWidth As Integer = 8
```

As for the character's font height, you use the `FontHeight` property inherited from the `Control` class, so you do not need a variable for it.

The `StyledTextArea` control allows the user to select part of or the whole text. The selected text will be painted in different colors defined by `highlightBackColor` and `highlightForeColor`:

```
Public highlightBackColor As Color = Color.DarkBlue
Public highlightForeColor As Color = Color.White
```

For the caret, the `caretThread` thread makes the caret blink:

```
Private caretThread As Thread
```

To indicate whether at one instance the caret is visible or invisible, you use a Boolean called `caretVisible`. The value of `caretVisible` toggles each time the method that draws the caret is called, giving the caret the needed blinking effect:

```
Private caretVisible As Boolean = True
```

Finally, to draw the caret, you use a `Pen` object called `pen` with a width of `penWidth`:

```
Private penWidth As Integer = 2
Private pen As New Pen(Color.Black, penWidth)
```

To change the width of the caret, you can change the value of `penWidth`. To change the color, you can change the `Color` property of the `Pen` object.

Constructing a View Object

Because a view is useless unless it has a reference to the `Model` object, the `View` class's only constructor accepts one argument of type `Model`, which is then passed to the model object variable:

```
Public Sub New(ByRef model As Model)
  Me.model = model
  .
  .
  .
End Sub
```

Afterward, the `Font` property is instantiated. This font draws each line of strings in the `Model` object:

```
fontHeight = 10
Font = New Font(fontFace, fontHeight)
```

The last piece of the code in the `View` class's constructor creates a `System.Threading.Thread` object, which manages the caret. You instantiate it by passing a `ThreadStart` delegate. This delegate references the methods to be invoked when this thread begins executing:

```
caretThread = New Thread(New ThreadStart(AddressOf DisplayCaret))
```

You then start the thread by calling its Start method:

```
caretThread.Start()
```

When the View object is destroyed, this thread must also be destroyed. Otherwise, the whole application (the form that incorporates the StyledTextArea control) cannot exit properly. To terminate the thread when the View object is destroyed, the View class overrides the Dispose method as follows:

```
Protected Overloads Overrides Sub Dispose(ByVal disposing As Boolean)
  caretThread.Abort()
  caretThread.Join()
  MyBase.Dispose(disposing)
End Sub
```

Understanding the View Class's Properties

The following sections discuss each property in the View class.

CaretColor

The CaretColor property specifies the color of the caret:

```
Public Property CaretColor() As Color
  Get
    Return pen.Color
  End Get
  Set(ByVal Value As Color)
    pen.Color = Value
  End Set
End Property
```

You can change the caret color by changing the value of the Color property of the Pen object used to draw the caret.

VisibleCharCount

The read-only `VisibleCharCount` property returns the number of characters that can span along the width of the screen:

```
Public ReadOnly Property VisibleCharCount() As Integer
  Get
    Return CInt(Math.Floor(Me.Width / characterWidth)) - 1
  End Get
End Property
```

VisibleLineCount

The read-only `VisibleLineCount` property returns the number of lines that can be displayed across the height of the screen:

```
Public ReadOnly Property VisibleLineCount() As Integer
  Get
    Return CInt(Me.Height / (lineSpace + GetFontHeight()))
  End Get
End Property
```

The number of visible lines in the view is the height of the view control divided by the number of pixels between lines plus the font height.

Understanding the View Class's Methods

The View class has the following methods.

DisplayCaret

`DisplayCaret` is a private method that is passed to the thread dedicated to making the caret flash on and off (`caretThread`). This method consists of an indefinite `While` loop that keeps on running as long as `caretThread` is still alive. The main thing this method does is toggle the `caretVisible` `Boolean` variable. The `DrawCaret` method then uses this variable to determine whether the caret should be visible at that instance. The other thing the method does is invalidate and update the region occupied by the caret to create the blinking effect of the caret.

The method implementation is as follows:

```
Private Sub DisplayCaret()
  Try
    While True
      ' call DrawCaret here
      Dim caretsLine As String = model.GetLine(controller.CaretLineNo)
      Dim x As Integer = GetStringWidth(caretsLine.Substring(0, _
        controller.CaretColumnNo - 1)) + _
        penWidth - (LeftInvisibleCharCount * characterWidth)
      Dim y As Integer = (controller.CaretLineNo - 1 - _
        controller.TopInvisibleLineCount) * (lineSpace + fontHeight)
      Dim caretRectangle As New Rectangle( _
        x - penWidth, y, 2 * penWidth, lineSpace + fontheight)

      Me.Invalidate(caretRectangle)
      Me.Update()
      If Not caretVisible Then
        Thread.Sleep(150)
      Else
        Thread.Sleep(350)
      End If
      caretVisible = Not caretVisible
    End While
  Catch
  End Try
End Sub
```

The coordinates x and y give the left-top point on the text area where the caret should be drawn. Note also that the thread is put to sleep for two different periods of time. When the caret is visible—in other words, when caretVisible is True—the Thread class's Sleep method is given the value 350 so that the caret will stay visible for 350 milliseconds. Conversely, when the caret is not visible, the Sleep method is given the value 150.

Dispose

The `Dispose` method is a protected method that overrides the `Dispose` method in the `Control` class and is used internally to ensure that the caret thread is terminated when the instance of this `View` object is destroyed. Its implementation is as follows:

```
Protected Overloads Overrides Sub Dispose(ByVal disposing As Boolean)
  caretThread.Abort()
  caretThread.Join()
  MyBase.Dispose(disposing)
End Sub
```

DrawCaret

The `DrawCaret` method actually draws the caret. The `DisplayCaret` method invalidates and updates the text area, causing the `OnPaint` method to be called. Toward the end of the `OnPaint` method, the `OnPaint` method calls the `DrawCaret` method to draw the caret. The `DrawCaret` method implementation is as follows:

```
Protected Sub DrawCaret(ByRef graphics As Graphics)
  'it's protected so that it can be overriden by subclass
  If caretVisible And Me.Focused Then
    'Measure string
    Dim caretsLine As String = model.GetLine(controller.CaretLineNo)
    Dim x As Integer = GetStringWidth(caretsLine.Substring(0, _
      controller.CaretColumnNo - 1)) + _
      penWidth - (LeftInvisibleCharCount * characterWidth)
    Dim y As Integer = (controller.CaretLineNo - 1 - _
      controller.TopInvisibleLineCount) * (lineSpace + fontHeight)
    graphics.DrawLine(pen, x, y, x, y + lineSpace + fontHeight)
  End If
End Sub
```

The first thing the `DrawCaret` method does is to check the value of `caretVisible`, a `Boolean` that is constantly being toggled by the `DisplayCaret` method. When the `caretVisible` is `True`, the `DrawCaret` method obtains the starting point for the caret, as in the following code:

```
Dim caretsLine As String = model.GetLine(controller.CaretLineNo)
Dim x As Integer = GetStringWidth(caretsLine.Substring(0, _
  controller.CaretColumnNo - 1)) + _
  penWidth - (LeftInvisibleCharCount * characterWidth)
Dim y As Integer = (controller.CaretLineNo - 1 - _
  controller.TopInvisibleLineCount) * (lineSpace + fontHeight)
```

It then uses x and y to draw the caret, using the DrawLine method of the Graphics object passed as the argument:

```
graphics.DrawLine(pen, x, y, x, y + lineSpace + fontHeight)
```

GetCaretXAbsolutePosition

The GetCaretXAbsolutePosition method obtains the x coordinate of the caret position in pixels:

```
Public Function GetCaretXAbsolutePosition() As Integer
  Dim caretsLine As String = controller.GetCurrentLine()
  If Not caretsLine Is Nothing Then
    Return _
      GetStringWidth(caretsLine.Substring(0, controller.CaretColumnNo - 1))
    Else
      Return 0
    End If
End Function
```

It first gets the current line and then returns the result of the GetStringWidth method.

GetFontHeight

The GetFontHeight method returns the value of the FontHeight property:

```
Public Function GetFontHeight() As Integer
  Return FontHeight
End Function
```

GetStringWidth

The GetStringWidth method returns the number of pixels that the specified string will occupy when drawn on the text area:

```
Private Function GetStringWidth(ByRef s As String) As Integer
  If Not s Is Nothing Then
    Return s.Length * characterWidth
  Else
    Return 0
  End If
End Function
```

The string width is easy to calculate because each character is given the same width—in other words, the font is forced to be monospaced.

IsCaretVisible

The IsCaretVisible method indicates whether the caret is visible. The caret can become invisible if the text area is scrolled because scrolling retains the caret at its relative position. The implementation of the IsCaretVisible method is as follows:

```
Public Function IsCaretVisible() As Boolean
  Dim xPosition As Integer = GetCaretXAbsolutePosition()
  Dim leftInvisibleWidth As Integer = LeftInvisibleCharCount * characterWidth
  If xPosition < leftInvisibleWidth Or _
    xPosition > leftInvisibleWidth + Me.Width - 5 Or _
    controller.CaretLineNo > _
    controller.TopInvisibleLineCount + VisibleLineCount Then
    Return False
  Else
    Return True
  End If
End Function
```

The LeftInvisibleCharCount variable contains the number of characters that are not visible because the text area has been scrolled to the left. The number of pixels the invisible characters take (leftInvisibleWidth) is the product of LeftInvisibleCharCount and the width of each character in pixels. The caret is invisible if the x coordinate of the caret position is less than leftInvisibleWidth or greater than leftInvisibleWidth plus the text area width plus 5. The caret can also become invisible if the line number of the line the caret is on (controller.CaretLineNo) is greater than TopInvisibleLineCount plus VisibleLineCount.

MoveScreen

The MoveScreen method scrolls the text area's x position to the right, where x is the value passed to the method. A positive x means that the text area should be scrolled to the right, and a negative value indicates scrolling to the left. The method implementation is as follows:

```
Public Sub MoveScreen(ByVal increment As Integer)
  'move screen horizontally by x character
  LeftInvisibleCharCount = Math.Max(LeftInvisibleCharCount + increment, 0)
  RedrawAll()
End Sub
```

OnPaint

The OnPaint method provides the GUI for the text area. It draws all the characters visible at this instance and the caret. It also calls the PaintSelectionArea method if the controller has some text selected. The implementation of the OnPaint method is as follows:

```
Protected Overrides Sub OnPaint(ByVal e As PaintEventArgs)

  Dim graphics As Graphics = e.Graphics
  Dim textBrush As SolidBrush = New SolidBrush(ForeColor)
  Dim highlightTextBrush As SolidBrush = New SolidBrush(highlightForeColor)

  If controller.HasSelection() Then
    PaintSelectionArea(graphics)
  End If

  Dim i, visibleLine As Integer
  Dim maxCharCount As Integer
  For i = 1 To model.LineCount
    Dim thisLine As String = model.GetLine(i)
    If i > controller.TopInvisibleLineCount Then
      Dim y As Integer = visibleLine * (lineSpace + fontHeight)
      Dim j As Integer
      For j = 1 To thisLine.Length
        If j > LeftInvisibleCharCount And _
          j <= LeftInvisibleCharCount + VisibleCharCount + 1 Then
          Dim x As Integer = GetStringWidth(thisLine.Substring(0, j - 1)) - _
            LeftInvisibleCharCount * characterWidth
          If controller.IsInSelection(j, i) Then
```

```
                graphics.DrawString(thisLine.Substring(j - 1, 1), Font, _
                    highlightTextBrush, x, y)
                Else
                  graphics.DrawString(thisLine.Substring(j - 1, 1), Font, _
                    textBrush, x, y)
                End If
            End If
          Next j
          visibleLine = visibleLine + 1
        End If
    Next i


    'draw caret here
    DrawCaret(graphics)
End Sub
```

The OnPaint method starts by obtaining the Graphics object for the control (the View object) and constructing a SolidBrush to draw the normal text (textBrush) and a SolidBrush to draw the selected text (highlightTextBrush):

```
Dim graphics As Graphics = e.Graphics
Dim textBrush As SolidBrush = New SolidBrush(ForeColor)
Dim highlightTextBrush As SolidBrush = New SolidBrush(highlightForeColor)
```

Next, it calls the PaintSelectionArea method if the controller has selection—in other words, if part of the text is selected. The PaintSelectionArea method receives the reference to the previous Graphics object. The PaintSelectionArea method paints the background area for the selected text. However, it does not draw the selected text:

```
If controller.HasSelection() Then
  PaintSelectionArea(graphics)
End If
```

Then, it draws each line of the data, character by character, using the DrawString method. Prior to drawing each character, the method checks whether the character is in the selection using the controller's IsInSelection method. If it is, it is drawn using the highlightTextBrush SolidBrush. Otherwise, it is drawn using the textBrush SolidBrush:

```
Dim i, visibleLine As Integer
Dim maxCharCount As Integer
For i = 1 To model.LineCount
```

```
  Dim thisLine As String = model.GetLine(i)
  If i > controller.TopInvisibleLineCount Then
    Dim y As Integer = visibleLine * (lineSpace + fontHeight)
    Dim j As Integer
    For j = 1 To thisLine.Length
      If j > LeftInvisibleCharCount And _
        j <= LeftInvisibleCharCount + VisibleCharCount + 1 Then
        Dim x As Integer = GetStringWidth(thisLine.Substring(0, j - 1)) - _
          LeftInvisibleCharCount * characterWidth
        If controller.IsInSelection(j, i) Then
          graphics.DrawString(thisLine.Substring(j - 1, 1), Font, _
            highlightTextBrush, x, y)
        Else
          graphics.DrawString(thisLine.Substring(j - 1, 1), Font, _
            textBrush, x, y)
        End If
      End If
    Next j
    visibleLine = visibleLine + 1
  End If
Next i
```

Finally, the OnPaint method calls the DrawCaret method:

```
DrawCaret(graphics)
```

PaintSelectionArea

The OnPaint method calls the PaintSelectionArea method to paint the background of the selected text:

```
Private Sub PaintSelectionArea(ByRef graphics As Graphics)
  Dim brush As New SolidBrush(highlightBackColor)
  ' representing start and end coordinates of selected text
  Dim x1, y1, x2, y2 As Integer
  Dim p1, p2 As ColumnLine
  p1 = controller.selectionStartLocation
  p2 = controller.selectionEndLocation
  x1 = p1.Column : y1 = p1.Line
  x2 = p2.Column : y2 = p2.Line

  If y1 > y2 Or (y1 = y2 And x1 > x2) Then
    'swap
```

```
      Dim t As Integer
      t = y1 : y1 = y2 : y2 = t
      t = x1 : x1 = x2 : x2 = t
    End If


    Dim i As Integer
    Dim beginLine As Integer = Math.Max(y1, 1)
    Dim endLine As Integer = Math.Min(y2, model.LineCount)


    If beginLine = endLine Then
      If x1 > x2 Then
        Dim t As Integer
        t = x1 : x1 = x2 : x2 = t
      End If
      Dim thisLine As String = model.GetLine(beginLine)
      graphics.FillRectangle(brush, _
        2 + GetStringWidth(thisLine.Substring(0, x1 - 1)) - _
        (LeftInvisibleCharCount * characterWidth), _
        (beginLine - 1 - controller.TopInvisibleLineCount) * _
        (lineSpace + fontHeight), _
        GetStringWidth(thisLine.Substring(x1 - 1, x2 - x1)), _
        (lineSpace + fontHeight))
  Else
      For i = beginLine To endLine
        Dim thisLine As String = model.GetLine(i)
        If i = beginLine Then
          ' first line may not be the whole line,
          ' but from initial position of selection to end of string
          graphics.FillRectangle(brush, _
            2 + GetStringWidth(thisLine.Substring(0, x1 - 1)) - _
            LeftInvisibleCharCount * characterWidth, _
            (i - 1 - controller.TopInvisibleLineCount) * _
            (lineSpace + fontHeight), GetStringWidth(thisLine) - _
            GetStringWidth(thisLine.Substring(0, x1 - 1)), _
            (lineSpace + fontHeight))

        ElseIf i = endLine Then
          graphics.FillRectangle(brush, _
            2 - LeftInvisibleCharCount * characterWidth, _
            (i - 1 - controller.TopInvisibleLineCount) * _
            (lineSpace + fontHeight), _
            GetStringWidth(thisLine.Substring(0, x2 - 1)), _
            (lineSpace + fontHeight))
```

```
      Else
        ' last line may not be the whole line,
        ' but from first column to initial position of selection
        graphics.FillRectangle(brush, _
          2 - LeftInvisibleCharCount * characterWidth, _
          (i - 1 - controller.TopInvisibleLineCount) * _
          (lineSpace + fontHeight), GetStringWidth(thisLine), _
          (lineSpace + fontHeight))
      End If
    Next i
  End If
  'don't dispose graphics!!
End Sub
```

The selection area is all the characters between two `ColumnLine` objects indicated by the controller's `selectionStartLocation` and `selectionEndLocation` variables. The background for the selected text is painted by drawing filled rectangles from the beginning of the selection toward the end. Rectangles are drawn in each line in the selection. Because the method always scans from the first visible line downward, it is important that the `selectionEndLocation` resides to the bottom of the `selectionStartLocation` or, if there is only one line selected, to the right of the `selectionStartLocation`. Therefore, before the painting, `selectionStartLocation` and `selectionEndLocation` are checked and swapped if necessary:

```
Dim x1, y1, x2, y2 As Integer
Dim p1, p2 As ColumnLine
p1 = controller.selectionStartLocation
p2 = controller.selectionEndLocation
x1 = p1.Column : y1 = p1.Line
x2 = p2.Column : y2 = p2.Line

If y1 > y2 Or (y1 = y2 And x1 > x2) Then
  'swap
  Dim t As Integer
  t = y1 : y1 = y2 : y2 = t
  t = x1 : x1 = x2 : x2 = t
End If
```

You can locate the end location at the top of the start location if the user drags the mouse upward when selecting the text.

You set the beginning line and the end line of the selection by using `beginLine` and `endLine`:

```
Dim beginLine As Integer = Math.Max(y1, 1)
Dim endLine As Integer = Math.Min(y2, model.LineCount)
```

The next lines of code do the painting. A filled rectangle for a line is the result of calling the `FillRectangle` method of the `Graphics` class.

RedrawAll

The `RedrawAll` method invalidates the whole text area and forces a repaint. Before invalidating, the method makes some necessary adjustments to the controller's `TopInvisibleLineCount` variable and its own `LeftInvisibleCharCount` variable. Its implementation is as follows:

```
Public Sub RedrawAll()
  'before redraw correct invisible line count
  controller.TopInvisibleLineCount = _
    Math.Min(controller.TopInvisibleLineCount, _
    model.LineCount - VisibleLineCount)
  If controller.TopInvisibleLineCount < 0 Then
    controller.TopInvisibleLineCount = 0
  End If
  LeftInvisibleCharCount = Math.Min(LeftInvisibleCharCount, _
    model.LongestLineCharCount - VisibleCharCount)
  If LeftInvisibleCharCount < 0 Then LeftInvisibleCharCount = 0
  Me.Invalidate()
  Me.Update()
End Sub
```

RepositionCaret

The `RepositionCaret` method moves the caret to the new location when the user clicks the text area. This method accepts the x and y coordinates of the point where the user clicks on the text area. The method implementation is as follows:

```
Public Sub RepositionCaret(ByVal x As Integer, ByVal y As Integer)
  'Get the (visible) line number
  Dim lineNumber As Integer = 1 + CInt(y / (fontHeight + lineSpace))
  controller.CaretLineNo = Math.Min(lineNumber + _
    controller.TopInvisibleLineCount, model.LineCount)
```

```
'Now calculate the closest position of the character in the current line
Dim thisLine As String = controller.GetCurrentLine()
Dim i As Integer, minDistance As Single = Width ' the width of this control
Dim j As Integer = 0

For i = 0 To thisLine.Length
  Dim distance As Integer = _
    Math.Abs(x + LeftInvisibleCharCount * characterWidth - _
    GetStringWidth(thisLine.Substring(0, i)))
  If distance < minDistance Then
    minDistance = distance
    j = i
  End If
Next i
controller.CaretColumnNo = j + 1
RedrawAll()
End Sub
```

You can calculate the y coordinate as follows:

```
Dim lineNumber As Integer = 1 + CInt(y / (fontHeight + lineSpace))
controller.CaretLineNo = Math.Min(lineNumber + _
  controller.TopInvisibleLineCount, model.LineCount)
```

Note that if the user clicks on the area below the last line, the caret will move to the last line because the caret indicates the insertion point and you cannot insert a character into a nonexistent line.

The x coordinate of the caret has to be calculated so that the new location will be before the closest character to the point the user clicks:

```
Dim i As Integer, minDistance As Single = Width ' the width of this control
Dim j As Integer = 0

For i = 0 To thisLine.Length
  Dim distance As Integer = _
    Math.Abs(x + LeftInvisibleCharCount * characterWidth - _
    GetStringWidth(thisLine.Substring(0, i)))
  If distance < minDistance Then
    minDistance = distance
    j = i
  End If
Next i
controller.CaretColumnNo = j + 1
```

Finally, the method calls the RedrawAll method to repaint the text area.

Scroll

The Scroll method scrolls the text area vertically by x lines, where x is indicated by the value of the argument increment. The text area scrolls down if x is a positive integer and scrolls up for a negative x.

The method implementation is as follows:

```
Public Sub Scroll(ByVal increment As Integer)
  controller.TopInvisibleLineCount = _
    controller.TopInvisibleLineCount + increment
  If controller.TopInvisibleLineCount < 0 Then
    controller.TopInvisibleLineCount = 0
  End If
  RedrawAll()
End Sub
```

You achieve scrolling by changing the value of the controller's TopInvisible-LineCount variable and calling the RedrawAll method.

TranslateIntoCaretLocation

The TranslateIntoCaretLocation method returns a ColumnLine object given a (x, y) coordinate of a point in the text area. This method is useful for determining what is the closest ColumnLine to the user click point. The method implementation is as follows:

```
Public Function TranslateIntoCaretLocation( _
  ByVal x1 As Integer, ByVal y1 As Integer) As ColumnLine
  Dim column, line As Integer ' the coordinate for the returned Point

  'set lowest value for y1 in case the use keeps dragging above the control
  If y1 < 1 Then
    y1 = 1
  End If
```

```
'Get the visible line number
line = Math.Min(1 + controller.TopInvisibleLineCount + _
  CInt(y1 / (fontHeight + lineSpace)), model.LineCount)
'Now calculate the closest position of the character in the current line
Dim thisLine As String = model.GetLine(line)
Dim i As Integer, minDistance As Single = Me.Width 'the width of this control
Dim j As Integer = 0
For i = 0 To thisLine.Length
  Dim distance As Single = _
    Math.Abs(x1 + LeftInvisibleCharCount * characterWidth - _
    GetStringWidth(thisLine.Substring(0, i)))
  If distance < minDistance Then
    minDistance = distance
    j = i
  End If
Next i
column = j + 1
Return New ColumnLine(column, line)
End Function
```

Using the LineNumberView Class

The LineNumberView class represents a view that displays the line numbers of the Model object. The LineNumberView class has the model and controller object variables that are assigned to the Model object and the controller:

```
Private model As model
Public controller As StyledTextArea
```

In addition, two more class variables determine how line numbers are displayed, lineSpace and fontFace:

```
Public lineSpace As Integer = 2
Public fontFace As String = "Courier New"
```

The integer lineSpace is the number of pixels between two line numbers, and fontFace is the font type used to draw the numbers.

Constructing a LineNumberView Object

The only constructor of the LineNumberView class accepts an argument of type
Model. When an instance of this class is created, it assigns this object to its model
variable. It also sets its FontHeight and Font properties. This is the LineNumberView
class's constructor:

```
Public Sub New(ByRef model As Model)
  Me.model = model
  FontHeight = 10
  Font = New Font(fontFace, FontHeight)
End Sub
```

Understanding the LineNumberView Class's Property

The LineNumberView class has one property: VisibleLineCount, which is similar to
the VisibleLineCount property of the View class. The following is the property
implementation:

```
  Public ReadOnly Property VisibleLineCount() As Integer
    Get
      Return CInt(Me.Height / (lineSpace + FontHeight))
    End Get
  End Property
```

Understanding the LineNumberView Class's Methods

The LineNumberView class has two methods: OnPaint and RedrawAll. The following
sections explain both.

OnPaint

The OnPaint method overrides the OnPaint method in the Control class. Its mission
is to provide a GUI for the LineNumberView object. In other words, it draws the line
numbers. Its implementation is as follows:

```
Protected Overrides Sub OnPaint(ByVal e As PaintEventArgs)
  Dim graphics As Graphics = e.Graphics
  Dim textBrush As SolidBrush = New SolidBrush(ForeColor)
  Dim characterWidth As Integer = 8
```

```
  Dim i, visibleLine As Integer
  For i = 1 To Math.Min(model.LineCount, VisibleLineCount)
    Dim number As Integer = i + controller.TopInvisibleLineCount
    Dim x As Integer = Me.Width - characterWidth - _
      (number).ToString().Length * characterWidth
    Dim y As Integer = (i - 1) * (lineSpace + fontheight)
    graphics.DrawString(number.ToString(), Font, textBrush, x, y)
  Next i
End Sub
```

The OnPaint method first obtains the Graphics object of the LineNumberView object from the PaintEventArgs argument:

```
Dim graphics As Graphics = e.Graphics
```

It then constructs a SolidBrush object that draws the line numbers:

```
Dim textBrush As SolidBrush = New SolidBrush(ForeColor)
```

Next, the OnPaint method iterates all the line numbers that need to be drawn in a For loop and uses the DrawString method of the Graphics class to draw the numbers:

```
For i = 1 To Math.Min(model.LineCount, VisibleLineCount)
  Dim number As Integer = i + controller.TopInvisibleLineCount
  Dim x As Integer = Me.Width - characterWidth - _
    (number).ToString().Length * characterWidth
  Dim y As Integer = (i - 1) * (lineSpace + fontheight)
  graphics.DrawString(number.ToString(), Font, textBrush, x, y)
Next i
```

RedrawAll

The RedrawAll method invalidates the text area and forces a repaint. Its implementation is as follows:

```
Public Sub RedrawAll()
  Me.Invalidate()
  Me.Update()
End Sub
```

Using the StyledTextArea Class

The `StyledTextArea` class represents the controller in the MVC architecture of the
`StyledTextArea` control. It is also the class that programmers see when they use the
control. The other two main parts, the model and views, are private objects of this
class. Therefore, they are not visible to the programmer who uses this control.

You declare the model and two views of the `StyledTextArea` control as private
members of the `StyledTextArea` class:

```
Private view As View          ' the view in the MVC pattern
lineNumberView As LineNumberView
Private model As Model   ' the model in the MVC pattern
```

You can obtain and set the width of the `LineNumberView` through the public
`LineNumberWidth` field:

```
Public LineNumberWidth As Integer = 50
```

There are also vertical and horizontal scrollbars that scroll the text area vertically and horizontally, respectively. Their widths are also fixed:

```
Private hScrollBar As New HScrollBar()
Private vScrollBar As New VScrollBar()
Const hScrollBarHeight As Integer = 15
Const vScrollBarWidth As Integer = 15
```

All parts of the user interface are packaged in a `Panel` control:

```
Private panel As New panel()  ' we use panel so we can set the borderstyle
```

The sole reason for using a `Panel` is so that you can use its nice border. For
details, see the "InitializeComponent" section.

As mentioned, the `StyledTextArea` class is the controller part in the MVC
design pattern. Its main function is to take care of the user interaction with the
user interface. The `StyledTextArea` control is a control that can receive the user's
key input. A caret indicates the character insertion point visually in the `View` class.
This caret is drawn at the location specified by the following `caretLocation` variable
of type `ColumnLine`:

```
Private caretLocation As New ColumnLine(1, 1)
```

In addition, the StyledTextArea control also allows part of the text to be selected. The starting point and the ending point of the selected text are denoted by the following two variables. Their scope is Friend so that they can be accessed from the View class:

```
Friend selectionStartLocation As New ColumnLine(0, 0)
Friend selectionEndLocation As New ColumnLine(0, 0)
```

A private Boolean (selecting) also internally indicates that the user is dragging the mouse to make a text selection. You use this variable in the view_MouseUp, view_MouseDown, and view_MouseMove event handlers:

```
Private selecting As Boolean   ' user selecting text
```

Another Boolean (keyProcessed) indicates if a key press should be handled by the KeyPress event handler. See the view_KeyPress event handler and the ProcessDialogKey method in this class:

```
' indicates that the key press has been processed by ProcessDialogKey,
' so KeyPressed does not have to process this.
Private keyProcessed As Boolean
```

Also, the edited private Boolean indicates if the text in the Model object has been edited—in other words, whether a character has been added or deleted:

```
' indicates whether the text has been edited
Private editedField As Boolean
```

The last class variable in the StyledTextArea class is the TopInvisibleLineCount. This value has the Friend scope so that it can be accessed from both the View class and the LineNumberView class:

```
' represents the number of lines not displayed
' because the screen was scrolled down
Friend TopInvisibleLineCount As Integer
```

Constructing the StyledTextArea Class

The StyledTextArea class has one constructor that accepts no arguments. It consists only of the line that calls the InitializeComponent method:

```
Public Sub New()
  InitializeComponent()
End Sub
```

Understanding the StyledTextArea Class's Properties

The StyledTextArea class has several properties. Those properties with the scope Public are meant to be used by the user of the StyledTextArea control to set some settings of the control. The CaretColumnNo and CaretLineNo properties, which have the scope Friend, are meant to be used from the View class only.

The properties are explained in the following sections.

CaretColor

The CaretColor property represents the caret color in the View object. The implementation of this property is as follows:

```
Public Property CaretColor() As Color
  Get
    Return view.CaretColor
  End Get
  Set(ByVal caretColor As Color)
    view.CaretColor = caretColor
  End Set
End Property
```

CaretColumnNo

The CaretColumnNo property represents the caret's column location. You use it from inside the View class. Its implementation is as follows:

```
Friend Property CaretColumnNo() As Integer
  Get
    Return caretLocation.Column
  End Get
  Set(ByVal newColumnNo As Integer)
```

```
    If newColumnNo > 0 And newColumnNo <= GetCurrentLine().Length + 1 Then
      Dim oldColumnNo As Integer = caretLocation.Column
      caretLocation.Column = newColumnNo
      If oldColumnNo <> newColumnNo Then
        OnColumnChanged(New ColumnEventArgs(oldColumnNo, newColumnNo))
      End If
    End If
  End Set
End Property
```

CaretLineNo

The CaretLineNo property represents the caret's line location. You use it from inside the View class. Its implementation is as follows:

```
Friend Property CaretLineNo() As Integer
  Get
    Return caretLocation.Line
  End Get
  Set(ByVal newLineNo As Integer)
    If newLineNo > 0 And newLineNo <= model.LineCount Then
      Dim oldLineNo As Integer = caretLocation.Line
      caretLocation.Line = newLineNo
      If oldLineNo <> newLineNo Then
        OnLineChanged(New LineEventArgs(oldLineNo, newLineNo))
      End If
    End If
  End Set
End Property
```

Edited

The Edited property indicates whether a character has been inserted or deleted since the last time this property was reset. A program using the StyledTextArea control to display a document's content can reset this property whenever the document is reset. The next time the user tries to save the document, the program can check this property and skip the save if this property value is still False.

The Edited property implementation uses a field called editedField to store its value.

Its implementation is as follows:

```
Public Property Edited() As Boolean
  Get
    Return editedField
  End Get
  Set(ByVal value As Boolean)
    'allows it to be reset/set,
    'for example if the document using this control is saved
    editedField = value
  End Set
End Property
```

HighlightBackColor

The HighlightBackColor property represents the background color of the selected text:

```
Public Property HighlightBackColor() As Color
  Get
    Return view.highlightBackColor
  End Get
  Set(ByVal color As Color)
    view.highlightBackColor = color
  End Set
End Property
```

HighlightForeColor

The HighlightForeColor property represents the color of the selected text:

```
Public Property HighlightForeColor() As Color
  Get
    Return view.highlightForeColor
  End Get
  Set(ByVal color As Color)
    view.highlightForeColor = color
  End Set
End Property
```

LineCount

The LineCount property obtains the number of lines:

```
Public ReadOnly Property LineCount() As Integer
  Get
    Return model.LineCount
  End Get
End Property
```

LineNumberBackColor

The LineNumberBackColor property represents the background color of the
LineNumberView object:

```
Public Property LineNumberBackColor() As Color
  Get
    Return lineNumberView.BackColor
  End Get
  Set(ByVal color As Color)
    lineNumberView.BackColor = color
  End Set
End Property
```

LineNumberForeColor

The LineNumberForeColor property represents the color used to draw line numbers:

```
Public Property LineNumberForeColor() As Color
  Get
    Return lineNumberView.ForeColor
  End Get
  Set(ByVal color As Color)
    lineNumberView.ForeColor = color
  End Set
End Property
```

SelectedText

The read-only `SelectedText` property represents the user-selected text:

```
Public ReadOnly Property SelectedText() As String
  Get
    If HasSelection() Then
      Dim x1, y1, x2, y2 As Integer
      x1 = selectionStartLocation.Column
      y1 = selectionStartLocation.Line
      x2 = selectionEndLocation.Column
      y2 = selectionEndLocation.Line

      'swap if necessary
      If y1 > y2 Or (y1 = y2 And x1 > x2) Then
        Dim t As Integer
        t = x1 : x1 = x2 : x2 = t
        t = y1 : y1 = y2 : y2 = t
      End If

      If y1 = y2 Then
        Return model.GetLine(y1).Substring(x1 - 1, x2 - x1)
      Else
        Dim sb As New StringBuilder(model.CharCount + 2 * model.LineCount)
        Dim lineCount As Integer = model.LineCount
        Dim i, lineNo As Integer
        For i = y1 To y2
          Dim thisLine As String = model.GetLine(i)
          If i = y1 Then
            sb.Append(thisLine.Substring(x1 - 1))
          ElseIf i = y2 Then
            sb.Append(Microsoft.VisualBasic.Constants.vbCrLf)
            sb.Append(thisLine.Substring(0, x2 - 1))
          Else
            sb.Append(Microsoft.VisualBasic.Constants.vbCrLf)
            sb.Append(thisLine)
          End If
        Next
        Return sb.ToString()
      End If
    Else
      Return ""
    End If
  End Get
End Property
```

Text

The Text property represents all text in the StyledTextArea control. Setting this property overwrites the previous text. Its implementation is as follows:

```
Public Overrides Property Text() As String
  Get
    Dim sb As New StringBuilder(model.CharCount + 2 * model.LineCount)
    Dim lineCount As Integer = model.LineCount
    Dim i As Integer
    For i = 1 To lineCount
      Dim thisLine As String = model.GetLine(i)
      sb.Append(thisLine)
      If i < lineCount Then
        sb.Append(Microsoft.VisualBasic.Constants.vbCrLf)
      End If
    Next
    Return sb.ToString()
  End Get
  Set(ByVal s As String)
    If Not s Is Nothing Then
      Dim initialColumn As Integer = caretLocation.Column
      Dim initialLine As Integer = caretLocation.Line

      'remove all lines
      Dim i As Integer
      Dim lineCount As Integer = model.LineCount
      For i = 2 To lineCount
        model.RemoveLine(2, False)
      Next
      model.SetLine(1, "") ' don't remove the first line
      caretLocation.Column = 1
      caretLocation.Line = 1
      caretLocation = model.InsertData(s, caretLocation)

      If caretLocation.Column <> initialColumn Then
        OnColumnChanged(New _
          ColumnEventArgs(initialColumn, caretLocation.Column))
      End If
      If caretLocation.Line <> initialLine Then
        OnLineChanged(New LineEventArgs(initialLine, caretLocation.Line))
      End If
      ResetSelection()
```

```
      If Not view.IsCaretVisible() Then
        ScrollToShowCaret()
      End If
      RedrawAll()
    End If
  End Set
End Property
```

TextBackColor

The TextBackColor property represents the background color of the View object:

```
Public Property TextBackColor() As Color
  Get
    Return view.BackColor
  End Get
  Set(ByVal color As Color)
    view.BackColor = color
  End Set
End Property
```

TextForeColor

The TextForeColor property represents the color used to draw text in the View object:

```
Public Property TextForeColor() As Color
  Get
    Return view.ForeColor
  End Get
  Set(ByVal color As Color)
    view.ForeColor = color
  End Set
End Property
```

Understanding the StyledTextArea Class's Methods

The StyledTextArea class has the following methods.

AdjustHScrollBar

The `AdjustHScrollBar` method adjusts the horizontal scrollbar to reflect the up-to-date values of the scrollbar's `Maximum` and `Value` properties. This method disables the scrollbar if the longest line is shorter than the screen width. It implementation is as follows:

```
Private Sub AdjustHScrollBar()
  If view.Width < model.LongestLineCharCount * view.characterWidth + 1 Then
    hScrollBar.Enabled = True
    hScrollBar.Maximum = model.LongestLineCharCount - _
        view.VisibleCharCount + 1   '10 is the margin
    hScrollBar.Value = Math.Min(hScrollBar.Maximum, _
      view.LeftInvisibleCharCount)
  Else
    hScrollBar.Enabled = False
  End If
End Sub
```

AdjustVScrollBar

The `AdjustVScrollBar` method adjusts the vertical scrollbar to reflect the current values of the scrollbar's `Maximum` and `Value` properties. This method disables the scrollbar if the number of lines is smaller than the number of lines the screen can display at a time. Its implementation is as follows:

```
Private Sub AdjustVScrollBar()
  'adjust vScrollBar
  If view.VisibleLineCount < model.LineCount Then
    vScrollBar.Enabled = True
    vScrollBar.Maximum = model.LineCount - view.VisibleLineCount + 1
    vScrollBar.Value = Math.Min(TopInvisibleLineCount, vScrollBar.Maximum)
  Else
    vScrollBar.Enabled = False
  End If

End Sub
```

Copy

The Copy method copies the selected text into the Clipboard:

```
Public Sub Copy()
  'copy selected text to clipboard
  If HasSelection() Then
    Clipboard.SetDataObject(SelectedText)
  End If
End Sub
```

Cut

The Cut method copies the selected text into the Clipboard and deletes the selection:

```
Public Sub Cut()
  If HasSelection() Then
    Copy()
    RemoveSelection()
    ResetSelection()
    RedrawAll()
  End If
End Sub
```

Find

The Find method searches a pattern in the text and highlights the matching part of the text:

```
Public Function Find(ByVal userPattern As String, _
  ByVal startColumn As Integer, ByVal startLine As Integer, _
  ByVal caseSensitive As Boolean, _
  ByVal wholeWord As Boolean, ByVal goUp As Boolean) As ColumnLine

  'make sure startColumn and startLine is greater than 0
  startColumn = Math.Max(startColumn, 1)
  Dim pattern As String = userPattern.Trim()
  Dim patternLength As Integer = pattern.Length
  Dim lineCount As Integer = model.LineCount
  Dim direction As Integer = 1
  If goUp Then direction = -1
  startLine = Math.Max(startLine, 1)
```

```vbnet
startLine = Math.Min(startLine, lineCount)
Dim lineNo As Integer = startLine
If Not caseSensitive Then
  pattern = pattern.ToUpper()
End If
While lineNo <= lineCount And lineNo > 0
  Dim thisLine As String = model.GetLine(lineNo)

  If Not caseSensitive Then
    thisLine = thisLine.ToUpper()
  End If

  Dim searchResult As Integer = -1
  If lineNo = startLine Then
    If startColumn - 1 < thisLine.Length Then
      searchResult = thisLine.IndexOf(pattern, startColumn - 1)
    End If
  Else
    searchResult = thisLine.IndexOf(pattern)
  End If

  If searchResult <> -1 And wholeWord Then
    'search successful but now test if the found pattern is a
    'whole word by checking the characters after and before
    'the match
    If searchResult > 0 Then
      'test the character before the match
      If Char.IsLetterOrDigit( _
        Convert.ToChar(thisLine.Substring(searchResult - 1, 1))) Then
        searchResult = -1
      End If
    End If
    If searchResult <> -1 And _
      thisLine.Length > searchResult + patternLength Then
      'test the character after the match
      If Char.IsLetterOrDigit( _
        Convert.ToChar(thisLine.Substring(searchResult + _
        patternLength, 1))) Then
        searchResult = -1
      End If
    End If
  End If
  If searchResult <> -1 Then    'successful
```

```
      'move caret to new position
      CaretLineNo = lineNo
      CaretColumnNo = searchResult + patternLength + 1
      Highlight(searchResult + 1, lineNo, _
        searchResult + patternLength + 1, lineNo)
      RedrawAll()
      Return New ColumnLine(searchResult + 1, lineNo)
    End If
    lineNo = lineNo + direction
  End While
  Return New ColumnLine(0, 0)
End Function
```

GetCurrentLine

The GetCurrentLine method returns the string representing the line the caret is on:

```
Public Function GetCurrentLine() As String
  'return the line where the caret is on
  Return model.GetLine(CaretLineNo)
End Function
```

GetLine

The GetLine method gets the line at the specified line number:

```
Public Function GetLine(ByVal lineNo As Integer) As String
  Return model.GetLine(lineNo)
End Function
```

HasSelection

The HasSelection method indicates whether there is part of the text that is selected:

```
Friend Function HasSelection() As Boolean
  If selectionStartLocation.Equals(selectionEndLocation) Then
    Return False
  Else
    Return True
  End If
End Function
```

Highlight

The `Highlight` method highlights the selected text:

```
Private Sub Highlight(ByVal x1 As Integer, ByVal y1 As Integer, _
  ByVal x2 As Integer, ByVal y2 As Integer)
  '(x1, y1) is the starting column,line of highlight
  '(x2, y2) is the end column,line of hightlight
  'swap (x1,y1) and (x2,y2) if necessary
  If y1 > y2 Or (y1 = y2 And x1 > x2) Then
    Dim t As Integer
    t = x1 : x1 = x2 : x2 = t
    t = y1 : y1 = y2 : y2 = t
  End If
  selectionStartLocation.Column = x1
  selectionStartLocation.Line = y1
  selectionEndLocation.Column = x2
  selectionEndLocation.Line = y2
End Sub
```

hScrollBar_Scroll

The `hScrollBar_Scroll` event handler handles the horizontal scrollbar's `Scroll` event. It adjusts the position of the horizontal scrollbar as well as scrolling the `View` object's screen, if necessary. Its implementation is as follows:

```
Private Sub hScrollBar_Scroll(ByVal sender As Object, _
  ByVal e As ScrollEventArgs)
  Select Case e.Type
    Case ScrollEventType.SmallIncrement
      If view.LeftInvisibleCharCount < _
        model.LongestLineCharCount - view.VisibleCharCount + 1 Then
        view.MoveScreen(hScrollBar.SmallChange)
      End If
    Case ScrollEventType.LargeIncrement
      If view.LeftInvisibleCharCount < _
        model.LongestLineCharCount - view.VisibleCharCount Then
        Dim maxIncrement As Integer = _
          Math.Min(hScrollBar.LargeChange, model.LongestLineCharCount - _
          view.VisibleCharCount - view.LeftInvisibleCharCount)
        view.MoveScreen(maxIncrement)
      End If
    Case ScrollEventType.SmallDecrement
```

```
      view.MoveScreen(-hScrollBar.SmallChange)
    Case ScrollEventType.LargeDecrement
      view.MoveScreen(-hScrollBar.LargeChange)
    Case ScrollEventType.ThumbTrack
      view.LeftInvisibleCharCount = e.NewValue
      RedrawAll()
    Case ScrollEventType.ThumbPosition
      view.LeftInvisibleCharCount = e.NewValue
      RedrawAll()
  End Select
End Sub
```

InitializeComponent

The IntializeComponent method initializes the controls and classes used in the StyledTextArea control. You call this method with the class's constructor. Its implementation is as follows:

```
Private Sub InitializeComponent()
  model = New Model()
  view = New View(model)
  view.controller = Me
  view.ForeColor = Color.Black
  view.BackColor = Color.White
  view.Cursor = Cursors.IBeam

  lineNumberView = New LineNumberView(model)
  lineNumberView.controller = Me
  lineNumberView.BackColor = Color.AntiqueWhite
  lineNumberView.ForeColor = Color.Black

  lineNumberView.TabStop = False
  vScrollBar.TabStop = False
  hScrollBar.TabStop = False
  ResizeComponents()
  panel.Dock = DockStyle.Fill
  panel.Controls.Add(lineNumberView)
  panel.Controls.Add(view)
  panel.Controls.Add(hScrollBar)
  panel.Controls.Add(vScrollBar)
  panel.BorderStyle = BorderStyle.Fixed3D
```

```
      Me.Controls.Add(panel)
      AddHandler view.KeyPress, AddressOf view_KeyPress
      AddHandler view.MouseDown, AddressOf view_MouseDown
      AddHandler view.MouseUp, AddressOf view_MouseUp
      AddHandler view.MouseMove, AddressOf view_MouseMove

      AddHandler model.LineCountChanged, AddressOf Model_LineCountChanged
      AddHandler model.LongestLineCharCountChanged, _
        AddressOf model_LongestLineCharCountChanged
      AddHandler vScrollBar.Scroll, AddressOf vScrollBar_Scroll
      AddHandler hScrollBar.Scroll, AddressOf hScrollBar_Scroll
      AddHandler panel.Resize, AddressOf panel_Resize

      hScrollBar.Enabled = False
      hScrollBar.SmallChange = 1 ' 1 character
      hScrollBar.LargeChange = 2
      vScrollBar.Enabled = False
      vScrollBar.SmallChange = 1
      vScrollBar.LargeChange = 2
    End Sub
```

IsCaretOnFirstColumn

The IsCaretOnFirstColumn method indicates whether the caret is on the first column of any line:

```
Private Function IsCaretOnFirstColumn() As Boolean
  Return (CaretColumnNo = 1)
End Function
```

IsCaretOnFirstLine

The IsCaretOnFirstLine method indicates whether the caret is on the first line:

```
Private Function IsCaretOnFirstLine() As Boolean
  Return (CaretLineNo = 1)
End Function
```

IsCaretOnFirstVisibleLine

The IsCaretOnFirstVisibleLine method indicates whether the caret is on the first visible line of the View object's text area:

```
Private Function IsCaretOnFirstVisibleLine() As Boolean
  Return (CaretLineNo = TopInvisibleLineCount + 1)
End Function
```

IsCaretOnLastColumn

The IsCaretOnLastColumn method indicates whether the caret is on the last column of the current line:

```
Private Function IsCaretOnLastColumn() As Boolean
  Return (CaretColumnNo = GetCurrentLine().Length + 1)
End Function
```

IsCaretOnLastLine

The IsCaretOnLastLine method indicates whether the caret is on the last line:

```
Private Function IsCaretOnLastLine() As Boolean
  Return (CaretLineNo = model.LineCount)
End Function
```

IsCaretOnLastVisibleLine

The IsCaretOnLastVisibleLine method indicates whether the caret is on the last visible line of the View object's text area:

```
Private Function IsCaretOnLastVisibleLine() As Boolean
  Return (CaretLineNo = view.VisibleLineCount + TopInvisibleLineCount)
End Function
```

IsInSelection

The IsInSelection method indicates whether the caret is in the selected text:

```
Public Function IsInSelection(ByVal column As Integer, _
  ByVal line As Integer) As Boolean
  'indicate that the character at (column, line) is selected
  If Not HasSelection() Then
    Return False
  Else
    Dim x1, y1, x2, y2 As Integer
    x1 = selectionStartLocation.Column
     y1 = selectionStartLocation.Line
    x2 = selectionEndLocation.Column
    y2 = selectionEndLocation.Line

    'swap if necessary to make (x2, y2) below (x1, y1)
    If (y1 > y2) Or (y1 = y2 And x1 > x2) Then
      Dim t As Integer
      t = x2 : x2 = x1 : x1 = t
      t = y2 : y2 = y1 : y1 = t
    End If

    If y2 > model.LineCount Then
      y2 = model.LineCount
      If y1 = y2 And x1 > x2 Then
        Dim t As Integer
        t = x2 : x2 = x1 : x1 = t
      End If
    End If
     f line < y2 And line > y1 Then
      Return True
    ElseIf y1 = y2 And line = y1 And column >= x1 And column < x2 Then
      'selection in one line
      Return True
    ElseIf line = y1 And line <> y2 And column >= x1 Then
      Return True
    ElseIf line = y2 And line <> y1 And column < x2 Then
      Return True
    Else
      Return False
    End If
  End If
End Function
```

model_LineCountChanged

The model_LineCountChanged event handler handles the LineCountChanged event of the Model object. It adjusts the vertical scrollbar by calling the AdjustVScrollBar method:

```
Private Sub model_LineCountChanged(ByVal sender As Object, _
  ByVal e As LineCountEventArgs)
  AdjustVScrollBar()
End Sub
```

model_LongestLineCharCountChanged

The model_LongestLineCharCountChanged event handler handles the LongestLineCharCountChanged event of the Model object. It checks if the number of characters the View object's text area can display is larger than the number characters of the longest line. If so, it sets the LeftInvisibleCharCount variable of the View object to zero. It then calls the AdjustHScrollBar method to adjust the horizontal scrollbar. The implementation of model_LongestLineCharCountChanged is as follows:

```
Private Sub model_LongestLineCharCountChanged(ByVal sender As Object, _
  ByVal e As LongestLineEventArgs)
  If e.LongestLineCharCount < view.VisibleCharCount Then
    view.LeftInvisibleCharCount = 0
  End If
  AdjustHScrollBar()
End Sub
```

OnColumnChanged

The OnColumnChanged method raises the ColumnChanged event:

```
Protected Overridable Sub OnColumnChanged(ByVal e As ColumnEventArgs)
  RaiseEvent ColumnChanged(Me, e)
End Sub
```

OnLineChanged

The OnLineChanged method raises the LineChanged event:

```
Protected Overridable Sub OnLineChanged(ByVal e As LineEventArgs)
  RaiseEvent LineChanged(Me, e)
End Sub
```

panel_Resize

The panel_Resize event handler handles the Resize event of the Panel object by calling the ResizeComponents method:

```
Private Sub panel_Resize(ByVal sender As Object, ByVal e As EventArgs)
  ResizeComponents()
End Sub
```

Paste

The Paste method pastes the content of the Clipboard starting from the caret location. If there is selected text when the Paste method is called, the selected text will be deleted. Only paste the content of the Clipboard if the format is Text. Its implementation is as follows:

```
Public Sub Paste()
  ' In this method, CaretLocation's Line and Column fields
  ' are accessed without going through the CaretLineNo and CaretColumnNo
  ' properties so as not to raise the OnLineChanged and OnColumnChanged
  ' events repeatedly.
  Dim buffer As IDataObject = Clipboard.GetDataObject()
  If buffer.GetDataPresent(DataFormats.Text) Then

    Dim initialColumn As Integer = caretLocation.Column
    Dim initialLine As Integer = caretLocation.Line

    If HasSelection() Then
      RemoveSelection()
    End If

    Dim s As String = buffer.GetData(DataFormats.Text).ToString()
    caretLocation = model.InsertData(s, caretLocation)
    If caretLocation.Column <> initialColumn Then
      OnColumnChanged(New ColumnEventArgs(initialColumn, caretLocation.Column))
    End If
    If caretLocation.Line <> initialLine Then
      OnLineChanged(New LineEventArgs(initialLine, caretLocation.Line))
    End If
    If HasSelection() Then
      ResetSelection()
    End If
    If Not view.IsCaretVisible() Then
```

```
      ScrollToShowCaret()
    End If
    RedrawAll()
  Else
    'MsgBox("Incompatible data format")
  End If
End Sub
```

ProcessDialogKey

The ProcessDialogKey method overrides the same method in the Control class to
capture the pressing of any keyboard key. If the key corresponds to a character
that needs to be displayed or inserted into the Model object, it resets the keyProcessed
flag and in effect lets the view_KeyPress method handle the key press. Its implementation is as follows:

```
Protected Overrides Function ProcessDialogKey(ByVal keyData As Keys) As Boolean
  keyProcessed = True
  Select Case keyData
    Case Keys.Down
      ResetSelection()
      If Not IsCaretOnLastLine() Then
        If IsCaretOnLastVisibleLine() Then
          view.Scroll(1)
        End If
        CaretLineNo = CaretLineNo + 1
        If CaretColumnNo > GetCurrentLine().Length + 1 Then
          CaretColumnNo = GetCurrentLine().Length + 1
        End If
        ScrollToShowCaret()
        RedrawAll()
      End If
      Return True
    Case Keys.Up
      ResetSelection()
      If Not IsCaretOnFirstLine() Then
        If IsCaretOnFirstVisibleLine() Then
          view.Scroll(-1)
        End If
        CaretLineNo = CaretLineNo - 1
        If CaretColumnNo > GetCurrentLine().Length + 1 Then
          CaretColumnNo = GetCurrentLine().Length + 1
        End If
```

```
        ScrollToShowCaret()
        RedrawAll()
      End If
      Return True
   Case Keys.Right
      ResetSelection()
      If IsCaretOnLastColumn() Then
        If Not IsCaretOnLastLine() Then
          If IsCaretOnLastVisibleLine() Then
            view.Scroll(1)
          End If
          CaretLineNo = CaretLineNo + 1
          CaretColumnNo = 1
        End If
      Else
        CaretColumnNo = CaretColumnNo + 1
      End If
      ScrollToShowCaret()
      RedrawAll()
      Return True
   Case Keys.Left
      ResetSelection()
      If IsCaretOnFirstColumn() Then
        If Not IsCaretOnFirstLine() Then
          If IsCaretOnFirstVisibleLine() Then
            view.Scroll(-1)
          End If
          CaretLineNo = CaretLineNo - 1
          CaretColumnNo = GetCurrentLine().Length + 1
        End If
      Else
        CaretColumnNo = CaretColumnNo - 1
      End If
      ScrollToShowCaret()
      RedrawAll()
      Return True
   Case Keys.Delete
      'Deleting character does not change caret position but
      'may change the longest line char count
      If HasSelection() Then
        RemoveSelection()
        ResetSelection()
        ' then don't delete anything
```

```
        Else
          If CaretColumnNo = GetCurrentLine().Length + 1 Then
            ' at the end of line
            If CaretLineNo < model.LineCount Then
              'concatenate current line and next line
              'and delete next line
              Dim nextLine As String = model.GetLine(CaretLineNo + 1)
              model.SetLine(CaretLineNo, GetCurrentLine() & nextLine)
              model.RemoveLine(CaretLineNo + 1, True)
            End If
          Else
            'delete one character
            model.DeleteChar(caretLocation)
          End If
        End If


      RedrawAll()
      Return True
    Case Else
      If CInt(Keys.Control And keyData) = 0 And _
        CInt(Keys.Alt And keyData) = 0 Then
        ' let KeyPress process the key
        keyProcessed = False
      End If
      Return MyBase.ProcessDialogKey(keyData)
  End Select
End Function
```

RedrawAll

The RedrawAll method redraws the views of this component by calling the RedrawAll methods of the View class and the LineNumberView class and then adjusts the vertical and horizontal scrollbars:

```
Private Sub RedrawAll()
  view.RedrawAll()
  lineNumberView.RedrawAll()
  AdjustVScrollBar()
  AdjustHScrollBar()

End Sub
```

RemoveSelection

The RemoveSelection method deletes the selected text:

```
Public Sub RemoveSelection()
  If Not HasSelection() Then
    Return
  End If

  Dim initialCaretLocation As ColumnLine = caretLocation
  ' after selection is removed, adjust CaretX position.
  Dim x1, y1, x2, y2 As Integer
  x1 = selectionStartLocation.Column
  y1 = selectionStartLocation.Line
  x2 = selectionEndLocation.Column
  y2 = selectionEndLocation.Line

  If y1 > y2 Or (y1 = y2 And x1 > x2) Then
    'swap (x1, y1) and (x2, y2)
    Dim t As Integer
    t = x1 : x1 = x2 : x2 = t
    t = y1 : y1 = y2 : y2 = t
  End If
  If y1 = y2 Then
    Dim thisLine As String = model.GetLine(y1)
    model.SetLine(y1, thisLine.Substring(0, x1 - 1) & _
      thisLine.Substring(x2 - 1, thisLine.Length - x2 + 1))
    'it's okay if event is raised when CaretColumnNo is set
    CaretColumnNo = x1
  Else
    'delete lines between y1 and y2
    Dim j As Integer
    For j = 1 To (y2 - y1 - 1)
      model.RemoveLine(y1 + 1, False) 'false means "do not raise event"
    Next
    'merge line y1 with line y2 and delete the original line y2
    Dim thisLine As String = model.GetLine(y1)
    Dim nextLine As String = model.GetLine(y1 + 1)
    model.SetLine(y1, thisLine.Substring(0, x1 - 1) & _
      nextLine.Substring(x2 - 1, nextLine.Length - x2 + 1))
    model.RemoveLine(y1 + 1, True)
    ' CaretLineNo must be adjusted before CaretColumnNo because
    ' CaretColumnNo property will use CaretLineNo. Therefore, it
```

```
    ' is important that CaretLineNo contains the correct value
    CaretLineNo = y1
    CaretColumnNo = x1
  End If
End Sub
```

ResetSelection

The ResetSelection method resets the selectionStartLocation and selectionEndLocation variables by setting their Column and Line fields to zero:

```
Public Sub ResetSelection()
  selectionStartLocation.Column = 0
  selectionStartLocation.Line = 0
  selectionEndLocation.Column = 0
  selectionEndLocation.Line = 0
End Sub
```

ResizeComponents

The ResizeComponents method resizes the components used in the StyledTextArea control. This method is called when the StyledTextArea control is first constructed and every time its size is changed:

```
Private Sub ResizeComponents()
  lineNumberView.Size = New Size(LineNumberWidth, panel.Height - _
    hScrollBarHeight - 4)
  lineNumberView.Location = New Point(0, 0)
  view.Size = New Size(panel.Width - lineNumberView.Width - _
    vScrollBarWidth - 4, panel.Height - hScrollBarHeight - 4)
  view.Location = New Point(lineNumberView.Width, 0)
  vScrollBar.Location = New Point(view.Width + lineNumberView.Width, 0)
  vScrollBar.Size = New Size(vScrollBarWidth, view.Height)
  hScrollBar.Location = New Point(0, view.Height)
  hScrollBar.Size = _
    New Size(view.Width + lineNumberView.Width, hScrollBarHeight)
  AdjustVScrollBar()
  AdjustHScrollBar()
End Sub
```

ScrollToShowCaret

The `ScrollToShowCaret` method scrolls the `View` object horizontally and/or vertically to make sure the caret is visible:

```
Private Sub ScrollToShowCaret()
  If Not view.IsCaretVisible() Then
    If model.GetLine(CaretLineNo).Length > view.VisibleCharCount Then
      view.LeftInvisibleCharCount = GetCurrentLine().Length - _
      view.VisibleCharCount
    Else
      view.LeftInvisibleCharCount = 0
    End If
    If CaretLineNo > TopInvisibleLineCount + view.VisibleLineCount Then
      TopInvisibleLineCount = CaretLineNo - view.VisibleLineCount + 1
    End If
  End If
End Sub
```

SelectAll

The `SelectAll` method selects all the text in the `Model` object:

```
Public Sub SelectAll()
  selectionStartLocation.Column = 1
  selectionStartLocation.Line = 1
  selectionEndLocation.Column = model.GetLine(model.LineCount).Length + 1
  selectionEndLocation.Line = model.LineCount
  RedrawAll()
End Sub
```

SelectLine

The `SelectLine` method returns the `String` object on the specified line number:

```
Public Sub SelectLine(ByVal lineNo As Integer)
  If lineNo <= model.LineCount Then
    Dim thisLine As String = model.GetLine(lineNo)
    Dim length As Integer = thisLine.Length
    selectionStartLocation = New ColumnLine(1, lineNo)
    selectionEndLocation = New ColumnLine(length + 1, lineNo)
    caretLocation = selectionStartLocation
    RedrawAll()
  End If
End Sub
```

view_KeyPress

The view_KeyPress event handler handles the key press of a key that corresponds to a character that is not processed by the ProcessDialogKey method:

```
Private Sub view_KeyPress(ByVal sender As Object, ByVal e As KeyPressEventArgs)
  If Not keyProcessed Then
    Dim c As Char = e.KeyChar
    Dim convertedChar As Integer = Convert.ToInt32(c)
    RemoveSelection()
    ResetSelection()

    Select Case convertedChar
      Case Keys.Back    'backspace
        If Not (IsCaretOnFirstColumn() And IsCaretOnFirstLine()) Then
          'not at beginning of Model
          If IsCaretOnFirstColumn() Then
            Dim oldLine As String = model.GetLine(CaretLineNo)
            Dim prevLine As String = model.GetLine(CaretLineNo - 1)
            Dim newLine As String = prevLine & oldLine
            model.SetLine(CaretLineNo - 1, newLine)
            model.RemoveLine(CaretLineNo, True)
            CaretLineNo = CaretLineNo - 1
            CaretColumnNo = prevLine.Length + 1
          Else
            Dim oldLine As String = model.GetLine(CaretLineNo)
            Dim newLine As String = oldLine.Remove(CaretColumnNo - 2, 1)
            model.SetLine(CaretLineNo, newline)
            CaretColumnNo = CaretColumnNo - 1
          End If
          editedField = True
        End If
      Case Keys.Return ' return key
        Dim oldLine As String = GetCurrentLine()
        Dim newLine As String = oldLine.Substring(0, CaretColumnNo - 1)
        Dim nextLine As String = oldLine.Substring(CaretColumnNo - 1)
        model.SetLine(CaretLineNo, newline)
        model.InsertLine(CaretLineNo + 1, nextLine)
        Dim needToScroll As Boolean = IsCaretOnLastVisibleLine()
        CaretColumnNo = 1
        CaretLineNo = CaretLineNo + 1
        If needToScroll Then
          view.Scroll(1)
```

```
        End If
        editedField = True


      Case Keys.Escape 'Escape
        'escape key, do nothing
      Case Else
        model.InsertChar(c, caretLocation)
        CaretColumnNo = CaretColumnNo + 1
        editedField = True
    End Select

    ScrollToShowCaret()
    RedrawAll()
    e.Handled = True
  End If
End Sub
```

view_MouseDown

This view_MouseDown event handler handles the MouseDown event of the View object.
A mouse down of the left button indicates the user is starting to select text in the View
object's text area. It sets the selecting flag to True and sets selectionStartLocation
and selectionEndLocation to the translated ColumnLine object of the mouse click's
location. Its implementation is as follows:

```
Private Sub view_MouseDown(ByVal sender As Object, ByVal e As MouseEventArgs)
  'move the caret
  If e.Button = MouseButtons.Left Then
    view.RepositionCaret(e.X, e.Y)
    selecting = True
    Dim cl As ColumnLine = view.TranslateIntoCaretLocation(e.X, e.Y)
    selectionStartLocation = cl
    selectionEndLocation = cl
    RedrawAll()
  End If
End Sub
```

view_MouseMove

The view_MouseMove event handler handles the MouseMove event of the View object. If the MouseMove event triggers when the value of selecting is True, it indicates the user is dragging the mouse to select text in the View object's text area. Its implementation is as follows:

```
Private Sub view_MouseMove(ByVal sender As Object, ByVal e As MouseEventArgs)
  'only respond when selecting, i.e. when the left button is pressed
  If selecting Then
    Dim cl As ColumnLine
    cl = view.TranslateIntoCaretLocation(e.X, e.Y)
    selectionEndLocation = cl
    RedrawAll()
  End If
End Sub
```

view_MouseUp

The view_MouseUp event handler handles the MouseUp event of the View object. If the MouseUp event triggers when the selecting value is True, it indicates the end of the selection by the user. Its implementation is as follows:

```
Private Sub view_MouseUp(ByVal sender As Object, ByVal e As MouseEventArgs)
  'move the caret
  If selecting And e.Button = MouseButtons.Left Then
    selecting = False 'reset selecting
    view.RepositionCaret(e.X, e.Y)
    RedrawAll()
  End If
End Sub
```

vScrollBar_Scroll

The vScrollBar_Scroll event handler handles the Scroll event of the vertical scrollbar vScrollBar:

```
Private Sub vScrollBar_Scroll(ByVal sender As Object, _
  ByVal e As ScrollEventArgs)
  Select Case e.Type
    Case ScrollEventType.SmallIncrement
      If TopInvisibleLineCount < model.LineCount - view.VisibleLineCount Then
        view.Scroll(vScrollBar.SmallChange)
```

```
            lineNumberView.RedrawAll()
        End If
    Case ScrollEventType.LargeIncrement
        If TopInvisibleLineCount < model.LineCount - view.VisibleLineCount Then
            Dim maxIncrement As Integer = _
                Math.Min(vScrollBar.LargeChange, _
                    model.LineCount - view.VisibleLineCount - TopInvisibleLineCount)
            view.Scroll(maxIncrement)
            lineNumberView.RedrawAll()
        End If
    Case ScrollEventType.SmallDecrement
        view.Scroll(-vScrollBar.SmallChange)
        lineNumberView.RedrawAll()
    Case ScrollEventType.LargeDecrement
        view.Scroll(-vScrollBar.LargeChange)
        lineNumberView.RedrawAll()
    Case ScrollEventType.ThumbTrack
        TopInvisibleLineCount = e.NewValue
        RedrawAll()
    Case ScrollEventType.ThumbPosition
        TopInvisibleLineCount = e.NewValue
        RedrawAll()
    End Select

End Sub
```

Understanding the StyledTextArea Class's Events

The StyledTextArea control has two events: ColumnChanged and LineChanged. With these events, the programmer who embeds the StyledTextArea control in a form will be notified when the user moves the caret. Programmers can then update the line and column position if they want. The following sections describe these events.

ColumnChanged

The ColumnChanged event raises every time the caret moves to another column:

```
Public Event ColumnChanged As ColumnEventHandler
```

LineChanged

The LineChanged event triggers every time the caret moves to another line:

```
Public Event LineChanged As LineEventHandler
```

Compiling the Component

If you are not using an IDE, you can compile the component by running the build.bat file in the Project directory. Here is the content of the file.

```
vbc /out:StyledTextArea.dll ColumnLine.vb LineNumberView.vb Model.vb
StyledTextArea.vb Support.vb View.vb /t:library
/r:System.dll,System.Windows.Forms.dll,System.Drawing.dll
```

The result will be a DLL file named StyledTextArea.dll.

Using the StyledTextArea Control

Using the StyledTextArea control is no different from using other standard controls. You need to construct an object of the StyledTextArea class and then set the values of the properties you want to use. You can also handle one or both of its two events: ColumnChanged and LineChanged.

The Form1.vb file in the project's directory contains a form class (Form1) that uses a StyledTextArea control named textArea. The whole source code will not be reproduced here to save space. However, I will explain some key events and methods.

In addition to a StyledTextArea control, the Form1 class (displayed in Figure 1-7) contains the following standard controls:

- A Label control (label1) to display the position of the caret in textArea.

- A Button control (copyButton) to copy the selected text in textArea to the Clipboard.

- A Button control (cutButton) to cut the selected text in textArea and copy it to the Clipboard.

- A Button control (pasteButton) to paste the content of the Clipboard to textArea.

- A Button control (selectButton) to select the text in textArea.

- A TextBox control (findPattern) to receive text as a pattern to be searched in textArea.

- A Button control (findButton) to conduct searching in textArea.

- Three CheckBox controls (caseCB, wholeWordCB, and goUpCB) that receive parameters in the searching. You must select the caseCB check box to specify that the search should take case sensitivity into account. You must select the wholeWordCB check box to indicate that the find pattern is a whole word. Finally, the goUpCB check box indicates the reverse direction of the search.

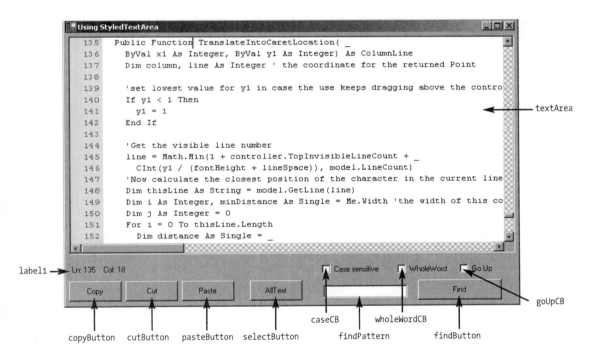

Figure 1-7. Using the StyledTextArea *control*

The form has four private variables, declared as follows:

```
Private x1 As Integer = 1
Private y1 As Integer = 1
Private column As Integer = 1
Private line As Integer = 1
```

You use the variables x1 and y1 in the event handler that handles the Click event of findButton, and line and column represent the line and column position of the caret in textArea (respectively).

When the Form1 class is instantiated, its class's constructor calls the InitializeComponent method, which constructs all the controls it uses and sets the controls' properties. Of particular interest is the part of the method that instantiates the StyledTextArea control and sets its properties:

```
textArea = New StyledTextArea()
textArea.Size = New Size(680, 345)
textArea.Location = New Point(5, 5)
textArea.CaretColor = Color.Red
textArea.LineNumberBackColor = Color.FromArgb(240, 240, 240)
textArea.LineNumberForeColor = Color.DarkCyan
textArea.HighlightBackColor = Color.Black
textArea.HighlightForeColor = Color.White
textArea.TabIndex = 0
```

The Size, Location, and TabIndex properties inherit from the Control class, and the rest are the properties defined and implemented in the StyledTextArea class itself.

At the end of the InitializeComponent method, you call the UpdateLabel method:

```
Me.Controls.AddRange(New Control() _
{Label1, selectButton, pasteButton, cutButton, copyButton, goUpCB, _
textArea, findPattern, findButton, wholeWordCB, caseCB, findButton, _
findPattern})
UpdateLabel()
```

The UpdateLabel method updates the text of label1, displaying the current position of the caret in the StyledTextArea control:

```
label1.Text = "Ln: " & line & "    Col: " & column
```

See that it simply uses the line and column variables? Initially, both line and column have the value of 1. Therefore, the Label control displays the following text:

```
Ln: 1    Col: 1
```

In this example, `column` gets updated every time the `StyledTextArea` control's caret moves to another column. You do this in the event handler `textArea_ColumnChanged` that handles the `ColumnChanged` event of the `StyledTextArea` control:

```
Private Sub textArea_ColumnChanged(ByVal sender As Object, _
  ByVal e As ColumnEventArgs) Handles textArea.ColumnChanged
  column = e.NewColumn
  UpdateLabel()
End Sub
```

The value of `line` is updated every time the `StyledTextArea` control's caret moves to another line. You do this in the event handler `textArea_LineChanged` that handles the `LineChanged` event of the `StyledTextArea` control:

```
Private Sub textArea_LineChanged(ByVal sender As Object, _
  ByVal e As LineEventArgs) Handles textArea.LineChanged
  line = e.NewLine
  UpdateLabel()
End Sub
```

The `copyButton_Click`, `cutButton_Click`, `pasteButton_Click`, and `selectButton_Click` event handlers handle the `Click` events of `copyButton`, `cutButton`, `pasteButton`, and `selectButton` (respectively). These four controls' functions are self-explanatory. They simply use the `Copy`, `Cut`, `Paste`, and `SelectAll` methods of the `StyledTextArea` class. Note that they also call the `StyledTextArea` class's `Focus` method to return focus to `textArea`:

```
Private Sub copyButton_Click(ByVal sender As Object, ByVal e As EventArgs) _
    Handles copyButton.Click
    textArea.Copy()
    textArea.Focus()
  End Sub

  Private Sub cutButton_Click(ByVal sender As Object, ByVal e As EventArgs) _
    Handles cutButton.Click
    textArea.Cut()
    textArea.Focus()
  End Sub

  Private Sub pasteButton_Click(ByVal sender As Object, ByVal e As EventArgs) _
    Handles pasteButton.Click
    textArea.Paste()
    textArea.Focus()
  End Sub
```

```
Private Sub selectButton_Click(ByVal sender As Object, ByVal e As EventArgs) _
  Handles selectButton.Click
  textArea.SelectAll()
  textArea.Focus()
End Sub
```

Finally, the findButton_Click event handler handles the Click event of findButton. It uses the text entered into the findPattern TextBox control to search in textArea. It also uses the x1 and y1 variables to store the position of the start column and the start line for searching. In addition, it uses the values of the three CheckBox controls as parameters for the Find method of the StyledTextArea class.

Compiling and Running the Application

To compile the application, you must first copy the StyledTextArea.dll file to the directory where the form file (form1.vb) resides. Then, change the directory to where form1.vb resides and type the following command:

```
vbc /t:winexe /r:System.dll,System.windows.forms.dll,System.Drawing.dll, ⤸
StyledTextArea.dll form1.vb
```

To run the program, type the following:

```
form1
```

Summary

This chapter featured the StyledTextArea control, which you can use in a form in a Windows application. You should now understand how to do the following:

- Use the Control and UserControl classes.

- Draw the user interface for a custom control.

- Handle key presses.

- Understand the Observer design pattern.

- Handle and create custom events.

- Use the MVC design pattern.

CHAPTER 2

Building an XML Document Editor

EXTENSIBLE MARKUP LANGUAGE (XML) has been a successful rising star in the computing industry. Developed by the World Wide Web Consortium (W3C) in 1996, XML is now a widely accepted standard for data exchange and extensible data structure.

As XML becomes more popular, a need arises to write and edit XML documents. The project in this chapter is an XML document editor that you can use to edit multiple XML documents, validate each document, build a tree based on elements in each document, and so on. This XML editor is a Multiple Document Interface (MDI) application, so you can open and work with multiple documents at the same time.

NOTE *The objectives of this project are twofold: demonstrating how to write an MDI application and showing how to program XML in the .NET Framework.*

Overview of the Chapter

The chapter starts by presenting some introductory topics that will help you understand each piece of the software. It then concludes by discussing the project. The main sections in this chapter are as follows:

- **"A Brief Theory of XML"**: This section introduces XML for those new to this standard. It is not a complete reference on XML but should help you understand the application developed in this chapter.

- **"XML Programming in the .NET Framework"**: This section explains the members of the System.Xml namespace and how to use the classes to read, write, and validate XML documents. In addition, there is also a discussion on how to manipulate nodes in an XML document.

- **"Writing MDI Applications"**: This section explains how to build an MDI application.

- **"The Singleton Design Pattern"**: This section discusses the Singleton design pattern, which you can use to create a class that can have only one instance.

- **"Printing in the .NET Framework Windows"**: This section covers the `System.Drawing.Printing` namespace. It explains how to print text and use the Print dialog box, Page Setup, printer settings, and Print Preview options.

- **"Implementing the Project"**: This section discusses the application built for this chapter in detail. It starts with the various parts of the application, such as the `XmlFiewer` custom control, the Find dialog box, and the `Document` class. It then continues by integrating the parts.

A Brief Theory of XML

An *XML document* is a plain text file. As such, you can use any text editor of your choice to write, view, and edit it. When you see an XML document for the first time, you will immediately notice that some words are enclosed in brackets: < … >. The words in brackets are called *tags*. If you know Hypertext Markup Language (HTML), then XML will remind you of it. However, unlike HTML, no predefined tags make up an XML document. Every tag is tailor-made—in other words, you create your own!

NOTE *This section does not offer you a complete reference of XML. XML is a broad topic that requires a thick book to describe it thoroughly. However, what is presented in this chapter should give you sufficient background knowledge to work through the project.*

The main use of XML is to store a data structure. Consider, for example, a table containing product information as given in Table 2-1.

Table 2-1. A Table Containing Some Product Information

PRODUCTID	NAME	DESCRIPTION	PRICE	SUPPLIERID
1	ChocChic	Mint chocolate, 100gr	1.50	1
2	Chocnuts	Chocolate with peanuts, 200gr	2.95	2

As you can see, Table 2-1 contains two records. If this data is to be written in XML, you will get the XML document shown in Listing 2-1.

Listing 2-1. An XML Document

```
<?xml version="1.0" standalone="yes" encoding="UTF-8"?>
<products>
  <product>
    <product_id>1</product_id>
    <name>ChocChic</name>
    <description>Mint chocolate, 100g</description>
    <price>1.50</price>
    <supplier_id>1</supplier_id>
  </product>
  <product>
    <product_id>2</product_id>
    <name>Chocnuts</name>
    <description>Chocolate with peanuts, 200gr</description>
    <price>2.95</price>
    <supplier_id>2</supplier_id>
  </product>
</products>
```

You might ask the following question: If relational databases work so well, why do you need XML at all? There are a number of answers:

- XML uses a standard and open format from the W3C (www.w3c.org), making data exchange easy. Compare this with proprietary data formats of relational databases that make exchanging data a complex process.

- XML can represent hierarchical data.

- You must comply with rules when writing XML. These rules make it possible to check the data integrity of an XML document.

- The same rules make it possible to validate XML documents.

- XML is extensible. You create your custom tags to accommodate any type of data you have.

NOTE *You can find the XML recommendation version 1.0 (the latest version) at* www.w3.org/TR/REC-xml.

Because there are rules in writing XML and because it is based on an open standard, there is no ambiguity in interpreting an XML document, even when trying to understand an XML document you have never seen before. For instance, you can describe the XML document shown in Listing 2-1 as follows:

- The first line specifies it is an XML document compliant to version 1.0 of XML, it is a stand-alone document (meaning it does not refer to any external entity), and it uses UTF-8 encoding.

- The second line begins the data, which is represented as a collection of elements. The first element in the XML document is <products>, which is self-explanatory. Clearly this XML document is a collection of products. The first element, which is always the topmost element in hierarchical data, is called the *root*. So, <products> is the root in Listing 2-1.

- An element can consist of other elements, which are called the *child elements* of that element. As mentioned, XML is suitable for hierarchical data. Therefore, elements with child elements that in turn have their own child elements are common in XML. For example, the <product> element is the child element of the <products> element. The <product> element has the child elements <product_id>, <name>, <description>, <price>, and <supplier_id>.

- An element in an XML document can contain *attributes*, which are similar to attributes of an HTML tag. For example, the following is a <product> element to which an in_stock attribute has been added:

```
<product in_stock="yes">
```

NOTE *Element names and values, as well as attribute names and values, are case sensitive.*

In determining whether data integrity has been maintained in an XML document, an XML writer should know two rules: well-formedness and validity. A valid XML document is always well-formed, but a well-formed document is not always valid.

A *well-formed* XML document follows the syntax rules governed by the World Wide Web Consortium (W3C) in the XML 1.0 Specification. Well-formedness means the following:

- An XML document must contain at least one element, the root element.

- There can be only one root element. All other elements are nested inside the root element.

- Each element must nest inside an *enclosing* element. For example, Listing 2-2 is *not* well-formed because the closing `</name>` element appears after the `<description>` opening tag.

Listing 2-2. An XML Document, Not Well-Formed

```
<product>
  <name>
    ChocChic
  <description>
    chocolate with mint 100g
  </name>
  </description>
</product>
```

A *valid* XML document is one that follows a set of grammatical rules. You can check the validity of an XML document against two sets of rules: Document Type Definitions (DTDs) and schemas. A valid XML document must have a DTD or a schema associated with it, against which the correctness and well-formedness of the XML document can be verified.

We now discuss how to write a well-formed XML document. Afterward, we look at the two rules that can guarantee the validity of the XML document.

Writing Well-Formed XML Documents

What does it take to write a well-formed XML document? The short answer is that the document must meet all the well-formedness constraints specified in the W3C's XML 1.0 recommendation. This translates into the following rule: An XML document has three parts—a prolog, an element, and a miscellaneous part. The following sections describe these parts.

Prolog

The *prolog* starts an XML document. It contains an XML declaration, miscellaneous part, and DTD. All the parts in the prolog are optional. Therefore, an XML document can still be well-formed even if the prolog is empty. However, an XML document with an empty prolog is not valid.

The XML declaration part of the prolog contains the version information, optional encoding declaration, and optional stand-alone document declaration. These prolog examples contain only the XML declaration part:

```
<?xml version="1.0"?>
<?xml version="1.0" encoding="UTF-8"?>
<?xml version="1.0" standalone="yes"?>
<?xml version="1.0" encoding="UTF-8" standalone="yes"?>
```

The only valid version number for an XML document is currently 1.0. The encoding declaration is the language encoding for the document. The default value for the encoding declaration is UTF-8. A value of "yes" for the stand-alone declaration means the XML document does not refer to any external document; "no" means the opposite.

The miscellaneous part of the prolog contains a comment or a processing instruction.

NOTE *An XML comment starts with* <!-- *and ends with* -->.

A processing instruction is an instruction to the XML processor and it is processor dependant. As such, you do not specify it in the XML 1.0 recommendation. A common processing instruction includes the `<?xml-stylesheet?>` instruction, which connects a style sheet with the XML document.

The "Writing Valid XML Documents" section discusses the DTD part of a prolog.

Element

An XML element begins with a start tag and ends with an end tag. A start tag begins with < and ends with >. An end tag starts with </ and ends with >. *Empty elements* are an exception, however. In addition to the normal syntax, an empty element can consist of only one tag.

For example, the following is an XML element:

```
<productId>1</productId>
```

And the following is an empty element:

```
<productId/>
```

A tag name, such as `productId` in the previous examples, starts with a letter, an underscore, or a colon. Following the first character are letters, digits, underscores, hyphens, periods, and colons. A tag name can contain no whitespace.

An element can have *attributes*, which are name-value pairs containing additional data for the element. You separate the name and the value in an attribute with an equal sign. Attribute names follow the same rule as tag names. You must enclose attribute values in quotation marks, either double quotes or single quotes. Using double quotes is more common, but you can use single quotes if the value itself contains double quotes. In a case where the attribute value contains both single quotes and double quotes, you can use ' to represent a single quote and " to represent a double quote.

NOTE *In addition to* ' *and* ", *you can use* & *for the ampersand (&) character,* < *for the left-bracket (<) character, and* > *for the right-bracket (>) character.*

For example, the following element whose tag name is product has an attribute called in_stock. The attribute has the value of 6:

```
<product in_stock="6">
  <name>ChicChoc</name>
</product>
```

Confusion often arises whether to write data related to an element as an attribute or a child element. In the case of the previous example, you can rewrite the elements as follows:

```
<product>
  <in_stock>6</in_stock>
  <name>ChicChoc</name>
</product>
```

Whether to use an attribute or a child element is entirely up to you. However, the general rule of thumb says that you should not have more than 10 attributes in one element.

Miscellaneous

This part can contain comments or processing instructions.

Writing Valid XML Documents

As mentioned, well-formedness alone is not enough to guarantee the data integrity of an XML document. For data integrity, you also have to make sure that an XML document is valid. For example, an XML document that contains the data structure for some products may define that the root element is <products> and there are five child elements under it: <name>, <description>, <product_id>, <price>, and <supplier_id>. If a document has a <products> element as its root, but the <supplier_id> element is missing, the document is not valid, even though it may be well-formed.

For validity, you can check the XML document against two rules: DTDs and schemas. Specifications for DTDs were published earlier than those of schemas, but schemas are more powerful than DTDs. However, both are still widely in use today. We look at both in turn.

Document Type Definition

You can define DTDs in the XML document itself or in an external file—or in both. The following sections first cover DTD basics in an internal DTD and then cover documents that have external DTDs. The last subsection talks about entities and attributes.

NOTE *You can find the formal rules for DTDs in the XML 1.0 at* `www.w3.org/TR/REC-xml`.

DTD Basics

To start with, you use `<!DOCTYPE>` to write a DTD, which always appears in the XML document prolog. There are a few syntaxes for `<!DOCTYPE>`; this chapter uses the following:

```
<!DOCTYPE rootName [DTD]>
```

where `rootName` is the name of the root in the document and `[DTD]` is the part that defines all elements—in other words, the root itself and all other elements nesting inside the root. Each element is defined by `<!ELEMENT>`. Because an XML document must have a root, the DTD must have at least one element that defines the root itself. For example, the following is an XML document with an internal DTD. The DTD dictates that the document must have a root called `products`, and `<products>` can have no elements nested inside it:

```
<?xml version="1.0" standalone="yes"?>
<!DOCTYPE products [
<!ELEMENT products (#PCDATA)>
]>
<products/>
```

Note that the XML declaration in the prolog contains the `standalone` attribute with the value of `"yes"`. This means that this XML document does not refer to any external document. Note also that the DTD defines the `<!ELEMENT>` for products. `#PCDATA` stands for parsed character data and indicates text that does not contain markup.

You can also declare that an element must be empty using the EMPTY keyword. An empty element cannot have a value or a child element, but it can have attributes. For example, the following is the previous XML document with a DTD that states that the root element (product) must be empty:

```
<?xml version="1.0" standalone="yes"?>
<!DOCTYPE products [
<!ELEMENT products EMPTY>
]>
<products></products>
```

An XML document with only the root and no other elements is not of much use. The <!ELEMENT> in a DTD allows you to define another element. For instance, the following is a DTD that states that the XML document must have <products> as its root and <products> must have a <product> element. The DTD next states that the <product> element must have the <name> and <product_id> elements:

```
<!DOCTYPE products [
<!ELEMENT products (product)>
<!ELEMENT product (name,product_id)>
<!ELEMENT name (#PCDATA)>
<!ELEMENT product_id (#PCDATA)>
]>
```

Listing 2-3 shows a valid XML document that uses the previous DTD.

Listing 2-3. A Valid XML Document with an Internal DTD

```
<?xml version="1.0" standalone="yes"?>
<!DOCTYPE products [
<!ELEMENT products (product)>
<!ELEMENT product (name,product_id)>
<!ELEMENT name (#PCDATA)>
<!ELEMENT product_id (#PCDATA)>
]>
<products>
  <product>
    <name>ChicChoc</name>
    <product_id>10</product_id>
  </product>
</products>
```

In declaring child elements, you can use the following operators that have special meanings. Here *x* denotes a child element:

- x*: Zero or more instances of x

- x+: One or more instances of x

- x?: Zero or one instance of x

- x, y: x followed by y

- x | y: x or y

For example, if you want to say in the previous DTD that `<products>` can have zero or more `<product>` elements and `<product>` can have an optional `<name>` but must have a `<product_id>`, use this modified DTD:

```
<!DOCTYPE products [
<!ELEMENT products (product)*>
<!ELEMENT product (name?,product_id)>
<!ELEMENT name (#PCDATA)>
<!ELEMENT product_id (#PCDATA)>
]>
```

External DTDs

Using an external DTD is useful because you can share the DTD with many XML documents. Also, for a long DTD, it makes the XML document that uses it tidier.

There are two kinds of external DTDs: private and public. Private DTDs are to be used privately by certain people or applications in a group. You specify an external private DTD using the SYSTEM keyword in the `<!DOCTYPE>`. On the other hand, a public external DTD can be used by anyone, thus making it public. To make an external DTD public, use the PUBLIC keyword in the `<!DOCTYPE>`.

Practically the only differences between using an external DTD from an internal DTD are that with external DTDs you have a separate file for the DTD and this DTD file is referenced from inside the XML document. Listing 2-4 shows an XML document that uses a private DTD called products.dtd. Because the products.dtd file is referenced without any information about its path, it must reside in the same directory as the XML document.

Listing 2-4. A Valid XML Document with a Private External DTD

```
<?xml version="1.0" standalone="no"?>
<!DOCTYPE products SYSTEM "products.dtd">
<products>
  <product>
    <name>ChocChic</name>
    <product_id>12</product_id>
  </product>
  <product>
    <name>Waftel Chocolate</name>
    <product_id>15</product_id>
  </product>
</products>
```

And, the following is the `products.dtd` file, which is an external DTD to the previous XML document:

```
<!ELEMENT products (product)+>
<!ELEMENT product (name, product_id)>
<!ELEMENT name (#PCDATA)>
<!ELEMENT product_id (#PCDATA)>
```

You can also reference a private external DTD using its Uniform Resource Locator (URL). In this case, you just specify a URL after the SYSTEM keyword:

```
<!DOCTYPE products SYSTEM "http://www.brainysoftware.com/dtd/products.dtd">
```

A public external DTD is quite similar, except that you must define a Formal Public Identifier (FPI) after the PUBLIC keyword in the <!DOCTYPE> element. The FPI has four fields, each of which is separated from each other using double forward slashes (//). The first field in an FPI indicates the formality of the DTD. For a DTD that you define yourself, you use a minus (-) sign. If the DTD has been approved by a nonstandard body, you use a plus (+) sign. For a formal standard, use the reference to the standard itself. The second field in an FPI is the name of the organization that maintains the DTD. The third field indicates the type of document being described, and the fourth field specifies the language that the DTD uses. For example, EN stands for English.

This is an example of a <!DOCTYPE> that references an external public DTD:

```
<!DOCTYPE products PUBLIC "-//bs//Exports//EN" 
"http://brainysoftware.com/products.dtd">
```

Entities

In a DTD, you can define *entities*. You will probably ask then, what is an entity? To explain it to a programmer like yourself, it is best to draw an analogy between an entity in an XML document and a constant in a computer program. You declare a constant (using the keyword Const in Visual Basic) and assign it a value so that you can reference the value through the constant from within your code. Likewise, you define an entity in a DTD so that you can use it from anywhere in the XML document. You define an entity using the following syntax:

```
<!ENTITY name definition>
```

When the XML document is parsed, the entity will be replaced by the value of the entity. To use the entity, you precede the entity name with the ampersand (&) and add a semicolon (;) after the name. For example, to refer to an entity called myEntity, you write &myEntity;.

As an example, Listing 2-5 shows an XML document in which an entity named company is declared in its DTD. The value of the entity is Cooper Wilson and Co.

Listing 2-5. An XML Document with an Entity

```
<?xml version="1.0" standalone="yes"?>
<!DOCTYPE products [
<!ELEMENT products (manufacturer, (product)*)>
<!ELEMENT manufacturer (#PCDATA)>
<!ELEMENT product (name, product_id)>
<!ELEMENT name (#PCDATA)>
<!ELEMENT product_id (#PCDATA)>
<!ENTITY company "Cooper Wilson and Co.">
]>
<products>
  <manufacturer>&company;</manufacturer>
  <product>
    <name>ChocChic</name>
    <product_id>12</product_id>
  </product>
  <product>
    <name>Waftel Chocolate</name>
    <product_id>15</product_id>
  </product>
</products>
```

When a parser, such as Internet Explorer, reads this XML document, it replaces the entity with its value, like in Listing 2-6.

Listing 2-6. An XML Document with an Entity's Value

```
<?xml version="1.0" standalone="yes" ?>
<!DOCTYPE products (View Source for full doctype...)>
<products>
  <manufacturer>Cooper Wilson and Co.</manufacturer>
  <product>
    <name>ChocChic</name>
    <product_id>12</product_id>
  </product>
  <product>
    <name>Waftel Chocolate</name>
    <product_id>15</product_id>
  </product>
</products>
```

You can use five predefined entities in your XML document without declaring them in the DTD: ', ", &, <, and >.

Attributes

You specify attributes that an element has using the following syntax:

```
<!ATTLIST elementName
  attributeName_1 type_1 defaultValue_1
  attributeName_2 type_2 defaultValue_2
  .
  .
  .
  attributeName_n type_n defaultValue_n>
```

For example, to define that the <product> element must have the id attribute, you write the code shown in Listing 2-7.

Listing 2-7. An XML Document with Elements and Attributes

```
<?xml version="1.0" standalone="yes"?>
<!DOCTYPE products [
<!ELEMENT products (product)*>
<!ELEMENT manufacturer (#PCDATA)>
<!ELEMENT product (name, product_id)>
<!ELEMENT name (#PCDATA)>
<!ELEMENT product_id (#PCDATA)>
<!ATTLIST product
  supplier_id CDATA #IMPLIED>
]>
<products>
  <product supplier_id="1">
    <name>ChocChic</name>
    <product_id>12</product_id>
  </product>
  <product supplier_id="2">
    <name>Waftel Chocolate</name>
    <product_id>15</product_id>
  </product>
</products>
```

The default value #IMPLIED means that the attribute is optional.

Schemas

Like DTDs, schemas validate XML documents. However, schemas are more powerful. Schemas provide the following advantages over DTDs:

- Additional data types are available using a schema.

- Schemas support custom data types.

- A schema uses XML syntax.

- A schema supports object-oriented concepts such as polymorphism and inheritance.

NOTE *Schemas are basically XML documents. By convention a schema has an* .xsd *extension. The term* instance document *is often used to describe an XML document that conforms to a particular schema. A schema does not have to reside in a file, though. It may be a stream of bytes, a field in a database record, or a collection of XML Infoset "information items."*

In discussing schemas, it is convenient to refer to elements as *simple types* and *complex types*. Elements that contain subelements or carry attributes are complex types, whereas elements that contain numbers (and strings, dates, and so on) but do not contain any subelements are simple types. Some elements have attributes; attributes always have simple types.

The W3C recommendation defines schemas in a three-part document at the following locations:

- www.w3.org/TR/xmlschema-0/

- www.w3.org/TR/xmlschema-1/

- www.w3.org/TR/xmlschema-2/

Each of the elements in the schema has a prefix xsd:, which is associated with the XML Schema namespace through the declaration xmlns:xsd="http://www.w3.org/2001/XMLSchema" that appears in the schema element. By convention, the prefix xsd: denotes the XML Schema namespace, although you can use any prefix. The same prefix, and hence the same association, also appears on the names of built-in simple types—for example, xsd:string. The purpose of the association is to identify the elements and simple types as belonging to the vocabulary of the XML Schema language rather than the vocabulary of the schema author. For clarity, I just mention the names of elements and simple types and omit the prefix.

NOTE *Like DTDs, schemas can appear inside an XML document or as external documents. The* schemaLocation *and* xsi:schemaLocation *attributes specify the location of an external schema referenced by an XML document. However, the project in this chapter does not support external schemas; therefore, I do not discuss them in detail. Interested readers should read the document at* www.w3.org/TR/xmlschema-0/.

In XML Schema, there is a basic difference between the complex types that allow elements in their content and can carry attributes and the simple types that cannot have element content and cannot carry attributes. There is also a major distinction between definitions that create new types (both simple and complex) and declarations that enable elements and attributes with specific names and types (both simple and complex) to appear in document instances. In this section, we focus on defining complex types and declaring the elements and attributes that appear within them.

You define new complex types using the complexType element; such definitions typically contain a set of element declarations, element references, and attribute declarations. The declarations are not themselves types, but rather an association between a name and the constraints that govern the appearance of that name in documents governed by the associated schema. You declare elements using the element element, and you declare attributes using the attribute element. Listing 2-8 is an example of an XML document that uses an inline schema.

Listing 2-8. Using an Inline Schema

```
<xs:schema
   xmlns:xs='http://www.w3.org/2001/XMLSchema'
   xmlns='xsdBook'
   targetNamespace='xsdBook'
>
   <xs:element name='Book'>
     <xs:complexType>
       <xs:sequence>
         <xs:element name='Title' type='xs:string' maxOccurs='1'/>
         <xs:element name='Author' type='xs:string' maxOccurs='1'/>
       </xs:sequence>
       <xs:attribute name='Edition' type='xs:string' use='optional'/>
     </xs:complexType>
   </xs:element>
</xs:schema>

<hc:Book Edition='1' xmlns:hc='xsdBook'>
   <Title>Dogs are from Mars, Cats are from Venus</Title>
   <Author>T. Sakhira</Author>
</hc:Book>
```

Related XML Resources

To conclude the discussion of XML basics, the following are links to useful documents to help you work with XML and understand it better:

- www.w3c.org/xml: The official Web site of XML

- www.w3c.org/TR/REC-xml/: The W3C XML 1.0 recommendation

- www.w3c.org/DOM/: The W3C Document Object Model

- www.w3.org/TR/REC-xml/: The formal rules for DTDs in XML 1.0

- www.w3.org/TR/xmlschema-0/: XML Schema Part 0: Primer

- www.w3.org/TR/xmlschema-1/: XML Schema Part 1: Structures

- www.w3.org/TR/xmlschema-2/: XML Schema Part 2: Datatypes

- www.xml.com/: A site dedicated to providing XML resources, discussions, and so on

- http://msdn.microsoft.com/xml/tutorial/default.asp: Microsoft's XML tutorial

Now that you have a good background of XML theory, it's time to learn how to program XML in the .NET Framework.

XML Programming in the .NET Framework

For working with XML in the .NET Framework, you mainly work with the classes in the System.Xml namespace. With these classes, you can read and write to XML documents, traverse and change the values of the elements in an XML document, validate the document, and so on. This section therefore discusses some important classes in the System.Xml namespace and provides examples on how to use them.

NOTE *For importing XML into a database or saving a database table into XML, you can use the* System.Data.DataSet *class.*

To read XML, you use the reader classes in the System.Xml namespace. There is the abstract XmlReader class with its three child classes: XmlNodeReader, XmlTextReader, and XmlValidatingReader. Of these, the XmlTextReader class provides the fastest access to XML data. However, you can only use this class to read XML in a non-cached, forward-only direction. An important class you can use to validate an XML document is the XmlValidatingReader class.

For writing to XML documents, you use the writer classes in the System.Xml namespace. There is the abstract XmlWriter class and its child class, XmlTextWriter. XmlWriter represents a writer for generating streams or files containing XML data. Like the XmlTextReader, XmlWriter and XmlTextWriter work only in a non-cached, forward-only direction.

When working with XML, you often want to access an individual node in the document—for example, when you need to traverse nodes in an XML document. For this purpose, you use the XmlNode class. As the name implies, XmlNode represents a node in an XML document.

Also, everyone working with XML in the .NET Framework needs to be familiar with the XmlDocument class, which represents an XML document. This class directly derives from XmlNode and has one child class: XmlDataDocument.

Reading XML

An important class that is frequently used for reading XML documents is the XmlTextReader class. Constructing an instance of this class is easy because XmlTextReader provides 13 constructors from which to choose. For example, you can pass a System.IO.Stream or the URL of the XML document you want to read.

You can find the complete list of members of this class in the class library reference of the .NET Framework Software Development Kit (SDK) documentation; however, the following are some of the important properties:

- Depth: The depth of the node.

- EOF: Indicates if the end of file has been reached.

- HasValue: Indicates whether the node can have a value.

- IsEmptyElement: Indicates whether the current node is an empty element.

- LineNumber: Returns the current line number.

- Name: The name of the node.

- NodeType: The type of the node. Its value is one of the members of the System.Xml.XmlNodeType enumeration: Attribute, CDATA, Comment, Document, DocumentFragment, DocumentType, Element, EndElement, EndEntity, Entity, EntityReference, None, Notation, ProcessingInstruction, SignificantWhiteSpace, Text, Whitespace, and XmlDeclaration.

- Value: The node's text value.

The XmlTextReader class has a number of methods; however, the most important method is Read, which you use to read the next node in the document. When Read is called, the node name is copied into the Name property and the node value is copied into the Value property. The Read method returns True if the next node was read successfully and False if it has reached the last node.

Listing 2-9 uses the XmlTextReader class to read an XML document's nodes in sequence and displays the name and the value of an element node.

Listing 2-9. Reading an XML Document

```
Imports System.Xml
Dim xmlReader As XmlTextReader
Try
  xmlReader = New XmlTextReader("test.xml")
  While xmlReader.Read()
    If xmlReader.NodeType = XmlNodeType.Element Then
      System.Console.WriteLine(xmlReader.Name & " : ")
    End If
    If xmlReader.NodeType = XmlNodeType.Text Then
      System.Console.WriteLine(xmlReader.Value)
    End If
  End While
Catch ex As Exception
End Try
If Not xmlReader Is Nothing Then
  xmlReader.Close()
End If
```

In Listing 2-9, you first open an XML document called test.xml. Then, you read each node in the XML document by repeatedly calling the Read method of the XmlTextReader class until it returns False.

Validating XML Documents

If you read the "A Brief Theory on XML" section earlier in the chapter, you know that being able to maintain data integrity is one reason why XML survives today. The mechanism for checking the data integrity through validating a document is solid in XML, and the System.Xml namespace has the XmlValidatingReader class that makes validating XML documents a piece of cake.

To use the XmlValidatingReader class, you first construct an instance of it and keep calling its Read method. This method throws a System.Xml.XmlException when it encounters an invalid line. You can then retrieve the message from the exception to find out what makes the document invalid. The XmlValidatingReader class has similar properties and methods to XmlTextReader. However, XmlValidatingReader does not have a constructor that accepts a System.IO.Stream object. Instead, you can pass an XmlReader object.

Listing 2-10 presents code that validates an XML document.

Listing 2-10. Validating an XML Document

```
Imports System.Xml
Dim xmlReader As XmlTextReader
Dim xmlValReader As XmlValidatingReader
Try
  xmlReader = New XmlTextReader("test.xml")
  xmlValReader = New XmlValidatingReader(xmlReader)
  While xmlValReader.Read()
  End While
  System.Console.WriteLine("document validated")
Catch ex As Exception
    System.Console.WriteLine(ex.ToString())
End Try
If Not xmlValReader Is Nothing Then
  xmlValReader.Close()
End If
```

Writing to XML Documents

You use the System.Xml.XmlTextWriter class to write to XML documents. This class has properties and methods that make it convenient to write to an XML document. The following are some important properties:

- Formatting: Indicates how the document is formatted. It can accept one of the two members of the System.Xml.Formatting enumeration: Indented or None.

- Indentation: Determines how many IndentChar characters to be written for each level in the node hierarchy.

- IndentChars: The character for indenting. The default is a space.

When working with the XmlTextWriter class, you will often use the following methods: WriteStartDocument, WriteEndDocument, WriteComment, WriteStartAttribute, WriteEndAttribute, WriteStartElement, WriteEndElement, and WriteString. All these methods are self-explanatory.

Listing 2-11 presents code that writes to an XML document using the XmlTextWriter class.

Listing 2-11. Writing to an XML Document

```
Imports System.Xml
Dim xmlWriter As XmlTextWriter
Try
  xmlWriter = New XmlTextWriter("test2.xml", Nothing)
  xmlWriter.WriteStartDocument()
  xmlWriter.Formatting = Formatting.Indented
  xmlWriter.Indentation = 4
  xmlWriter.WriteStartElement("books")
  xmlWriter.WriteStartElement("book")
  xmlWriter.WriteAttributeString("id", "1")
  xmlWriter.WriteElementString("author", "Holzner, Charles")
  xmlWriter.WriteElementString("title", _
    "English-Japanese Dictionary")
  xmlWriter.WriteElementString("price", "59.95")
  xmlWriter.WriteEndElement()
  xmlWriter.WriteEndElement()
  xmlWriter.WriteEndDocument()
Catch ex As Exception
```

```
Finally
  xmlWriter.Close()
End Try
```

When run, this is the resulting XML document:

```xml
<?xml version="1.0"?>
<books>
    <book id="1">
        <author>Holzner, Charles</author>
        <title>English-Japanese Dictionary</title>
        <price>59.95</price>
    </book>
</books>
```

Traversing XML Nodes

XML is a hierarchical data structure. As such, it is often desirable to be able to traverse through each individual node in an XML document. You can easily do this in the .NET Framework thanks to the System.Xml.XmlNode and the System.Xml.XmlDocument classes.

The XmlNode class represents a node in an XML document. As a node can have child nodes, the XmlNode class is equipped with the ChildNodes property that returns a System.Xml.XmlNodeList containing all the child nodes of the current node. Then, it also has the FirstChild property from which you can obtain the first child node. You can obtain the node name from the Name property and the node's value from the Value property. You can find a complete list of properties in the documentation.

As to the methods, the following are some important methods of the XmlNode class:

- AppendChild: Adds a node to the end of the list of child nodes

- InsertAfter: Inserts a node right after a reference node

- InsertBefore: Inserts a node right before a reference node

- RemoveChild: Removes a child node

The XmlDocument class represents an XML document. The following are some of the properties of the XmlDocument class:

- DocumentElement: Returns the root XmlDocument for the document

- Name: The name of the node

- NodeType: The type of the node

The following are some of the methods in the XmlDocument class, all of which are self-explanatory: CreateAttribute, CreateComment, CreateElement, CreateNode, Load, LoadXml, ReadNode, and Save.

As an example, consider Listing 2-12, which you can use to traverse an XML document and display its nodes' names and values. Listing 2-13 shows the input that produces the output shown in Listing 2-14.

Listing 2-12. Traversing Nodes in an XML Document

```
Imports System.Xml
Dim xmlDocument As New XmlDocument()
Try
  xmlDocument.Load("test.xml")
  DrawNode(xmlDocument.DocumentElement, 1)
Catch ex As Exception
End Try
.

.

.

Sub DrawNode(ByVal node As XmlNode, ByVal level As Integer)
  'Draw only if node.NodeType is Element or Text
  'Draw the line
  System.Console.Write(New String("-"c, level * 2))
  'If node.NodeType = Text, we don't want to display
  'the node.Name
  If node.NodeType = XmlNodeType.Element Then
    System.Console.Write(node.Name)
  End If
  System.Console.WriteLine(node.Value)
  If (node.HasChildNodes) Then
    node = node.FirstChild
    While Not IsNothing(node)
      If node.NodeType = XmlNodeType.Element Or _
```

```
        node.NodeType = XmlNodeType.Text Then
          DrawNode(node, level + 1)
      End If
      node = node.NextSibling
    End While
  End If
End Sub
```

Listing 2-13. The Input

```
<?xml version="1.0" standalone="yes"?>
<!DOCTYPE products [
<!ELEMENT products (product)*>
<!ELEMENT manufacturer (#PCDATA)>
<!ELEMENT product (name, product_id)>
<!ELEMENT name (#PCDATA)>
<!ELEMENT product_id (#PCDATA)>
]>
<products>
  <product>
    <name>ChocChic</name>
    <product_id>12</product_id>
  </product>
  <product>
    <name>Waftel Chocolate</name>
    <product_id>15</product_id>
  </product>
</products>
```

Listing 2-14. The Output

```
--products
----product
------name
--------ChocChic
------product_id
--------12
----product
------name
--------Waftel Chocolate
------product_id
--------15
```

Listing 2-12 features the recursive DrawNode subroutine to draw all the element nodes. When called, this method is passed the root element of the XML document and a level of 1.

For each node, the DrawNode draws a line consisting of a number of hyphen characters. The number of hyphen characters is proportional to the value of level.

For each node whose type is Element, the node's name is output to the console:

```
'If node.NodeType = Text, we don't want to display
'the node.Name
If node.NodeType = XmlNodeType.Element Then
  System.Console.Write(node.Name)
End If
System.Console.WriteLine(node.Value)
```

Then, it checks if the current node has child nodes. If it has, the node is assigned the first child of children:

```
If (node.HasChildNodes) Then
  node = node.FirstChild
```

And then, for each child node that is an element, it calls the DrawNode method again and increments the level:

```
While Not IsNothing(node)
  If node.NodeType = XmlNodeType.Element Or _
    node.NodeType = XmlNodeType.Text Then
    DrawNode(node, level + 1)
  End If
  node = node.NextSibling
End While
```

Now that you know how to manipulate XML documents in .NET, it is time to discuss MDI applications.

Writing Multiple-Document Interface Applications

Many Windows applications allow you to work with multiple documents at the same time, with each document displayed in its own window. This type of application is called a *Multiple-Document Interface* (MDI) application. Examples of MDI applications are Microsoft Word and Microsoft Excel. In contrast, Microsoft Notepad and Microsoft Paint are *Single-Document Interface* (SDI) applications because there can only be one document open at a time.

In the .NET Framework, writing MDI applications is easy. Basically, you have a form that acts as the parent form. From this parent form you allow the user to create other forms, which will become the child forms of the parent form. The parent form is also called the *MDI container*. For a form to be an MDI container, you must set the Form class's IsMdiContainer property to True, like the following:

```
Me.IsMdiContainer = True
```

For a child document, usually you extend the System.Windows.Forms.Form class to get a new class that represents a child document. This child class also has its own user interface, menus, and so on.

To create or open a new child document, such as when the user clicks the New or Open menu item from the File menu in a typical Windows MDI application, you write the following code inside the MDI container. In this example, doc represents a child form and Me refers to the MDI container itself:

```
Dim doc As New System.Windows.Forms.Form()
doc.MdiParent = Me
doc.Show()
```

That's the least you need to do to create an MDI application. However, there are features you may want to add, so read on.

The MDI container needs to monitor its children. For example, it needs to know for sure how many child documents are currently open and which one is the active document. When the user closes a child document, the MDI container needs to know it. Also, when another child document is activated, the MDI container may want to do something in response.

The Form class is rich enough to cater for these needs. For example, the Closed event triggers every time a user closes a form (and consequently, a child document extending the Form class). You might want to do something when a child document is closed—for example, delete a tab page associated with that child document. To know the number of child documents, you do not need to have a counter that you increment when a new child document is created and decrement when a child document is closed. The Form class's MdiChildren property represents an array of Form objects. You can obtain the number of child documents from the Length property of the MdiChildren property:

```
Dim childCount As Integer = Me.MdiChildren.Length
```

It is also often the case that you need to override the `OnMdiChildActivate` method so that you can customize what the MDI container needs to do when a child document is activated. To override this method, you write the following:

```
Protected Overrides Sub OnMdiChildActivate(ByVal e As EventArgs)
  MyBase.OnMdiChildActivate(e)
  . . .
End Sub
```

Note that you should call the `OnMdiChildActivate` method of the base class. Failure to do this will result in failed menu merging. (You can read more about menu merging in the later "Menu Merging" section.)

Now that you know the basic things to do to write an MDI application, the next few sections discuss related topics.

Setting the Parent-Child Relationship

The relationship between an MDI container and its child document is one of the most important things to think about when designing an MDI application. The questions are always as follows: How well do you want the child to know the parent? Do you want the child to be independent from its container so that the child document can be reused in other MDI applications? Or, do you not care if the child document depends on the MDI container?

Let's discuss these two options carefully.

Code reuse is one of the main objectives of object-oriented programming. Therefore, if you can write a child document class that does not need to know about its container, it will be a good thing because it means the child document can be used in other MDI applications. However, developing this kind of MDI application is more difficult because there is no direct way to call a method or access a property in the MDI container. For example, if the container assigns a tab page for each MDI document, as shown in Figure 2-1, the tab page's text is normally the same as the title of the child document. If the child document's title is changed, the tab page's text must change too. How does the child document tell the tab page associated with it—which resides in the MDI container—that its title has changed?

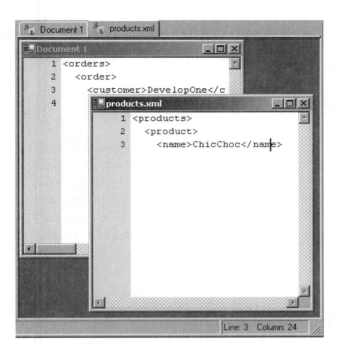

Figure 2-1. Tab pages are often associated with child documents.

Thanks to delegates, however, you can create a custom event raised from the child document. A child document can use this custom event to notify something to its container without the child document needing to know anything about the container.

NOTE *Chapter 1, "Creating a Custom Control: StyledTextArea," discusses creating custom events.*

The second option to the parent-child relationship is to let the child know about its parent by passing a reference to the parent. This really makes programming easier because now the child has access to certain properties and methods in the parent. However, the child will then have to know about the parent's type.

The XML editor project in this chapter takes the first approach, retaining the child document independence of its container. It is not the easiest design, but it promotes code reuse.

Setting Menu Merging

In an MDI application, some functions are only available when there is at least one child document open. For example, the Save function saves a child document into a file. When there is no child document open, then there is nothing to be saved. Ideally, the menu or button that executes this function should also only be available if it makes sense to call that function. The Save menu item under the File menu should only be visible if there is at least one child document open in the MDI application. When the application first starts, the Save menu item should not be visible. Also, after all child documents are closed, the Save menu item should disappear.

In the .NET Framework, the menus to execute functions that manipulate child documents should reside in the child document class itself, not in the MDI container. On the other hand, functions that can be executed without at least a child document open lie in the MDI container class. These functions include the Open function, which opens a document, and the Exit function. The menus to these functions should be available at all all times. Figure 2-2 shows an example of the File menu in an MDI application when no child document is open, and Figure 2-3 shows the File menu in the same application when at least one child document is open.

Figure 2-2. The File menu when no child document is open

Figure 2-3. The File menu when at least one child document is open

Now the question is this: How do you do that?

There are at least two answers. The first is through showing and hiding menu items. The second is through menu merging. The first approach is messy, and the second is elegant and easy. Therefore, this project uses menu merging. Before discussing menu merging, however, let's briefly discuss menus and menu items in the .NET Framework.

It is hard to find a decent Windows application that has no menu. Menus make it easy to access certain functionality in the application and, in most circumstances, minimize the use of controls such as buttons. Using menus is often preferable to button controls because menus take less space and make your application look more organized.

In the `System.Windows.Forms` namespace, all menu-related controls are child classes of the `Menu` class. This class is an abstract class, however, so you cannot instantiate it. The `Menu` class has three child classes: `ContextMenu`, `MainMenu`, and `MenuItem`.

The `ContextMenu` class represents shortcut menus that can be displayed when the user clicks the right mouse button over a control or area of the form. Shortcut menus typically combine different menu items from a `MainMenu` of a form that are useful for the user given the context of the application.

The `MainMenu` class represents the "conventional" menu on the top part of your form. It is a container for the menu structure of a form. A menu is composed of menu items represented by the `MenuItem` class. Each menu item is normally a command for your application or a parent menu for other submenu items.

The `Form` class has the `Menu` property to which you can assign a `MainMenu` object to bind the `MainMenu` object to the form.

The first thing you need to do to have a menu in your form is create a `MainMenu` object that will be bound to the form:

```
Dim mainMenu As New MainMenu()
```

However, nothing is visible in the `MainMenu` object until you add a menu item. You also must set the `Text` property of the `MenuItem` object. An ampersand (&) character in the `Text` property value indicates the character to be underlined when a user presses the Alt key. Adding a `MenuItem` object to a `MainMenu` or another `MenuItem` object is done by calling the `Add` method of the `MenuItemCollection` of the `Menu` object. You can access this collection from the `MenuItems` property of the Menu class. For example:

```
Dim fileMenuItem As New MenuItem()
mainMenu.MenuItems.Add(fileMenuItem)
```

You can add another menu item to a menu item to form a hierarchical structure of menu items. The menu item added to another menu item becomes a submenu of the latter menu item.

The interesting part of the MenuItem class is that it has several constructors, some of which allow you to create a MenuItem object and pass a handler for an event as well as assign a shortcut for the menu item. For example, the following is a menu item called fileOpenMenuItem. You construct it using the constructor that accepts a string for the Text property value, an event handler, and a shortcut:

```
Private fileOpenMenuItem As New MenuItem("&Open", _
  New EventHandler(AddressOf fileOpenMenuItem_Click), Shortcut.CtrlO)
```

NOTE *Those familiar with design patterns will recognize a* Command *pattern here, in which a command (the pointer to the* fileOpenMenuItem_Click *function) is encapsulated in an object (*fileOpenMenuItem*).*

To add a separator to a menu, you add a hyphen to its MenuItems collection, such as the following:

```
fileMenuItem.MenuItems.Add("-"); // add a separator
```

With an MDI application, some menu items are in the MDI container and some are in the child document class. The technique to work with menu items in both the MDI container and child documents is the same. However, you need to set the MergeOrder property of the menu items that belong to the same menu.

For instance, the MDI container has a File menu item (a menu item whose Text property is set to File) added to the main menu. Added to this File menu item are the New item, the Open item, a separator, and the Exit item. The File menu item in the child document class has the Save, Save As, Page Setup, Print Preview, and Print menu items. When a user opens a child document in the MDI application, the menu items under the File menu item in the child document must merge with other menu items under the File menu item in the container.

This is surprisingly easy to do. All you need to do is set the MergeOrder and MergeType properties of the MenuItem objects.

The MergeOrder property indicates the relative position of the menu item when it is merged with another. The MergeType property indicates the behavior of the menu item when its menu is merged with another.

The `MergeType` property can have one of the following members of the `System.Windows.Forms.MenuMerge` enumeration:

- `Add`: This adds the `MenuItem` to the collection of existing `MenuItem` objects in a merged menu.

- `MergeItems`: This merges all submenu items of this `MenuItem` with those of existing `MenuItem` objects at the same position in a merged menu.

- `Remove`: This excludes the `MenuItem` in a merged menu.

- `Replace`: This replaces an existing `MenuItem` with the `MenuItem` at the same position in a merged menu.

For example, Listing 2-15 constructs the menu items in the File menu item in an MDI container.

Listing 2-15. Creating the Menu Items in an MDI Container

```
Dim fileMenuItem As New MenuItem()
Dim fileNewMenuItem As New MenuItem("&New", _
    New System.EventHandler(AddressOf Me.fileNewMenuItem_Click), Shortcut.CtrlN)
Dim fileOpenMenuItem As New MenuItem("&Open", _
    New EventHandler(AddressOf fileOpenMenuItem_Click), Shortcut.CtrlO)

Dim fileExitMenuItem As New MenuItem("E&xit", _
    New System.EventHandler(AddressOf Me.fileExitMenuItem_Click))

fileMenuItem.Text = "&File"
fileMenuItem.MergeType = MenuMerge.MergeItems
fileMenuItem.MergeOrder = 0
mainMenu.MenuItems.Add(fileMenuItem)
fileOpenMenuItem.MergeOrder = 101
fileNewMenuItem.MergeOrder = 100
fileExitMenuItem.MergeOrder = 120
fileMenuItem.MenuItems.Add(fileNewMenuItem)
fileMenuItem.MenuItems.Add(fileOpenMenuItem)

Dim separatorFileMenuItem As MenuItem = _
  fileMenuItem.MenuItems.Add("-")
separatorFileMenuItem.MergeOrder = 119
fileMenuItem.MenuItems.Add(fileExitMenuItem)
```

And, Listing 2-16 constructs the menu items in the File menu item in the child document class.

Listing 2-16. Constructing the Menu Items in the Child Document

```
Dim fileMenuItem As New MenuItem()
Dim fileSaveMenuItem As New MenuItem("&Save", _
  New EventHandler(AddressOf fileSaveMenuItem_Click), _
  Shortcut.CtrlS)
Dim fileSaveAsMenuItem As New MenuItem("Save &As...", _
  New EventHandler(AddressOf fileSaveAsMenuItem_Click))
Dim filePageSetupMenuItem As New MenuItem("Page Set&up...", _
  New EventHandler(AddressOf filePageSetupMenuItem_Click))
Dim filePrintPreviewMenuItem As New MenuItem("Print Pre&view", _
  New EventHandler(AddressOf filePrintPreviewMenuItem_Click))
Dim filePrintMenuItem As New MenuItem("&Print...", _
  New EventHandler(AddressOf filePrintMenuItem_Click), _
    Shortcut.CtrlP)
Dim fileSeparatorMenuItem As New MenuItem("-")
fileMenuItem.Text = "&File"
fileMenuItem.MergeType = MenuMerge.MergeItems
fileMenuItem.MergeOrder = 0
fileSaveMenuItem.MergeOrder = 113
fileSaveAsMenuItem.MergeOrder = 114
fileSeparatorMenuItem.MergeOrder = 115
filePageSetupMenuItem.MergeOrder = 116
filePrintPreviewMenuItem.MergeOrder = 117
filePrintMenuItem.MergeOrder = 118
fileMenuItem.MenuItems.Add(fileSaveMenuItem)
fileMenuItem.MenuItems.Add(fileSaveAsMenuItem)
fileMenuItem.MenuItems.Add(filePageSetupMenuItem)
fileMenuItem.MenuItems.Add(filePrintPreviewMenuItem)
fileMenuItem.MenuItems.Add(filePrintMenuItem)
fileMenuItem.MenuItems.Add(fileSeparatorMenuItem)
```

You do not have to do anything else. All menu items will merge beautifully when a child document is created in the MDI container.

Setting Child Document Layout

Arranging child documents cannot be easier in the .NET Framework. You do this in a single line of code by calling the LayoutMdi method of the System.Windows.Forms.Form class. This method accepts a member of the System.Windows.Forms.MdiLayout enumeration. Its members are as follows:

- ArrangeIcons: This arranges all MDI child icons within the client region of the MDI container.

- Cascade: This cascades all MDI child windows within the client region of the MDI container.

- TileHorizontal: This tiles all MDI child windows horizontally within the client region of the MDI container.

- TileVertical: This tiles all MDI child windows vertically within the client region of the MDI container.

Figures 2-4, 2-5, and 2-6 show the layout of the child documents after calling the LayoutMdi method by passing a different member of the MdiLayout enumeration. Specifically, Figure 2-4 shows a Cascade layout, Figure 2-5 shows a TileHorizontal layout, and Figure 2-6 shows a TileVertical layout.

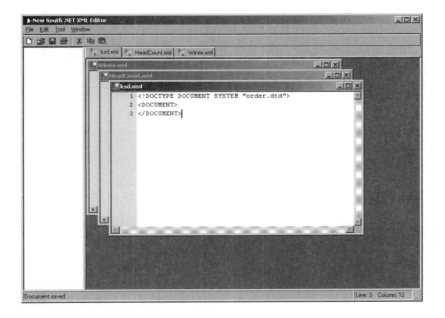

Figure 2-4. Cascade *layout*

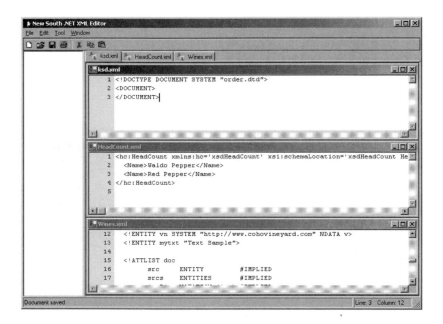

Figure 2-5. TileHorizontal *layout*

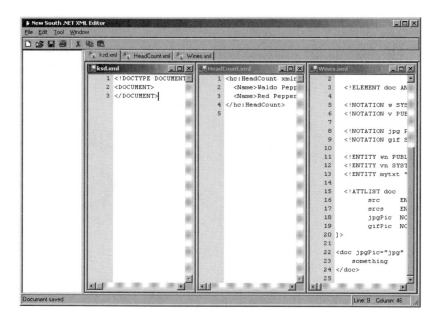

Figure 2-6. TileVertical *layout*

Building a Status Bar

The MDI container in an MDI application normally has a status bar, represented by the System.Windows.Forms.StatusBar class. It is a nice addition to the bottom of the form to display messages. To be useable, a status bar must have one or more status bar panels. The System.Windows.Forms.StatusBarPanel class represents each status bar panel. You must add a status bar panel to the StatusBarPanelCollection of the StatusBar object. The Panels property represents this collection. This code constructs a status bar having two status bar panels:

```
Dim statusBar As New StatusBar()
Dim statusBarPanel1 As New StatusBarPanel()
Dim statusBarPanel2 As New StatusBarPanel()
statusBar.Panels.Add(statusBarPanel1);
statusBar.Panels.Add(statusBarPanel2);
```

To get the appearance that you want, you set the BorderStyle and AutoSize properties of the StatusBarPanel. The text to display is the value of the Text property of the StatusBarPanel object.

In an MDI application, there is often a need for the child document to display a message in a status bar. However, an MDI application normally only has one status bar, which is in the MDI container. How do you write a message on the status bar without sacrificing the independence of the child document of the MDI container?

The answer to this question is simple. You just declare a reference variable of a status bar in the child document class. When a child document is created, you pass the object reference to the status bar in the MDI container to the child document. Now the child document has access to it. There is one thing to remember, though: Because you cannot guarantee that an MDI container always passes a status bar to a child document, every time you want to write to the status bar from within a child document, you need to check that the status bar is not null.

Tab Control and Tab Pages

As you saw in Figure 2-1 of this chapter, an MDI application often has a tab control, represented by the System.Windows.Forms.TabControl class. A tab control is a bar that spans horizontally at the bottom or at the top of the client area of an MDI container. A child document is often associated with a tab page, represented by the System.Windows.Forms.TabPage class. When a child document is created, a tab page is added to the tab control. When the child document is closed, the tab page associated with it is also destroyed.

Each tab page in the tab control can have an image as well as text. The text displayed is the value of the Text property of the TabPage object. To display an image, however, you need to assign an ImageList object to the TabControl, then select an image in the ImageList by setting the ImageIndex property of the TabPage control. Therefore, tab pages in the same tab control can have different images.

This code creates a TabPage object and adds it to a TabControl called tabControl:

```
Dim tabPage As New IndexedTabPage()
tabPage.Text = "New Document"
tabPage.ImageIndex = 1
tabControl.Controls.Add(tabPage)
'Activate the new tabPage
tabControl.SelectedIndex = tabControl.TabCount - 1
```

Note that the last line of the code selects the recently created tab page by setting the TabControl object's SelectedIndex to the TabCount property minus 1. The TabCount property returns the number of tab pages. In this example, the code uses TabCount minus 1 because SelectedIndex is zero-based. Therefore, the first tab page is tab page number 0, and the last tab page is numbered (TabCount - 1).

As mentioned previously, because a tab page is associated with a child document, it must be destroyed when the child document is closed. With the Closed event in the System.Windows.Forms.Form class, this is not a difficult task. You can wire the Closed event with an event handler. This event handler gets called when a child document is closed. However, there remains a problem. The Closed event passes a System.EventArgs object. It does not tell you which child document has closed. The event simply notifies that a child document has been closed.

Often you need to maintain a unique number assigned to both a tab page and an associated child document. When a child document is closed, you simply check all the child documents for this unique number and delete any tab page having a number not found in any child document. This is the approach that this project takes. You will see the code that does this in the "Implementing the Project" section.

Creating a Toolbar

A *toolbar* is a horizontal bar containing buttons that your user can click to perform certain functions. Generally, each individual button on the toolbar duplicates a function that can also be invoked from one of the menus. However, a toolbar's buttons are always visible and can be invoked by a single click. A toolbar also tends to give the impression that your application is user-friendly.

In the .NET Framework, the System.Windows.Forms.Toolbar class represents a toolbar. The System.Windows.Forms.ToolBarButton class represents a toolbar button. Each button normally displays one of the images in the ImageList object passed to the toolbar. Therefore, after the toolbar is instantiated, you assign an ImageList object to its ImageList property, such as in the following code:

```
toolBar.ImageList = imageList
```

Then, use the ImageIndex of each individual toolbar button to assign an image in the ImageList control:

```
toolBarButton1.ImageIndex = 0
toolBarButton2.ImageIndex = 1
toolBarButton3.ImageIndex = 2
toolBarButton4.ImageIndex = 3
```

Of course, you then have to add the toolbar buttons to the ToolBar control:

```
toolBar.Buttons.Add(toolBarButton1)
toolBar.Buttons.Add(toolBarButton2)
toolBar.Buttons.Add(toolBarButton3)
toolBar.Buttons.Add(toolBarButton4)
```

And, add the ToolBar control to the form:

```
Me.Controls.Add(toolBar)
```

An astute reader will notice that it is not that simple in an MDI application. Remember that the toolbar always resides in the MDI container and some of the functions that need to be performed are methods of the child document class. How do you invoke the function inside the child document object from the MDI container?

Although this is certainly an issue, fortunately it is not a big one. In fact, you can attack the problem with a number of approaches. However, always remember that you do not want to compromise the child document class independence of the MDI container.

The following are your options:

- You can make the child document class's methods public. Because the MDI container has access to each instance of its child document, it can always call these public methods. However, this approach might not be desirable if you do not want to expose those methods to the outside world.

- You can invoke those methods by clicking the menus in the child document objects. When a child document is created, its menus are merged so the user can click on them to invoke what they are meant to do. With a toolbar, you can send the same key combination to the current application to invoke a function inside the child document. For example, the user would press Alt+F followed by the O key to open a document. With a toolbar, you can send this key combination to the application using the Send method of the System.Windows.Forms.SendKeys class. For example, to send Alt+F followed by O, you write the following:

```
SendKeys.Send("%FO")
```

Another issue when using a toolbar is detecting which toolbar button is being clicked. When a toolbar is clicked, the event handler will accept a ToolBarButtonClickEventArgs object. This class has the Button property, and you use it as in Listing 2-17.

Listing 2-17. Using the Button *Property*

```
Protected Sub toolBar_ButtonClick(ByVal sender As Object, _
  ByVal e As ToolBarButtonClickEventArgs)

  ' Evaluate the Button property to determine
  ' which button was clicked.
  If e.Button.Equals(newToolBarButton) Then
    fileNewMenuItem.PerformClick()
  ElseIf e.Button.Equals(openToolBarButton) Then
    fileOpenMenuItem.PerformClick()
  ElseIf e.Button.Equals(saveToolBarButton) Then
    If Me.MdiChildren.Length > 0 Then
  .
  .
  .
```

Understanding the Singleton Design Pattern

Even beginners of object-oriented programming know that they can instantiate a class using the New keyword followed by the class's constructor, such as the following:

```
New MyClass()
```

or as follows:

```
New MyClass(123)
```

You get one object each time a constructor is called. If you call a class's constructor three times, you get three instances of the class.

NOTE *Even if you do not write a constructor in your class, the Visual Basic compiler creates a no-argument constructor in the absence of one. However, if a class does have a constructor, whether it is a no argument constructor or one that accepts argument(s), the Visual Basic compiler does not create a new one. These constructors are accessible because they have a public access modifier.*

However, there are cases where you want to limit the number of instances of a class to one. For example, recall that in Microsoft Word you can press Ctrl+F to display a Find dialog box. However, for the whole life of Microsoft Word, there can only be one Find dialog box. If you press Ctrl+F two times, there is still only one Find dialog box. Even when there are multiple documents open, there can only be one Find dialog box that works with any active document. Indeed, you do not need more than one instance of the Find dialog box. In fact, having more than one probably will make programming harder.

For cases such as this, you use the Singleton pattern. This pattern is effective for limiting the maximum number of instances of a class to exactly one. In this case if more than one object need to use an instance of the class, those objects share the same instance. One of the reasons why you want to share an instance is to share data.

How do you do that? Because the absence of a constructor will make the compiler create a no-argument public constructor, a class applying the Singleton pattern has a private or protected constructor. Because the constructor is private or protected, there is no way you can create an instance of that class by calling its constructor. The constructor is not accessible from outside the class.

The question that arises then is this: If the only constructor cannot be accessed, how do you get an instance of that class? The answer lies in a static (*shared*) method in the class. A Singleton class will have a static method that calls the constructor to create an instance of the class and return this instance to the caller of the static method. But, isn't the constructor private? That's right. However, remember that the static method is also in the same class; therefore, it has access to all members of the class, including the private constructor.

You might ask the following question: "You can't create an instance of a class by calling its constructor, so how do you call the static method without having an object?" Note, though, you can use a static member of a class without having an instance of that class.

To limit the number of instances to one, the static method has to check if an instance has been created before. If it has, it simply returns a reference to the previous created instance. If it has not, it calls the constructor to create one. It is as simple as that.

As an example, consider the form whose class is called SingletonForm in Listing 2-18. This class represents a Singleton form.

Listing 2-18. A Singleton Form

```
Imports System
Imports System.Windows.Forms
Imports System.ComponentModel

Public Class SingletonForm : Inherits Form
  Private Shared myInstance As SingletonForm
  Private Sub New()
    Me.Text = "Singleton Form"
  End Sub

  Protected Overrides Sub OnCLosing(ByVal e As CancelEventArgs)
    e.Cancel = True
    Me.Hide()
  End Sub

  Public Shared Function GetInstance() As SingletonForm
    If myInstance Is Nothing Then
      myInstance = New SingletonForm()
    End If
    Return myInstance
  End Function
End Class
```

First, notice that the class only has one constructor and its access modifier is private. Second, to get an instance of that class, you have the static GetInstance method, and there is also a static variable called myInstance (of type SingletonForm). The GetInstance method returns the myInstance variable. The method checks if myInstance is null (Nothing) and, if yes, calls the constructor:

```
If myInstance Is Nothing Then
    myInstance = New SingletonForm()
End If
```

The method then returns myInstance.

To obtain a reference to the only instance of the SingletonForm class, you do not use its constructor. Instead, you call its GetInstance method, as in the following snippet:

```
Dim myForm As SingletonForm = SingletonForm.GetInstance()
```

Once you get the instance, you can call its public members just as you would a normal class's object. For example, because SingletonForm extends the Form class, you can call its Show method:

```
myForm.Show()
```

This application uses the Singleton pattern in the Find dialog box. Therefore, you should understand the concept well.

Why Not Use a Static (Shared) Object Reference?

You know that if you declare an object reference as shared, you also only have one single instance of that object. So, why bother using the Singleton pattern? Because the Singleton pattern guarantees that even if you have two or more reference variables of a Singleton class, you can only create one instance. Also, using a Singleton pattern makes it easier to change a design to allow more than one instance of a class.

Printing in the .NET Framework Windows

Simple printing, such as sending a string to the printer, in the .NET Framework is easy. However, the .NET Framework lacks a ready-to-use class that encapsulates complex printing tasks. For example, you must do some coding if you want to enable your user to set the page and printer, change the margins, print more than one copy, and so on. This section offers a brief tutorial on printing using the .NET Framework class library. It starts from printing a simple string and then proceeds with some coding for Page Setup and Print Preview.

The .NET Framework provides the `System.Drawing.Printing` namespace for printing. The main class in this namespace is the `PrintDocument` class, which represents an object that sends output to the printer. The role of this class is so central that you can achieve simple and complex printing tasks by using this class alone. However, as you shall see, other classes in this and other namespaces help make coding easier.

You use the `System.Drawing.Printing.PrintDocument` class to print by calling its `Print` method after constructing an instance of this class. One of the events the `Print` method invokes is the `PrintPage` event. You need to wire an event handler to the `PrintPage` event and write the code to send output to the printer. The event handler will receive an argument of type `System.Drawing.Printing.PrintPageEventArgs` containing data related to the `PrintPage` event. One of the properties in `PrintPageEventArgs` is `Graphics`, from which you can obtain a `System.Drawing.Graphics` object. This `Graphics` object represents a print page. To send a string to the printer, for example, you use the `Graphics` class's `DrawString` method. Of course you can also call other methods of the `Graphics` class, such as `FillRectangle`, `DrawLine`, and so on.

To illustrate how you print using members of the `System.Drawing.Printing` namespace, see the form in Listing 2-19. This is basically a blank form without any printing capability. You will gradually add code to this class to add printing features. Listing 2-19 is a form class with a menu having a menu item called `fileMenuItem`. `fileMenuItem` in turn has three sub menu items: `filePageSetupMenuItem`, `filePrintPreviewMenuItem`, and `filePrintMenuItem`.

Listing 2-19. The Template for Printing

```
Imports System
Imports System.Windows.Forms
Imports System.Drawing
Imports System.Drawing.Printing
Imports System.IO
```

```vb
Public Class Form1 : Inherits Form

  Public Sub New()
    Me.Menu = New MainMenu()
    Dim fileMenuItem As New MenuItem("&File")
    Dim filePageSetupMenuItem As New MenuItem("Page Set&up...", _
      New EventHandler(AddressOf filePageSetupMenuItem_Click))
    Dim filePrintPreviewMenuItem As New MenuItem("Print Pre&view", _
      New EventHandler(AddressOf filePrintPreviewMenuItem_Click))
    Dim filePrintMenuItem As New MenuItem("&Print...", _
      New EventHandler(AddressOf filePrintMenuItem_Click), Shortcut.CtrlP)

    fileMenuItem.MenuItems.Add(filePageSetupMenuItem)
    fileMenuItem.MenuItems.Add(filePrintPreviewMenuItem)
    fileMenuItem.MenuItems.Add(filePrintMenuItem)

    Me.Menu.MenuItems.Add(fileMenuItem)
  End Sub

' -------------- event handlers --------------------------------------------
  Private Sub filePrintMenuItem_Click(ByVal sender As Object, ByVal e As EventArgs)
  End Sub

  Private Sub filePrintPreviewMenuItem_Click(ByVal sender As ⤶
Object, ByVal e As EventArgs)
  End Sub

  Private Sub filePageSetupMenuItem_Click(ByVal sender As ⤶
Object, ByVal e As EventArgs)
  End Sub
' -------------- end of event handlers ----------------------------------------

  <STAThread()> Shared Sub Main()
    Application.Run(New Form1())
  End Sub

End Class
```

Note that each of the three menu items in fileMenuItem is wired with an event handler in its declaration. The event handlers for the three menu items are filePageSetupMenuItem_Click, filePrintPreviewMenuItem_Click, and filePrintMenuItem_Click, as shown in the following code that is part of the class's constructor:

```
Dim filePageSetupMenuItem As New MenuItem("Page Set&up...", _
  New EventHandler(AddressOf filePageSetupMenuItem_Click))
Dim filePrintPreviewMenuItem As New MenuItem("Print Pre&view", _
  New EventHandler(AddressOf filePrintPreviewMenuItem_Click))
Dim filePrintMenuItem As New MenuItem("&Print...", _
  New EventHandler(AddressOf filePrintMenuItem_Click), Shortcut.CtrlP)
```

As you can see from the code in Listing 2-19, the three event handlers are currently blank:

```
Private Sub filePrintMenuItem_Click(ByVal sender As Object, ByVal e As EventArgs)
End Sub
Private Sub filePrintPreviewMenuItem_Click(↩
  ByVal sender As Object, ByVal e As EventArgs)
End Sub
Private Sub filePageSetupMenuItem_Click(ByVal sender As↩
  Object, ByVal e As EventArgs)
End Sub
```

If you compile and run this class, you will see something like the form in Figure 2-7.

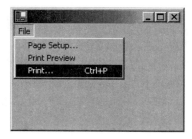

Figure 2-7. The blank printing template

Now, you are ready to add code to the template in Listing 2-19. Follow these steps:

1. Add a class-level variable called printDoc of type
   `System.Drawing.Printing.PrintDocument`:

   ```
   Private printDoc As New PrintDocument()
   ```

2. In the class's constructor, wire the PrintPage event of printDoc with an
   event handler called printDoc_PrintPage:

   ```
   AddHandler printDoc.PrintPage, AddressOf printDoc_PrintPage
   ```

3. Add code to the filePrintMenuItem_Click event handler:

   ```
   Private Sub filePrintMenuItem_Click(ByVal sender As Object, ByVal e As EventArgs)
     printDoc.Print()
   End Sub
   ```

4. Add code to printDoc_PrintPage:

   ```
   Private Sub printDoc_PrintPage(ByVal sender As Object, ↵
   ByVal e As PrintPageEventArgs)
     Dim textToPrint = ".NET Printing is easy"
     Dim printFont As New Font("Courier New", 12)
     e.Graphics.DrawString(textToPrint, printFont, Brushes.Black, 0, 0)
   End Sub
   ```

Listing 2-20 shows the resulting form. The code in bold is the code you added.

Listing 2-20. The Form with Code That Prints

```
Imports System
Imports System.Windows.Forms
Imports System.Drawing
Imports System.Drawing.Printing
Imports System.IO

Public Class Form1 : Inherits Form

  Private printDoc As New PrintDocument()

  Public Sub New()
    Me.Menu = New MainMenu()
    Dim fileMenuItem As New MenuItem("&File")
```

```
    Dim filePageSetupMenuItem As New MenuItem("Page Set&up...", _
      New EventHandler(AddressOf filePageSetupMenuItem_Click))
    Dim filePrintPreviewMenuItem As New MenuItem("Print Pre&view", _
      New EventHandler(AddressOf filePrintPreviewMenuItem_Click))
    Dim filePrintMenuItem As New MenuItem("&Print...", _
      New EventHandler(AddressOf filePrintMenuItem_Click), Shortcut.CtrlP)

    fileMenuItem.MenuItems.Add(filePageSetupMenuItem)
    fileMenuItem.MenuItems.Add(filePrintPreviewMenuItem)
    fileMenuItem.MenuItems.Add(filePrintMenuItem)

    Me.Menu.MenuItems.Add(fileMenuItem)

    AddHandler printDoc.PrintPage, AddressOf printDoc_PrintPage
  End Sub

  '----------- event handlers -----------------------------
  Private Sub filePrintMenuItem_Click(ByVal sender As Object,
ByVal e As EventArgs)
    printDoc.Print()
  End Sub

  Private Sub filePrintPreviewMenuItem_Click(ByVal sender As
Object, ByVal e As EventArgs)
  End Sub

  Private Sub filePageSetupMenuItem_Click(ByVal sender As
Object, ByVal e As EventArgs)
  End Sub

  Private Sub printDoc_PrintPage(ByVal sender As Object,
ByVal e As PrintPageEventArgs)
    Dim textToPrint = ".NET Printing is easy"
    Dim printFont As New Font("Courier New", 12)
    e.Graphics.DrawString(textToPrint, printFont, Brushes.Black, 0, 0)
  End Sub
  '----------- end of event handlers ------------------------

  <STAThread()> Shared Sub Main()
    Application.Run(New Form1())
  End Sub

End Class
```

If you run the form now and press Ctrl+P—and, of course, assuming a printer is connected to your computer and the correct driver is installed—the printer will print the string ".NET Printing is easy." Easy, isn't it?

Using PrintDialog

Usually in a Windows application, you will see the Print dialog box prior to printing. This dialog box gives the user the chance to cancel the printing, change the printer properties, select the number of copies, select the pages to print, and so on. If you modify the filePrintMenuItem_Click in Listing 2-20 with the one in Listing 2-21, a Print dialog box will display prior to printing. The System.Windows.Forms.PrintDialog class represents a Print dialog box.

Listing 2-21. Using PrintDialog

```
Private Sub filePrintMenuItem_Click(ByVal sender As Object, ByVal e As EventArgs)
  Dim dlg As New PrintDialog()
  dlg.Document = printDoc
  If (dlg.ShowDialog = DialogResult.OK) Then
    printDoc.Print()
  End If
End Sub
```

Figure 2-8 shows a Print dialog box.

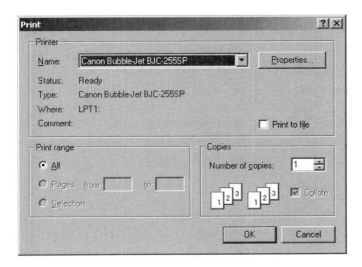

Figure 2-8. The Print dialog box

The filePrintMenuItem_Click event handler in Listing 2-21 only sends output to the printer if the user clicks the Print dialog box's OK button. However, the settings your user changes in the Print dialog box will not take effect until you write the code to take into account those options.

Page Setup

The following section adds the feature to set up the page used for printing. For this, you must follow these steps:

1. Construct an instance of the System.Drawing.Printing.PageSettings class. For this example, add the following to the Declarations part of the form class:

    ```
    Private pgSettings As New PageSettings()
    ```

2. Set pgSettings to the DefaultPageSettings property of printDoc before printing. Therefore, add the highlighted code to the filePrintMenuItem_Click event handler in your form:

    ```
    Private Sub filePrintMenuItem_Click(ByVal sender As
    Object, ByVal e As EventArgs)
      printDoc.DefaultPageSettings = pgSettings
      Dim dlg As New PrintDialog()
      dlg.Document = printDoc
      If (dlg.ShowDialog = DialogResult.OK) Then
        printDoc.Print()
      End If
    End Sub
    ```

3. Allow the user to change the setting of the page. For this example, add the following code to the filePageSetupMenuItem_Click event handler:

    ```
    Private Sub filePageSetupMenuItem_Click(ByVal sender As Object, _
      ByVal e As EventArgs)
      Dim pageSetupDialog As New PageSetupDialog()
      pageSetupDialog.PageSettings = pgSettings
      pageSetupDialog.AllowOrientation = True
      pageSetupDialog.AllowMargins = True
      pageSetupDialog.ShowDialog()
    End Sub
    ```

4. Modify the printDoc_PrintPage event handler to take into account the top and left margins. This is the code for your form:

```
Private Sub printDoc_PrintPage(ByVal sender As Object, _
  ByVal e As PrintPageEventArgs)
  Dim textToPrint = ".NET Printing is easy"
  Dim printFont As New Font("Courier New", 12)
  Dim leftMargin As Integer = e.MarginBounds.Left
  Dim topMargin As Integer = e.MarginBounds.Top
  e.Graphics.DrawString(textToPrint, printFont,
Brushes.Black, leftMargin, topMargin)
End Sub
```

Now you can select Page Setup from the File menu. It will display the dialog box shown in Figure 2-9. How it looks depends on your printer type.

Figure 2-9. Page Setup dialog box

Listing 2-22 shows the complete code for the form that includes page setup.

Listing 2-22. The Form Class That Allows the User to Change the Page Setup

```
Imports System
Imports System.Windows.Forms
Imports System.Drawing
Imports System.Drawing.Printing
Imports System.IO


Public Class Form1 : Inherits Form

  Private printDoc As New PrintDocument()
  Private pgSettings As New PageSettings()

  Public Sub New()
    Me.Menu = New MainMenu()
    Dim fileMenuItem As New MenuItem("&File")
    Dim filePageSetupMenuItem As New MenuItem("Page Set&up...", _
      New EventHandler(AddressOf filePageSetupMenuItem_Click))
    Dim filePrintPreviewMenuItem As New MenuItem("Print Pre&view", _
      New EventHandler(AddressOf filePrintPreviewMenuItem_Click))
    Dim filePrintMenuItem As New MenuItem("&Print...", _
      New EventHandler(AddressOf filePrintMenuItem_Click), Shortcut.CtrlP)

    fileMenuItem.MenuItems.Add(filePageSetupMenuItem)
    fileMenuItem.MenuItems.Add(filePrintPreviewMenuItem)
    fileMenuItem.MenuItems.Add(filePrintMenuItem)

    Me.Menu.MenuItems.Add(fileMenuItem)

    AddHandler printDoc.PrintPage, AddressOf printDoc_PrintPage
  End Sub

  '----------- event handlers ------------------------------
  Private Sub filePrintMenuItem_Click(ByVal sender As Object, _
    ByVal e As EventArgs)
    printDoc.DefaultPageSettings = pgSettings

    Dim dlg As New PrintDialog()
    dlg.Document = printDoc
    If (dlg.ShowDialog = DialogResult.OK) Then
      printDoc.Print()
    End If
  End Sub
```

```
Private Sub filePrintPreviewMenuItem_Click(ByVal sender As Object, _
  ByVal e As EventArgs)
End Sub

Private Sub filePageSetupMenuItem_Click(ByVal sender As Object, _
  ByVal e As EventArgs)
  Dim pageSetupDialog As New PageSetupDialog()
  pageSetupDialog.PageSettings = pgSettings
  pageSetupDialog.AllowOrientation = True
  pageSetupDialog.AllowMargins = True
  pageSetupDialog.ShowDialog()
End Sub

Private Sub printDoc_PrintPage(ByVal sender As Object, _
  ByVal e As PrintPageEventArgs)
  Dim textToPrint = ".NET Printing is easy"
  Dim printFont As New Font("Courier New", 12)
  Dim leftMargin As Integer = e.MarginBounds.Left
  Dim topMargin As Integer = e.MarginBounds.Top
  e.Graphics.DrawString(textToPrint, printFont, Brushes.Black, _
    leftMargin, topMargin)
End Sub
'----------- end of event handlers -----------------------

<STAThread()> Shared Sub Main()
  Application.Run(New Form1())
End Sub

End Class
```

Printer Setting

You can also enable the user to change printer settings by doing the following:

1. Create an instance of the System.Drawing.Printing.PrinterSettings class.
    For your form, add the following line of code:

    ```
    Private prtSettings As New PrinterSettings()
    ```

2. Set prtSettings to the PrinterSettings property of the PageSetupDialog:

```
Private Sub filePageSetupMenuItem_Click(ByVal sender As
Object, ByVal e As EventArgs)
  Dim pageSetupDialog As New PageSetupDialog()
  pageSetupDialog.PageSettings = pgSettings
  pageSetupDialog.PrinterSettings = prtSettings
  pageSetupDialog.AllowOrientation = True
  pageSetupDialog.AllowMargins = True
  pageSetupDialog.ShowDialog()
End Sub
```

Now the Printer button in the Page Setup dialog box is enabled (see Figure 2-10).

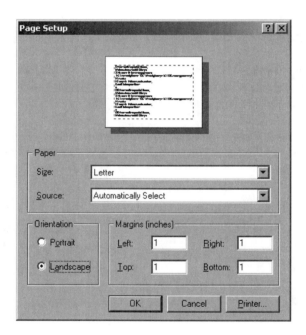

Figure 2-10. Page Setup dialog box with enabled Printer button

If you click the Printer button, you will see the Printer settings page (see Figure 2-11).

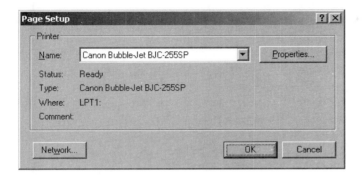

Figure 2-11. The Printer settings page from the Page Setup dialog box

Print Preview

In a Windows application, before users print, they can normally print a preview of how the printout will look on paper. You can also provide this feature by adding the following code to the filePrintPreviewMenuItem_Click event handler:

```
Private Sub filePrintPreviewMenuItem_Click(ByVal sender As Object, _
  ByVal e As EventArgs)
  Dim dlg As New PrintPreviewDialog()
  dlg.Document = printDoc
  dlg.ShowDialog()
End Sub
```

The System.Windows.Forms.PrintPreviewDialog class represents the Print Preview dialog box. You can create an instance of this dialog box by using its no-argument constructor. Then you must assign the PrintDocument object to print to the Document property of the PrintPreviewDialog object. When the ShowDialog method is called, it will invoke the PrintPage event of the PrintDocument object. However, the output will not be sent to the printer but to the PrintPreviewDialog object.

Figure 2-12 shows the Print Preview dialog box.

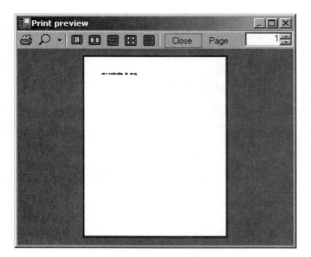

Figure 2-12. Print Preview dialog box

Listing 2-23 gives the complete code.

Listing 2-23. The Complete Code with Page Setup and Print Preview

```
Imports System
Imports System.Windows.Forms
Imports System.Drawing
Imports System.Drawing.Printing
Imports System.IO

Public Class Form1 : Inherits Form

  Private printDoc As New PrintDocument()
  Private pgSettings As New PageSettings()
  Private prtSettings As New PrinterSettings()

  Public Sub New()
    Me.Menu = New MainMenu()
    Dim fileMenuItem As New MenuItem("&File")
    Dim filePageSetupMenuItem As New MenuItem("Page Set&up...", _
      New EventHandler(AddressOf filePageSetupMenuItem_Click))
```

```vbnet
  Dim filePrintPreviewMenuItem As New MenuItem("Print Pre&view", _
    New EventHandler(AddressOf filePrintPreviewMenuItem_Click))
  Dim filePrintMenuItem As New MenuItem("&Print...", _
    New EventHandler(AddressOf filePrintMenuItem_Click), Shortcut.CtrlP)

  fileMenuItem.MenuItems.Add(filePageSetupMenuItem)
  fileMenuItem.MenuItems.Add(filePrintPreviewMenuItem)
  fileMenuItem.MenuItems.Add(filePrintMenuItem)

  Me.Menu.MenuItems.Add(fileMenuItem)

  AddHandler printDoc.PrintPage, AddressOf printDoc_PrintPage
End Sub

'----------- event handlers ----------------------------
Private Sub filePrintMenuItem_Click(ByVal sender As Object, _
  ByVal e As EventArgs)
  printDoc.DefaultPageSettings = pgSettings

  Dim dlg As New PrintDialog()
  dlg.Document = printDoc
  If (dlg.ShowDialog = DialogResult.OK) Then
    printDoc.Print()
  End If
End Sub

Private Sub filePrintPreviewMenuItem_Click(ByVal sender As Object, _
  ByVal e As EventArgs)
  Dim dlg As New PrintPreviewDialog()
  dlg.Document = printDoc
  dlg.ShowDialog()
End Sub

Private Sub filePageSetupMenuItem_Click(ByVal sender As Object, _
  ByVal e As EventArgs)
  Dim pageSetupDialog As New PageSetupDialog()
  pageSetupDialog.PageSettings = pgSettings
  pageSetupDialog.PrinterSettings = prtSettings
  pageSetupDialog.AllowOrientation = True
  pageSetupDialog.AllowMargins = True
  pageSetupDialog.ShowDialog()
End Sub
```

```
  Private Sub printDoc_PrintPage(ByVal sender As Object, _
    ByVal e As PrintPageEventArgs)
    Dim textToPrint = ".NET Printing is easy"
    Dim printFont As New Font("Courier New", 12)
    Dim leftMargin As Integer = e.MarginBounds.Left
    Dim topMargin As Integer = e.MarginBounds.Top
    e.Graphics.DrawString(textToPrint, printFont,
Brushes.Black, leftMargin, topMargin)
  End Sub
  '----------- end of event handlers -----------------------

  <STAThread()> Shared Sub Main()
    Application.Run(New Form1())
  End Sub
End Class
```

Up to this point, you already know how to provide basic features for printing from your Windows form. There is still a lot to talk about, but you will revisit printing in the "Using the TextPrinter Class" section.

Implementing the Project

The XML editor application you will build in this chapter is an MDI application. The user can open any number of XML documents and get those documents validated. For each document, the user can also build a tree for the elements in the document. Each document encapsulates the StyledTextArea control discussed in Chapter 1, "Creating a Custom Control: StyledTextArea."

The MDI container uses the following components:

- XmlViewer

- TextPrinter

- Document

In turn the Document component uses the FindDialog component. The following sections discuss each of these components before dissecting the MDI container.

Using the XmlViewer Component

The XmlViewer component displays the tree representing an XML document's hierarchical data structure. Figure 2-13 shows an example of an XML viewer component.

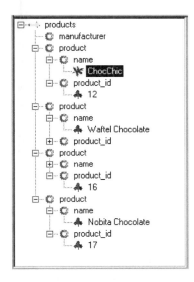

Figure 2-13. An XMLViewer *component*

Note that a different image can represent each node type. For example, the image representing the root is different from the ones representing a branch and a leaf. Also, you can customize these images, meaning you choose your own images to pass to the XML viewer component. Also, a selected element has a yet different image.

The class that represents XML viewer components is XmlViewer. It inherits the System.Windows.Forms.TreeView class. As a result, XmlViewer automatically supports scrolling. You can find the code for the XmlViewer class in the XmlViewer.vb file.

The class has only two public methods: BuildTree and Clear. The BuildTree method builds a tree by passing a string representing the content of an XML document. The Clear method clears the component.

At the declarations part of the class, there are six integers representing the image indexes:

```
Public RootImageIndex As Integer
Public RootSelectedImageIndex As Integer
Public LeafImageIndex As Integer
Public LeafSelectedImageIndex As Integer
Public BranchImageIndex As Integer
Public BranchSelectedImageIndex As Integer
```

The client must pass an ImageList object to the XmlViewer and then set the indexes for each of the previous six fields, such as in the following code:

```
xmlViewer.ImageList = imageList
xmlViewer.RootImageIndex = 8
xmlViewer.RootSelectedImageIndex = 9
xmlViewer.BranchImageIndex = 10
xmlViewer.BranchSelectedImageIndex = 11
xmlViewer.LeafImageIndex = 12
xmlViewer.LeafSelectedImageIndex = 13
```

After you construct an instance of the XmlViewer class, the client calls the BuildTree method by passing the content of an XML document. This method will then build the tree. Nothing will be displayed if the XML document is not well-formed.

The BuildTree method will first clear the component by calling the Clear method:

```
Clear()
```

It then creates a System.Xml.XmlDocument:

```
Dim xmlDocument As New XmlDocument()
```

Next, the BuildTree method needs to call the Load method of the XmlDocument class to load the document. The Load method has four overloads to allow you to pass one of the following: a System.IO.Stream object, a String object, a System.IO.TextReader object, or a System.Xml.XmlReader object. You have a string that is passed to the BuildTree method, so naturally your choice to load an XML document will be to use the second overload that accepts a String object.

However, looking up the documentation, you will see the following signature
of the second overload:

```
Overridable Overloads Public Sub Load (ByVal filename As String)
```

The method overload expects a filename to the XML document, not the
content of the document. Therefore, you cannot use this one.

Our second choice is to use the first overload of the Load method that accepts
a System.IO.TextReader. You can obtain a TextReader object from a String by constructing a System.IO.StringReader object because the System.IO.StringReader class
is a child class of the System.IO.TextReader class. Therefore, you have the following:

```
xmlDocument.Load(New StringReader(xmlText))
```

The BuildTree method draws the tree by calling the private DrawNode method.
However, the DrawNode method needs the root element. Therefore, you create a
root that is of type System.Windows.Forms.TreeNode. The TreeNode class has several
constructors. Which constructor you choose largely depends on whether you
want the element to display text and an image or text only. If you want the root to
display both text and an image, the constructor that allows you to do so has the
following signature:

```
Public Sub New( _
    ByVal text As String, _
    ByVal imageIndex As Integer, _
    ByVal selectedImageIndex As Integer _
)
```

You obtain the text for the root from the name of the XML document's
root. In a System.Xml.XmlDocument object, the root element is represented by the
DocumentElement property, which is of type System.Xml.XmlElement. The XmlElement
class has the Name property representing the name of the element. Therefore,
the following code creates a TreeNode object with some text and the appropriate
indexes of the images to be displayed when the element is selected and when it is
not selected:

```
Dim root As New TreeNode(xmlDocument.DocumentElement.Name, _
  RootImageIndex, rootselectedimageindex)
```

Having a root, you can then call the DrawNode method, passing to the method the root of the XML document (xmlDocument.DocumentElement) the TreeNode object that represents the root and 0. The latter represents the level of depth of the XML element. The root has the level of 0.

What the DrawNode method does is to create a visual representation of the XML document. It will traverse the nodes in the XmlDocument object passed as the first argument and create a System.Windows.Forms.TreeNode object for each node in the document:

```
DrawNode(xmlDocument.DocumentElement, root, 0)
```

The call to the DrawNode method will create a hierarchical structure for the TreeNode root. Next, you need to add the root to the Nodes property of the current instance of the XmlViewer class. The Nodes property (which represents the collection of nodes) inherits from the TreeView class:

```
Me.Nodes.Add(root)
```

Finally, you call the ExpandAll method to expand all the nodes:

```
Me.ExpandAll()
```

Using the Find Dialog Box

The XML Editor application supports the searching and replacing of words, just like Microsoft Word lets you find and replace a word or a phrase. For this purpose, you will create a Find dialog box that will be called from a child document.

The application, which acts as an MDI container, can have multiple child documents, but all the child documents share the same Find dialog box because there needs only to be one anyway, just like all documents in Microsoft Word share the same Find and Replace dialog boxes.

To build a Find dialog box that can be shared, you use the Singleton pattern as explained previously. Figure 2-14 shows the Find dialog box. Note that for this application, the Find and Replace functions use the same dialog box.

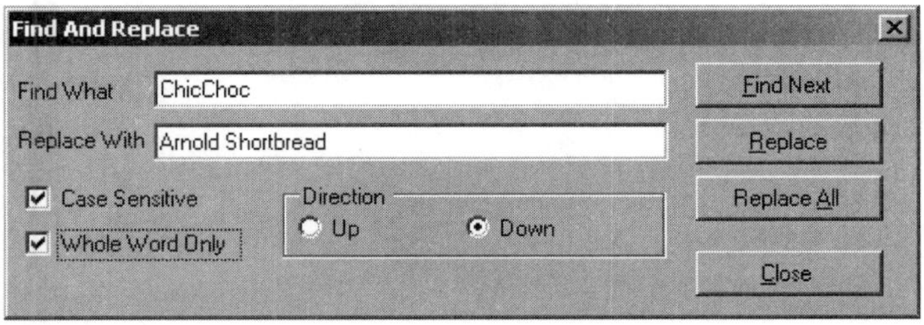

Figure 2-14. The Find dialog box

Note also that the Find dialog box does not have Minimize and Restore buttons.

You can find the FindDialog class, which represents the Find dialog box, in the FindDialog.vb file in the chapter's project directory.

First and foremost, as a Singleton the FindDialog class only has a private constructor:

```
Private Sub New()
  . . .
End Sub
```

To obtain an instance of this class, you use an object factory such as the following:

```
Public Shared Function GetInstance()
  If findDialog Is Nothing Then
    findDialog = New FindDialog()
  End If
  Return findDialog
End Function
```

The GetInstance method returns an instance of the FindDialog class. Because this method is static (shared), you can call it without having to have an instance of its class. In fact, this method must be static or no instance can be created otherwise. The object reference returned by this method (findDialog) is also declared shared:

```
Private Shared findDialog As findDialog
```

Another important thing to note is that the FindDialog object will remain in existence even when it is closed. Therefore, you override the OnClosing method as follows:

```
Protected Overrides Sub OnClosing(ByVal e As CancelEventArgs)
  e.Cancel = True 'doesn't allow the user to close
  Me.Hide()
End Sub
```

Note that the Cancel property of the CancelEventArgs is set to True to cancel the closing. Instead of closing, you simply hide the form. When the Find dialog box is called again, the hidden instance reappears. As a result, it retains the previous states set by the user. For instance, if the Case Sensitive box was checked, that box will remain checked. If there is a value in the Find box, the value will also be displayed again.

You will also notice that you override the Dispose method in the FindDialog class, and you set the static object reference findDialog to Nothing:

```
Protected Overloads Overrides Sub Dispose(ByVal disposing As Boolean)
  findDialog = Nothing
  MyBase.Dispose(disposing)
End Sub
```

The reason why you need to set the findDialog to Nothing when the findDialog object is disposed is this: The GetInstance method is called from inside the child document represented by the Document class. To be exact, the code that calls it resides inside the overridden OnGotFocus method. This means a FindDialog instance is obtained every time that child document gets a focus, including when the child document is first created:

```
Protected Overrides Sub OnGotFocus(ByVal e As EventArgs)
  findDialog = FindDialog.GetInstance()
  findDialog.Owner = Me
  findDialog.SetTextArea(textArea)
End Sub
```

See that the child document that received focus always gets hold of the instance of the FindDialog class. You then set its Owner property to the child document itself, making the child document owner of the findDialog object. In addition, you pass the current child document's TextArea to the FindDialog instance for the FindDialog instance to work on. When the current child document with focus closes, the focus moves to another child document, and this next child document will be the owner of the FindDialog instance. Now, what if the last child document is closed? The FindDialog instance will belong to no child document, and because its owner is disposed, the FindDialog instance will also be disposed.

If you do not set the findDialog object reference to Nothing, it will still reference the disposed FindDialog object. As a result, when a new child document is created, it will call the following code in its OnGotFocus method:

```
findDialog = FindDialog.GetInstance()
```

This will call the GetInstance method of the FindDialog class:

```
Public Shared Function GetInstance()
  If findDialog Is Nothing Then
    findDialog = New FindDialog()
  End If
  Return findDialog
End Function
```

Remember that the findDialog object reference is shared, so it is still in memory. If you do not set the findDialog object reference to Nothing when the instance of the FindDialog class is disposed, the findDialog in the GetInstance method will not evaluate to True in the If statement and the GetInstance method will simply return the findDialog object reference, which still references a disposed object.

Now, look at the second line of the OnGotFocus method in the Document class:

```
findDialog.Owner = Me
```

Trying to access the Owner property of a disposed object will throw an exception.

On the other hand, if the findDialog object reference is set to Nothing when the instance of the last FindDialog class is disposed, the GetInstance method will create a new instance and return this instance.

Now that you know the lifecycle of the class, shift your attention to the three important methods of the FindDialog class: Find, Replace, and ReplaceAll.

Using the Find Method

The Find method collects search options and calls the Find method of the StyledTextArea class. The FindDialog class's Find method collects search options from the following controls:

- findTextBox: The search pattern

- caseCheckBox: Whether case sensitivity matters

- wholeWordCheckBox: Whether the search is to find the whole word only

- upRadioButton: The direction of the search

In addition, the method also uses the x1 and y1 class variables to determine the start column and start line of the searching.

If the method finds a match, it highlights the matching pattern in the StyledTextArea control and the Find method returns True. If no match is found, the method returns False. Listing 2-24 shows the Find method.

Listing 2-24. The Find Method

```
Private Function Find() As Boolean
  If Not textArea Is Nothing Then
    Dim pattern As String = findTextBox.Text
    If pattern.Length > 0 Then
      Dim p As ColumnLine = textArea.Find(pattern, x1, y1, _
        caseCheckBox.Checked, wholeWordCheckBox.Checked, upRadioButton.Checked)

      If p.Equals(New ColumnLine(0, 0)) Then
        'search not found
        If upRadioButton.Checked Then
          y1 = textArea.LineCount
          x1 = textArea.GetLine(y1).Length + 1
        Else
          y1 = 1
          x1 = 1
        End If
        MessageBox.Show("Search Pattern Not Found")
        Return False
      Else
        If Not upRadioButton.Checked Then
          x1 = p.Column + 1
```

```
      y1 = p.Line
    Else
      x1 = p.Column - pattern.Length - 1
      If x1 <= 1 Then
        x1 = 1
        y1 = p.Line - 1
      Else
        y1 = p.Line
      End If
    End If
    Return True
  End If
 End If
End If
Return False
End Function
```

The Find method starts by examining the length of the search pattern. It only does the search if the pattern is not blank. Searching is straightforward by calling the Find method of the StyledTextArea class, passing the search options you have collected:

```
If pattern.Length > 0 Then
  Dim p As ColumnLine = textArea.Find(pattern, x1, y1, _
    caseCheckBox.Checked, wholeWordCheckBox.Checked, upRadioButton.Checked)
    .
    .
    .
```

The Find method of the StyledTextArea class returns a ColumnLine object indicating the start column and line of the matching pattern, if it finds one. Otherwise, the ColumnLine object is equal to ColumnLine(0, 0).

If no matching pattern is found, the FindDialog class's Find method will reposition x1 and y1 to the beginning or the end of the text in the StyledTextArea control, depending on whether the upRadioButton is checked:

```
If upRadioButton.Checked Then
  y1 = textArea.LineCount
  x1 = textArea.GetLine(y1).Length + 1
Else
  y1 = 1
  x1 = 1
End If
```

Then, it will display a message box saying that the search pattern was not found and return False:

```
MessageBox.Show("Search Pattern Not Found")
Return False
```

If a matching pattern is found, the Find method will reposition the x1 and y1 variables for the next invocation of the Find method:

```
If Not upRadioButton.Checked Then
  x1 = p.Column + 1
  y1 = p.Line
Else
  x1 = p.Column - pattern.Length - 1
  If x1 <= 1 Then
    x1 = 1
    y1 = p.Line - 1
  Else
    y1 = p.Line
  End If
End If
```

It will then return True:

```
Return True
```

Using the Replace Method

The Replace method replaces the highlighted text in the StyledTextArea control with the string in the replaceTextBox. Normally, the Replace method is called after the Find method is called and finds a match. Listing 2-25 shows the Replace method.

Listing 2-25. The Replace *Method*

```
Private Function Replace() As Boolean
  If Not textArea Is Nothing Then
    If textArea.SelectedText.Equals("") Then
      Return Find()
```

```
    Else
      Dim replacePattern As String = replaceTextBox.Text
      Dim buffer As IDataObject = Clipboard.GetDataObject()
      textArea.Cut()
      Clipboard.SetDataObject(replacePattern)
      textArea.Paste()
      Clipboard.SetDataObject(buffer)
      Return Find()
    End If
  End If
End Function
```

The Replace method starts by checking whether there is some highlighted text in the StyledTextArea control. If there is not, it calls the Find method. The user will then have to invoke the Replace method again once the Find method finds a matching pattern. This time it will do the code in the Else block. What it does is the following:

1. Saves the current content of the Clipboard to a System.Windows.Forms.IDataObject object

2. Calls the Cut method of the StyledTextArea class to remove the selected text from the StyledTextArea control

3. Calls the SetDataObject method of the System.Windows.Forms.Clipboard class to copy replacePattern to the Clipboard

4. Calls the Paste method of the StyledTextArea class to paste the data in the Clipboard at the position of the caret

5. Calls the SetDataObject method again to copy the content of buffer (the original content of the Clipboard) back to the Clipboard

6. Calls the Find method so that the next matching pattern is highlighted and ready to be replaced

Like the Find method, the Replace method returns True when a replace was successfully executed, or False otherwise.

Using the ReplaceAll Method

The ReplaceAll method repeatedly calls the Replace method to replace all matching patterns in the StyledTextArea control:

```
Private Sub ReplaceAll()
  While Replace()
  End While
End Sub
```

Using the TextPrinter Class

The TextPrinter class offers text printing functionality that can be reused in various applications. The main advantage of using the TextPrinter class is that the code for printing will not scatter the main application classes. You will find the TextPrinter class in the TextPrinter.vb file. There are three public methods you can use: PrintPreview, SetupPage, and Print.

The PrintPreview and SetupPage methods are straightforward. If you have read the section "Printing in the .NET Framework Windows," you surely will understand it. The PrintPreview method declares and creates a System.Windows.Forms.PrintPreviewDialog object, sets its Document property with a PrintDocument object (printDoc), and calls its ShowDialog method:

```
Dim dlg As New PrintPreviewDialog()
dlg.Document = printDoc
dlg.ShowDialog()
```

Calling the ShowDialog method triggers the PrintPage event of the System.Drawing.Printing.PrintDocument object, which then executes the code in the PrintPage event handler (printDoc_PrintPage). This event handler will be explained later when discussing the Print method.

The SetupPage method declares and creates a System.Windows.Forms.PageSetupDialog object, sets some of its properties, and calls its ShowDialog method.

The Print method uses a System.Windows.Forms.PrintDialog class to let the user choose some options and then calls the Print method of the PrintDocument object. This captures two of the events that are raised when the Print method is called: BeginPrint and PrintPage. The BeginPrint event raises once at the beginning of the printing process. Its event handler (printDoc_BeginPrint) sets the startPrinting Boolean to True and prepares a StringReader textToPrint. The printDoc_PrintPage event handler(explained next) uses the startPrinting Boolean.

The PrintPage event triggers for each page printed. The printDoc_PrintPage event handler first checks the value of startPrinting. If startPrinting is True, the event handler calculates certain values that will be used throughout the printing of pages. It then iterates the StringReader textToPrint to print each line of the string.

Using the Document Class

The Document class represents a child document in the MDI container. Each instance of this class is assigned a unique number that is stored in its public field ChildIndex. The MDI container users this index mainly to synchronize the child document with its associated tab page.

You can use an instance of the Document class to edit and validate an XML document as well as to build the tree of the elements in the XML document. Three shortcuts are provided: F5 and F6 for validating the XML document and F9 for building the tree. F5 validates XML documents that do not contain a schema. F6 validates XML documents having an inline schema. The main method of this class is the ValidateDocument function.

Before delving into the class, however, you should look at the delegate TitleEventHandler and the event argument class TitleEventArgs used by the Document class. You can find both in the Document.vb file.

You use TitleEventHandler and TitleEventArgs when you trigger the custom event TitleChanged. Why you need these two is explained shortly.

The MDI container creates a tab page for each child document opened or each child document created. Each tab page is associated with one child document. The text in a tab page is the same as the text shown on the title bar of the child document. The child document title is the name of the XML document file. The child document title can change in two cases:

- A new document is given a temporary name starting with "Document"; for example, the first new document is called *Document 1*. When the user saves a document, the user can give it a filename that is different from its temporary name, and this will be reflected in the title bar.

- The user can save a document as another name. This too will change the name.

The tab page associated with a child document resides in the MDI container, and the child document knows nothing about it. When the child document's title changes, the text in the associated tab page must change too. The child document notifies the MDI container by raising the `TitleChanged` event. This event must then be captured in the MDI form.

The `Document` class extends the `System.Windows.Forms.Form` class and uses the `StyledTextArea` control discussed in Chapter 1, "Creating a Custom Control: StyledTextArea." You can find the `Document` class in the `Document.vb` file.

The `Document` class also uses the `FindDialog` class for searching and the `TextPrinter` class for printing the text.

Additionally, the `Document` class has an object reference to an `XmlViewer` and an object reference to a `StatusBar` control. When a `Document` object is constructed, the MDI container passes the references of its `XmlViewer` and `StatusBar` objects to the child document. Having an `XmlViewer`, the child document can build a tree of the XML elements. With a status bar, it can also write to the MDI container's status bar panels. The child document needs to know nothing about the MDI container, which promotes its code reuse.

The object reference to an `XmlViewer` is passed to the constructor. You pass the status bar by setting the `StatusBar` property. Because there is no guarantee that an MDI container will set the `StatusBar` property, access to the status bar object is always first, making sure that the object is not null.

The `Document` class has two constructors. Their signatures are as follows:

```
Public Sub New(ByVal childIndex As Integer, ByVal filePath As String, _
  ByRef xmlViewer As xmlViewer)
Public Sub New(ByVal childIndex As Integer, ByRef xmlViewer As xmlViewer)
```

The two constructors enforce that a `Document` object always has a child index and a reference to the `XmlViewer` control.

The following sections describe the `Document` class's members.

Understanding the Document Class's Properties

The `Document` class has three properties: `StatusBar`, `Text`, and `Title`.

StatusBar

The MDI container uses the write-only `StatusBar` property to pass an object reference to a `StatusBar` object so that the child document can write to the panels of the MDI container's status bar.

Text

The Text property represents the text in the StyledTextArea control. This property overloads the Text property inherited from the System.Windows.Forms.Control class.

Title

The Title property represents the text displayed on the document title bar. In the System.Windows.Forms.Control class this is represented by the Text property; therefore this Title property reads from and writes to the base class's Text property.

Understanding the Document Class's Methods

The following are the Document class's methods, not including the event handlers, which are self-explanatory.

Find

You invoke the Find public method when the user needs to use the Find and Replace facility. What this method does is display the FindDialog object, which was obtained or created in the OnGotFocus method.

GetTextPrinter

The private GetTextPrinter method returns a TextPrinter object that can be used to print and print preview the document's text or set the page. You call this method from the Print, PrintPreview, and SetupPage methods.

InitializeComponent

The private InitializeComponent method initializes components that are used from the Document object. The constructors call this method.

IsFilenameUsed

The private IsFilenameUsed method checks if a filename has been used by other child documents. To do this, the method needs to access the parent form through the MdiParent property. The MdiParent property returns a System.Windows.Forms.Form object. Once obtained, all the child documents can be obtained using the MdiChildren property. A call to the CType function converts a Form object (representing a child document) into a Document object. Because the Document class has the public FilePath field that holds the value of its file path (or null if the child document has not been saved), the IsFilenameUsed method can check the FilePath value of all child documents of the MDI container.

OnClosing

The protected OnClosing method overrides the same method in the base class. The reason why you override this method is to avoid an unsaved document closed without first warning the user that the document has not been saved. If a document has been changed but not saved, the Edited property of the StyledTextArea control will be True. If this is the case, a message box is displayed, prompting the user to either save it or confirm that they want to close the document without saving.

OnGotFocus

You call the OnGotFocus method when the document gets the focus. When it does, it needs to grab the singleton FindDialog method from another child document.

OnTitleChanged

The OnTitleChanged method raises the TitledChanged event.

Print

The private Print method calls the Print method of the TextPrinter class.

PrintPreview

The private PrintPreview method calls the PrintPreview method of the TextPrinter class.

RebuildTree

The private RebuildTree method calls the BuildTree method of the XmlViewer object and passes to it the Text property.

Save

The private Save method saves a document into a file. First it checks if the document has been saved before. A document that has been saved will have a file path; therefore a document whose file path is null has not been saved before. In this case, it calls the SaveAs method:

```
If FilePath Is Nothing Then
  Return SaveAs()
Else
  .
  .
  .
End If
```

If the document has been saved, you create a System.IO.StreamWriter object, passing the file path:

```
Dim sw As New StreamWriter(FilePath)
```

You then use its Write method to write it to the file, passing the string to be written:

```
sw.write(Text)
```

Afterward, you close the StreamWriter object, you set the Edited property of the StyledTextArea control to False, and you call the WriteToLeftPanel method:

```
sw.Close()
textArea.Edited = False
WriteToLeftPanel("Document saved")
```

On a successful save, the method returns True. Otherwise, it returns False.

SaveAs

The private SaveAs method saves a document that has not been saved before. It returns True if the document is saved successfully and False if the user cancels the saving.

To save a document, the user will be prompted to enter a filename using a System.Windows.Forms.SaveFileDialog:

```
Dim saveFileDialog As New SaveFileDialog()
saveFileDialog.Filter = "Xml Documents (*.xml)|*.xml|All files (*.*)|*.*"
saveFileDialog.FilterIndex = 1
```

Then, if the user clicks OK after entering a filename, it will check if the filename has been used in another child document by calling the IsFilenameUsed method:

```
If saveFileDialog.ShowDialog = DialogResult.OK Then
  'does not allow the doc to be saved as a name
  'of a file that is opened as another child document
  If IsFilenameUsed(saveFileDialog.FileName) Then
    MessageBox.Show ( _
      "The name is identical with one of the open documents. " & _
      "Please use another name")
    Return False
    .
    .
    .
```

If the filename is acceptable, the entered FileName will be set to the FilePath variable and the document title changed, and it invokes the OnTitleChanged to raise the TitleChanged event:

```
Else
  FilePath = saveFileDialog.FileName
  Me.Title = Path.GetFileName(FilePath)
  OnTitleChanged(New TitleEventArgs(Me.Title))
```

Lastly, it calls the Save method to do the actual saving of the document:

```
Return Save()
```

SelectLine

The public SelectLine method returns a string in the specified line number.

UpdateLineAndColumnNumbers

The private `UpdateLineAndColumnNumbers` method writes the line and column position of the caret in the `StyledTextArea` control to the right panel of the status bar.

SetupPage

The private `SetupPage` method calls the `SetupPage` method of the `TextPrinter` object.

ValidateDocument

The `ValidateDocument` method validates the current document. You can validate two types of XML documents: documents with an internal or external DTD and documents with an inline schema. This method accepts a `Boolean` to switch between the two validation types. A `True` value means that the document to be validated contains an inline schema; a `False` value means that the document to be validated uses a DTD.

   This method first checks that the document has been saved. Otherwise, the `SaveAs` method is called and, upon a successful save, calls itself:

```
If FilePath Is Nothing Then
  If SaveAs() Then
    Return ValidateDocument(withInlineSchema)
  Else
    Return False
  End If
End If
```

An XML document often references an external DTD document. It is always assumed that this external document resides in the same directory as the XML document. Therefore, the first thing to do is to set the `CurrentDirectory` property of the `System.Environment` object to the XML document file path:

```
Environment.CurrentDirectory = Path.GetDirectoryName(FilePath)
```

It then makes sure that the document is not empty:

```
Dim xmlText As String = Me.Text
If xmlText.Trim().Equals("") Then
  MessageBox.Show("Document is empty.", "Error")
  Return False
End If
```

Next, it does the validating using the System.Xml.XmlValidatingReader class's Read method. Listing 2-26 shows the code that does the validation.

Listing 2-26. Validating Using Read

```
Dim xmlReader As XmlTextReader
Dim xmlValReader As XmlValidatingReader
Try
  xmlReader = New XmlTextReader(New StringReader(xmlText))
  If withInlineSchema Then
    xmlValReader = New _
      XmlValidatingReader(xmlText, XmlNodeType.Element, Nothing)
  Else
    xmlValReader = New XmlValidatingReader(xmlReader)
  End If
  While xmlValReader.Read()
  End While
  MessageBox.Show("Document validated.", "Validating Document")
  Return True
```

This catches any exception during the validation process so that the user can find where the error is. An error message can include the line and column position of where the error occurs. In this case, you can notify the user by parsing the error message and highlighting the line (see Listing 2-27).

Listing 2-27. Parsing the Error

```
Catch ex As Exception
  Dim errorMessage As String = ex.Message
  ' it ends with "Line x, position y" or "(x, y)"
  MessageBox.Show(errorMessage, "Error validating document")
  Dim index1, index2 As Integer
  Dim line As String
  index1 = errorMessage.LastIndexOf("Line")
```

```
Try
  If index1 = -1 Then
    index1 = errorMessage.LastIndexOf("(")
    index2 = errorMessage.LastIndexOf(",")
    line = errorMessage.Substring(index1 + 1, index2 - index1 - 1)
  Else
    index2 = errorMessage.LastIndexOf(", position")
    line = errorMessage.Substring(index1 + 5, index2 - index1 - 5)
  End If
  SelectLine(CInt(line))
Catch
```

WriteToLeftPanel

The private `WriteToLeftPanel` method writes to the first panel in the status bar,
should a status bar be passed to the `Document` object. Because there is no guarantee
an MDI container will pass a status bar, the `WriteToLeftPanel` method checks the
`statusBarField` before it writes to its first panel:

```
If Not statusBarField Is Nothing Then
  If statusBarField.Panels.Count > 0 Then
    statusBarField.Panels(0).Text = s
  End If
End If
```

WriteToRightPanel

The private `WriteToRightPanel` method writes to the second panel in the status bar,
should a status bar be passed to the `Document` object. Because there is no guarantee
an MDI container will pass a status bar, the `WriteToRightPanel` method checks the
`statusBarField` before it writes to its second panel:

```
If Not statusBarField Is Nothing Then
  If statusBarField.Panels.Count > 1 Then
    statusBarField.Panels(1).Text = s
  End If
End If
```

Understanding the Document Class's Event

The Document class has one event: TitleChanged. This event raises when the text in the title bar of the document changes.

Creating the MDI Container

The last part of the project is the XMLEditor class, which represents the MDI container. This class integrates all other parts. Figure 2-15 shows the XML editor application.

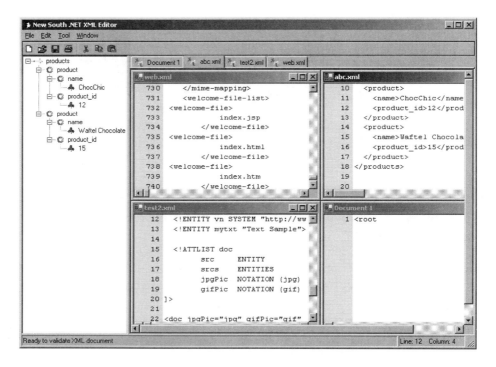

Figure 2-15. An XML editor application

You can find the code for the XMLEditor class in the form1.vb file.

The XMLEditor class uses several images that are stored in the images subdirectory of the application directory. These images are for the parent form icon, the child document icon, the toolbar buttons, and the elements in the XmlViewer control.

The XMLEditor class manages its child documents with the help of the private childIndex field that is initialized as 1. Each child document is assigned a unique index number and is linked with a tab page having the same index number.

Because a TabPage does not have a property to hold an index number, you define a class called IndexedTabPage as an inner class of the XMLEditor class. You make IndexedTabPage an inner class because only the XMLEditor class uses IndexedTabPage.

Listing 2-28 shows the IndexTabPage class.

Listing 2-28. IndexTabPage

```
Class IndexedTabPage : Inherits TabPage
  Private childIndexField As Integer
  Public Property ChildIndex() As Integer
    Get
      Return childIndexField
    End Get
    Set(ByVal index As Integer)
      childIndexField = index
    End Set
  End Property
End Class
```

The IndexedTabPage class does not do much except add a property called ChildIndex to the TabPage class.

The declaration part of the XMLEditor class contains variables for the menu, menu items, toolbar, toolbar buttons, status bar, status bar panels, bitmaps, an XmlViewer, a Splitter, and an ImageList. (The use of these controls will not be explained again here.)

The XMLEditor class inherits the System.Windows.Forms.Form class; therefore, XMLEditor is a form. In order for it to be an MDI container, its IsMdiContainer is set to True, as in the first line of the InitializeComponent method:

```
Me.IsMdiContainer = True
```

The following sections mention some important methods of the XMLEditor class. Some of the methods, including most of the event handlers, are self-explanatory and will not be repeated here.

Understanding the XMLEditor Class's Methods

The following are the methods in the XMLEditor class.

AddTabPage

The private AddTabPage method adds an IndexedTabPage to the tabControl control. It accepts a String containing the filename of the child document associated with this tab page. Every tab page has an icon that is the eighth icon in the TabControl's ImageList.

The AddTabPage method starts by instantiating an IndexedTabPage object:

```
Dim tabPage As New IndexedTabPage()
```

It then sets its Text property of the TabPage with the filename of the path passed to this method, its ImageIndex to 7, and its ChildIndex with the current sequential index number:

```
tabPage.Text = Path.GetFileName(text)
tabPage.ImageIndex = 7
tabPage.ChildIndex = childIndex
```

Next, the method increments the child index so that the next tab page will have a different index number:

```
childIndex += 1
```

The tab page is ready to be added to the tab control. You add a tab page to a tab control by calling the Add method of the tab control's Controls collection:

```
tabControl.Controls.Add(tabPage)
```

The new tab page will be the one selected. So, you set the tab control's SelectedIndex property with the tab page position in the Controls collection. Because the new tab page is the most recently added tab page, it will be last in the position—or the same as the number of tab pages in the tab control's Controls collection, which is represented by the TabCount property. However, the SelectedIndex property is zero-based, so the last position will be the number of tab pages minus one:

```
tabControl.SelectedIndex = tabControl.TabCount - 1
```

child_TitleChanged

The child_TitleChanged event handler invokes every time a child document's title changes. This event handler handles the Document class's TitleChanged event. The reason why you need to capture this event is to update the tab page's Text when its associated child document has a new title.

The first thing to do, of course, is to obtain the Document object that sends the event message. This is readily available from the first argument to the child_TitleChanged event handler. Using CType, you can convert the Object object to a Document object:

```
Dim doc As Document = CType(sender, Document)
```

Then, you can get the child index of the child document:

```
Dim childIndex As Integer = doc.ChildIndex
```

Now you need to find the tab page that corresponds to the child document that sends the event message. You do this by comparing the child index of the document with that of each of the tab pages. When a match is found, you know the corresponding tab page has been found, so you can change its Text property with the new title of the child document:

```
  Dim tabPage As IndexedTabPage
  For Each tabPage In tabControl.TabPages
    If tabPage.ChildIndex = childIndex Then
      tabPage.Text = e.Title
      Exit For
    End If
  Next
End Sub
```

child_Closed

The child_Closed event handler handles the Close event of every child document. child_Closed therefore is called every time a child document is closed. The purpose of capturing this event is to remove the tab page associated with the closed child document.

It starts by converting the sender (the closed document) to an object of type Document using the CType function and obtains the ChildIndex property of the closed document:

```
Dim doc As Document = CType(sender, Document)
Dim childIndex As Integer = doc.ChildIndex
```

Once you get the child index, you have to find the corresponding tab page by iterating the TabPages collection of the tab control and matching its child index with the closed document's child index. Once a match is found, the tab page is removed from the TabPages collection using the Remove method:

```
'now remove tabpage with the same childIndex
Dim tabPage As IndexedTabPage
For Each tabPage In tabControl.TabPages
  If tabPage.ChildIndex = childIndex Then
    tabControl.TabPages.Remove(tabPage)
    Exit For
  End If
Next
```

GetDocumentByFilepath

The GetDocumentByFilepath method returns a Document object having the specified path. It iterates the MdiChildren property and compares its FilePath field with the specified path:

```
Dim childCount As Integer = Me.MdiChildren.Length
Dim i As Integer
For i = 0 To childCount - 1
  Dim doc As Document = CType(Me.MdiChildren(i), Document)
  Dim docPath As String = doc.FilePath
  If Not docPath Is Nothing Then
    'docPath could be null in the case of a new document
    If docPath.Equals(path) Then
      Return doc
    End If
  End If
Next
Return Nothing
```

NewDocument

The NewDocument method creates a new child document and adds a corresponding
tab page for the added child document.

The first line of the NewDocument method uses the Document constructor, passing
the current child index and the object reference to the XmlViewer object:

```
Dim doc As Document = New Document(childIndex, xmlViewer)
```

For each child document, you wire two events: Closed and TitledChanged:

```
AddHandler doc.Closed, AddressOf child_Closed
AddHandler doc.TitleChanged, AddressOf child_TitleChanged
```

Then, you must set the child document's MdiParent to the MDI container. You
also pass the reference of the parent form's status bar to the child document so
that the child document can write to the status bar:

```
doc.MdiParent = Me
doc.StatusBar = Me.statusBar
```

Next, you show the child document using the Show method:

```
doc.Show()
```

Last, you add a tab page by calling the AddTabPage method:

```
AddTabPage("Document " & childIndex.ToString())
```

OnMdiChildActivate

The OnMdiChildActivate method overrides the OnMdiChildActivate method in the
base class. The reason you need to override this method is so you can select
the tab page associated with the active child document.

One thing to be cautious about is to avoid the infinite loop caused by the
tabControl_SelectedIndexChanged that triggers when the selected tab page changes.
The tabControl_SelectedIndexChanged activates the child document associated with
the tab control with the selection. A flag (childFormActivated) is used and its value
is set to True in this method. The tabControl_SelectedIndexChanged event handler
will not activate a child document if this flag is True.

The OnMdiChildActivea method starts by calling the overridden method in the base class:

```
MyBase.OnMdiChildActivate(e)
```

It then sets the childFormActivated Boolean to True so that the tabControl_SelectedIndexChanged event handler will not try to activate a child document, which in turn will cause the OnMdiChildActivate to be invoked, causing an infinite loop:

```
childFormActivated = True
```

Then it obtains the active child document, gets the child index of the active child document, and sets the focus to the active child document:

```
Dim activeChildDocument As Document = CType(Me.ActiveMdiChild, Document)
'Get the ChildIndex of the active MdiChild
Dim activeChildIndex As Integer = activeChildDocument.ChildIndex
activeChildDocument.Focus()
```

Next, it goes through the tab pages collection to find the tab page with the same child index and selects the tab page:

```
Dim tabPage As IndexedTabPage
Dim i As Integer
Dim tabPageCount As Integer = tabControl.TabCount
For i = 0 To tabPageCount - 1
  tabPage = tabControl.TabPages(i)
  If tabPage.ChildIndex = activeChildIndex Then
    tabControl.SelectedIndex = i
    Exit For
  End If
Next i
```

Lastly, the OnMdiChildActivate rebuilds the tree in the XmlViewer object so it draws the hierarchical data of the active child document:

```
xmlViewer.BuildTree(CType(Me.ActiveMdiChild, Document).Text)
```

OpenDocument

You use the private OpenDocument method to open an XML document. The method enables the user to navigate the file system using System.Windows.Forms.OpenFileDialog. If the user tries to open a document that is already open, the method will activate the existing document instead.

The method starts by constructing an OpenFileDialog object and setting some of its properties:

```
Dim openFileDialog As New OpenFileDialog()
'you can set an initial directory if you want, such as this
'openFileDialog.InitialDirectory = "c:\"
openFileDialog.Filter = "Xml Documents (*.xml)|*.xml|All files (*.*)|*.*"
openFileDialog.FilterIndex = 1
```

After the user clicks the OK button, the method first tries to retrieve a document having the same file path from the collection of all child documents using the GetDocumentByFilePath method. If there is already an open document by that name, the document is activated instead:

```
If openFileDialog.ShowDialog() = DialogResult.OK Then
  'check if the document already opened by this app.
  Dim doc As Document = GetDocumentByFilepath(openFileDialog.FileName)
  If Not doc Is Nothing Then
    doc.Activate()
  Else
```

Otherwise, the OpenDocument method tries to open that document into a System.IO.Stream object:

```
Dim stream As Stream ' the current XML document
xmlDocumentFilePath = openFileDialog.FileName
stream = openFileDialog.OpenFile()
```

To read the document, you create a System.IO.StreamReader object, passing the stream resulting from the OpenFile method of the OpenFileDialog object:

```
Dim sr As New StreamReader(stream)
```

Then, you create a Document object and write the Closed and TitleChanged events to the child_Closed and child_TitleChanged event handlers, respectively:

```
doc = New Document(childIndex, xmlDocumentFilePath, xmlViewer)
AddHandler doc.Closed, AddressOf child_Closed
AddHandler doc.TitleChanged, AddressOf child_TitleChanged
```

Next, you populate the child document's StyledTextArea control by reading the StreamReader object:

```
doc.Text = sr.ReadToEnd()
sr.Close()
```

Afterward, you set the MdiParent property of the child document, pass the status bar to the StatusBar property, and call the Show method to display the child document:

```
doc.MdiParent = Me
doc.StatusBar = Me.statusBar
doc.Show()
```

Lastly, you add a tab page that is associated with the child document using the AddTabPage method:

```
AddTabPage(xmlDocumentFilePath)
```

tabControl_SelectedIndexChanged

The tabControl_SelectedIndexChanged event handler invokes every time a different tab page is selected in the tab control—for example, when the user clicks one of the tab pages. When a tab page is selected, the child document associated with it must also been activated. Therefore, you need to first obtain the child index of the selected tab page and then find the child document having the same child index and activate it.

Note that the SelectedIndexChanged can also raise when the user selects a child document. Selecting a child document will cause the OnMdiChildActivate method to be executed, and the overridden OnMdiChildActivate method in the XMLEditor class sets the SelectedIndex property of the Tab control, causing the SelectedIndexChange event to be raised. To prevent this infinite loop, the tabControl_SelectedIndexChanged changed event handler is only executed when the childFormActivated flag is False:

```
If Not childFormActivated Then ' this is to avoid infinite loop
```

The `tabControl_SelectedIndexChanged` event handler obtains the child index of the tab page selected, iterates through the collection of the child documents, and compares the child index with the child index of each child document:

```
'get the ChildIndex of the active tab page
If tabControl.SelectedIndex <> -1 Then '-1 when if is no tabpage
  Dim tabPage As IndexedTabPage = _
    CType(tabControl.TabPages(tabControl.SelectedIndex), IndexedTabPage)
  Dim activeChildIndex As Integer = tabPage.ChildIndex '

  ' Now activate the MdiChild with the same ChildIndex
  Dim mdiChild As Document
  For Each mdiChild In Me.MdiChildren
    If mdiChild.ChildIndex = activeChildIndex Then
```

Once a match is found, the child document activates:

```
mdiChild.Activate()
Exit For
```

At the end of the event handler, you set the `childFormActivated` flag to `False`:

```
childFormActivated = False
```

toolBar_ButtonClick

The `toolBar_ButtonClick` event handler executes when a user clicks a toolbar button. It first finds out which button was clicked and then does a specific task depending on the button clicked:

```
' Evaluate the Button property to determine which button was clicked.
    If e.Button.Equals(newToolBarButton) Then
      fileNewMenuItem.PerformClick()
    ElseIf e.Button.Equals(openToolBarButton) Then
      fileOpenMenuItem.PerformClick()
    ElseIf e.Button.Equals(saveToolBarButton) Then
      If Me.MdiChildren.Length > 0 Then
        SendKeys.Send("%FS")
      End If
    ElseIf e.Button.Equals(printToolBarButton) Then
      If Me.MdiChildren.Length > 0 Then
        SendKeys.Send("%FP")
      End If
```

```
ElseIf e.Button.Equals(cutToolBarButton) Then
  If Me.MdiChildren.Length > 0 Then
    SendKeys.Send("%ET")
  End If
ElseIf e.Button.Equals(copyToolBarButton) Then
  If Me.MdiChildren.Length > 0 Then
    SendKeys.Send("%EC")
  End If
ElseIf e.Button.Equals(pasteToolBarButton) Then
  If Me.MdiChildren.Length > 0 Then
    SendKeys.Send("%EP")
  End If
End If
```

Compiling and Running the Application

To compile the project files, follow these steps:

1. Create a working directory.

2. Copy StyledTextArea.dll from Chapter 1 to the working directory.

3. Copy the XmlViewer.vb, FindDialog.vb, Document.vb, TextPrinter.vb, and Form1.vb files into the working directory.

4. Create the images directory in that directory and copy all the image files into the images directory.

5. Run the build.bat file to build the project.

Listing 2-29 shows the content of the build.bat file.

Listing 2-29. `build.bat`

```
vbc /t:library /r:System.dll,System.Windows.Forms.dll, _
System.Drawing.dll,StyledTextArea.dll FindDialog.vb
vbc /t:library /r:System.dll,System.Windows.Forms.dll, _
System.Drawing.dll,System.Xml.dll XmlViewer.vb
vbc /t:library /r:System.dll,System.Windows.Forms.dll, _
System.Drawing.dll,System.Xml.dll TextPrinter.vb
vbc /t:library /r:System.dll,System.Windows.Forms.dll, _
System.Drawing.dll,mscorlib.dll,System.Xml.dll, _
StyledTextArea.dll,XmlViewer.dll,TextPrinter.dll, _
FindDialog.dll Document.vb
vbc /t:winexe/r:System.dll,System.Windows.Forms.dll, _
System.Drawing.dll,mscorlib.dll,System.Xml.dll,StyledTextArea.dll, _
XmlViewer.dll,TextPrinter.dll,FindDialog.dll,Document.dll form1.vb
```

To run the application, type `form1.exe` in the command prompt.

Summary

In this chapter you saw the topics that you need to understand to build an MDI application that validates an XML document. Those topics are as follows:

- A brief theory of XML

- How to work with XML documents in the .NET Framework

- How to develop MDI applications

- The Singleton pattern

- How to print in the .NET Framework

Finally, you learned how to develop the XML editor project.

CHAPTER 3

Writing Games

COMPUTER GAMES ARE one of the most exciting Windows applications to write and are at the same time one of the most difficult. Modern games, such as Quake or DOOM, also usually consume a lot of computing resources and normally require the most powerful processors to run. More important, you must write each line of the code by considering efficiency, even if this means more memory will be used. Speed is more important than memory! For this reason, not surprisingly, C and C++ have been the two languages of choice when developing computer games. For speed, speed, and speed.

Writing popular games is even more difficult. Not only do you need to be a skillful programmer, but popular games are more the child of high creativity and imagination than technical expertise. The figure is something like this: Out of 10,000 game developers, 9,900 go bankrupt because they do not get the required market acceptance. In other words, their games are not interesting and exciting enough.

Now, before starting, I would like to say the following in relation to your expectation: This chapter explains how a computer game works. However, it does not have the pretension to make you a commercial game developer. Also, it does not provide you with the techniques required to write games that can compete with the most modern games. Therefore, you will not be able to write Quake just by reading this chapter.

The main objective of this chapter is to teach how to write multithreaded programs using the classes in the System.Threading namespace. A game application is selected as the project to make the learning process more fun.

Not only that, but games, even simple ones, are exciting. A game is very different from the rest of the projects in this book. Testing the project, for example, means you need to play the game. And, you also play the game when you are debugging. How fun is that?

And, did I mention creativity and imagination? I must confess I am not a person with much of each of them. Therefore, for the project, I clone a simple popular game that you have probably played before: Pac-Man.[1] For those of you who have not heard about this exciting game, the following is a brief history of Pac-Man.

Pac-Man was one of the most popular games in the early and late 80s. It was the fruit of Toru Iwatani's imagination and creativity. Iwatani worked as a game designer at Namco Limited, a video game company in Tokyo, Japan. Born on January 25, 1955, Iwatani is self-taught, never having any formal training as a game programmer..

Iwatani joined Namco in 1977, at the age of 22. Three years later, he thought of Pac-Man for the first time, when one day he was eating a pizza. He ate a one slice and the shape of the remaining pizza gave him the idea.

With the help of four other Namco employees, Iwatani completed Pac-Man in one year and five months. The game was first introduced in Japan, where it became an instant success. It then invaded America and Europe in no time.

 NOTE *If you are interested to know the story behind Pac-Man's invention, this is a useful URL:* http://retrogamer.merseyworld.com/iwatani.htm.

The Pac-Man clone you will build in this chapter is called *Doggie*. The idea is simple. Doggie is a shy dog who is afraid of cats. So, all his life he has to run from the four cats who like to bully him. There are magic bones, however, that can help Doggie gain strength and confidence. For a few seconds after Doggie eats a magic bone, he will feel confident and brave and stronger than the cats who chase him. In those few seconds, the cats change to a paler color and Doggie can chase them to get more points. After the few seconds elapse, Doggie will lose its strength and courage and has to run away again until he finds another magic bone.

---

1.   PAC-MAN® ©1980 Namco Ltd., All Rights Reserved.

Overview of the Chapter

As usual, this chapter starts with introductory materials you need to master before you can begin the coding. The following are the main sections to come:

- **"Working with Threads"**: This section explains what a thread is and how to use the System.Threading.Thread class and other classes in the System.Threading namespace to create multithreaded applications.

- **"Using Timers"**: A timer is a device for activating another device after a certain period of time. Timers, in application programming, are useful tools, and the .NET Framework provides a way for manipulating timers easily. This section explains how to do that.

- **"Understanding Game Theory"**: To write computer games, you need to know the theory. This section provides a brief theory that a game developer must know.

- **"Implementing the Project"**: The last section in this chapter presents the Doggie game itself. It explains all the classes used and the interaction of each class with another.

Working with Threads

I had been playing computer games before I got into computer programming. When I started to take programming more seriously, this was the question that came to my mind one day when I was playing games: How do the bad guy and the hero move together at the same time? Didn't I have a single-processor PC?

You must forgive me for asking such a naïve question. After all, it was the DOS era and all the programs I had written were simple applications that did not incorporate very complicated programming logic.

Later on I found the answer.

A program can allocate processor time to units in its body. Each unit is then given a portion of the processor time. Even if your computer only has one processor, it can have multiple units that work at the same time. The trick is to slice processor time and give each slice to each processing unit. The smallest unit that can take processor time is called a *thread*. A program that has multiple threads is referred to as a *multithreaded application*. Therefore, a computer game is often multithreaded. If you have two threads, you can use one thread to move the hero and another thread to move the bad guy. In the end, both will seem to move together.

Clever, isn't it?

NOTE *You can write a computer game even using a language that does not support the concept of threads. However, using threads, writing this kind of program will be easier. The project in this chapter therefore uses threads generously.*

But what exactly is a thread?

The .NET Framework documentation defines a thread as follows:

Threads are the basic units to which an operating system allocates processor time, and more than one thread can be executing code inside a process. Each thread maintains exception handlers, a scheduling priority, and a set of structures the system uses to save the thread context until it is scheduled. The thread context includes all of the information the thread needs to seamlessly resume execution, including the thread's set of CPU registers and stack, in the address space of the thread's host process.

However, prior to the .NET era, Visual Basic (VB) programmers could not easily write multithreaded programs. Sometimes, they had to switch to C++, and sometimes they could only do it with the help of third-party tools. If you used VB to write games, well, you chose the wrong language.

With the emergence of .NET, gone are the days where multithreaded applications were the domain of C++ programmers. With the .NET Framework, developing multithreaded applications cannot be easier, regardless of the language you use, whether it is VB, C#, or other .NET languages. The class library provides the System.Threading namespace that contains classes that support multithreading. The central class in this namespace is Thread, which represents a thread. This is the topic of the next discussion.

Using the System.Threading.Thread Class

The System.Threading.Thread class has one constructor whose signature is as follows:

```
Public Sub New( start As ThreadStart )
```

To instantiate a Thread object, you pass a System.Threading.ThreadStart. ThreadStart is a delegate used to specify the program code executed by the Thread object. ThreadStart has the following signature:

```
Public Delegate ThreadStart()
```

For example, to assign a method called Run to a Thread, you construct the Thread object using the following statement:

```
Dim myThread As Thread = New Thread(New ThreadStart(AddressOf Run))
```

And then, to start the thread, you call its Start method:

```
myThread.Start()
```

In this case, after you call the Start method, the code in the Run method will execute.

The Start method is an asynchronous method, therefore it returns immediately.

A Thread object can have many possible states. Understanding these states is crucial in working with Thread objects properly. The possible states for a Thread object are members of the System.Threading.ThreadState enumeration. Table 3-1 summarizes them.

Table 3-1. Members of the System.Threading.ThreadState *Enumeration*

MEMBER	DESCRIPTION
Aborted	The thread is in the Stopped state.
AbortRequested	The ThreadAbort method has been invoked on the thread, but the thread has not yet received the pending System.Threading.ThreadAbortException that will attempt to terminate it.
Background	The thread is being executed as a background thread, as opposed to a foreground thread. This state is controlled by setting the IsBackground property of the Thread class.
Running	The thread has been started, it is not blocked, and there is no pending ThreadAbortException.
Stopped	The thread has stopped.
StopRequested	The thread is being requested to stop. This is for internal use only.
Suspended	The thread has been suspended.
SuspendRequested	The thread is being requested to suspend.
Unstarted	The Thread.Start method has not been invoked on the thread.
WaitSleepJoin	The thread is blocked as a result of a call to Wait, Sleep, or Join methods.

When first created, a thread is in the Unstarted state. After the Start method is called, the thread's state will become Running. You can suspend a thread by calling the Thread class's Suspend method. After the Suspend method is called, the thread will be in the SuspendRequested state. A suspended thread resumes when the Resume method of Thread class is called. When a thread is resumed, its state gets back to the Running state.

The Sleep method is used often. As the name implies, it sends a thread to sleep for a specified period of time. After the time elapses, you do not have to wake up the thread because it will continue running automatically.

You should terminate a Thread object when the application exits. To do this, you use the Abort method. When this method is invoked, the system throws a System.Threading.ThreadAbortException in the thread to abort it. Calling the Abort method does not guarantee that the thread aborts immediately or at all. If a thread does an unbounded amount of computation in the finally block called as part of the abort procedure, for example, the thread will be delayed from being aborted indefinitely. To make sure a thread has aborted, call the Join method after calling Abort.

The Thread class has the IsAlive property that you can use to inquire about the state of a Thread object. If IsAlive property is True, the thread has been started and has not been aborted.

A thread can also run in the background or foreground. A background thread is the same as a foreground thread, except that background threads do not prevent a process from terminating. You make a thread a background thread by setting the Thread class's IsBackground property to True.

Pros and Cons of Using Threads

In a computer game, it is obvious that you need a way to fool the user into thinking that more than one part of the program is being executed simultaneously. In non-game applications, threads are also useful, especially because using threads increases the level of responsiveness of your program.

For example, if your program is doing something time consuming, such as writing to a disk or waiting for a connection to a Web server, your program can still do something else, such as taking user input. This way, your user does not have to spend time waiting for that particular resource-extensive task to finish. In fact, you can create threads with different priorities. For instance, automatic saving to a disk can happen only when the user is not busy typing.

However, threads consume resources. You should be aware of this and not be too generous with using more threads than necessary. In addition, keeping track of many threads is a taxing programming task.

Using the Thread Class in a Ticker Application

To illustrate the use of the Thread class in a multithreaded application, consider Listing 3-1. The example features a form with two Label controls. It uses two Thread objects (thread1 and thread2) to turn the labels into news tickers. The first ticker flashes three news items in the newsItems array of strings. The second ticker features four items in the businessItems array of strings.

Listing 3-1. The News Tickers Example

```
Imports System
Imports System.Windows.Forms
Imports System.Drawing
Imports System.IO
Imports System.Threading

Public Class Form1 : Inherits Form

  Private label1, label2 As New Label()
  Private newsItems() As String = _
    {"Safest Aerobic Machine Launched", _
      "First Dog Cloning Is Only Days Away", _
      "Reviving the Extinct Tasmanian Tiger"}

  Private businessItems() As String = _
    {"FirstMeasure Software to Go Nasdaq", _
      "MFMF Directors To Meet For The First Time", _
      "First Sign of Economic Recovery Finally At Sight", _
      "Euro Hits Record Low (Again)"}

  Private thread1, thread2 As Thread

  Public Sub New()
    label1.Width = 280
    label1.Height = 30
    label1.Location = New Point(1, 10)
    label1.TextAlign = ContentAlignment.MiddleRight

    label2.Width = 280
    label2.Height = 30
    label2.Location = New Point(1, 40)
```

```
    Me.Controls.Add(label1)
    Me.Controls.Add(label2)

    thread1 = New Thread(New ThreadStart(AddressOf MoveLeft))
    thread1.Start()

    thread2 = New Thread(New ThreadStart(AddressOf MoveRight))
    thread2.Start()

End Sub

Private Sub MoveLeft()
  Dim counter As Integer = 0
  Dim max As Integer = newsItems.Length

  While (True)
    ' get news headline
    Dim headline As String = newsItems(counter)
    counter += 1
    If counter = max Then
      counter = 0
    End If
    Dim i As Integer
    For i = 0 To headline.Length
      label1.Text = headline.Substring(0, i)
      Thread.Sleep(60)
    Next
    Thread.Sleep(100)
  End While
End Sub

Private Sub MoveRight()
  Dim counter As Integer = 0
  Dim max As Integer = businessItems.Length

  While (True)
    ' get news headline
    Dim headline As String = businessItems(counter)
    counter += 1
    If counter = max Then
      counter = 0
    End If
    Dim i As Integer
```

```
    For i = 0 To headline.Length
      label2.Text = headline.Substring(0, i)
      Thread.Sleep(100)
    Next

    Thread.Sleep(100)
  End While
End Sub

Protected Overrides Sub OnClosed(ByVal e As EventArgs)
  thread1.Join(0)
  thread2.Join(0)
  Environment.Exit(0)
End Sub

<STAThread()> Shared Sub Main()
  Application.Run(New Form1())
End Sub

End Class
```

To compile this application, from the directory where the listing-03.01.vb file resides, type the following:

```
vbc /t:winexe /r:System.dll,System.Windows.Forms.dll, ↵
System.Drawing.dll listing-03.01.vb
```

Figure 3-1 shows what the application looks like when run.

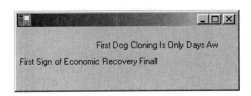

Figure 3-1. Headline ticker application

Now, let's explain how this simple multithreaded application works.

First, look at the following part of the class's constructor:

```
thread1 = New Thread(New ThreadStart(AddressOf MoveLeft))
thread1.Start()

thread2 = New Thread(New ThreadStart(AddressOf MoveRight))
thread2.Start()
```

In this example, thread1 and thread2 are instantiated and started. When thread1 is started, it will begin executing the MoveLeft method. When thread2 is started, the MoveRight method will start running.

The MoveLeft method consists of a While loop that runs indefinitely, until the Thread is aborted:

```
While (True)
    .
    .
    .
End While
```

The MoveLeft method displays the items in newsItems in turn. When the thread first starts, the MoveLeft method gets the first string into headline because counter is 0:

```
Dim headline As String = newsItems(counter)
```

Then it increments counter so that the next time the code in the While loop is called, the code will get the next string:

```
counter += 1
```

However, there are only a certain number of strings. So, when the last string in the array is reached, it must go back to the first string:

```
If counter = max Then
  counter = 0
End If
```

Then, for each string, it does a For loop that goes from zero to the length of the string, constructing a substring starting from an empty string. For each loop, it gets a substring that is one character longer than the substring in the previous loop. As a result, the text on the label looks like it is running:

```
Dim i As Integer
For i = 0 To headline.Length
  label1.Text = headline.Substring(0, i)
  Thread.Sleep(60)
Next
```

For each substring to be readable, it must move slowly enough for the reader to read. Therefore, you call the Sleep method of the Thread class and pass 60 to put the thread to sleep for 60 milliseconds. For each string, it will sleep for 100 milliseconds:

```
Thread.Sleep(100)
```

The MoveRight method is similar to MoveLeft. However, MoveRight works on the business headlines and moves from right to left.

Finally, the two threads terminate when the form is closed. You achieve this by overriding the OnClose method of the Form class. In the OnClose method, you call the Join method of both thread1 and thread2, causing both threads to be blocked:

```
thread1.Join(0)
thread2.Join(0)
```

Using Timers

In the world of electronics, a timer is a device you can use to activate another device after a certain period of time. For example, you can use a timer to switch on an electronic kettle for 15 minutes at 6:00 A.M. (so by the time you get out of the bed, you have boiling water for coffee). Or, you can install a timer in a car to trigger the alarm 20 seconds after the engine is started. (This gives the driver enough time to switch off the alarm.)

In .NET programming, you have several timer controls you can use for many different purposes. The classic example of the use of a timer is for displaying a splash screen. When the main application loads and initializes, the user is "entertained" by the splash screen that appears for five seconds and closes in time when the main application is ready. Or, as another example, in a video game, the bad guy will start chasing the hero two seconds after the hero's first move.

You can also use a timer to trigger recurring events. For instance, you can create an application that uses a timer to check every few seconds if a certain server is up and running. If it's not, the application can send a notification email to the administrator.

The .NET Framework class library provides several Timer classes. One is the member of the System.Windows.Forms namespace and is known as the *Windows-based timer*. The other one belongs to the System.Timers namespace and is called the *server-based timer*.

NOTE *There is another* Timer *class in the* System.Threading *namespace; however, it is not discussed in this chapter.*

The System.Windows.Forms.Timer class is optimized for Windows applications and can only be used in a Windows application. The server-based timer is for a server environment. To use any of the timer classes, you wire an event handler that is to be executed when the timer goes off. You also set the Interval property to indicate the number of milliseconds the timer will go off after it is started. Both classes are explained in the next two subsections with examples.

Using the Windows-Based Timer

The Windows-based timer works in a single-threaded environment and uses the User Interface (UI) thread to perform processing. These timers require that the user code have a UI message pump available and always operate from the same thread. Windows-based timers have accuracy limited to 55 milliseconds.

The System.Windows.Forms.Timer class has one event: Tick. When the timer is on, this event is raised repeatedly every specified amount of time. The value of the class's Interval property indicates the specified amount of time. For instance, if the value of the Interval property is 3000, the Tick event is raised once every 3,000 milliseconds.

By default, the Timer is off when it is instantiated. As such, the Tick event will not be raised regardless of the value of the Interval property. To switch on the timer, you can either set the Timer class's Enabled property to True or call its Start method.

To switch it off, you set the Enabled property to False or invoke the Timer class's Stop method.

As an example, Listing 3-2 is a form that displays a splash screen for five seconds. The splash screen is displayed two seconds after the form is instantiated. To achieve this, it uses the System.Windows.Forms.Timer class.

Listing 3-2. A Splash Screen Using the Windows-Based Timer

```
Imports System
Imports System.Windows.Forms

Public Class Form1 : Inherits Form
  Private theTimer As New Timer()
  Private splash As New Form()
  Private splashShown As Boolean = False

  Public Sub New()
    AddHandler theTimer.Tick, AddressOf theTimer_Tick
    theTimer.Interval = 2000
    theTimer.Start()
  End Sub

  Private Sub theTimer_Tick(ByVal sender As Object, ByVal e As EventArgs)
    If Not splashShown Then
      splash.Text = "Splash screen"
      splash.Show()
      ' show the splash screen for 5 seconds
      theTimer.Interval = 5000
      splashShown = True
    Else
      'close the splash screen
      splash.Close()
      theTimer.Enabled = False
    End If
  End Sub

  <STAThread()> Shared Sub Main()
    Application.Run(New Form1())
  End Sub

End Class
```

To compile this application, from the directory where the `listing-03.02.vb` file resides, type the following:

```
vbc /t:winexe /r:System.dll,System.Windows.Forms.dll, ↵
System.Drawing.dll listing-03.02.vb
```

When run, you will first see a Windows form. After two seconds, another form appears. The second form will disappear in five seconds.

To understand how the application works, first note the declaration part of the `Form1` class:

```
Private theTimer As New Timer()
Private splash As New Form()
Private splashShown As Boolean = False
```

The `theTimer` variable is an object reference to a Windows-based timer control. `splash` is a form that is to be displayed as a splash screen. `splashShown` is a `Boolean` that will be used to switch off the timer.

When the `Form1` class's constructor is called, it wires the `Timer` class's `Tick` event with an event handler called `theTimer_Tick`:

```
AddHandler theTimer.Tick, AddressOf theTimer_Tick
```

The timer's `Interval` property is then set to 2000, indicating that the timer will go off once in every two seconds, triggering the timer's `Tick` event. As a result, the `theTimer_Tick` event handler will execute every two seconds:

```
theTimer.Interval = 2000
```

To start the timer, you call the `Timer` class's `Start` method:

```
theTimer.Start()
```

You see that the code in the `Form1` class's constructor will make the `Timer` object's `Tick` event trigger repeatedly. However, you only want the timer to be executed twice: once to display the splash screen and once to close it. You achieve this using the `splashShown` `Boolean` in the `theTimer_Tick` event handler.

The initial value of `splashShown` is `False`. Therefore, when the `Tick` event is raised for the first time, the `theTimer_Tick` event handler executes the code in the `If` block. It first sets the `Text` property of the splash screen form and displays the splash screen by calling the `Show` method:

```
splash.Text = "Splash screen"
splash.Show()
```

You want the splash screen to appear for five seconds, so you set the `Interval` property of the `Timer` object to 5000 and set `splashShown` to `True`:

```
' show the splash screen for 5 seconds
theTimer.Interval = 5000
splashShown = True
```

Five seconds later, the timer's `Tick` event is raised again. This time the value of `splashShown` is `True`, so the code in the `Else` block in the `theTimer_Tick` event handler is executed.

It first calls the splash screen's `Close` method to close the splash screen:

```
'close the splash screen
splash.Close()
```

Then, it sets the `Timer` class's `Enabled` property to `False`, in effect deactivating the timer:

```
theTimer.Enabled = False
```

Because its `Enabled` property is set to `False`, the timer will not go off again. Therefore, during the life of the application, the timer only goes off twice.

Using the Server-Based Timer

The server-based timer uses worker threads in a multithreaded environment and are more accurate than Windows-based timers because of their architecture. Best of all, server-based timers can move among threads to handle the raised events. You can also use server-based timers in a Windows application, as in this chapter's Doggie project.

The `System.Timers.Timer` class has one event, `Elapsed`, which is raised when a specified amount of time elapses after the timer is started. The `Timer` class's `Interval` property indicates the amount of time. For instance, if the value of the `Interval` property is 4000, the `Elapsed` event triggers 4,000 milliseconds after the timer is started.

The value of the `AutoReset` property determines whether the `Elapsed` event will trigger again. If its value is `True`, the `Elapsed` event will be raised again. If the value of the `AutoReset` property is `False`, the `Elapsed` event will not be triggered again. By default, the value of the `AutoReset` property is `True`.

Like the Windows-based timer, you can switch on the server-based timer by calling its Start method or setting its Enabled property to True. You switch it off by calling its Stop method or setting its Enabled property to False.

Another difference between the System.Timers.Timer class and the System.Windows.Forms.Timer class is the type of event argument passed to the event handler that handles the method when the Tick event or Elapsed event is raised. With the Windows-based timer, it is a System.EventArgs object. With the server-based timer, it is a System.Timers.ElapsedEventArgs object.

The System.Timers.ElapsedEventArgs class has one property: SignalTime. This property returns a System.DateTime object indicating the time the Elapsed event was raised. You need this property because the System.Timers.Timer class is multi-threaded, so the call to its event handler may run on one thread while a call to the Stop method runs on another thread. This means that the Elapsed event might trigger after the Stop method is called. To prevent this from happening, you can use the SignalTime property to compare the time the event is raised with the time the Stop method is called. If the event is raised after the Stop method is called, you have the disposal not to process the event.

Listing 3-3 offers a similar example to display a splash screen. However, this example uses a server-based timer.

Listing 3-3. Displaying a Splash Screen Using a Server-Based Timer

```
Imports System
Imports System.Windows.Forms

Public Class Form1 : Inherits Form
  Private theTimer As New System.Timers.Timer()
  Private splash As New Form()
  Private splashShown As Boolean = False

  Public Sub New()
    AddHandler theTimer.Elapsed, AddressOf theTimer_Elapsed
    theTimer.Interval = 2000
    theTimer.Start()
  End Sub

  Private Sub theTimer_Elapsed(ByVal sender As Object, _
    ByVal e As System.Timers.ElapsedEventArgs)
    If Not splashShown Then
      splash.Text = "Splash screen"
      splash.Show()
      ' show the splash screen for 5 seconds
```

```
      theTimer.Interval = 5000
      splashShown = True
    Else
      'close the splash screen
      splash.Close()
      theTimer.AutoReset = False
    End If
  End Sub

  <STAThread()> Shared Sub Main()
    Application.Run(New Form1())
  End Sub
End Class
```

To compile this application, from the directory where the listing-03.03.vb file resides, type the following:

```
vbc /t:winexe /r:System.dll,System.Windows.Forms.dll, ↵
System.Drawing.dll listing-03.03.vb
```

In the Form1 class's constructor, you wire the Elapsed event of the Timer class with an event handler theTimer_Elapsed. Note that the event handler receives a System.Timers.ElapsedEventArgs.

Also, when the Elapsed event is raised for the second time, you set the AutoReset property to False, instead of resetting the Enabled property.

Understanding Game Theory

A video game is basically a movie. It consists of frames that change with a rate fast enough to make our brains think the pictures are continuous. Unlike a movie, though, the frames in a video game are composed on the fly. What happens next depends on a number of factors, including the user input.

The steps that make up the lifecycle of the game application is what differentiates a game from other Windows applications:

1. **Initialize**: In this step you prepare for the game itself. This includes instantiating the game actors, drawing the initial playing ground, setting the timers, and so on.

2. **Start game loop**: After the initialization, the game loop begins. The user (player) can start playing.

3. **Process user input**: The user input is taken from the input device, be it keyboard, mouse, or joystick. In Doggie, this is the keyboard press that will move Doggie, the hero in the game.

4. **Perform the game logic**: This includes performing the artificial intelligence in response to the user input. For example, in Doggie this is the step that determines the next location of the bad guys.

5. **Draw the next frame**: Based on the user input in step 3 and the game logic in step 4, render the next frame. In Doggie, this is the redrawing of the game actors in their new locations.

6. **Synchronize display**: Depending on the number of CPU cycles spent for steps 3 and 4, the next frame will be ready sooner or later than the previous frame. This results in a varying frame rate, something that is not acceptable. This step basically calculates the time spent on steps 3 and 4 and delays the computer action accordingly. In other words, if a frame must change every 30 milliseconds and steps 3 and 4 took 20 milliseconds, the thread that takes care of the frame drawing is put to sleep for 10 milliseconds. Consequently, if steps 3 and 4 took 10 milliseconds to complete, the thread is put to sleep for 20 seconds. This way, every frame will be changed in 30 milliseconds, making the game have a steady frame rate. Here is how it is done:

```
While True
    ' the use of t1 and t2 below is to make the frame rate steady
    Get t1 (the start time)
    Do Step 3 and 4
    Draw the next frame (Step 5)
    Get tw (the end time)
    Process time = t2 - t1
    If Process time < time for each frame,
    wait until (time for each frame) elapses
    End While
Loop. Go back to Step 2.
```

7. **Shut down:** The game has reached its end. In this step, the application releases any resource and does some cleaning up. With .NET Framework, this is equipped with a garbage collector; however, you could skip this step safely.

Implementing the Project

Trying to understand how the Doggie application works will be much easier if you have played Pac-Man before. If you have not, I encourage you to try Doggie first before you read this section. The following section is a description of how you play the game. If you are already a Pac-Man addict, it is still a good idea to read the following to familiarize yourself with the terms used throughout this section.

NOTE *In describing how the application works, I have tried to adopt the easiest way possible. So, I do not explain each class in turn like I do in some other chapters. Instead, I start with the easiest part first. I explain the most difficult part of the application, the artificial intelligence that moves the cats, last.*

NOTE *Do not panic if you do not understand when you first read this. This is not an easy topic, especially if this is your first game project. Depending on how good you are at programming, chances are you will have to read it more than once to understand the whole system.*

Playing the Game

To play the game, you must first extract the Ch03Codes.zip file that you downloaded. You will find an EXE file after the extraction, and there will also be a subdirectory called images that contains all image files needed by the application.

To run the application, run this EXE file. You will see something like Figure 3-2.

It is basically a form with two menus: File and About. The File menu has two menu items: New Game and Exit. The About menu will display the About dialog box when clicked.

The client area consists of three parts:

- The top part, which is 25-pixels high, where the score and other instructions display.

- The maze, or the playing ground, which covers the whole client area excluding the top part and the bottom part.

- The bottom part, 31-pixels high, where the current game level and the remaining Doggie's "lives" display.

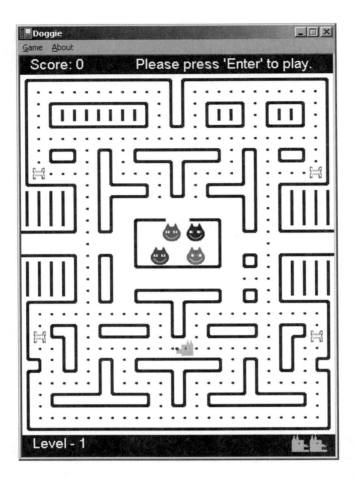

Figure 3-2. The Doggie game

When the application is first started, you will see Doggie (the dog in pink color). There is also the cat house at the center of the maze. There are four cats inside. The cats are the bad guys in this game. The colors of the cats are blue, green, red, and black. These cats are simply referred to as *blue cat, green cat, red cat,* and *black cat.*

The black bullets scattered around the maze are the foods. There are also four bones at the corners of the maze. You get 10 points for eating each food and bone. The blue structures that look like the letter T and squares represent walls.

To start, press the Enter key. You then use the four arrow keys (up, down, left, right) to move Doggie. Doggie can move along the paths surrounded by the walls. The aim of this game is to get the highest score by eating the foods and catching the cats.

At first the cats will chase Doggie around, and Doggie has to avoid collision with them. However, after Doggie eats one of the bones, the situation is reversed for a few seconds. Doggie becomes stronger and faster than the cats, and Doggie should catch the cats to get higher points. When Doggie catches a cat, it will change color and move to the cat house. The caught cat will then turn back into a normal cat inside the cat house. The cat in the cat house will stay there until the reversed situation is over.

When all the foods have been eaten, the current game level is over and you move to a higher level.

Classes in the Projects

The following are the classes and other types in the Doggie project:

- The Constants class

- The GameState enumeration

- The Direction enumeration

- The Form1 class

- The GameManager class

- The Maze class

- The GameActor abstract class

- The Doggie class

- The Cat abstract class

- The BlueCat class

- The GreenCat class

- The BlackCat class

- The RedCat class

Figure 3-3 shows the class diagram.

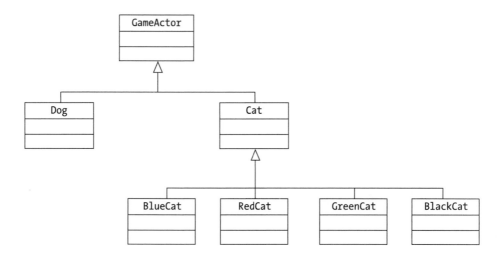

Figure 3-3. The class diagram

Doggie and Cat are the direct child classes of GameActor. Cat has four child classes: BlueCat, GreenCat, RedCat, and BlackCat.

During the life of the application, there is one instance of the Maze class, one instance of the GameManager class, one instance of the Form1 class, one instance of the Doggie class, one instance of the BlueCat class, one instance of the GreenCat class, one instance of the BlackCat class, and one instance of the RedCat class.

Each instance of the game actor (Doggie and the four cats) has its own thread that takes care of the movement of the game actor. There is also another thread called game that draws the frames. In addition, there is the application thread itself.

NOTE *You can find the code listings in the project's directory.*

Some of these classes depend on each other. Therefore, explaining how the program works by discussing each class in turn will not be effective. Instead, I explain functionality starting from the functions that have least dependence. I will start from the maze.

Creating the Maze

The maze, represented by the Maze class, is the playing ground in this game. It consists of 26 columns and 31 rows, so there are 26 × 31 = 806 cells. Each cell is drawn as a 16 × 16 pixels square. Figure 3-4 shows the maze, with white lines added to indicate the partition between two maze cells.

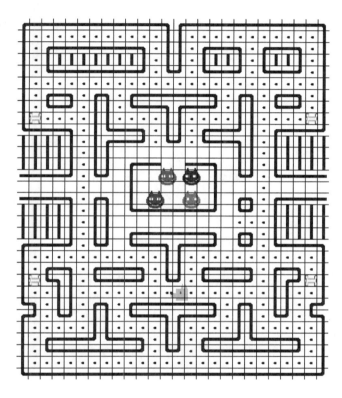

Figure 3-4. The maze

You can refer to each cell by its row number and its column number. For example, the cell at the first column in the first row is cell(0, 0), and the cell in the last column and the last row is cell(30, 25). As you can see, the four bones are respectively in cell(2, 1), cell(2, 24), cell(22, 1), and cell(22, 24). In the beginning of every game level, Doggie is positioned in cell(25, 13), and the four cats are in cell(13, 12), cell(13, 14), cell(15, 11), and cell(15, 14).

The blue lines represent the walls. Both Doggie and the cats can move around the maze by moving from one cell to another. However, they cannot go through the walls.

Let's start with an explanation of how to draw the maze.

Drawing the Maze

You draw the maze by drawing each cell using the DrawMaze method of the Maze class. The DrawMaze method uses the following For loops to draw each cell:

```
For i = 0 To mazeRowCount - 1         'mazeRowCount = 31
  For j = 0 To mazeColumnCount - 1    'mazeColumnCount = 26
    DrawCell(j, i, g)
  Next
Next
```

For each cell, it calls the DrawCell method, passing the column number (j), the row number (i), and the graphics object to draw the cells on (g).

Drawing the Cells

If you look at the maze cells in Figure 3-4, you will see that not all cells are identical. Some contain horizontal or vertical parts of a wall, some contain nothing but the food, and some are a different kind of a block. How does the DrawCell method know how to draw each cell of the maze? The answer to this lies in the maze array of strings that is declared and initialized in the Maze class (see Listing 3-4).

Listing 3-4. The String Representing the Maze

```
Private maze() As String = { _
    "a-----------ba-----------b", _
    "|**********||**********|", _
    "|$a-b*a---b*||*a---b*a-b$|", _
    "|*| |*|   |*||*|   |*| |*|", _
    "|*d-c*d---c*dc*d---c*d-c*|", _
    "|*********************|", _
    "|*a-b*ab*a------b*ab*a-b*|", _
    "|*d-c*||*d--ba--c*||*d-c*|", _
    "|*****||****||****||*****|", _
    "d---b*|d--b*||*a--c|*a---c", _
```

```
    "     |*|a--c*dc*d--b|*|    ",  _
    "     |*||            ||*|    ",  _
    "     |*|| a--##--b ||*|    ",  _
    "----c*dc |%%%%%| dc*d----",  _
    "<    *   |%%%%%|    *   >",  _
    "----b*ab |%%%%%| ab*a----",  _
    "     |*|| d------c ||*|    ",  _
    "     |*||            ||*|    ",  _
    "     |*|| a------b ||*|    ",  _
    "a---c*dc d--ba--c dc*d---b",  _
    "|**********||**********|",  _
    "|*a-b*a---b*||*a---b*a-b*|",  _
    "|$db|*d---c*dc*d---c*|ac$|",  _
    "|**||***************||**|",  _
    "db*||*ab*a------b*ab*||*ac",  _
    "ac*dc*||*d--ba--c*||*dc*db",  _
    "|*****||****||****||*****|",  _
    "|*a---cd--b*||*a--cd---b*|",  _
    "|*d-------c*dc*d-------c*|",  _
    "|**********************|",  _
    "d----------------------c"  _
}
```

The maze array contains 31 strings, and each string consists of 26 characters. It is not a coincidence that the number of strings is the same as the number of rows in the maze. Each string represents a row in the maze. The first string therefore represents the cells in the first row.

In turn, each character in each string represents a cell in the maze row. It is not surprising that the number of characters in each string is the same as the number of columns in the maze row. There are several different characters in all the strings: spaces, *a*'s, *b*'s, *c*'s, *d*'s, dollar ($) signs, pipe (|) characters, asterisks (*), percent (%) signs, brackets (> and <), and hyphens (-). The same character in maze represents the same cell. To understand this more fully, you will look at the code that draws the cell (the DrawCell method) shortly.

However, note that you do not use maze to draw each cell. Instead, you use the mazeData variable, which is also an array of strings that initially contains the same exact value as maze. I will explain later why you employ two arrays of strings. For now, remember that the value of mazeData is the same as the value of maze.

Here is the `DrawCell` method. Recall that this method accepts the cell column number, the cell row number, and the reference to the `Graphics` object on which the maze will be drawn.

```
Sub DrawCell(ByVal x As Integer, ByVal y As Integer, ByRef g As Graphics)
  Dim value As Char = mazeData(y).Chars(x)
  Select Case value
    Case " "c
      g.FillRectangle(emptyBrush, x * square, y * square, square, square)
    Case "*"c
      g.FillRectangle(emptyBrush, x * square, y * square, square, square)
      g.FillEllipse(foodBrush, x * square + 6, y * square + 6, 4, 4)
    Case "J"c
      g.FillRectangle(emptyBrush, x * square, y * square, square, square)
      g.FillEllipse(foodBrush, x * square + 6, y * square + 6, 4, 4)
    Case "$"c
      g.FillRectangle(emptyBrush, x * square, y * square, square, square)
      g.FillEllipse(superBrush, x * square + 2, y * square + 2, 12, 12)
    Case "-"c
      g.FillRectangle(emptyBrush, x * square, y * square, square, square)
      g.DrawImage(images(0), x * square, y * square, square, square)
    Case "|"c
      g.FillRectangle(emptyBrush, x * square, y * square, square, square)
      g.DrawImage(images(1), x * square, y * square, square, square)
    Case "a"c
      g.FillRectangle(emptyBrush, x * square, y * square, square, square)
      g.DrawImage(images(2), x * square, y * square, square, square)
    Case "b"c
      g.FillRectangle(emptyBrush, x * square, y * square, square, square)
      g.DrawImage(images(3), x * square, y * square, square, square)
    Case "c"c
      g.FillRectangle(emptyBrush, x * square, y * square, square, square)
      g.DrawImage(images(4), x * square, y * square, square, square)
    Case "d"c
      g.FillRectangle(emptyBrush, x * square, y * square, square, square)
      g.DrawImage(images(5), x * square, y * square, square, square)
    Case "#"c
      g.FillRectangle(emptyBrush, x * square, y * square, square, square)
      g.DrawImage(images(6), x * square, y * square, square, square)
    Case "<"c
      g.FillRectangle(emptyBrush, x * square, y * square, square, square)
    Case ">"c
      g.FillRectangle(emptyBrush, x * square, y * square, square, square)
```

```
    Case "%"c
      g.FillRectangle(emptyBrush, x * square, y * square, square, square)
    End Select
End Sub
```

The first line of the DrawCell method obtains the character at the specified position passed to this method. For instance, for x = 6 and y = 3, the cell to be drawn is the cell in the fourth row of the maze at the seventh column. In other words, it is cell (3, 6). The character to be obtained is from the fourth string of mazeData and character number 7:

```
Dim value As Char = mazeData(y).Chars(x)
```

Having the right character, it will then go through a Select Case block to determine what to draw. As an example, an asterisk character represents a food. Therefore, if the character is an asterisk, the following two lines of code execute:

```
g.FillRectangle(emptyBrush, x * square, y * square, square, square)
g.FillEllipse(foodBrush, x * square + 6, y * square + 6, 4, 4)
```

This draws a rectangle with a Brush object called emptyBrush (which is a Brush with a black color) starting at position (x * square, y * square), where square is the width and the height of the cell. The value of square is 16 (pixels).

The second line of the previous code draws a circle that represents a food using foodBrush.

Figure 3-5 shows the characters and the cell types they represent.

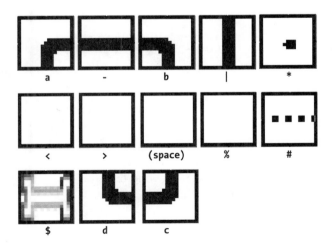

Figure 3-5. The characters and the cell types they represent

Now, let's discuss why you need both maze and mazeData.

As you know, as Doggie moves along, it can eat the foods in the maze. When a food in a cell has been eaten, the cell becomes empty. The program must remember which cells Doggie has visited and removes the foods in those cells because Doggie has eaten them. The program remembers this because it makes a copy of the content of maze in mazeData. Therefore, maze contains the initial structure of the maze cells, but mazeData contains the "value" of each cell as the game proceeds. This means, every time Doggie eats a food in a cell, you modify the value of the character that represents the cell in mazeData.

When the DrawMaze method is called, it draws the maze at its initial stage. It also counts the number of foods in the maze and copies each individual string of maze to mazeData:

```
Private Sub DrawMaze()
  food = 0
  Dim g As Graphics = Graphics.FromImage(image)
  Dim i As Integer
  For i = 0 To mazeRowCount - 1
    ' copy the ith string from maze to mazeData
    mazeData(i) = maze(i)
    Dim j As Integer
    For j = 0 To mazeColumnCount - 1
      If mazeData(i).Chars(j) = "*" Or _
        mazeData(i).Chars(j) = "$" Then
        food += 1
      End If
      DrawCell(j, i, g)
    Next
  Next
  g.Dispose()

End Sub
```

Look at the part of the code that is printed in bold. Because * represents a food and $ represents a bone, both are counted as "food," and the integer food is incremented when one of them is encountered.

The Graphics object g in the DrawMaze method is created from a Bitmap called image using the shared FromImage method of the System.Drawing.Graphics class. You construct image at the declaration section of the Maze class:

```
image = New Bitmap(Width, Height)
```

where Width is the width of the maze and Height is the height of the maze.

At this point, you can conclude that you can draw a different maze by simply changing the value of maze at initialization. I review other methods of the Maze class at the later sections.

Understanding Game States

A video game is basically a movie that consists of frames. These frames are drawn continually many times every second to fool human eyes into thinking that the video is continuous. Normally, the rate of 30 frames per second is sufficient. Unlike a movie, however, the sequence of frames in a video game is created on the fly, based on the previous user input. Once a game starts, the application executes a While loop that keeps drawing these frames. What is being drawn at a particular instance of time depends on what happened prior to drawing. Specifically, the Doggie game uses members of the GameState enumeration:

```
Public Enum GameState As Integer
    Init
    [New]
    Begin
    Run
    Win
    Lose
    GameOver
    [Stop]
End Enum
```

 NOTE *The members* New *and* Stop *are in brackets because* New *and* Stop *are keywords in Visual Basic.*

In fact, in most classes there is a variable called currentState that retains the current state of the game. The currentState variable values in all objects will be updated when the state of the game changes.

These states are as follows:

Init: This is the state when the application is first started. In this state a GameManager object is constructed. Instantiating a GameManager object will construct the Maze object and all the game actors (Doggie and the four cats) because the GameManager class's constructor contains code that does so. After the object instantiation, the state will change to New.

New: This is a new game. In this state, the application draws or redraws the maze, displays the string *Please press 'Enter' to play* on the top part of the client area and waits for the user to press Enter. When the user presses the Enter key, the state will change to Begin.

Begin: The application draws a string *Ready* on the top part of the client area, initializes the game actors (Doggie and the four cats), waits for two seconds, and changes the state to Run.

Run: In this state the application checks for collision between Doggie and one of the cats. If collision occurs in a normal circumstance, Doggie dies. However, if the collision occurs at the "reverse" situation (in other words, when Doggie is being stronger after eating a bone), the cat dies. If Doggie dies, the state switches to Lose. If Doggie eats all the foods in the maze, the state goes to Win. If a user presses an arrow key during this state, Doggie changes direction.

Win: The application draws the string *YOU WIN!!!* on the top part of the client area, redraws the maze, increments the game level by one, and changes the state to Begin.

Lose: The application draws the string *YOU LOSE!!!* on the top part of the client area, decrements the lives by one if it is not yet zero, or changes the state to GameOver if there are no more lives.

GameOver: The application draws the string *Game Over* on the top part of the client area, resets the score and lives, waits two seconds, and changes the state to New.

Stop: This state occurs when the form closes. In this state, the game thread aborts.

Working with the Threads

There are seven threads used in this application: one in each of the game actors (Doggie and the four cats), one in the application's thread, and one used for drawing frames.

Starting the Application

When the application is first started, the Form1 class's constructor is called. The constructor consists of only one line: InitializeComponent(). This method is as follows:

```
Public Sub InitializeComponent()
  Dim mainMenu As New MainMenu()
  Dim gameMenuItem As New MenuItem("&Game")

  Dim gameNewGameMenuItem As New MenuItem("&New Game", _
    New EventHandler(AddressOf gameNewGameMenuItem_Click))
  Dim gameExitMenuItem As New MenuItem("E&xit", _
    New EventHandler(AddressOf gameExitMenuItem_Click))

  gameMenuItem.MenuItems.Add(gameNewGameMenuItem)
  gameMenuItem.MenuItems.Add(gameExitMenuItem)

  Dim aboutMenuItem As New MenuItem("&About", _
    New EventHandler(AddressOf aboutMenuItem_Click))

  mainMenu.MenuItems.Add(gameMenuItem)
  mainMenu.MenuItems.Add(aboutMenuItem)

  Me.Menu = mainMenu
  Me.MaximizeBox = False
  Me.FormBorderStyle = FormBorderStyle.Fixed3D
  Me.Text = "Doggie"

  GameManager.SetState(GameState.Init)
  Me.ClientSize = New Size(GameManager.Width, GameManager.Height)
  game = New Thread(New ThreadStart(AddressOf Run))
  AddHandler Me.KeyDown, AddressOf DetectKeyDown
  game.Start()
End Sub
```

The `InitializeComponent` method sets up the two menus and wires some event handlers to the menu items. It also sets the `Icon` and the `FormBorderStyle` properties. The important part of this method is in the last five lines:

```
GameManager.SetState(GameState.Init)
Me.ClientSize = New Size(GameManager.Width, GameManager.Height)
game = New Thread(New ThreadStart(AddressOf Run))
AddHandler Me.KeyDown, AddressOf DetectKeyDown
game.Start()
```

It calls the static `SetState` of the `GameManager` class passing `GameState.Init`, sets the `ClientSize` property, instantiates the game `Thread` objects passing a `ThreadStart` delegate, wires the `KeyDown` event of the form with the `DetectKeyDown` method and start the game `Thread`.

Note that the `ThreadStart` delegate that is passed to the `Thread` class's constructor passes the address of `Run`. It causes the `Run` method to execute when the game thread's `Start` method is called. The `Run` method contains a `While` loop, which is the main loop of the game. "The Game's Main Loop" covers this method. However, before doing that, let's discuss the `SetState` method of the `GameManager` class, which is called in the `InitializeComponent` method passing the `GameState.Init`. This will construct a `GameManager` object:

```
GameManager.SetState(GameState.Init)
```

Calling the SetState Method and Constructing the GameManager Object

The `GameManager` object is constructed when the `InitializeComponent` method in the `Form1` class calls the static `SetState` method of the `GameManager` class. The following code is the `SetState` method of the `GameManager` class. Remember that in the `Form1` class's `InitializeComponent` method, the `SetState` method is passed `GameState.Init`:

```
Public Shared Sub SetState(ByVal state As GameState)
  If state = GameState.Init Then
    gameMgr = New GameManager()
  End If

  gameMgr.currentState = state
  gameMgr.theMaze.SetState(state)
  gameMgr.doc.SetState(state)
  Dim i As Integer
```

```
  For i = 0 To Constants.catCount - 1
    gameMgr.cats(i).SetState(state)
  Next

  Select Case state
    Case GameState.Init
      SetState(GameState.[New])
    Case GameState.[New]
      gameMgr.level = 1
      gameMgr.lives -= 1
    Case GameState.Begin
      gameMgr.timer.Interval = 2000
      gameMgr.timer.Start()
    Case GameState.Win
      gameMgr.timer.Interval = 2000
      gameMgr.timer.Start()
    Case GameState.Lose
      gameMgr.timer.Interval = 2000
      gameMgr.timer.Start()
    Case GameState.GameOver
      gameMgr.timer.Interval = 2000
      gameMgr.timer.Start()
  End Select
End Sub
```

The SetState method instantiates the GameManager object if the argument passed is GameState.Init. After that it sets the states in the Maze object, Doggie object, and the four cat objects. Then, it enters a Select block, which does the thing explained in the earlier "Understanding Game States" section.

Let's now concentrate on the GameManager class's constructor that gets called when GameState.Init is passed to the SetState method.

The GameManager class's constructor is as follows:

```
Public Sub New()
  dog = New Doggie()
  cats(0) = New RedCat(dog)
  cats(1) = New BlueCat(dog)
  cats(2) = New BlackCat(dog)
  cats(3) = New GreenCat(dog)

  theMaze = New Maze(dog, cats)
```

```
        Const topImageHeight As Integer = 25
        Const bottomImageHeight As Integer = 30

        topImage = New Bitmap(theMaze.Width, topImageHeight)
        boardImage = New Bitmap(theMaze.Width, theMaze.Height)
        bottomImage = New Bitmap(theMaze.Width, bottomImageHeight)

        Height = theMaze.Height + topImageHeight + bottomImageHeight
        Width = theMaze.Width

        timer = New System.Timers.Timer()
        AddHandler timer.Elapsed, AddressOf OnTimedEvent
        timer.AutoReset = False

        f14 = New Font("Arial", 14)
        f16 = New Font("Arial", 16)
        f18 = New Font("Arial", 18)

        green = New SolidBrush(Color.Green)
        white = New SolidBrush(Color.White)
        red = New SolidBrush(Color.Red)

        dogImage = New Bitmap("images/doggie/right2.gif")
    End Sub
```

The GameManager class's constructor instantiates the following objects:

- The Dog object.

- The four Cat objects. The constructor of the Cat class accepts a Dog object.

- The Maze object by passing the Dog object and an array of Cat objects.

- Three images (for the top part, the maze, and the bottom part).

- The Timer object. It also wires its Elapsed event with the OnTimedEvent event handler.

- Three Font objects (f14, f16, and f18).

- Four SolidBrush objects (blue, green, white, and red).

The Game's Main Loop

The main loop is in the Run method of the Form1 class. The Run method is as follows:

```
Public Sub Run()
  Thread.Sleep(100)
  While True
    ' the use of t1 and t2 below is to make the frame rate
    ' steady
    Dim t1 As Integer = Environment.TickCount
    Dim g As Graphics = Me.CreateGraphics()
    GameManager.Draw(g)
    Dim t2 As Integer = Environment.TickCount
    g.Dispose()
    Thread.Sleep(Math.Max(0, 30 - (t2 - t1)))
  End While
End Sub
```

NOTE *The game's main loop in the* Run *method runs in a separate thread. Meanwhile, the main thread of the application still works to detect user input.*

The loop starts after a delay of 100 milliseconds. It starts by obtaining the reference to the form's Graphics object:

```
Dim g As Graphics = Me.CreateGraphics()
```

It then calls the GraphicManager class's Draw method. This Draw method draws a frame. Note that the Draw method accepts the Graphics object on which the frame is to be drawn.

The TickCount property of the System.Environment class returns the number of milliseconds that elapsed since the system started. You are interested in the value of the TickCount property before and after the Draw method is called. The difference between them is the number of milliseconds taken to execute the Draw method. You want every frame to be changed every 30 milliseconds; therefore, you use the following line of code:

```
Thread.Sleep(Math.Max(0, 30 - (t2 - t1)))
```

This will make the thread sleep for (30 – time taken to draw) milliseconds. If the time taken to draw is more than 30 milliseconds, the value of (30 – time taken to draw) will be negative. In this case, the Max method of the Math class will return 0 and the thread will not sleep at all.

The Draw method of the GameManager class draws the current frame. Let's look at how it does it in the following section, "Drawing the Current Frame."

Drawing the Current Frame

The application's client area consists of three parts: the top part, the maze, and the bottom part. The GameManager class's Draw method draws each frame by drawing these three parts in turn. For each part the method employs a temporary Graphics object gTemp. The Draw method is given as follows:

```
Public Shared Sub Draw(ByRef g As Graphics)
  ' --- Drawing the top part ---
  Dim gTemp As Graphics = Graphics.FromImage(gameMgr.topImage)
  gTemp.Clear(Color.Black)
  gTemp.DrawString("Score: " & gameMgr.theMaze.score * 10, _
    gameMgr.f14, gameMgr.white, 10, 0)

  Select Case gameMgr.currentState
    Case GameState.[New]
      gTemp.DrawString("Please press 'Enter' to play.", _
        gameMgr.f14, gameMgr.white, 150, 0)
    Case GameState.Begin
      gTemp.DrawString("Ready!", gameMgr.f16, gameMgr.white, 150, 0)
    Case GameState.Run
      gameMgr.theMaze.CheckCollission()
      If gameMgr.dog.dead Then
        SetState(GameState.Lose)
      ElseIf gameMgr.theMaze.food = 0 Then
        SetState(GameState.Win)
      End If
    Case GameState.Win
      gTemp.DrawString("YOU WIN!!!", gameMgr.f16, gameMgr.green, 150, 0)
    Case GameState.Lose
      gTemp.DrawString("YOU LOSE!!!", gameMgr.f16, gameMgr.red, 150, 0)
    Case GameState.GameOver
      gTemp.DrawString("GAME OVER", gameMgr.f18, gameMgr.red, 150, 0)
  End Select
```

```
gTemp.Dispose()

' --- Drawing the maze ---
gTemp = Graphics.FromImage(gameMgr.boardImage)
gameMgr.theMaze.Draw(gTemp)
gTemp.Dispose()

' --- Drawing the bottom part ---
gTemp = Graphics.FromImage(gameMgr.bottomImage)
gTemp.Clear(Color.Black)

gTemp.DrawString("Level - " & gameMgr.level, gameMgr.f14, _
  gameMgr.white, 10, 0)

Dim i As Integer
For i = 0 To gameMgr.lives - 1
  gTemp.DrawImage(gameMgr.pacImage, (Width - 10) - (i + 1) * 24, 0, 24, 24)
Next
gTemp.Dispose()

' putting all three parts together
g.DrawImage(gameMgr.topImage, 0, 0)
g.DrawImage(gameMgr.boardImage, 0, 25)
g.DrawImage(gameMgr.bottomImage, 0, gameMgr.theMaze.Height + 25)
End Sub
```

Note that the maze is drawn by calling the Draw method of the Maze class. At the end of the method, the frame is completed by putting all three parts together.

Of the three, the maze is the most complicated because it includes drawing the game actors.

The Draw method of the Maze class draws the maze. It is passed a Graphics object from the GameManager object. This Graphics object is a reference to the Graphics object of the Form1 object. The Draw method is as follows:

```
Public Sub Draw(ByRef g As Graphics)
  If rebuild Then
    reverse = False
    DrawMaze()
    rebuild = False
    g.Clear(Color.Black)
    g.DrawImage(image, 0, 0)
  End If
```

```
    RemoveActor(CType(pac, GameActor), g)
    Dim i As Integer
    For i = 0 To Constants.catCount - 1
      RemoveActor(CType(cats(i), GameActor), g)
    Next
    DrawActor(CType(pac, GameActor), g)
    For i = 0 To Constants.catCount - 1
      DrawActor(CType(cats(i), GameActor), g)
    Next
End Sub
```

The Draw method first checks if rebuilding is necessary by testing the value of the rebuild Boolean. The rebuild Boolean is set to True when the game state changes to GameState.New or GameState.Begin. When rebuild is True, the method sets the reverse Boolean to False, calls the DrawMaze method to draw the maze, resets rebuild, clears the Graphics object, and draws the image image onto the Graphics object.

 NOTE *The "Drawing the Maze" section explains the* DrawMaze *method.*

The Boolean reverse indicates whether the situation is reversed. When True, it indicates that Doggie has just eaten a bone and is being stronger than the cats. The DrawMaze method draws the maze on the image image, which is initialized as follows at the class's constructor:

```
image = New Bitmap(Width, Height)
```

Note that most of the time the DrawMaze is not called. If the maze has to be redrawn for each frame, the game thread will work hard and the whole application will become very slow if the user's computer is not powerful enough. The cells that are occupied by the game actors are updated because the game actors (at least the cats) move all the time.

You do this in the second part of the Draw method:

```
RemoveActor(CType(pac, GameActor), g)
Dim i As Integer
For i = 0 To Constants.catCount - 1
```

```
      RemoveActor(CType(cats(i), GameActor), g)
Next
DrawActor(CType(pac, GameActor), g)
For i = 0 To Constants.catCount - 1
  DrawActor(CType(cats(i), GameActor), g)
Next
```

The RemoveActor method removes the image of the actor from the previous position in the maze, and the DrawActor method draws the actor in the current position. The RemoveActor and the DrawActor are the topics of the next discussion.

The following is the RemoveActor method:

```
Private Sub RemoveActor(ByRef a As GameActor, ByRef g As Graphics)
  Dim x As Integer = a.oldXScreen \ square
  Dim y As Integer = a.oldYScreen \ square

  If x = 0 Or y = 0 Then
    Return
  End If

  Dim actualX As Integer = a.oldXScreen - 4
  Dim actualY As Integer = a.oldYScreen - 4

  Dim i As Integer = actualX \ square
  Dim j As Integer = actualY \ square

  Dim upperBound As Integer = (actualX + 24) \ square

  While i <= upperBound
    For j = actualY \ square To (actualY + 24) \ square
      DrawCell(i, j, g)
    Next
    i += 1
  End While
End Sub
```

NOTE *In VB, the \ operator is a division operator that rounds down the result. Therefore, 19 \ 5 = 3.*

Each maze cell is a square of 16 × 16 pixels, and an image actor has a dimension of 24 × 24 pixels. If an actor is exactly on top of a single cell (see Figure 3-6), there are nine cells that need to be redrawn when the actor is removed. On the other hand, if the actor occupies two adjacent cells (like in Figure 3-7), six cells need to be redrawn.

Figure 3-6. The actor is exactly on top of a single cell.

Figure 3-7. The actor occupies two adjacent cells.

And this is the DrawActor method:

```
Private Sub DrawActor(ByRef a As GameActor, ByRef g As Graphics)
  SyncLock (a)
    If Not a.frameReady Then
      Try
        Monitor.Wait(a)
      Catch e As SynchronizationLockException
      Catch e As ThreadInterruptedException
      End Try
    End If
    a.Draw(g)
    a.frameReady = False
    Monitor.Pulse(a)
  End SyncLock
End Sub
```

Driving Doggie

First of all, Doggie and all cats always move along a straight line. Even when the player is not doing anything, Doggie will move on until it hits the wall. In this case, the player can then "turn" Doggie to another direction. So, the player does not really move Doggie, but only tells Doggie the next "turn direction." The turn direction can be left, right, up, or down. The player notifies Doggie of the next turn direction using one of the arrow keys. If the player presses one of the arrow keys when Doggie is still moving, the turn direction will be remembered and takes effect when Doggie can do the turn—for example, if Doggie is right on top of a junction. The information about the turn direction is kept in the turnDirection Boolean variable in the Doggie class.

To capture a key press, in the Form1 class you write the following code in the InitializeComponent method to wire the form's KeyDown event with the DetectKeyDown event handler:

```
AddHandler Me.KeyDown, AddressOf DetectKeyDown
```

And the following is the DetectKeyDown method in the Form1 class. Note that game is a Thread object that takes care of the main loop that draws frames:

```
Protected Sub DetectKeyDown(ByVal sender As Object, ByVal e As KeyEventArgs)
  If e.KeyCode = Keys.Space Then
    If game.ThreadState = ThreadState.Suspended Then
      game.Resume()
    ElseIf game.ThreadState = ThreadState.Running Then
      game.Suspend()
    End If
  Else
    GameManager.KeyDown(sender, e)
  End If
End Sub
```

The method first checks if the key pressed is the spacebar. The spacebar acts as a toggle bar that pauses and resumes the game:

```
If e.KeyCode = Keys.Space Then
```

If the key is the spacebar, it checks the state of the game Thread. If game is suspended, game is resumed by calling the Resume method of the Thread class. If game is running, game is suspended by calling the Suspend method:

```
If game.ThreadState = ThreadState.Suspended Then
  game.Resume()
ElseIf game.ThreadState = ThreadState.Running Then
  game.Suspend()
End If
```

If the key pressed is not the spacebar, the key press simply passes to the KeyDown method of the GameManager class, passing the sender and the KeyEventArgs argument:

```
Else
  GameManager.KeyDown(sender, e)
```

The following is the KeyDown method of the GameManager class:

```
Public Shared Sub KeyDown(ByVal o As Object, ByVal e As KeyEventArgs)
  If Not gameMgr Is Nothing Then
    If gameMgr.currentState = GameState.Run Then
      gameMgr.pac.KeyDown(o, e)
    ElseIf gameMgr.currentState = GameState.[New] And _
      e.KeyCode = Keys.Enter Then
      SetState(GameState.Begin)
    End If
  End If
End Sub
```

The code in the KeyDown method only executes if the static gameMgr has been instantiated. In this case, the code checks the value of the currentState Boolean. If its value is GameState.Run (the game is running), it calls the KeyDown method of the Doggie class:

```
If gameMgr.currentState = GameState.Run Then
  gameMgr.dog.KeyDown(o, e)
```

In the previous code, dog is an object variable of type Dog. You will have a look at the Dog class's KeyDown method in a moment.

If the currentState of the gameMgr is GameState.New and the key pressed is the Enter key, then the state of the game changes to GameState.Begin:

```
ElseIf gameMgr.currentState = GameState.[New] And _
  e.KeyCode = Keys.Enter Then
  SetState(GameState.Begin)
```

Now shift your attention to the KeyDown method of the Dog class, which actually moves Doggie. This is the method:

```
Public Sub KeyDown(ByVal o As Object, ByVal e As KeyEventArgs)
  Select Case e.KeyCode
    Case Keys.Up
      turnDirection = 0
    Case Keys.Down
      turnDirection = 2
    Case Keys.Left
      turnDirection = 1
    Case Keys.Right
      turnDirection = 3
  End Select
End Sub
```

As you can see, the KeyDown method in the Dog class is only used to change the value of turnDirection, a Boolean variable in the Dog class. The valid value of turnDirection can be 0, 1, 2, or 3. A value of -1 means that Doggie is not turning anywhere.

Doggie itself will move when the next frame is drawn.

Now, let's see how the game thread in the Form1 class actually moves Doggie (and the cats). Recall that the Run method in the Form1 class calls the Draw method of the GameManager class:

```
GameManager.Draw(g)
```

Somewhere in the Draw method in the GameManager class, it calls the Draw method of the Maze class:

```
' --- Drawing the maze ---
gTemp = Graphics.FromImage(gameMgr.boardImage)
gameMgr.theMaze.Draw(gTemp)
gTemp.Dispose()
```

The following are the last lines of the Draw method of the Maze class:

```
RemoveActor(CType(pac, GameActor), g)
Dim i As Integer
For i = 0 To Constants.catCount - 1
  RemoveActor(CType(cats(i), GameActor), g)
Next
DrawActor(CType(dog, GameActor), g)
For i = 0 To Constants.catCount - 1
  DrawActor(CType(cats(i), GameActor), g)
Next
```

The last part in bold in the code is the call to the DrawActor method that passes the Dog instance. Let's look at the DrawActor method:

```
Private Sub DrawActor(ByRef a As GameActor, ByRef g As Graphics)
  SyncLock (a)
    If Not a.frameReady Then
      Try
        Monitor.Wait(a)
      Catch e As SynchronizationLockException
      Catch e As ThreadInterruptedException
      End Try
    End If
    a.Draw(g)
    a.frameReady = False
    Monitor.Pulse(a)
  End SyncLock
End Sub
```

The DrawActor method locks the actor and then calls the Draw method of the GameActor class. The method is an abstract method:

```
Public MustOverride Sub Draw(ByVal g As Graphics)
```

So, thanks to polymorphism, it will call the overriding Draw method in the child class—in this case, the Dog class. This is the Draw method of the Dog class:

```
Public Overrides Sub Draw(ByVal g As Graphics)
  g.DrawImage(image, xScreen - 4, yScreen - 4)
End Sub
```

Updating Positions

The Dog class and all the cats derive from the GameActor class. The GameActor class has the following four integer variables:

```
Public xScreen, yScreen As Integer
Public oldXScreen, oldYScreen As Integer
```

xScreen and yScreen indicate the coordinate of the Doggie instance in the maze. Remember that the maze consists of 31 rows and 26 columns of cells and each cell is a square of 16 × 16 pixels. Therefore, the maze is 26 × 16 = 416 pixels wide and 31 × 16 = 496 pixels high. The top-left corner of the cell in the first column and the first row is on coordinate (0, 0) of the maze. Its bottom-right corner is on coordinate (15, 15).

To move completely from one cell to the next cell on the right, a game actor's xScreen must be incremented by 16. To move from one cell to the next cell on the left, a game actor's xScreen must be decremented by 16. By the same token, to move one cell to the next cell below the current cell, the game actor's yScreen must be incremented by 16.

Between two frames a game actor does not move 16 pixels at a time because such a move would create a very rough video. Instead, it moves 2 pixels. Therefore, a game actor will need 8 frames to move to the next adjacent cell. There is an exception to this rule, however. In the reversed situation, Doggie moves 4 pixels at a time so that it will be able to catch the cats.

The step integer variable in the GameActor class indicates the number of pixels the game actor moves.

Note that the possible values of step are 2 and 4. In theory, it could be anything that is divisible by 16 (the maze cell width)—in other words, it could be 1, 2, 4, 8, or 16. The values are not arbitrary. Remember that a game actor needs to turn when it hits the wall. Before it turns, its screen positions will be evaluated. It is only allowed to turn if its position matches the edge of the cell. For example, suppose that the Doggie is moving to the right. After four frames, its screen position will be in perfect line with the next cell's side and if there is no wall on top of it, it will be able to turn upward, should the user instruct Doggie to do so.

NOTE *In the discussion of a game actor's turning, you differentiate those turns into two turns: an L turn and a 180-degree turn. An L turn is turning 90 degrees—in other words, from right to up or right to down. A 180-degree turn is from right to left, left to right, up to down, and down to up. A game actor can do a 180-degree turn anytime, regardless of its screen position.*

On the other hand, if the step has a value of 3, for example, a game actor will never be able to turn until $3 \times 16 = 48$ frames!

Each game actor is moved by a separate thread in the GameActor class:

```
' the thread that moves the actor
  Private thread As thread
```

You instantiate this Thread object in the class's constructor by passing a ThreadStart delegate that receives the address of the Run method:

```
Public Sub New()
  thread = New Thread(New ThreadStart(AddressOf Run))
End Sub
```

The Run method of the GameActor class is as follows:

```
Private Sub Run()
  While True
    SyncLock Me
      If frameReady Then
        Try
          Monitor.Wait(Me)
        Catch e As SynchronizationLockException
        Catch e As ThreadInterruptedException
        End Try
      End If
      Update()
      frameReady = True
      Monitor.Pulse(Me)
    End SyncLock
  End While
End Sub
```

Pay special attention to the Update abstract method. Because it is abstract, when the method is called, the overriding Update method in the child class is executed. In the Dog class, the Update method is as follows:

```
Public Overrides Sub Update()
  If currentState = GameState.Lose Then
    image = images(2, anim)
    anim += 1
    anim = anim Mod 4
    Return
  End If

  If currentState <> GameState.Run Then
    Return
  End If

  If turnDirection = Direction.Invalid Then
    Return
  End If

  Dim ok As Boolean = GameManager.MoveRequest(Me, _
    walkDirection, turnDirection)
  If ok Then
    walkDirection = turnDirection
  Else
    GameManager.MoveRequest(Me, walkDirection, walkDirection)
  End If

  'choose the image.
  image = images(movement, walkDirection)
  movement += 1
  movement = movement Mod 3
End Sub
```

The method basically checks the game's state and assigns to image an appropriate image. It first checks if the game's state is GameState.Lose:

```
If currentState = GameState.Lose Then
    image = images(2, anim)
    anim += 1
    anim = anim Mod 4
    Return
End If
```

If it is, it will display one of the following images in Figure 3-8.

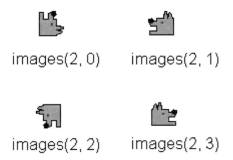

images(2, 0)   images(2, 1)

images(2, 2)   images(2, 3)

Figure 3-8. Animation effect caused by displaying four images in turn

If the game's state is not GameState.Run, or turnDirection is Direction.Invalid, then it returns.

Next, the game actor has the walk direction. However, you need to check if the next move is permitted. You do this by calling the MoveRequest method. This method returns True if the next move is permitted. Otherwise, it returns False.

The following is the GameManager class's MoveRequest, which simply calls the MoveRequest method in the Maze class:

```
Public Shared Function MoveRequest(ByRef actor As GameActor, _
    ByVal old_dir As Integer, ByVal dir As Integer) As Boolean
    Return gameMgr.theMaze.MoveRequest(actor, old_dir, dir)
  End Function
```

The following is the MoveRequest method in the Maze class. This method returns True if the game actor is permitted to move and False otherwise. The method accepts the game actor, the old direction, and the intended direction.

The following is the MoveRequest method of the Maze class:

```
Public Function MoveRequest(ByVal actor As GameActor, _
  ByVal oldDir As Integer, ByVal dir As Integer) As Boolean
  Dim xMove As Integer = 0
  Dim yMove As Integer = 0

  Dim x As Integer = actor.xScreen
  Dim y As Integer = actor.yScreen
  Dim xFood As Integer = x
  Dim yFood As Integer = y

  If (x Mod square <> 0 Or y Mod square <> 0) And _
    Math.Abs(oldDir - dir) Mod 2 <> 0 Then
    Return False
  End If
  Select Case dir
    Case Direction.Up
      y -= actor.step
      yMove = -actor.step
      yFood += yMove
    Case Direction.Left
      x -= actor.step
      xMove = -actor.step
      xFood += xMove
    Case Direction.Down
      y += square + actor.step - 1
      yMove = actor.step
      yFood += yMove
    Case Direction.Right
      x += square + actor.step - 1
      xMove = actor.step
      xFood += xMove
  End Select

  Dim xOff As Integer = x \ square
  Dim yOff As Integer = y \ square

  Dim val As Char = mazeData(yOff).Chars(xOff)

  If val = "a"c Or val = "b"c Or val = "c"c Or val = "d"c Or _
    val = "-"c Or val = "|"c Then
    Return False
  End If
```

```
            If val = "#"c And dir = 2 And (Not actor.dead) Then
              Return False
            End If

            If val = "#"c And dir = 0 And doorClosed Then
              Return False
            End If

            If val = "<"c Then
              actor.SetPos(24, 14)
            Else
              If val = ">"c Then
                actor.SetPos(1, 14)
              Else
                actor.Move(xMove, yMove)
              End If
            End If
            If xFood Mod square <> 0 Or yFood Mod square <> 0 Then
              Return True
            End If

            xOff = xFood \ square
            yOff = yFood \ square

            If actor.GetType().ToString().EndsWith("Doggie") And _
              (mazeData(yOff).Chars(xOff) = "*"c Or _
              mazeData(yOff).Chars(xOff) = "$") Then

              food -= 1
              score += 1
              If val = "$"c Then
                reverse = True
                Cat.scared = True
                actor.step = 4
                doorClosed = True
                timer.Interval = 10000
                timer.Start()
              End If

              mazeData(yOff) = mazeData(yOff).Remove(xOff, 1)
              mazeData(yOff) = mazeData(yOff).Insert(xOff, " ")
            End If

            Return True
          End Function
```

The `MoveRequest` method starts by the following declaration:

```
Dim xMove As Integer = 0
Dim yMove As Integer = 0

Dim x As Integer = actor.xScreen
Dim y As Integer = actor.yScreen
Dim xFood As Integer = x
Dim yFood As Integer = y
```

For now, you are interested in x and y, which represent the screen coordinate of the actor. Recall that an actor can only make an L turn if its screen position is on a cell's corner. Therefore, you check the screen position with the following:

```
If (x Mod square <> 0 Or y Mod square <> 0) And _
  Math.Abs(oldDir - dir) Mod 2 <> 0 Then
  Return False
End If
```

If both x or y are not evenly divisible by square (16 pixels), then the screen position does not permit the actor to make an L turn. You then check if the actor is trying to make an L turn or a 180-degree turn or is just trying to move straight.

If you look at the `Direction` enumeration, you will notice that the difference in value of no turn and a 180-degree turn is either 0 or 2. Therefore, if the remainder of (oldDir - dir) / 2 is not 0, then the actor is trying to make an L turn.

If the game actor is making an L turn but the position is not good for the game actor to do so, the `MoveRequest` method returns `False` straight away.

Otherwise, it flows to the next lines:

```
Select Case dir
  Case Direction.Up
    y -= actor.step
    yMove = -actor.step
    yFood += yMove
  Case Direction.Left
    x -= actor.step
    xMove = -actor.step
    xFood += xMove
  Case Direction.Down
    y += square + actor.step - 1
    yMove = actor.step
    yFood += yMove
  Case Direction.Right
```

```
        x += square + actor.step - 1
        xMove = actor.step
        xFood += xMove
End Select
```

The code in the Select blocks updates the x or y according to the value of step. However, you now need to check if the destination of the next move is a wall:

```
Dim xOff As Integer = x \ square
Dim yOff As Integer = y \ square

Dim val As Char = mazeData(yOff).Chars(xOff)

If val = "a"c Or val = "b"c Or val = "c"c Or val = "d"c Or _
  val = "-"c Or val = "|"c Then
  Return False
End If

If val = "#"c And dir = 2 And (Not actor.dead) Then
  Return False
End If

If val = "#"c And dir = 0 And doorClosed Then
  Return False
End If

If val = "<"c Then
  actor.SetPos(24, 14)
Else
  If val = ">"c Then
    actor.SetPos(1, 14)
  Else
    actor.Move(xMove, yMove)
  End If
End If
If xFood Mod square <> 0 Or yFood Mod square <> 0 Then
  Return True
End If

xOff = xFood \ square
yOff = yFood \ square
```

```
If actor.GetType().ToString().EndsWith("Doggie") And _
   (mazeData(yOff).Chars(xOff) = "*"c Or _
   mazeData(yOff).Chars(xOff) = "$") Then

    food -= 1
    score += 1
    If val = "$"c Then
       reverse = True
       actor.step = 4
       doorClosed = True
       timer.Interval = 10000
       timer.Start()
    End If

    mazeData(yOff) = mazeData(yOff).Remove(xOff, 1)
    mazeData(yOff) = mazeData(yOff).Insert(xOff, " ")
  End If

  Return True
End Function
```

Moving the Cats

The movement of the cats is the most difficult part of the program logic. Here, some artificial intelligence determines the next position of each cat.

First of all, recall that the cats are there to catch Doggie and kill it. Therefore, the cat needs to know Doggie's position in the maze. This is not hard because the Cat class's constructor receives the instance of the Dog class. In other words, each of the four Cat objects has a reference to the instance of the Dog class. The Dog class is a child class of the GameActor class, and the GameActor class has the xScreen and yScreen variables that denote the position of the game actor in the maze. Because both xScreen and yScreen are public, once you get a reference of a game actor, you can access its xScreen and yScreen values. Therefore, because the cats have a reference to the Dog object, they can easily know where Doggie is in the maze.

However, if all the four cats start to chase Doggie because they leave the cat house, it would be hard for the player to win, and the game would be frustratingly difficult. To make the game more exciting, each cat has its own time to attack and time where it just wanders around randomly. In the Cat class, there is a Boolean variable named attack that indicates whether the cat is in the attack state. If the value of attack in a cat is True, the cat will try to approach Doggie. If it is False, the cat moves randomly. You toggle the value of attack by a server-based timer named timer. The timer variable in the Cat class is protected so it can be accessed by the child classes.

In the Cat class's constructor, the server-based timer's Elapsed event is wired to the method SwapAttack and its AutoReset property is set to True, causing the Elapsed event to be raised repeatedly:

```
timer = New System.Timers.Timer()
AddHandler timer.Elapsed, AddressOf SwapAttack
timer.AutoReset = True
```

The frequency with which the Elapsed event triggers is determined by the value of the Interval property of the System.Timers.Timer class and is set in the child classes (BlueCat, GreenCat, RedCat, and BlackCat). The value of the Interval property of this timer is different in each instance of the Cat subclass to make each cat behave differently.

The Interval property is assigned value in the Init method of each cat child class. For example, this is the Init method of the BlueCat class:

```
Public Overrides Sub Init()
  SetPos(11, 15)
  walkDirection = Direction.Left
  image = normalImages(walkdirection, state)
  Timer.Interval = 25000
  Timer.Start()
  attack = False
End Sub
```

And this is the Init method of the GreenCat class:

```
Public Overrides Sub Init()
  SetPos(14, 15)
  walkdirection = Direction.Right
  image = normalimages(walkdirection, state)
  Timer.Interval = 8000
  Timer.Start()
  attack = False
End Sub
```

The `Init` method of the RedCat class is as follows:

```
Public Overrides Sub Init()
  SetPos(12, 13)
  walkdirection = Direction.Up
  image = normalimages(walkdirection, state)
  Timer.Interval = 20000
  Timer.Start()
  attack = True
End Sub
```

And the following is the `Init` method of the BlackCat class:

```
Public Overrides Sub Init()
  SetPos(14, 13)
  walkdirection = Direction.Down
  image = normalimages(walkdirection, state)
  Timer.Interval = 2000
  Timer.Start()
  attack = True
End Sub
```

You call the `Init` method from the `InitActor` method of the Maze class. From the `Init` method of each subclass of the Cat class, you will notice the following:

- The `SetPos` method is called and given different arguments in each `Init` method of the Cat subclass. The `SetPos` method sets the initial position of the cat in the cat house. It inherits from the GameActor class and is defined as follows:

  ```
  Public Sub SetPos(ByVal x As Integer, ByVal y As Integer)
    xScreen = x * Maze.square
    yScreen = y * Maze.square
  End Sub
  ```

- The `walkDirection` variable in each cat is assigned a different value so that each cat will have a different walk direction from each other.

- The `Interval` property of the Timer class in each cat is assigned a different value.

- The attack Boolean in the BlueCat and the GreenCat classes is set to False. This Boolean is set to True in the RedCat and BlackCat classes. Therefore, the red and black cats are programmed to attack when the game starts, before the SwapAttack method toggles it. The blue cat and the green cat are not in the attack state initially, until the SwapAttack method toggles it.

The event handler SwapAttack is simple, its function being to toggle attack. It only consists of the following code:

```
Public Sub SwapAttack(ByVal o As Object, ByVal e As ElapsedEventArgs)
  attack = Not attack
End Sub
```

There is also another Boolean in the Cat class that determines the next position of each individual cat instance: scared. This Boolean is a shared variable; therefore, every cat instance will have the same scared value. This Boolean is public so it can be set from outside the class. It is set to True when Doggie has just eaten a bone and the situation is reversed (so, the cats are scared). It is set back to False when the "reverse" situation has expired.

You set the scared Boolean to True in the MoveRequest method of the Maze class, in the following If block:

```
If actor.GetType().ToString().EndsWith("Doggie") And _
  (mazeData(yOff).Chars(xOff) = "*"c Or _
  mazeData(yOff).Chars(xOff) = "$") Then
      food -= 1
  score += 1
  If val = "$"c Then
    reverse = True
    Cat.scared = True
    actor.step = 4
    doorClosed = True
    timer.Interval = 10000
    timer.Start()
  End If
End If
```

You set the scared Boolean to False in the ReverseExpired method of the Maze class:

```
Public Sub ReverseExpired(ByVal o As Object, ByVal e As ElapsedEventArgs)
  doorClosed = False
  reverse = False
  pac.step = 2
  Cat.scared = False
End Sub
```

Note that in both methods (MoveRequest and ReverseExpired), the scared Boolean needs only to be set once because it is a shared field.

The last Boolean that affects how a cat moves is dead. A cat dies if it collides with Doggie when the situation is reversed. When it is dead, the cat changes color and moves back to the cat house.

Now let's see how the positions of the four cats are updated.

Updating the Cat's Position

The Update method in the Cat class determines the next position of a cat and the next image that will be used to represent the cat in the next frame. If you understand how the Update method in the Dog class works, you should not find it hard to understand how the similar method in the Cat class works.

First of all, this is the Update method in the Cat class:

```
Public Overrides Sub Update()
  If currentState <> GameState.Run Then
    Return
  End If
  If delay = 1 Then
    state += 1
    state = state Mod 2
  End If
  delay += 1
  delay = delay Mod 3

  If dead Then
    image = deadCat(walkDirection)
    MoveDeadCat()
  Else
    If scared Then
      image = scaredImages(state)
    Else
      image = normalImages(normalImageSequence)
      normalImageSequence = (normalImageSequence + 1) Mod 4

    End If
    MoveCat()
  End If

End Sub
```

First, it only makes sense to worry about a cat position if the game's state is GameState.Running. If this is not the case, return from the method:

```
If currentState <> GameState.Run Then
  Return
End If
```

The next few lines deal with the animation of the cat image. Each state and delay determines the selection of image files:

```
If delay = 1 Then
    state += 1
    state = state Mod 2
End If
delay += 1
delay = delay Mod 3
```

Next, this is where the cat's position is actually determined:

```
If dead Then
  image = deadCat(walkDirection)
  MoveDeadCat()
Else
  If scared Then
    image = scaredImages(state)
  Else
    image = normalImages(normalImageSequence)
    normalImageSequence = (normalImageSequence + 1) Mod 4

  End If
  MoveCat()
```

If the cat is dead, the image is assigned an image of a dead cat. In this application, I only use one image to represent a dead cat. However, the program itself animates a dead cat by using four different images of dead cats.

Figure 3-9 shows a dead cat.

Figure 3-9. A dead cat

It then calls the MoveEye method.

If the cat is not dead, the image of the cat will depend on whether the shared scared Boolean is True or False. If the value of scared is True, the image will be one of the two images in Figure 3-10.

Figure 3-10. Two different images of scared looks

If the scared Boolean value is False, the image will be one of the four images in Figure 3-11.

Figure 3-11. Four different images of normal looks

Either way, the Update method calls the MoveCat method.

Now, let's look at the MoveCat method and the MoveDeadCat method. However, before doing that, you will look at the two methods called from both the MoveCat and the MoveDeadCat methods: the RandomWalk and WalkToTarget methods.

The RandomWalk Method

The RandomWalk method creates an array of integers dirs. dirs contains four elements, and each of the elements is populated with a random number between 0 and 3 inclusive. Each of the elements will have a different value. The RandomWalk method then calls the Walk method passing dirs.

The RandomWalk method is as follows:

```
Public Sub RandomWalk()
  Dim rand As Integer = random.Next(4)
  Dim dirs(4) As Integer
  dirs(0) = rand
  rand = random.Next(1)
  If rand = 0 Then
    dirs(1) = (dirs(0) + 1) Mod 4
    dirs(2) = (dirs(1) + 1) Mod 4
    dirs(3) = (dirs(2) + 1) Mod 4
  Else
    dirs(1) = ((dirs(0) - 1) + 4) Mod 4
    dirs(2) = ((dirs(1) - 1) + 4) Mod 4
    dirs(3) = ((dirs(2) - 1) + 4) Mod 4
  End If
  Walk(dirs)
End Sub
```

And here is the Walk method:

```
Public Sub Walk(ByRef dirs() As Integer)
    'this sub sets the walkDirection value
  Dim ok As Boolean
  If dirs(0) <> ((walkDirection - 2) + 4) Mod 4 Then
    ok = GameManager.MoveRequest(Me, walkDirection, dirs(0))
    If ok Then
      walkDirection = dirs(0)
      Return
    End If
  End If
  If dirs(1) <> ((walkDirection - 2) + 4) Mod 4 Then
    ok = GameManager.MoveRequest(Me, walkDirection, dirs(1))
    If ok Then
      walkDirection = dirs(1)
      Return
    End If
  End If
```

```
  If dirs(2) <> ((walkDirection - 2) + 4) Mod 4 Then
    ok = GameManager.MoveRequest(Me, walkDirection, dirs(2))
    If ok Then
      walkDirection = dirs(2)
      Return
    End If
  End If
  If dirs(3) <> ((walkDirection - 2) + 4) Mod 4 Then
    ok = GameManager.MoveRequest(Me, walkDirection, dirs(3))
    If ok Then
      walkDirection = dirs(3)
      Return
    End If
  End If
End Sub
```

The aim of calling the `Walk` method is to change the value of `walkDirection`. The `walkDirection` variable can have one of the following members of the `Direction` enumeration: `Up`, `Down`, `Left`, and `Right`.

In changing the value of `walkDirection`, the `Walk` method avoids making the game actor make a 180-degree turn. Remember that the value of `Direction.Up`, `Direction.Down`, `Direction.Left`, and `Direction.Right` are 0, 2, 1, and 3 respectively? A 180-degree turn happens if the value of `walkDirection` changes from `Direction.Down` to `Direction.Up`, from `Direction.Up` to `Direction.Down`, from `Direction.Left` to `Direction.Right`, or from `Direction.Right` to `Direction.Left`.

Converting the members of the `Direction` enumeration to integers, you can say that a 180-degree turn happens if `walkDirection` - 2 is either 2 or –2. For example, if the current `walkDirection` value is `Direction.Up` (integer 0) and the next value is `Direction.Down` (integer 2), then `Direction.Up` - `Direction.Down` = 0 – 2 = –2. However, if the current `walkDirection` value is `Direction.Up` and the next value is `Direction.Left`, it is not a 180-degree turn because `Direction.Up` - `Direction.Left` = 0 – 1 = –1.

Therefore, the following line of the `Walk` method

```
If dirs(0) <> ((walkDirection - 2) + 4) Mod 4 Then
```

translates into the following: "If changing the current value of `walkDirection` with the content of the first element in `dirs` does not make the game actor have a 180-degree turn, then…".

If the If statement is satisfied, it calls the MoveRequest method of the GameManager class to find out if such a turn is permitted. If it is, then change the value of walkDirection with dirs(0) and return:

```
ok = GameManager.MoveRequest(Me, walkDirection, dirs(0))
If ok Then
  walkDirection = dirs(0)
  Return
End If
```

If the If statement is not satisfied, the Walk method will try changing the current value of walkDirection with the next element of the dirs array.

The WalkToTarget Method

The WalkToTarget method causes the cat to move to the specified target. The target could be Doggie or the cat house:

```
Public Sub WalkToTarget(ByVal tx As Integer, ByVal ty As Integer)
  Dim dirs(4) As Integer
  RequestDirection(dirs, tx, ty)
  Walk(dirs)
End Sub
```

The WalkToTarget method accepts the screen coordinate of the target. If the target is Doggie, tx will be Dog.xScreen and ty will be Dog.yScreen.

The WalkToTarget method calls the RequestDirection that will populate an array of integers (dirs) with possible values of turn direction. The populated dirs will then be passed to the Walk method for a possible change of the value of walkDirection.

The MoveCat Method

If you understand the Walk and the WalkToTarget methods, understanding the MoveCat method is not difficult. This method changes the screen position of the cat in the next frame. When moving, the cats use a map as defined by the map array of string in the Maze class.

The map array of string is initialized with the following strings:

```
Private map() As String = { _
    "+-----------++-----------+", _
    "|    J      ||     J     |", _
    "| a-b a---b || a---b a-b |", _
    "| | | |  | || |  | | | |", _
    "| d-c d---c dc d---c d-c |", _
    "|J   J  J  J J  J  J   J|", _
    "| a-b ab a------b ab a-b |", _
    "| d-c || d--ba--c || d-c |", _
    "|   J||   ||   ||J   |", _
    "d---b |d--b || a--c| a---c", _
    "      | |a--c dc d--b| |     ", _
    "      | ||   JJJJ   || |     ", _
    "      | || a--##--b || |     ", _
    "----c dc |%%%%%| dc d----", _
    "      J  J|%%%%%|J  J     ", _
    "----b ab |%%%%%| ab a----", _
    "      | || d------c || |     ", _
    "      | ||J        J|| |     ", _
    "      | || a------b || |     ", _
    "a---c dc d--ba--c dc d---b", _
    "|    J  J  ||  J  J    |", _
    "| a-b a---b || a---b a-b |", _
    "| db| d---c dc d---c |ac |", _
    "| ||J  J  J  J  J  J|| |", _
    "db || ab a------b ab || ac", _
    "ac dc || d--ba--c || dc db", _
    "| J   ||    ||    ||   J |", _
    "| a---cd--b || a--cd---b |", _
    "| d-------c dc d-------c |", _
    "|          J  J          |", _
    "d----------------------c" _
}
```

This is similar to the maze array of Strings. Note that the percent (%) sign represents a block inside the cat house and J denotes a junction.

NOTE *A junction is a cell from which a game actor can move in three or four directions. The cells in the four corners allow a game actor to move in only two directions and therefore are not junctions.*

You pass the map array of strings to the Cat class by calling the Cat class's SetMap method:

```
Public Sub SetMap(ByVal m() As String)
  map = m
End Sub
```

First, the MoveCat method tries to detect if the cat is in a cell inside the cat house:

```
Public Sub MoveCat()
  Dim y As Integer = yScreen \ Maze.square
  If map(y).Chars(xScreen \ Maze.square) = "%"c And _
    yScreen Mod Maze.square = 0 And xScreen Mod Maze.square = 0 Then
    ' cat in cat house
    If (scared) Then
      RandomWalk()
    Else
      'walk to the cat house door (to get out)
      WalkToTarget(12 * Maze.square, 11 * Maze.square)
    End If
  ElseIf map(y).Chars(xScreen \ Maze.square) = "J"c Then
    If (scared) Then
      RandomWalk()
    ElseIf (attack) Then
      WalkToTarget(pac.xScreen, pac.yScreen)
    Else
      RandomWalk()
    End If
  Else
    If (GameManager.MoveRequest(Me, walkDirection, walkDirection)) Then
      Return
    End If

    If (GameManager.MoveRequest(Me, walkDirection, _
      (walkDirection + 1) Mod 4)) Then
      ' make an L-turn is okay
      walkDirection = (walkDirection + 1) Mod 4
      Return
```

```
     End If
     If (GameManager.MoveRequest(Me, walkDirection, _
       (walkDirection + 3) Mod 4)) Then
       ' make an L-turn is okay
     walkDirection = (walkDirection + 3) Mod 4
       Return
     End If
   End If
 End Sub
End Sub
```

The MoveDeadCat Method

The MoveDeadCat method is called from the Update method of the Cat class when the cat is dead—in other words, when the dead field of the cat object is True. This method is defined as follows:

```
Sub MoveDeadCat()
  If map(yScreen \ Maze.square).Chars(xScreen \ Maze.square) = "%"c _
    And (yScreen Mod Maze.square = 0) _
    And (xScreen Mod Maze.square = 0) Then
    'the cat is in the cat house
    dead = False
    RandomWalk()
  ElseIf map(yScreen \ Maze.square). _
    Chars(CInt(xScreen \ Maze.square)) = "J" Then
    WalkToTarget(12 * Maze.square, 13 * Maze.square)
  Else
    If GameManager.MoveRequest(Me, walkDirection, walkDirection) Then
      Return
    End If
    If GameManager.MoveRequest(Me, walkDirection, _
      (walkDirection + 1) Mod 4) Then
      walkDirection = (walkDirection + 1) Mod 4
      Return
    End If
    If GameManager.MoveRequest(Me, walkDirection, _
      (walkDirection + 3) Mod 4) Then
      walkDirection = (walkDirection + 3) Mod 4
      Return
    End If
  End If
End Sub
```

First the method checks whether the cat is in the cat house. If it is, change its dead field value to `False`. By changing this, the next frame will display the cat in a normal appearance, not as a pair of eyes. Then, just do a random walk until the reverse situation is back to normal:

```
If map(yScreen \ Maze.square).Chars(xScreen \ Maze.square) = "%"c _
  And (yScreen Mod Maze.square = 0) _
  And (xScreen Mod Maze.square = 0) Then
  'the cat is in the cat house
  dead = False
  RandomWalk()
```

If the cat is not in the cat house, check if it is on a junction. If it is, call the `WalkToTarget` method, passing the location of the cat house for the arguments. A *junction* is a cell that allows the cat to make an L turn. In other words, if a cat is in a *junction*, it can turn in three or four directions. The cells at the corner only allow the cat to turn 90 degrees, and they are not junctions:

```
ElseIf map(yScreen \ Maze.square). _
  Chars(CInt(xScreen \ Maze.square)) = "J" Then
  WalkToTarget(12 * Maze.square, 13 * Maze.square)
```

If the cat is not in the cat house and not in a junction, it tries to walk straight:

```
If GameManager.MoveRequest(Me, walkDirection, walkDirection) Then
  Return
End If
```

If it cannot walk straight, that is when it hits the wall (at a cell in the corner); it will attempt to make an L turn:

```
If GameManager.MoveRequest(Me, walkDirection, _
  (walkDirection + 1) Mod 4) Then
  walkDirection = (walkDirection + 1) Mod 4
  Return
End If
```

If it still cannot walk (because it tries to make the wrong L turn), it will attempt another L turn in another direction:

```
If GameManager.MoveRequest(Me, walkDirection, _
  (walkDirection + 3) Mod 4) Then
  walkDirection = (walkDirection + 3) Mod 4
  Return
End If
```

NOTE *You can find the code listings in the project's directory.*

Compiling and Running the Application

All source files can be found in the Project directory. To compile the application, run the build.bat file.

The result will be a `DoggieGame.exe` file.

To run the program, type `DoggieGame` from the command prompt or double-click the icon in Windows Explorer. Note that the `images` folder containing all the image files must reside in the same directory as the `DoggieGame.exe` file.

Summary

In this chapter you have learned how to create a game. As an introduction, you have also learned how to use threads in a multithreaded application and timers. You first saw a news ticker application and later a Pac-Man clone called Doggie.

CHAPTER 4

Creating a UML Class Diagram Editor

THIS CHAPTER PRESENTS a drawing application that can create a Unified Modeling Language (UML) class diagram, save it to a disk file, and then retrieve it. The main goal of this project is to illustrate the .NET Framework's Application Programming Interface (API), which enables the use of graphics and text on the video display and the printer. This API is called *Graphics Device Interface Plus (GDI+)*. GDI+ is an improvement on the GDI, the underlying technology of Windows graphics used by programmers prior to the .NET Framework era. The project is a pure drawing application. For example, do not expect to generate code once you finish your class diagram.

Overview of the Chapter

Like in other projects in this book, you need to understand a number of under-lying technologies before developing this application. Each of these technologies gets its own section. Afterward, you will develop the project. These are the main sections:

- **"Drawing in the .NET Framework"**: This section describes various members of the System.Drawing namespace used for drawing in the .NET Framework.

- **"Creating a Simple Drawing Application"**: This section presents an appli-cation that lets the user to draw simple shapes. This section demonstrates the use of the classes in the System.Drawing namespace.

- **"Understanding Object Serialization for Persisting the Graphics Objects"**: This section explains how to persist graphics objects such as lines and rec-tangles into the file system to be retrieved later when the user needs them.

- **"Understanding the Memento Design Pattern"**: This section explains how you can use the Memento pattern to help with object serialization.

- **"Exploring the UML Class Diagram"**: This section introduces the UML class diagram.

- **"Implementing the Project"**: This section explains how the project works and describes each class in detail.

Drawing in the .NET Framework

There are two types of drawing applications: raster based and vector based. *Raster-based* drawing applications work on bitmap images. Examples of these include the Microsoft Paint application that you can find in every computer with the Windows operating system. Shapes you draw in a raster-based drawing application blend into the drawing surface. Once drawn, the shape becomes part of the image. You cannot manipulate it as an object. *Vector-based* drawing applications, on the other hand, treat each shape drawn as an object. This means, once drawn, a shape can still be manipulated. You can resize it, change its color, fill it with a different color, and so on. Corel Draw is a popular example of a vector-based drawing application.

As mentioned previously, the main technology for working with graphics and text in the .NET Framework is GDI+. The beauty of GDI+ is that it is device independent. You use the same function to draw a particular shape without having to be concerned about the details of the device hardware to which you are drawing. All you need to do is call the methods in the classes that encapsulate GDI+ functionality.

GDI+ provides three categories of services:

- Two-dimensional (2D) vector graphics

- Imaging

- Typography

The 2D vector graphics service deals with drawing shapes using points on a coordinate system. The shapes can be as primitive as a line (specified by two points on a coordinate system) and a rectangle (defined by four points). However, they can also be as complex as polygon splines and Bézier splines.

You use the imaging service to manipulate bitmap images, and you use the typography service to manipulate text.

NOTE *The project in this chapter only uses the 2D vector graphics service.*

The three GDI+ services are encapsulated in various classes in the .NET Framework class library. You can use a number of namespaces for working with graphics and text. The main one is the System.Drawing namespace. The other namespaces are System.Drawing.Design, System.Drawing.Drawing2D, System.Drawing.Imaging, System.Drawing.Printing, and System.Drawing.Text. The project uses a few classes and structures in the System.Drawing and the System.Drawing.Drawing2D namespaces. Therefore, you will look at these classes and structures in the following subsections.

The System.Drawing.Point Structure

A Point object represents a coordinate in a 2D plane. The easiest way to construct a Point is by passing two integers as the abscissa and the ordinate parts (the x and y parts) of the coordinate, such as the following:

```
Dim point As Point = New Point(14, 200)
```

Point is frequently used not only when drawing a shape but also when writing a form-based application. For example, to adjust the position of a Button control on a form, you can assign a Point object to the button's Location property to indicate the position of the top-left corner of the button on the form. As an example, the following code places the button's top-left corner at coordinate (100, 30) in a form that contains the button—in other words, 100 pixels from the left edge of the form and 30 pixels from the upper edge of the form's client area:

```
button.Location = New Point(100, 30)
```

The Point structure has the X and Y properties from which you can obtain the abscissa and ordinate of the coordinate that a Point object represents. Also, IsEmpty is a read-only property that returns True only when both the X and Y properties of a Point object have the value of zero. (Note, though, that this can be misleading; (0, 0) can represent a valid coordinate for a Point object.)

Another way of constructing a Point is by passing an Integer. The low-order 16 bits of the integer will become the value of the Point object's abscissa, and the high-order 16 bits the value of the Point object's ordinate.

If you need more precision in your `Point` object, you can use the `PointF` structure. Instead of representing a coordinate with a pair of integers, `PointF` takes `Singles` as the x and y parts of a coordinate. `PointF` has only a single constructor with the following signature:

```
Public Sub New ( ByVal x as Single, ByVal y as Single )
```

The System.Drawing.Size Structure

The `Size` structure represents the width and height of a rectangular area. The easiest way to construct a `Size` object is by passing two integers as its width and height, like in the following code:

```
Dim size As Size = New Size(10, 30)
```

This `Size` object has a width of 10 pixels and a height of 30 pixels. In a form-based Windows application, the `Size` structure often sets or changes the size of a control. The `Control` class has the `Size` property to which you can assign a `Size` object. For instance, the following code sets the size of a button so that it will be 80-pixels wide and 30-pixels tall:

```
button1.Size = New Size(80, 30)
```

In addition, you can also construct a `Size` object by passing a `Point` object, like in the following code:

```
Dim point As Point = New Point(50, 30)
Dim size As Size = New Size(point)
```

In this case, the width and height of the resulting `Size` object will have the value of X and Y properties of the `Point` object, respectively.

You can obtain the width and height values of a `Size` object by retrieving the value of its `Width` and `Height` properties. Another property, `IsEmpty`, is a read-only property that returns `True` only if both the `Width` and `Height` properties have the value of zero.

If you need more precision, you can use the `System.Drawing.SizeF` structure. `SizeF` is similar to `Size` except that `Singles` represents its width and height.

The `System.Drawing.Rectangle` Structure

The `Rectangle` structure represents a rectangle. You can use an instance of this structure for multiple purposes. For example, to draw a rectangle, you can pass a `Rectangle` object to the `DrawRectangle` method of the `Graphics` object (discussed in "The System.Drawing.Graphics Class" section).

An instance of the `Rectangle` structure stores the location of its top-left coordinate and its size. You can construct an instance of this structure by passing a `Point` and a `Size` of four integers, using the following two constructors of the `Rectangle` structure:

```
Public Sub New( ByVal location As Point, ByVal size As Size)
Public Sub New( _
  ByVal x As Integer, _
  ByVal y As Integer, _
  ByVal width As Integer, _
  ByVal height As Integer _
)
```

In this example, `location` in the first constructor, and `x` and `y` in the second constructor denote the top-left coordinate of the `Rectangle`.

The `System.Drawing.Color` Structure

The `Color` structure represents a color that you can use to draw shapes or to assign to the `BackColor` or `ForeColor` properties of a control. To construct a `Color` object, you do not use any constructor because this structure does not have one. Instead, the structure includes a large number of static (shared) properties that represent various colors. For example, the `Brown` property represents a brown `Color` object.

The following code shows how to use the `Brown` property of the `Color` structure to assign a brown color to the `BackColor` property of a `Button` control:

```
Dim myColor As Color = Color.Brown
button1.BackColor = myColor
```

In addition to some common colors such as green, blue, yellow, red, white, and black, you can choose more exotic colors such as azure, beige, coral, or powder blue. There are more than 140 properties representing different colors!

If that is not enough, you can compose a custom color by passing the R, G, and B components of an RGB color to the FromArgb static method. Again, because this method is static, you can use it without having a Color object. As an example, the following code constructs a Color object whose R, G, and B components are all 240:

```
Dim myColor As Color = Color.FromArgb(240, 240, 240)
```

Note that even though the arguments are all integers, the values passed must be in the range of 0 and 255; this will result in a 32-bit color, in which the first eight bits are not used.

In fact, you can also specify all the 32 bits of a Color object through another overload of the FromArgb method that accepts four integers:

```
Overloads Public Shared Function FromArgb( _
  ByVal alpha As Integer, _
  ByVal red As Integer, _
  ByVal green As Integer, _
  ByVal blue As Integer _
)
```

You can retrieve the individual alpha, red, green, and blue components of a Color object by calling its ToArgb method, which returns an Integer representing all the four components (alpha, red, green, and blue). This Integer indicates the Color object's color values as shown in Table 4-1.

Table 4-1. The Color *Object's Color Values*

BITS	VALUE
0–7	Blue
8–15	Green
16–23	Red
24–31	Alpha

Another way of constructing a Color object is by using the Color structure's FromName method. For example, the following code constructs a blue color by passing the string "blue" to the FromName method:

```
Dim myColor As Color = Color.FromName("blue")
```

The System.Drawing.Pen Class

The Pen class represents a pen that you can use for drawing a shape or writing text. A Pen object can have a color, a width, a brush, and other properties. The easiest way to construct a Pen is by passing a Color object to one of the Pen class's constructors. For instance, the following code creates a yellow pen:

```
Dim pen As Pen = New Pen(Color.Yellow)
```

A Pen object constructed using this code has a default width of 1 and a default brush. Another constructor lets you specify a width as well as a color. For example, the following Pen object is yellow with a width of 1.8:

```
Dim pen As Pen = New Pen(Color.Yellow, 1.8)
```

In addition, you can pass a Brush object, or a Brush object and a width, using two other constructors of the Pen class:

```
Public Sub New( ByVal brush as Brush )
Public Sub New( ByVal brush as Brush, ByVal width As Single )
```

NOTE *For information on how to construct a* Brush *object, see "The System.Drawing.Brush Class" section.*

The Pen class also provides some advanced properties to customize your Pen object. For example, you can create a Pen that draws a dashed line by specifying a value for the DashStyle property, as shown in the following code:

```
pen.DashStyle = Drawing.Drawing2D.DashStyle.DashDot
```

The System.Drawing namespace also provides an easy way to construct a Pen object with a width of 1: by using the Pens class. The Pens class has more than 100 properties whose names indicate a predefined color. From these properties you can get a Pen object in the specified color. For instance, the Green property of the Pens class returns a green Pen object with a width of 1. The Pens class's Red property gives you a red pen.

The System.Drawing.Brush Class

You use a Pen object to draw the lines of a shape or to write text on it. To fill the interior of a shape you draw, you use a brush, which in the .NET Framework class library is represented by the System.Drawing.Brush class and its five derived classes. The Brush class itself is an abstract class; therefore, you cannot directly instantiate it. You can, however, instantiate one of its child classes: HatchBrush, LinearGradientBrush, PathGradientBrush, SolidBrush, and TextureBrush. HatchBrush represents a hatch-styled rectangular brush, LinearGradientBrush represents a brush that paints with a linear gradient, PathGradientBrush fills a GraphicPath with a gradient, SolidBrush represents a brush that fills an area evenly, and TextureBrush represents a brush with a texture image to fill an area. For example, the following code draws a filled rectangle on a form using a SolidBrush:

```
' get the Graphics of a form
Dim g As Graphics = form.CreateGraphics()
Dim solidBrush As SolidBrush = New SolidBrush(Color.Blue)
g.FillRectangle(solidBrush, 10, 20, 100, 100)
```

The System.Drawing.Brushes class provides an easy way of obtaining a Brush object the same way the Pens class provides Pen objects in a specified color. For example, the Red property of the Brushes class returns a red Brush object. The other properties of a Brush object obtained from one of the properties of the Brushes class are system-defined.

The System.Drawing.Graphics Class

The System.Drawing.Graphics class represents a rectangular area on which various shapes can be drawn and text can be written. The constructor of this class is private, so there is no way you can instantiate a Graphics class using the New keyword. However, you can obtain a Graphics object from a form or another control. These Graphics objects represent the drawing surface of that control. Once you obtain a Graphics object, you can use its various methods to draw many different shapes on it. For example, if you want to draw on a form, you first need to obtain the Graphics object of that form and then call the methods of the Graphics object. The System.Windows.Forms.Control class provides the CreateGraphics method, which returns a Graphics object representing the drawing surface of that control.

The methods of the `Graphics` class often require you to pass a `Pen` or a `Brush` object to create a shape. As one example, you can use the `DrawLine` method of the `Graphics` class to draw a line. One of its overloads has the following signature:

```
Overloads Public Sub DrawLine( _
  ByVal pen As Pen, _
  ByVal x1 As Integer, _
  ByVal y1 As Integer, _
  ByVal x2 As Integer, _
  ByVal y2 As Integer _
)
```

This overload accepts a `Pen` object and four integers representing the starting coordinate (x1, y1) and the end coordinate (x2, y2) of the line. For example, the following code obtains the `Graphics` object of a form, creates a `Pen` object, and passes the `Pen` object to the `DrawLine` method to draw a line on the form:

```
Dim g As Graphics = Me.CreateGraphics()
Dim pen As Pen = New Pen(Color.Yellow, 1.9)
' set the pen's DashStyle to dash - dot
pen.DashStyle = Drawing.Drawing2D.DashStyle.DashDot
g.DrawLine(pen, 0, 0, 100, 200)
```

The code draws the line from the coordinate (0, 0) to the coordinate (100, 200). Figure 4-1 shows a number of shapes you can draw using the methods of the `Graphics` class.

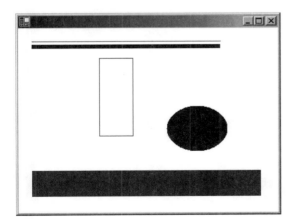

Figure 4-1. Drawing simple shapes

The Graphics Class's Methods

The following are some other methods of the Graphics class.

DrawLines

The DrawLines method draws lines that connect a series of points in an array, which is passed as the second parameter to the method. The first parameter is a Pen object. For example, the following code declares and instantiates an array of four points and draws lines connecting those points on a form:

```
Dim points(4) As Point
points(0) = New Point(0, 0)
points(1) = New Point(0, 120)
points(2) = New Point(20, 120)
points(3) = New Point(20, 0)

Dim g As Graphics = Me.CreateGraphics()
Dim pen As Pen = New Pen(Color.Yellow, 1.9)
g.DrawLines(pen, points)
```

DrawRectangle

The DrawRectangle method draws a rectangle. For example, the following code draws a rectangle on a form by passing a Pen object and four integers. The first two integers represent the coordinate of the top-left corner of the rectangle, the third coordinate is the width of the rectangle, and the last integer the height of the rectangle:

```
Dim g As Graphics = Me.CreateGraphics
Dim pen As Pen = New Pen(Color.Aquamarine, 1.9)
g.DrawRectangle(pen, 10, 10, 100, 20)
```

The top-left corner of the rectangle is at coordinate (10, 10), and it has a width of 100 pixels and a height of 20 pixels.

DrawEllipse

The DrawEllipse method draws an ellipse within an imaginary rectangle. For example, the following code draws an ellipse having a width of 100 pixels and a height of 20. The top-left corner of the imaginary rectangle is at coordinate (10, 10):

```
Dim g As Graphics = Me.CreateGraphics()
Dim pen As Pen = New Pen(Color.Bisque, 1.9)
g.DrawEllipse(pen, 10, 10, 100, 20)
```

FillRectangle

The FillRectangle method draws a filled rectangle. For example, the following code draws a filled rectangle on a form by passing a SolidBrush object and four integers. The first two integers represent the coordinate of the top-left corner of the rectangle. The rectangle has a width of 100 pixels and a height of 30 pixels:

```
Dim g As Graphics = Me.CreateGraphics()
Dim solidBrush As SolidBrush = New SolidBrush(Color.DarkCyan)
g.FillRectangle(solidBrush, 10, 10, 100, 30)
```

FillEllipse

The FillEllipse method draws a filled ellipse. This method is similar to DrawEllipse, but the resulting ellipse is filled. Instead of passing a Pen object, the method requires a Brush object. The following code draws a filled ellipse on a form:

```
Dim g As Graphics = Me.CreateGraphics()
Dim solidBrush As SolidBrush = New SolidBrush(Color.DeepPink)
g.FillEllipse(solidBrush, 10, 10, 100, 30)
```

DrawString

The DrawString method writes a string of text at a specified location on the Graphics object. For an example, see "The System.Drawing.Font Class" section later in this chapter.

Save

The Save method persists the current Graphics object into a System.Drawing.Drawing2D.GraphicsState object. Later, you can retrieve the persisted object using the Restore method.

Restore

The Restore method restores a previously persisted Graphics object from a System.Drawing.Drawing2D.GraphicState object. For example, the following code saves the state of a Graphics object into a System.Drawing.Drawing2D.GraphicState object, does something, and restores it:

```
Dim g As Graphics = Me.CreateGraphics()
' save the state of the current Graphics object
Dim graphicsState As GraphicsState = g.Save
' do something here
    .
    .
    .
' restore it
g.Restore(graphicsState)
```

The Graphics Class's Properties

The following are some of the most important properties of the Graphics class.

DpiX

DpiX is the horizontal resolution of the current Graphics object.

DpiY

DpiX is the vertical resolution of the current Graphics object.

PageUnit

By default, the measurement unit of a Graphics object is a pixel. You can change this by setting the PageUnit property. This property takes one of the members of the GraphicsUnit enumeration: Display, Document, Inch, Millimeter, Pixel, Point, and World. For example, the following changes the PageUnit property of a Graphics object to inches:

```
graphics.PageUnit = GraphicsUnit.Inch
```

The System.Drawing.Font Class

The System.Drawing.Font class represents a font. The easiest way to construct a Font object is by passing a String containing the font name and the font size. For instance, the following obtains the Graphics object of a form, creates an Arial font with the size of 14, creates a SolidBrush called solidBrush, and writes a String on the Graphics object in 14-point Arial:

```
Dim g As Graphics = Me.CreateGraphics()
Dim font As Font = New Font("Arial", 14)
Dim solidBrush As SolidBrush = New SolidBrush(Color.Chartreuse)
g.DrawString("Hello", font, solidBrush, 10, 100)
```

If the font name passed to the constructor does not correspond to an available font, the default font is used.

The Font class has read-only Bold and Italic properties that indicate whether the Font is bold or italic.

The System.Drawing.Drawing2D.GraphicsPath Class

The System.Drawing.Graphics class provides methods to draw various shapes. However, you can create your own custom shape if none of the methods meets your needs. To do this, you use the System.Drawing.Drawing2D.GraphicsPath class. The GraphicsPath class, as the name implies, represents a graphics path. A graphics path consists of a series of connected points. After you construct a GraphicsPath object, you can draw it using the Graphics class's DrawPath method.

Besides for creating a custom shape, you can also use the GraphicsPath to create a custom cap for your Pen object, as discussed in the "Pen Caps" section.

As an example, the following code creates a GraphicsPath object and draws it using the DrawPath method of the Graphics class:

```
Dim gp As New GraphicsPath()
gp.AddLine(New Point(80, 20), New Point(10, 30))
gp.AddArc(New Rectangle(10, 30, 80, 160), 40, 130)
gp.AddLine(New Point(150, 30), New Point(80, 20))
graphics.DrawPath(Pens.Blue, gp)
```

Figure 4-2 shows the result of this code.

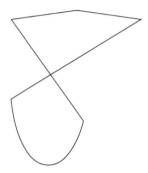

Figure 4-2. A GraphicsPath *object*

Pen Caps

You have seen that you can construct a Pen object and use it to draw lines and other shapes. What you have not learned is that the Pen class has the StartCap and EndCap properties, which represent the cap styles when the Pen object draws a line. The StartCap property determines the cap style at the beginning of the line, and the EndCap property the cap style at the end of the line.

The StartCap and the EndCap properties can accept a member of the System.Drawing.Drawing2D.LineCap enumeration: AnchorMask, ArrowAnchor, Custom, DiamondAnchor, Flat, NoAnchor, Round, RoundAnchor, Square, SquareAnchor, and Triangle.

As an example, Listing 4-1 creates Font and Brush objects and uses different end caps with the Pen object named pen.

Listing 4-1. Using Different Caps

```
Dim font As New Font("Courier New", 10)
Dim brush As New SolidBrush(Color.Black)

pen.EndCap = LineCap.AnchorMask
g.DrawLine(pen, 5, 10, 40, 10)
g.DrawString("AnchorMask", font, brush, 75, 5)

pen.EndCap = LineCap.ArrowAnchor
g.DrawLine(pen, 5, 30, 40, 30)
g.DrawString("ArrowAnchor", font, brush, 75, 25)

pen.EndCap = LineCap.DiamondAnchor
g.DrawLine(pen, 5, 50, 40, 50)
g.DrawString("DiamondAnchor", font, brush, 75, 45)

pen.EndCap = LineCap.Flat
g.DrawLine(pen, 5, 70, 40, 70)
g.DrawString("Flat", font, brush, 75, 65)

pen.EndCap = LineCap.NoAnchor
g.DrawLine(pen, 5, 90, 40, 90)
g.DrawString("NoAnchor", font, brush, 75, 85)

pen.EndCap = LineCap.Round
g.DrawLine(pen, 5, 110, 40, 110)
g.DrawString("Round", font, brush, 75, 105)

pen.EndCap = LineCap.RoundAnchor
g.DrawLine(pen, 5, 130, 40, 130)
g.DrawString("RoundAnchor", font, brush, 75, 125)

pen.EndCap = LineCap.Square
g.DrawLine(pen, 5, 150, 40, 150)
g.DrawString("Square", font, brush, 75, 145)

pen.EndCap = LineCap.SquareAnchor
g.DrawLine(pen, 5, 170, 40, 170)
g.DrawString("SquareAnchor", font, brush, 75, 165)

pen.EndCap = LineCap.Triangle
g.DrawLine(pen, 5, 190, 40, 190)
g.DrawString("Triangle", font, brush, 75, 185)
```

Figure 4-3 shows the result.

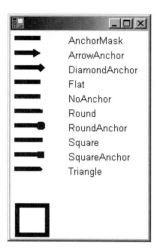

Figure 4-3. Using different caps

Note that the nondefault caps do not affect other shapes than lines, as shown by the rectangle at the bottom of Figure 4-3.

However, the available caps are only apparent when the pen width is large enough. If you choose a width of 1, for example, the caps are not that obvious, as demonstrated in Figure 4-4.

Figure 4-4. Line caps are not obvious if the pen width is not large enough.

You can create your own cap by creating a
System.Drawing.Drawing2D.CustomLineCap object and assigning it to the
CustomStartCap and/or the CustomEndCap properties of a Pen object. You create a
CustomLineCap by passing a GraphicsPath object. As an example, Listing 4-2 constructs a CustomLineCap object and assigns it to the CustomEndCap of a Pen object.

Listing 4-2. Drawing Your Own Cap

```
Dim g As Graphics = Me.CreateGraphics()
Dim pen As New Pen(Color.Black, 1)

Dim gp As New GraphicsPath()
gp.AddLine(New Point(-20, 0), New Point(20, 0))
gp.AddLine(New Point(20, 0), New Point(0, 20))
gp.AddLine(New Point(0, 20), New Point(-20, 0))

Dim customCap As New CustomLineCap(Nothing, gp)
pen.CustomEndCap = customCap
g.DrawLine(pen, 50, 100, 50, 35)
g.DrawLine(pen, 50, 150, 150, 100)
g.DrawLine(pen, 50, 170, 150, 170)
g.DrawLine(pen, 50, 180, 50, 250)
```

Figure 4-5 shows the result.

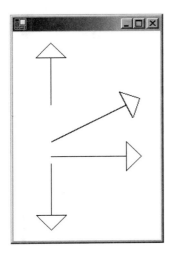

Figure 4-5. Creating your own cap

Anti-Aliasing

When you draw a line or another shape, sometimes the shape appears jagged.
GDI+ provides a way to smooth this out by applying anti-aliasing. Precisely, the
Graphics class has a property called SmoothingMode. This property value is one of
the System.Drawing.Drawing2D.SmoothingMode enumeration members: AntiAlias,
Default, HighQuality, HighSpeed, Invalid, and None. You assign
SmoothingMode.AntiAlias to apply anti-aliasing.

Listing 4-3 draws a number of lines. The first four lines drawn have no anti-
aliasing applied to them. The lines afterward do.

Listing 4-3. Applying Anti-Aliasing

```
Dim g As Graphics = Me.CreateGraphics()
Dim pen As New Pen(Color.Black, 1)

Dim gp As New GraphicsPath()
gp.AddLine(New Point(-20, 0), New Point(20, 0))
gp.AddLine(New Point(20, 0), New Point(0, 20))
gp.AddLine(New Point(0, 20), New Point(-20, 0))

Dim customCap As New CustomLineCap(Nothing, gp)
pen.CustomEndCap = customCap
g.DrawLine(pen, 50, 100, 60, 35)
g.DrawLine(pen, 50, 150, 150, 100)
g.DrawLine(pen, 50, 170, 150, 190)
g.DrawLine(pen, 50, 180, 70, 250)

g.SmoothingMode = SmoothingMode.AntiAlias
' the following lines will be smoothed out
g.DrawLine(pen, 250, 100, 260, 35)
g.DrawLine(pen, 250, 150, 350, 100)
g.DrawLine(pen, 250, 170, 350, 190)
g.DrawLine(pen, 250, 180, 270, 250)
```

Figure 4-6 shows the difference.

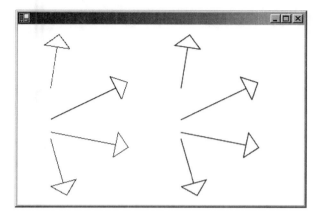

Figure 4-6. Applying anti-aliasing

Rotation

The Graphics class allows you to rotate the drawing plane. You do this by using the RotateTransform method of the Graphics class. To return the plane to normal, use the ResetTransform method.

Listing 4-4 illustrates how rotation affects the drawing.

Listing 4-4. Applying Rotation

```
Dim g As Graphics = Me.CreateGraphics()
Dim pen As New Pen(Color.Black, 1)
Dim font As New Font("Courier", 12)
Dim x As Integer = 120
Dim y As Integer = 20
g.DrawString("Advanced .NET Drawing", font, Brushes.Black, x, y)
g.DrawLine(pen, x, y + 20, x + 180, y + 20)

g.RotateTransform(30)
g.DrawString("Advanced .NET Drawing", font, Brushes.Black, x, y)
g.DrawLine(pen, x, y + 20, x + 180, y + 20)

' Rotate another 30 degrees
g.RotateTransform(30)
g.DrawString("Advanced .NET Drawing", font, Brushes.Black, x, y)
g.DrawLine(pen, x, y + 20, x + 180, y + 20)
```

Figure 4-7 shows the result.

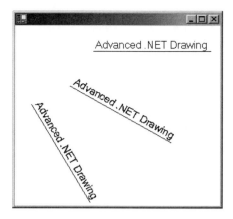

Figure 4-7. Applying rotation

Translate Transform

By default, all the coordinates you pass to the Graphics class's drawing methods are relative to the origin—which is coordinate (0,0). You can, however, translate the origin to another point in the coordinate so that the coordinates passed to the drawing methods are measured relative to the new point.

Listing 4-5 moves the origin to the coordinate (200, 200). Anything drawn will be measured to be relative to (200, 200).

Listing 4-5. Applying Translation

```
Dim g As Graphics = Me.CreateGraphics()
Dim pen As New Pen(Color.Black, 1)
Dim font As New Font("Courier", 8)

' draw a circle at the center of rotation
g.FillEllipse(Brushes.Red, 200, 200, 9, 9)
g.TranslateTransform(200, 200)

Dim i As Integer
For i = 0 To 11
  g.DrawString("Advanced .NET Drawing", font, Brushes.Black, 20, 20)
  g.DrawLine(pen, 20, 35, 150, 35)
  g.RotateTransform(30)
Next
```

Figure 4-8 shows the result of this code.

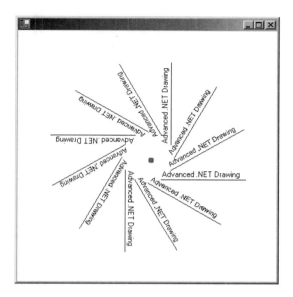

Figure 4-8. Applying translation

Creating a Simple Drawing Application

Before discussing the UML class diagram editor project in detail, let's look at a much-simplified version of the project. In fact, this simple drawing application can draw one shape only: rectangles. Understanding this simple application will help you understand the project.

The application has two classes: the DrawArea class that extends System.Windows.Forms.Panel and the form. The draw area fills the whole client area of the form. To draw a rectangle, the user clicks on the draw area and drags the mouse along. The first click point is the top-left corner of the rectangle. The point where the user releases the mouse becomes the bottom-right corner of the rectangle. Because you cannot guarantee that the user will drag the mouse to the left and down when drawing a rectangle, the release point could be located left of the starting point. If this is the case, then you have a problem because the two constructors of the System.Drawing.Rectangle class require you to pass a Point object representing the upper-left corner of the rectangle or the coordinate of that point.

The solution to this problem is the DrawArea class's GetRectangleFromPoints method, which you can use to obtain a System.Drawing.Rectangle object. The two points passed to this method can be any points in the draw area. You will see the GetRectangleFromPoints method after looking at the DrawArea class.

The DrawArea class extends the System.Windows.Forms.Panel class (see Listing 4-6).

Listing 4-6. The DrawArea *Class*

```
Imports System.Drawing
Imports System.Collections
Imports System.Windows.Forms

Public Class DrawArea : Inherits Panel
  Private shapes As New ArrayList()
  Private startPoint As Point

  Public Sub New()
    AddHandler Me.MouseDown, AddressOf me_MouseDown
    AddHandler Me.MouseUp, AddressOf me_MouseUp
  End Sub

  Protected Overrides Sub OnPaint(ByVal e As PaintEventArgs)
    Dim g As Graphics = e.Graphics
    Dim shapeEnum As IEnumerator = shapes.GetEnumerator
    Dim blackPen As Pen = Pens.Black
    While shapeEnum.MoveNext
      Dim rectangle As Rectangle = CType(shapeEnum.Current, Rectangle)
      g.DrawRectangle(blackPen, rectangle)
    End While
  End Sub

  Private Sub me_MouseDown(ByVal sender As System.Object, _
    ByVal e As MouseEventArgs)
    If e.Button = MouseButtons.Left Then
      startPoint = New Point(e.X, e.Y)
    End If
  End Sub

  Private Sub me_MouseUp(ByVal sender As System.Object, _
    ByVal e As MouseEventArgs)
    If e.Button = MouseButtons.Left Then
      Dim endPoint As New Point(e.X, e.Y)
      Dim r As Rectangle = GetRectangleFromPoints(startPoint, endPoint)
      shapes.Add(r)
      Me.Refresh()
    End If
  End Sub
```

```
Public Shared Function GetRectangleFromPoints(ByVal p1 As Point, _
  ByVal p2 As Point) As Rectangle
  Dim x1, x2, y1, y2 As Integer
  If p1.X < p2.X Then
    x1 = p1.X
    x2 = p2.X
  Else
    x1 = p2.X
    x2 = p1.X
  End If

  If p1.Y < p2.Y Then
    y1 = p1.Y
    y2 = p2.Y
  Else
    y1 = p2.Y
    y2 = p1.Y
  End If
  ' x2 > x1 and y2 > y1
  Return New Rectangle(x1, y1, x2 - x1, y2 - y1)
  End Function

End Class
```

NOTE *To compile the* DrawArea *class in Listing 4-6, use the following command from the directory in which the* listing-04.06.vb *file resides:* vbc /t:library /r:System.dll,System.Windows.Forms.dll, System.Drawing.dll listing-04.06.vb *(all on one line).*

The DrawArea class has a private System.Collection.ArrayList object in which all Rectangle objects drawn are stored. The DrawArea class overrides the OnPaint method so that all rectangles can be redrawn whenever the Paint event triggers.

In the constructor, the DrawArea class wires the MouseDown event with the me_MouseDown event handler and the MouseUp event with the me_MouseUp event handler:

```
AddHandler Me.MouseDown, AddressOf me_MouseDown
AddHandler Me.MouseUp, AddressOf me_MouseUp
```

The me_MouseDown event handler is called whenever the user clicks on the DrawArea object. The event handler is passed a MouseEventArgs object, from which you can obtain the Button object of the mouse and the coordinate of the click point (in the form of X and Y properties). What the me_MouseDown event does is check if the mouse button clicked was MouseButton.Left. If it was, it constructs a Point object containing the clicked point coordinate and assigns the Point object to the startPoint variable:

```
If e.Button = MouseButtons.Left Then
  startPoint = New Point(e.X, e.Y)
End If
```

The me_MouseUp event handler is invoked when the user releases the mouse button. It first checks if the mouse button released was MouseButtons.Left. If it was, it constructs a Point object containing the point at which the user released the mouse button and assigns it to the local variable endPoint.

```
Dim endPoint As New Point(e.X, e.Y)
```

It then passes both points to the GetRectangleFromPoints method to obtain a Rectangle object and add the Rectangle object to the shapes ArrayList:

```
Dim r As Rectangle = GetRectangleFromPoints(startPoint, endPoint)
shapes.Add(r)
```

Finally, it calls the Refresh method to force the surface to be repainted:

```
Me.Refresh()
```

You need the GetRectangleFromPoints method because you cannot guarantee that the startPoint will be on the top-left of the end point. The GetRectangleFromPoints method checks the coordinate of the two points and creates new points, if necessary, so that the first point will have an x coordinate and a y coordinate whose values are less than the values of the x and y coordinates of the second point.

Then, it constructs a Rectangle object by passing the two new coordinates and returns the Rectangle object.

The form in the application adds a DrawArea object as its child control and sets its Dock property to DockStyle.Fill. It also changes the background color of the DrawArea object to white.

Listing 4-7 shows the form.

Listing 4-7. The Form

```
Imports System
Imports System.Windows.Forms
Imports System.Drawing
Imports System.Drawing.Drawing2D

Public Class Form1 : Inherits Form
  Private drawArea As New DrawArea()

  Public Sub New()
    Me.ClientSize = New System.Drawing.Size(740, 585)
    drawArea.Dock = DockStyle.Fill
    Me.Controls.Add(drawArea)
    drawArea.BackColor = Color.White
  End Sub

  <STAThread()> Shared Sub Main()
    Dim f As New Form1()
    Application.Run(f)
  End Sub

End Class
```

NOTE *To compile the form in Listing 4-7, use the following command from the directory in which the* listing-04.07.vb *file resides:* vbc /t:winexe /r:System.dll,System.Windows.Forms.dll, System.Drawing.dll,listing-04.06.dll listing-04.07.vb *(all on one line).*

If you run the application, you can click and drag to draw a Rectangle object.

However, you probably notice one thing. When you drag your mouse, there is nothing to remind you of where the start point is. You also cannot see the size of the rectangle you are drawing.

To make it look more professional, you can add a feature so that you can see the rectangle you are drawing. The main thing you need to do is capture one more event: MouseMove.

To add the new feature, do the following steps to the DrawArea class:

1. Add the movingEndPoint variable of type Point in the class declaration:

    ```
    Private movingEndPoint As Point
    ```

2. Wire the MouseMove event to the me_MouseMove event handler in the constructor. The new constructor will look like this:

    ```
    Public Sub New()
        AddHandler Me.MouseDown, AddressOf me_MouseDown
        AddHandler Me.MouseMove, AddressOf me_MouseMove
        AddHandler Me.MouseUp, AddressOf me_MouseUp
    End Sub
    ```

3. Assign the movingEndPoint value to the startPoint every time the mouse is clicked. In the me_MouseDown event handler, add the line of code in bold:

    ```
    Private Sub me_MouseDown(ByVal sender As System.Object, _
      ByVal e As MouseEventArgs)
      If e.Button = MouseButtons.Left Then
        startPoint = New Point(e.X, e.Y)
        movingEndPoint = startPoint
      End If
    End Sub
    ```

4. Add the me_MouseMove event handler to handle the MouseMove event. This event triggers when the user drags the mouse. You need to draw a temporary rectangle and remove the previous temporary rectangle. This is the me_MouseMove event handler:

    ```
    Private Sub me_MouseMove(ByVal sender As System.Object, _
      ByVal e As MouseEventArgs)
      If e.Button = MouseButtons.Left Then
        Dim endPoint As New Point(e.X, e.Y)
        Dim graphics As Graphics = Me.CreateGraphics
        'remove the previous rectangle
        graphics.DrawRectangle(Pens.White, _
          GetRectangleFromPoints(startPoint, movingEndPoint))
        movingEndPoint = endPoint
        Me.Refresh()
        'draw a temporary rectangle
        graphics.DrawRectangle(Pens.Black, _
          GetRectangleFromPoints(startPoint, movingEndPoint))
      End If
    End Sub
    ```

Listing 4-8 gives the updated `DrawArea` class. The `Form1` class remains unchanged.

Listing 4-8. The `DrawArea` *Class That Captures the* `MouseMove` *Event*

```vb
Imports System.Drawing
Imports System.Collections
Imports System.Windows.Forms

Public Class DrawArea : Inherits Panel
  Private shapes As New ArrayList()
  Private startPoint As Point
  Private movingEndPoint As Point

  Public Sub New()
    AddHandler Me.MouseDown, AddressOf me_MouseDown
    AddHandler Me.MouseMove, AddressOf me_MouseMove
    AddHandler Me.MouseUp, AddressOf me_MouseUp
  End Sub

  Protected Overrides Sub OnPaint(ByVal e As PaintEventArgs)
    Dim g As Graphics = e.Graphics
    Dim shapeEnum As IEnumerator = shapes.GetEnumerator
    Dim blackPen As Pen = Pens.Black
    While shapeEnum.MoveNext
      Dim rectangle As Rectangle = CType(shapeEnum.Current, Rectangle)
      g.DrawRectangle(blackPen, rectangle)
    End While
  End Sub

  Private Sub me_MouseDown(ByVal sender As System.Object, _
    ByVal e As MouseEventArgs)
    If e.Button = MouseButtons.Left Then
      startPoint = New Point(e.X, e.Y)
      movingEndPoint = startPoint
    End If

  End Sub

  Private Sub me_MouseMove(ByVal sender As System.Object, _
    ByVal e As MouseEventArgs)
    If e.Button = MouseButtons.Left Then
```

```
      Dim endPoint As New Point(e.X, e.Y)
      Dim graphics As Graphics = Me.CreateGraphics
      graphics.DrawRectangle(Pens.White, _
        GetRectangleFromPoints(startPoint, movingEndPoint))
      movingEndPoint = endPoint
      Me.Refresh()
      graphics.DrawRectangle(Pens.Black, _
        GetRectangleFromPoints(startPoint, movingEndPoint))
    End If
  End Sub

  Private Sub me_MouseUp(ByVal sender As System.Object, _
    ByVal e As MouseEventArgs)
    If e.Button = MouseButtons.Left Then
      Dim endPoint As New Point(e.X, e.Y)
      Dim r As Rectangle = GetRectangleFromPoints(startPoint, endPoint)
      shapes.Add(r)
      Me.Refresh()
    End If
  End Sub

  Public Shared Function GetRectangleFromPoints(ByVal p1 As Point, _
    ByVal p2 As Point) As Rectangle
    Dim x1, x2, y1, y2 As Integer
    If p1.X < p2.X Then
      x1 = p1.X
      x2 = p2.X
    Else
      x1 = p2.X
      x2 = p1.X
    End If

    If p1.Y < p2.Y Then
      y1 = p1.Y
      y2 = p2.Y
    Else
      y1 = p2.Y
      y2 = p1.Y
    End If
    ' x2 > x1 and y2 > y1
    Return New Rectangle(x1, y1, x2 - x1, y2 - y1)
  End Function

End Class
```

Understanding Object Serialization for Persisting the Graphics Objects

When working with an object-oriented programming language, you sometimes need to persist the state of an object. The .NET Framework class library provides four namespaces to support object serialization: System.Runtime.Serialization, System.Runtime.Serialization.Formatters, System.Runtime.Serialization.Formatters.Binary, and System.Runtime.Serialization.Formatters.Soap.

To serialize an object, you need to either mark it with the <Serializable> attribute or implement the ISerializable interface. The following is a class that is marked with the <Serializable> attribute:

```
<Serializable()> Public Class Line
End Class
```

If a class to be serialized contains references to other objects, the classes of those other objects must also be marked <Serializable>.

Alternatively, your class can implement the ISerializable interface. See the following section for more information about this interface.

You can see examples of how to serialize objects into both binary data and SOAP formats in the sections "The BinaryFormatter Class" and "The SoapFormatter Class."

The ISerializable Interface

Unless you mark the class with the <Serializable> attribute, all classes whose instances are serialized must implement this interface. You use the ISerializable interface if you want your class to control its own serialization and deserialization.

The ISerializable interface only has one method, GetDataObject, to which you pass a SerializationInfo object and a StreamingContext object. The GetDataObject method will then populate the SerializationInfo object with data necessary for the serialization of the target object.

Listing 4-9 illustrates a class named MySerializableClass that implements the System.Runtime.Serialization.ISerializable interface. A SerializationInfo object and a StreamingContext object are available from the GetObjectData method.

Listing 4-9. A Class Implementing the ISerializable *Interface*

```
Imports System.Runtime.Serialization

Public Class MySerializableClass
  Implements ISerializable

  Dim info As SerializationInfo
  Dim context As StreamingContext

  Sub  GetObjectData(info As SerializationInfo, _
    context As StreamingContext) _
    Implements ISerializable.GetObjectData

    Me.info = info
    Me.context = context

    ' implementation code here

  End Sub

End Class
```

Classes that implement this interface include System.Data.DataSet, System.Drawing.Font, System.Collections.Hashtable, System.Drawing.Icon, and System.Drawing.Image.

The IFormatter Interface

IFormatter is a member of the System.Runtime.Serialization namespace. Both the BinaryFormatter class and the SoapFormatter class implement this interface. This interface has only two methods, Serialize and Deserialize.

The Serialize method serializes an object or an object containing other objects. The signature of this method is as follows:

```
Sub Serialize( _
  ByVal serializationStream As Stream, _
  ByVal graph As Object _
)
```

The Deserialize method deserializes an object or an object containing other objects. This method has the following signature:

```
Function Deserialize( _
  ByVal serializationStream As Stream _
) As Object
```

Because the return value of the Deserialize method is an object of type Object, you need to downcast the object into the appropriate type.

Two formats are available to store your persisted objects: binary and Extensible Markup Language (XML). Normally, you upcast either a BinaryFormatter object or a SoapFormatter object as an IFormatter object, depending on the format you use for the serialization.

Listing 4-10 illustrates how you can serialize an object called serializableObject. First the user is asked to select a file to serialize to using a SaveFileDialog and then the object is serialized in the SOAP format.

Listing 4-10. Serializing Objects

```
Protected Sub Serialize()
  Dim myStream As Stream
  Dim saveFileDialog As SaveFileDialog = New SaveFileDialog()
  saveFileDialog.Filter = "All files (*.*)|*"

  If saveFileDialog.ShowDialog() = DialogResult.OK Then
    ' get a Stream object
    myStream = saveFileDialog.OpenFile()
    If Not (myStream Is Nothing) Then
      ' ready to serialize
      Dim formatter As IFormatter
      formatter = CType(New SoapFormatter(), IFormatter)
      formatter.Serialize(myStream, serializableObject)
      'serializableObject is an object whose class has
      'been marked with the <serializable> attribute or
      'implements the ISerializable interface
      myStream.Close()
    End If
  End If
End Sub
```

The BinaryFormatter Class

The BinaryFormatter class is the only member of the
System.Runtime.Serialization.Formatters.Binary namespace. You use this class
to serialize and deserialize an object or a graph of objects in a binary file. For
performance, you need this format when serializing your objects. The resulting
file is also more compact than the XML format.

Listing 4-11 provides a class named SerializableClass that is marked for
serialization.

Listing 4-11. BinaryFormatter *Example*

```
Imports System
Imports System.IO
Imports System.Runtime.Serialization
Imports System.Runtime.Serialization.Formatters.Binary

<Serializable()> Class SerializableClass
  Private value As Integer
  Public Function GetValue() As Integer
    GetValue = value
  End Function

  Public Sub SetValue(ByVal value As Integer)
    Me.value = value
  End Sub
End Class

Public Module modMain
Public Sub Serialize()
  Dim myObject As SerializableClass = _
    New SerializableClass()
  myObject.SetValue(888)

  Dim stream As Stream = File.Create("C:\MyObject.bin")
  Dim formatter As IFormatter
  formatter = CType(New BinaryFormatter(), IFormatter)
  formatter.Serialize(stream, myObject)
  stream.Close()

End Sub
```

```
Public Sub Deserialize()
  Dim stream As Stream = File.OpenRead("C:\MyObject.bin")
  Dim formatter As IFormatter
  formatter = CType(New BinaryFormatter(), IFormatter)
  Dim myObject As SerializableClass
  myObject = CType(formatter.Deserialize(stream), SerializableClass)

  stream.Close()
  Console.WriteLine(myObject.GetValue)
End Sub

Public Sub Main()
    Serialize
    Deserialize
End Sub

End Module
```

The class is very simple, containing only one private field called value. There are two methods, GetValue and SetValue, respectively, to obtain and set the private field value. The code also provides two methods, Serialize and Deserialize. The Serialize method will persist an instance of SerializableClass into a file called MyObject.bin. The Deserialize method does the reverse, reading the SerializableClass object from the file and then printing its value.

The SoapFormatter Class

This is the only member of the System.Runtime.Serialization.Formatters.Soap namespace. You use this class to serialize and deserialize an object or a graph of objects in XML format.

Listing 4-12 shows an example that uses the SerializableClass class from the previous example. This class is marked for serialization. The class is very simple, containing only one private field called value. There are two methods, GetValue and SetValue, to obtain and set the private field value, respectively.

The code provides two methods, Serialize and Deserialize. The Serialize method will persist an instance of SerializableClass into a file called MyObject.bin. The Deserialize method does the reverse, reading the SerializableClass object from the file and then printing its value.

Listing 4-12. SoapFormatter *Example*

```vb
Imports System
Imports System.IO
Imports System.Runtime.Serialization
Imports System.Runtime.Serialization.Formatters.Soap

<Serializable()> Class SerializableClass
  Private value As Integer
  Public Function GetValue() As Integer
    GetValue = value
  End Function

  Public Sub SetValue(ByVal value As Integer)
    Me.value = value
  End Sub
End Class

Public Module modMain

Public Sub Serialize()
  Dim myObject As SerializableClass = New SerializableClass()
  myObject.SetValue(678)

  Dim stream As Stream = File.Create("C:\MyObject.xml")
  Dim formatter As IFormatter
  formatter = CType(New SoapFormatter(), IFormatter)
  formatter.Serialize(stream, myObject)
  stream.Close()
End Sub

Public Sub Deserialize()
  Dim stream As Stream = _
    File.OpenRead("C:\MyObject.xml")
  Dim formatter As IFormatter
  formatter = CType(New SoapFormatter(), IFormatter)
  Dim myObject As SerializableClass
  myObject = CType(formatter.Deserialize(stream), SerializableClass)
  stream.Close()
  Debug.WriteLine(myObject.GetValue)
End Sub
```

```
Public Sub Main
   Serialize()
   Deserialize()
End Sub

End Module
```

Understanding the Memento Design Pattern

When persisting an object, you sometimes face the following problem: Some or all of the object's internal states are private. Therefore, there is no way to obtain the values of those states without violating encapsulation.

However, you might argue, the object serialization technique in the .NET Framework allows you to persist objects into a file stream or other device. Yes, that is true. Nonetheless, the classes of some objects do not implement the ISerializable interface or are not marked with the <Serializable> attribute. For example, you may want to persist an instance of a class that inherits from the System.Windows.Forms.Control class, as is the case in our drawing application. The System.Windows.Forms.Control class is not marked with the <Serializable> attribute, and it does not implement the ISerializable interface. Attempting to serialize an object of this class will throw an exception.

In addition, there are two other problems to solve. The first relates to efficiency. Suppose you have a large object that you want to persist, but only a small fraction of the states inside the objects need to be persisted. Serializing the whole object will require greater space than necessary, not to mention that it will take longer time to serialize it and later retrieve it.

The second problem has to do with security. You may want to protect some internal state of the object. In other words, you may want to persist some states but not some other states.

The aforementioned issues make the object serialization technique seem useless, doesn't it? Not really. You can still use the .NET Framework object serialization technique with the help of the Memento design pattern.

The idea of the Memento pattern is simple. In this pattern, the object whose state you want to persist is called the *originator*. To apply the pattern, you create another object called the *memento*. The memento object is an external object that will hold the states of the originator. Therefore, if you need to save the states of the variables a, b, c, and d from the originator, the Memento pattern will have the same variables a, b, c, and d. But, hold on a second. What if some of the states are private fields, which of course are not accessible from outside the originator? The solution to this problem is the beauty of this pattern. The originator will have two extra methods: One is called CreateMemento, and the other is SetMemento.

The CreateMemento method instantiates a memento object, copies all its states that need to be persisted to the memento object, and then returns the memento object. Therefore, to persist the originator, you call its CreateMemento to obtain a memento object and then serialize the memento object.

The SetMemento method gets the states back. After you deserialize the previously saved memento object, you call the SetMemento object of the originator by passing the memento object obtained from the deserialization.

Clever, isn't it?

In the project in this chapter, you will modify the Memento design pattern a bit. The CreateMemento is called GetMemento, and instead of providing the SetMemento method, you will use a constructor that accepts a memento object. You can then use this constructor to instantiate the object as well as to restore the previous states.

Exploring the UML Class Diagram

UML is the standard language for object-oriented software visualization, specification, construction, and documentation. Grady Booch, Ivar Jacobson, and Jim Rumbaugh at Rational Software Corporation developed UML, with contributions from other methodologists, software vendors, and users. UML is a combined methodology of the Booch, OMT, and Jacobson methods.

NOTE *You can find various documents at* www.rational.com/uml/index.jsp. *A good tutorial book on UML is* The Unified Modeling Language User Guide *(Addison-Wesley, 1998).*

There are three kinds of building blocks in the UML vocabulary:

- Things

- Relationships

- Diagrams

You can group things in UML into four categories:

- Structural things

- Behavioral things

- Grouping things

- Annotational things

There are also four kinds of relationships in UML:

- Dependency

- Association

- Generalization

- Realization

The UML includes nine types of diagrams:

- Class diagram

- Object diagram

- Use case diagram

- Sequence diagram

- Collaboration diagram

- Statechart diagram

- Activity diagram

- Component diagram

- Deployment diagram

As you can see, UML addresses all the views needed to build and deploy object-oriented applications and therefore is very extensive. As such, tools for manipulating all aspects of the UML are also large applications. Understandably, such applications are not cheap. The most popular UML tools are the various products from Rational Software Corporation (www.rational.com). Alternatives include the Poseidon for UML Professional Edition and the Poseidon for UML Community Edition from Gentleware (www.gentleware.com). The latter is freely downloadable from the Web site.

NOTE *You can also use UML to model nonsoftware systems.*

The project in this chapter addresses a tiny fraction of UML: the class diagram.

Implementing the Project

You will start the project by defining the project specification. In plain English, it is a Windows application that can do the following:

- Draw two types of rectangular structures and four types of lines. A line always connects two rectangular structures and cannot stand alone.

- Write labels on the rectangular structure and attach labels on the line.

- Resize and move each rectangular structure around the draw area.

- Automatically adjust the line position when either of its rectangular structure is resized or moved.

- Allow the user to manually move a line around its rectangular structure.

The two rectangular structures available are the class structure and the interface structure. Figure 4-9 shows the class structure, and Figure 4-10 shows the interface structure.

Figure 4-9. The class structure

Figure 4-10. The interface structure

As shown in Figure 4-9, a class structure has three partitions. The top-most partition is for the class name. The one in the middle is for the class's list of attributes, and the bottom one is for the list of operations. Figure 4-11 illustrates a class with a name (Rectangle), four attributes (left, top, height, and width) and two operations (Draw() and Move()).

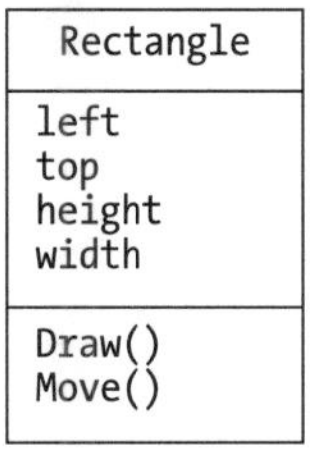

```
Rectangle
left
top
height
width
Draw()
Move()
```

Figure 4-11. A class with a name, attributes, and operations

An interface structure is similar to a class structure, but it only has two partitions. The top partition is for the interface name, which always follows the word <Interface>. The bottom partition is for the interface's list of operations. Figure 4-12 shows an interface called IButtonControl with two operations: NotifyDefault and PerformClick.

Figure 4-12. An interface with a name and operations

Two structures can have a relationship between them. A line represents a relationship. Four types of relationships are provided using one of the lines in Figure 4-13.

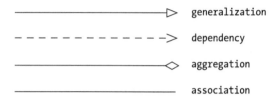

Figure 4-13. Types of relationships

As an example, Figure 4-14 shows a generalization relationship between the class Rectangle and the class Shape. In the figure, Rectangle is a child class of Shape.

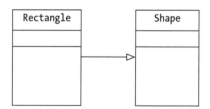

Figure 4-14. A generalization relationship

NOTE *A line always has two structures at its ends. It cannot stand alone. If one of the structures it connects is deleted, the line will be automatically removed, too.*

By default, a line connecting two structures will move automatically when one of the structures is moved. The position of the line will depend on the relative position between the two structures it connects. Figure 4-15 shows the line positions in four relative positions of the two structures.

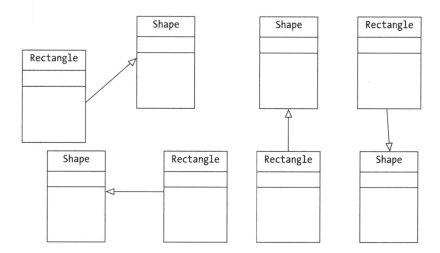

Figure 4-15. Automatic adjustments of the line positions

Automatic adjustment of a line's position that is caused by moving one of its structures always places the line at the center of one of the structure's edges. The user is allowed to adjust the line manually by dragging the line. Figure 4-16 shows a line that has been moved manually.

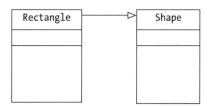

Figure 4-16. Manually positioning a line

A line can have zero to three labels. You can place each label on the left, center, and the right of the line. Figure 4-17 shows a line with labels.

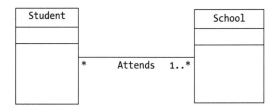

Figure 4-17. Line with labels

Finally, you can select a structure and a line to manipulate individually. For example, to add a name to a class structure, you must first select that class. A selected structure or line will be the active object and have handles. Figure 4-18 shows a selected class, and Figure 4-19 shows a selected line.

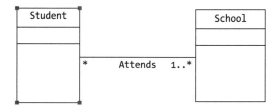

Figure 4-18. A selected class structure

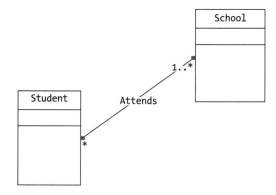

Figure 4-19. A selected line

The UML class diagram editor project is a Windows application. Figure 4-20 shows the class diagram for this application.

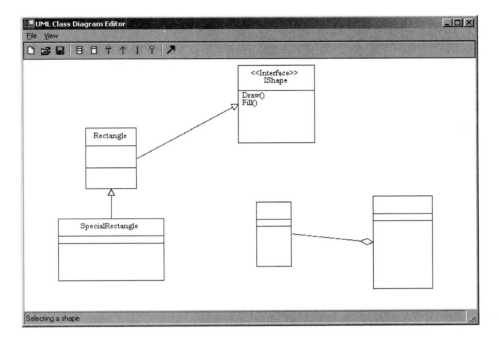

Figure 4-20. The class diagram

The main form has a number of menu items, a toolbar, a status bar, and a draw area. The draw area is represented by the DrawArea class, which derives from the System.Windows.Forms.Panel class. The draw area fills the entire client area of the main form.

The class structure is represented by the ClassRect class, and the interface structure is represented by the InterfaceRect class. Both ClassRect and InterfaceRect are direct child classes of the Rect class. The Line class represents a line.

The Rect class derives from the System.Windows.Forms.UserControl class and can draw itself. Every rectangular shape is added as a child control of the DrawArea object.

The Line class, on the other hand, does not inherit from any Windows control class. Therefore, it does not have a drawing surface to draw itself. As a result, it must use the Graphics object of the DrawArea control to draw itself. Every line drawn is added to an ArrayList of the DrawArea object.

Both rectangular shapes and lines have an internal state called selected that indicates whether the shape is being selected. In addition, each shape has the index field that stores a number that is unique to that shape. This unique number is passed to the constructor of both the Rect class and the Line class.

You can persist the shapes drawn into a file and later retrieve them from the same file.

The types used in this application are as follows:

- The ShapeType enumeration

- The RectHandle enumeration

- The LineHandle enumeration

- The RectPart enumeration

- The States class

- MathUtil

- Rect

- ClassRect

- InterfaceRect

- ClassRectMemento

- InterfaceRectMemento

- Line

- LineMemento

- InputBox

- PropertyForm

- DrawArea

- Form1

The following sections discuss each type, from the simplest classes to the more complex.

The ShapeType Enumeration

The ShapeType enumeration provides a way to enumerate the shapes that can be drawn plus None. Listing 4-13 gives the ShapeType enumeration, which you can find in the Misc.vb file in the project directory.

Listing 4-13. The ShapeType *Enumeration*

```
Imports System.Windows.Forms
Public Enum ShapeType As Integer
  [Class]
  [Interface]
  Generalization
  Dependency
  Association
  Aggregation
  None
End Enum
```

The RectHandle Enumeration

When selected, a class structure or an interface structure has four handles. Each handle is denoted by one of the members of the RectHandle enumeration. Listing 4-14 gives the RectHandle enumeration, which you can find in the Misc.vb file in the project directory.

Listing 4-14. The RectHandle *Enumeration*

```
Public Enum RectHandle As Integer
  TopLeft
  TopRight
  BottomLeft
  BottomRight
  None
End Enum
```

Figure 4-21 shows a selected class structure.

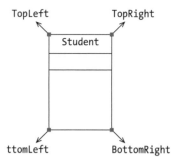

Figure 4-21. A selected class structure

The LineHandle Enumeration

When selected, a line has two handles. LineHandle.FromHandle denotes the handle on the start point. LineHandle.ToHandle denotes the handler on the end point. Listing 4-15 shows the LineHandle enumeration, which you can find in the Misc.vb file in the project directory.

Listing 4-15. The LineHandle *Enumeration*

```
Public Enum LineHandle As Integer
   FromHandle
   ToHandle
   None
End Enum
```

The RectPart Enumeration

When manipulating the parts of a class or interface, you need to refer to that part by using the RectPart enumeration. Listing 4-16 shows RectPart, which you can find in the Misc.vb file in the project directory.

Listing 4-16. The RectPart *Enumeration*

```
Public Enum RectPart As Integer
   Name
   Attributes
   Operations
End Enum
```

A class has three parts: name, attributes, and operations. An interface has two parts: name and operations.

The States Class

The States class stores two values that are shared by other classes in the application. Listing 4-17 shows this class, which you can find in the Misc.vb file in the project directory.

Listing 4-17. The States Class

```
Public Class States
  Public Shared ShapeDrawn As ShapeType = ShapeType.None
  Public Shared RectPart As RectPart
End Class
```

The first value is ShapeDrawn of type ShapeType. Its value can be one of the members of the ShapeType enumeration. It tells the application what shape the user is drawing. The user can choose which shape to be drawn by clicking one of the toolbar buttons representing those shapes. For example, if a user clicks the toolbar button representing the class structure, the event handler of that click event changes the value of States.ShapeDrawn. The DrawArea object then uses this value to respond to the user mouse click and drag.

The second value is RectPart of type RectPart. It tells which part of a class structure or an interface structure is being manipulated. The user can edit the label in those parts.

The MathUtil Class

The MathUtil class contains three methods, all of which are static. The first two methods are public static methods: GetRectangleFromPoints and GetSquareDistance. The third method is a private overload of GetSquareDistance. The private static method GetSquareDistance is used by the public GetSquareDistance method. Listing 4-18 shows the MathUtil class. Each method is explained after the code.

Listing 4-18. The MathUtil *Class*

```
Option Explicit On
Option Strict On

Imports System
Imports System.Drawing

Public Class MathUtil
  Public Shared Function GetSquareDistance(ByVal p1 As Point, _
    ByVal p2 As Point, ByVal p3 As Point) As Double
    ' calculate the distance between P3 and the line passing P1 and P2
    Dim aSquare, bSquare, cSquare, d, eSquare As Double
    aSquare = GetSquareDistance(p1, p3)
    bSquare = GetSquareDistance(p2, p3)
    cSquare = GetSquareDistance(p1, p2)
    ' c should not be zero, otherwise it means p1 = p2
    ' if it is so, return the distance of p3 and p1
    If cSquare = 0 Then
      Return Math.Sqrt(aSquare)
    End If

    d = (bSquare - aSquare + cSquare) / (2 * Math.Sqrt(cSquare))
    eSquare = bSquare - d ^ 2
    Return Math.Abs(eSquare)
  End Function

  Private Shared Function GetSquareDistance(ByVal p1 As Point, _
    ByVal p2 As Point) As Double
    Return ((p2.X - p1.X) ^ 2 + (p2.Y - p1.Y) ^ 2)
  End Function

  Public Shared Function GetRectangleFromPoints(ByVal p1 As Point, _
    ByVal p2 As Point) As Rectangle
    Dim x1, x2, y1, y2 As Integer
    If p1.X < p2.X Then
      x1 = p1.X
      x2 = p2.X
    Else
      x1 = p2.X
      x2 = p1.X
    End If
```

```
  If p1.Y < p2.Y Then
    y1 = p1.Y
    y2 = p2.Y
  Else
    y1 = p2.Y
    y2 = p1.Y
  End If
  ' x2 > x1 and y2 > y1
  Return New Rectangle(x1, y1, x2 - x1, y2 - y1)

 End Function

End Class
```

The `GetRectangleFromPoints` method is the same method explained
in the section "Creating a Simple Drawing Application." It returns a
`System.Drawing.Rectangle` object given two `Point` objects.

The public `GetSquareDistance` method obtains the square distance between a
point (p1) and a line passing two points (p2 and p3). The private `GetSquareDistance`
returns the square distance between two points. Before delving into these two
methods, however, let's have a look at some math. Those who are allergic to math-
ematics should not worry because there is only one simple mathematical formula:
Pythagoras's Theorem. It says that in a right-angled triangle, the area of the square
on the hypotenuse is the sum of the areas of the squares on the other two sides
(see Figure 4-22).

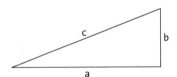

Figure 4-22. Pythagoras's Theorem

NOTE *Pythagoras's Theorem is $c^2 = a^2 + b^2$.*

The following shows how you can use Pythagoras's Theorem to find the distance between a point and a line if you know the coordinate of the point and the two points passed by the line.

The distance between point P3 and the line is the closest distance to the line at the tangent to the line that passes through P3. In Figure 4-23, the distance between P3 and the line passing P1 and P2 is e.

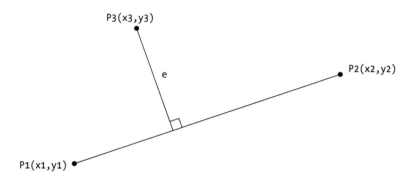

Figure 4-23. The distance between a point and a line

Applying Pythagoras's Theorem, you get the illustration in Figure 4-24.

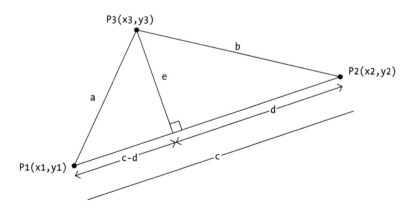

Figure 4-24. Using Pythagoras's Theorem to find the distance between a point and a line

Using Pythagoras's Theorem on the two triangles in Figure 4-24, you get the following:

$$e^2 = a^2 - (c-d)^2 \quad \text{(i)}$$
$$e^2 = b^2 - d^2 \quad \text{(ii)}$$

Equating (i) and (ii), you get the following:

```
a2 - (c-d) 2 = b2 - d2
a2 - c2 + 2cd - d2 = b2 - d2
a2 - c2 + 2cd = b2
2cd = b2 - a2 + c2
d = (b2 - a2 + c2) / 2c     (iii)
```

From (ii) you know the following:

$$e^2 = b^2 - d^2$$

Therefore, the distance is as follows:

$$e = \text{sqrt}(b^2 - d^2) \quad \text{(iv)}$$

where d is known from (iii).

Because you know the coordinates of the start point and the end point of a line in the class diagram, you know the distance between the two points P1 (x1, y1) and P2 (x2, y2) in Figure 4-24 is as follows:

$$\text{Sqrt}((x1 - x2)^2 + (y1 - y2)^2)$$

Therefore, you know c in (iii) previously. You also know a and b by using the same formulae to obtain the distance between P1 and P3 and the distance between P2 and P3. Therefore, you know a and b in (iii).

You use the private GetSquareDistance method to obtain the square distance between two points:

```
Private Shared Function GetSquareDistance(ByVal p1 As Point, _
  ByVal p2 As Point) As Double
  Return ((p2.X - p1.X) ^ 2 + (p2.Y - p1.Y) ^ 2)
End Function
```

Using (iii) and (iv), you can get the square distance of point P3 and the line passing P1 and P2 and calculate it using the public GetSquareDistance method in the MathUtil class. Both methods return the square of the distance to avoid rounding. In fact, knowing the square distance is as useful as knowing the distance itself.

The shared public GetSquareDistance method determines which line is closest to a click point on the draw area. It is called by the GetNearestLine method in the DrawArea class to determine which line is closest to a click point.

The Rect Class

The Rect class is an abstract class that represents a rectangular area and derives from the System.Windows.Forms.UserControl class. It has two child classes: ClassRect and InterfaceRect. ClassRect represents the class structure, and the InterfaceRect represents the interface structure.

Listing 4-19 shows the Rect class.

Listing 4-19. The Rect Class

```
Option Explicit On
Option Strict On

Imports System
Imports System.Windows.Forms
Imports System.Drawing
Imports System.Collections
Imports Microsoft.VisualBasic

Public MustInherit Class Rect : Inherits UserControl
    Public StartPoint As Point
    Public EndPoint As Point
    Public selected As Boolean = True
    Private handleColor As Color = Color.Red
    Public Const handleWidth As Integer = 6
    Public minimumWidth As Integer = 50
    Public minimumHeight As Integer = 100
    Protected foregroundPen As New Pen(Color.Black)
    Private handleBrush As New SolidBrush(handleColor)
    Protected textBrush As New SolidBrush(Color.Black)
    Public Shared Shadows fontHeight As Integer = 12
    Public Shared textTopMargin As Integer = 5
    Public index As Integer
```

```vb
Protected yPos As Integer
Protected xPos As Integer = 5
Public operations As New ArrayList()

Public Sub New(ByVal startPoint As Point, ByVal endPoint As Point, _
  ByVal index As Integer)
  Me.StartPoint = startPoint
  Me.EndPoint = endPoint
  Me.index = index
  Dim r As Rectangle = MathUtil.GetRectangleFromPoints(startPoint, endPoint)
  Dim currentWidth As Integer = _
    CInt(IIf(r.Width > minimumWidth, r.Width, minimumWidth))
  Dim currentHeight As Integer = _
    CInt(IIf(r.Height > minimumHeight, r.Height, minimumHeight))
  Me.SetBounds(r.X, r.Y, currentWidth, currentHeight)
  Font = New Font("Times New Roman", 10)
End Sub

Public Sub Delete()
  ' call Dispose to remove me from parent's Controls collection
  Me.Dispose()
  Me.DestroyHandle() 'trigger the HandleDestroyed event
End Sub

Protected Overrides Sub OnPaint(ByVal e As PaintEventArgs)
  Dim g As Graphics = e.Graphics
  If selected Then
    g.DrawRectangle(foregroundPen, _
      CInt(handleWidth / 2), CInt(handleWidth / 2), Me.Width - handleWidth, _
      Me.Height - handleWidth)
    DrawHandles(g)
  Else
    g.DrawRectangle(foregroundPen, _
      0, 0, Me.Width - 1, Me.Height - 1)
  End If
  DrawName(g)
  'draw the line that partition the name part and the next part
  yPos += fontHeight
  If selected Then
    Dim x1 As Integer = CInt(handleWidth / 2)
    Dim x2 As Integer = x1 + Me.Width - handleWidth
    g.DrawLine(foregroundPen, x1, yPos, x2, yPos)
  Else
    Dim x1 As Integer = 0
```

```vbnet
      Dim x2 As Integer = x1 + Me.Width
      g.DrawLine(foregroundPen, x1, yPos, x2, yPos)
    End If
    DrawMembers(g)
  End Sub

  Private Sub DrawHandles(ByRef g As Graphics)
    'draw handles
    g.FillRectangle(handleBrush, _
      0, 0, handleWidth, handleWidth)
    g.FillRectangle(handleBrush, _
      Me.Width - handleWidth, 0, handleWidth, handleWidth)
    g.FillRectangle(handleBrush, _
      0, Me.Height - handleWidth, handleWidth, handleWidth)
    g.FillRectangle(handleBrush, _
      Me.Width - handleWidth, Me.Height - handleWidth, _
      handleWidth, handleWidth)
  End Sub

  Protected MustOverride Sub DrawName(ByRef g As Graphics)
  Protected MustOverride Sub DrawMembers(ByRef g As Graphics)

  Public Function OnWhichHandle(ByVal p As Point) As RectHandle
    If Not selected Then
      Return RectHandle.None
    End If
    Dim x As Integer = p.X
    Dim y As Integer = p.Y
    If x <= handleWidth And y <= handleWidth Then
      Return RectHandle.TopLeft
    ElseIf x >= Me.Width - handleWidth And y <= handleWidth Then
      Return RectHandle.TopRight
    ElseIf x <= handleWidth And y >= Me.Height - handleWidth Then
      Return RectHandle.BottomLeft
    ElseIf x >= Me.Width - handleWidth And y >= Me.Height - handleWidth Then
      Return RectHandle.BottomRight
    Else
      Return RectHandle.None
    End If
  End Function

  Public Sub SetTop(ByVal top As Integer)
    If top >= 0 Then
```

```
      Me.Top = top
    End If
    StartPoint.Y = Me.Top
    EndPoint.Y = StartPoint.Y + Me.Height
  End Sub

  Public Sub SetLeft(ByVal left As Integer)
    If left >= 0 Then
      Me.Left = left
    End If
    StartPoint.X = Me.Left
    EndPoint.X = StartPoint.X + Me.Width
  End Sub

  Public Sub SetWidth(ByVal width As Integer)
    If width > minimumWidth Then
      Me.Width = width
    Else
      Me.Width = minimumWidth
    End If
    EndPoint.X = StartPoint.X + Me.Width
  End Sub

  Public Sub SetHeight(ByVal height As Integer)
    If height > minimumHeight Then
      Me.Height = height
    Else
      Me.Height = minimumHeight
    End If
    EndPoint.Y = StartPoint.Y + Me.Height
  End Sub
End Class
```

The Rect Class's Constructor

The user draws a class structure or an interface structure by clicking the mouse on the draw area and dragging the mouse and then releasing the mouse. Therefore, there are two important Point objects when drawing: the Point object representing the click point on the draw area and the Point object representing the point on which the mouse click is released. The first point is called the *start point,* and the second point is called the *end point.*

The Rect class's child class constructor will invoke the Rect class's constructor, passing the start point and the end point as well as an integer that will become a unique identifier for the constructed Rect object. The index is generated in the DrawArea object and is a sequential number.

The startPoint, endPoint, and index arguments are assigned to the class-level variables:

```
Me.StartPoint = startPoint
Me.EndPoint = endPoint
Me.index = index
```

Again, because you cannot predict how users drag the mouse when drawing, you use the GetRectangleFromPoints method of the MathUtil class to obtain a Rectangle object from the start point and the end point:

```
Dim r As Rectangle = MathUtil.GetRectangleFromPoints(startPoint, endPoint)
```

You impose a minimum width and a minimum height for a Rect object. If the Rectangle object's width is narrower than the minimum width, the minimum width is used. If the Rectangle object's height is shorter than the minimum height, the minimum height is used. You get two values: currentWidth and currentHeight. For example:

```
Dim currentWidth As Integer = _
  CInt(IIf(r.Width > minimumWidth, r.Width, minimumWidth))
Dim currentHeight As Integer = _
  CInt(IIf(r.Height > minimumHeight, r.Height, minimumHeight))
```

Next, set the bounds for the Rect object using the Rectangle object and currentWidth and currentHeight:

```
Me.SetBounds(r.X, r.Y, currentWidth, currentHeight)
```

Next, construct a Font object used for drawing the labels in the Rect object:

```
Font = New Font("Times New Roman", 10)
```

The OnPaint Method

You draw the rectangular area by overriding the OnPaint method. First you draw the rectangle around the Rect object and then around the name (by calling the DrawName method) and the members (by calling the DrawMembers method). To draw, you need to first obtain the Graphics object from the PaintEventArgs argument:

```
Dim g As Graphics = e.Graphics
```

The rectangle will depend on whether the Rect object is selected—in other words, it depends on the value of the selected field. If it is not selected, it draws the rectangle that has the same dimension as the Rect object:

```
g.DrawRectangle(foregroundPen, _
  0, 0, Me.Width - 1, Me.Height - 1)
```

If it is selected, the rectangle is slightly smaller because you need to draw the four handles:

```
g.DrawRectangle(foregroundPen, _
  CInt(handleWidth / 2), CInt(handleWidth / 2), Me.Width - handleWidth, _
  Me.Height - handleWidth)
DrawHandles(g)
```

Afterward, you need to draw the name by calling the DrawName method:

```
DrawName(g)
```

Then, you need to draw the partition line that separates the name and the next part (the attributes if the Rect object is a class structure, and the operation if it is an interface structure). Note that you keep the y position in the yPos variable:

```
yPos += fontHeight
```

Again, the line drawn will depend on whether the object is being selected:

```
If selected Then
  Dim x1 As Integer = CInt(handleWidth / 2)
  Dim x2 As Integer = x1 + Me.Width - handleWidth
  g.DrawLine(foregroundPen, x1, yPos, x2, yPos)
Else
  Dim x1 As Integer = 0
  Dim x2 As Integer = x1 + Me.Width
  g.DrawLine(foregroundPen, x1, yPos, x2, yPos)
End If
```

At the end, you call the DrawMembers method to draw the members:

```
DrawMembers(g)
```

Both the DrawName and the DrawMembers methods are abstract methods and must be overridden by the child class.

The SetTop, SetLeft, SetWidth, and SetHeight Methods

When a Rect object is moved, its Left and Top property values must also change. When the Rect object is resized, its Width and Height property values must also update. Rather than accessing these properties directly, you use the SetTop, SetLeft, SetWidth, and SetHeight methods so that you can restrict as well as modify some other values.

For instance, when the user tries to move the Rect object up further than the top edge of the DrawArea, the value of the top argument will be negative and the SetTop method will not allow it to happen because it checks the top argument:

```
Public Sub SetTop(ByVal top As Integer)
  If top >= 0 Then
    Me.Top = top
  End If
  StartPoint.Y = Me.Top
  EndPoint.Y = StartPoint.Y + Me.Height
End Sub
```

Also, when the user tries to move the `Rect` object past the left edge of the `DrawArea`, the left argument value of the `SetLeft` method will be negative and it will not allow it to happen:

```
Public Sub SetLeft(ByVal left As Integer)
  If left >= 0 Then
    Me.Left = left
  End If
  StartPoint.X = Me.Left
  EndPoint.X = StartPoint.X + Me.Width
End Sub
```

The `SetWidth` and `SetHeight` method restrict the smallest width and height a `Rect` object can get:

```
Public Sub SetWidth(ByVal width As Integer)
  If width > minimumWidth Then
    Me.Width = width
  Else
    Me.Width = minimumWidth
  End If
  EndPoint.X = StartPoint.X + Me.Width
End Sub

Public Sub SetHeight(ByVal height As Integer)
  If height > minimumHeight Then
    Me.Height = height
  Else
    Me.Height = minimumHeight
  End If
  EndPoint.Y = StartPoint.Y + Me.Height
End Sub
```

The OnWhichHandle Method

When the `Rect` object is selected, the user can resize it by dragging one of the four handles. The first thing to check is whether the mouse is over any handle and, if it is, which handle. The `OnWhichHandle` method returns a member of the `RectHandle` enumeration. If the mouse is over the `Rect` object but not over one of the handles, or if the `Rect` object is not selected, the method returns `RectHandle.None`.

The Delete Method

The Delete method is called when the DrawArea object receives a Delete input key when the Rect object is selected. The Delete method calls two methods:

```
Me.Dispose()
Me.DestroyHandle() 'trigger the HandleDestroyed event
```

The Dispose method removes it from the Controls collection of the DrawArea method. The DestroyHandle method is called so that the HandleDestroyed event triggers. The HandleDestroyed event will be caught by any Line object connecting this Rect object to another Rect object. When the Line object receives this event, the Line object knows that one of its structures is deleted and therefore will remove itself.

The ClassRect Class

The ClassRect class represents a class structure. It derives from the Rect class. Listing 4-20 shows the ClassRect class.

Listing 4-20. The ClassRect Class

```
Option Explicit On
Option Strict On

Imports System
Imports System.Windows.Forms
Imports System.Drawing
Imports System.Collections
Imports Microsoft.VisualBasic

Public Class ClassRect : Inherits Rect
  Public attributes As New ArrayList()

  Public Sub New(ByVal startPoint As Point, ByVal endPoint As Point, _
    ByVal index As Integer)
    MyBase.new(startPoint, endPoint, index)
  End Sub
```

```vb
Public Sub New(ByVal memento As ClassRectMemento)
  MyBase.New(memento.StartPoint, memento.EndPoint, memento.index)
  Me.Name = memento.name
  Me.attributes = memento.attributes
  Me.operations = memento.operations
  Me.selected = memento.selected
End Sub

Public ReadOnly Property AttributeCount() As Integer
  Get
    Return attributes.Count
  End Get
End Property

Protected Overrides Sub DrawName(ByRef g As Graphics)
  yPos = textTopMargin
  ' center text
  Dim x As Integer = _
    CInt((Me.Width - g.MeasureString(Me.Name, Font).Width) / 2)
  If x > xpos Then
    g.DrawString(Name, Font, textBrush, x, yPos)
  Else
    g.DrawString(Name, Font, textBrush, xPos, yPos)
  End If
  yPos += fontHeight
End Sub

Protected Overrides Sub DrawMembers(ByRef g As Graphics)
  'draw attributes here
  Dim attrEnum As IEnumerator = attributes.GetEnumerator
  While attrEnum.MoveNext
    Dim attribute As String = CType(attrEnum.Current, String)
    g.DrawString(attribute, Font, textBrush, xpos, ypos)
    yPos += fontHeight
  End While
  'draw the line that partition the attributes and operations
  yPos += fontHeight
  If selected Then
    Dim x1 As Integer = CInt(handleWidth / 2)
    Dim x2 As Integer = x1 + Me.Width - handleWidth
    g.DrawLine(foregroundPen, x1, yPos, x2, yPos)
  Else
    Dim x1 As Integer = 0
```

```
      Dim x2 As Integer = x1 + Me.Width
      g.DrawLine(foregroundPen, x1, yPos, x2, yPos)
    End If
    'draw operations
    Dim opsEnum As IEnumerator = operations.GetEnumerator
    While opsEnum.MoveNext
      Dim operation As String = CType(opsEnum.Current, String)
      g.DrawString(operation, Font, textBrush, xpos, ypos)
      yPos += fontHeight
    End While

  End Sub

  Public Function GetMemento() As ClassRectMemento
    Dim memento As New ClassRectMemento()
    memento.index = Me.index
    memento.name = Me.Name
    memento.attributes = Me.attributes
    memento.operations = Me.operations
    memento.StartPoint = Me.StartPoint
    memento.EndPoint = Me.EndPoint
    memento.selected = Me.selected
    Return memento
  End Function
End Class
```

The ClassRect Class's Constructors

The ClassRect class has two constructors. The first constructor is as follows:

```
Public Sub New(ByVal startPoint As Point, ByVal endPoint As Point, _
  ByVal index As Integer)
  MyBase.new(startPoint, endPoint, index)
End Sub
```

This constructor is called when the user has just drawn a class structure. This constructor simply calls the constructor in the base class (the Rect class).

The second constructor is called when the ClassRect object needs to be restored from the ClassRectMemento object. It accepts a ClassRectMemento object. This constructor calls the base class's constructor and restores any needed states from the RectMemento object:

```
MyBase.New(memento.StartPoint, memento.EndPoint, memento.index)
Me.Name = memento.name
Me.attributes = memento.attributes
Me.operations = memento.operations
Me.selected = memento.selected
```

The GetMemento Method

The GetMemento method returns a ClassRectMemento object for object serialization.

The DrawName Method

The DrawName method draws the name for this class structure.

The DrawMembers Method

The DrawMembers method draws the list of attributes and operations in this class structure.

The ClassRectMemento Class

The ClassRectMemento class is the memento for the ClassRect object (see Listing 4-21). Note that it is marked with the <Serializable> attribute so that it can be serialized.

Listing 4-21. The ClassRectMemento *Class*

```
Imports System
Imports System.Drawing
Imports System.Collections
<Serializable()> Public Class ClassRectMemento
  Public index As Integer
  Public name As String
  Public StartPoint As Point
  Public EndPoint As Point
  Public selected As Boolean = True
  Public operations As ArrayList
  Public attributes As ArrayList
End Class
```

The InterfaceRect Class

The InterfaceRect class represents a UML interface structure. It derives from the Rect class (see Listing 4-22).

Listing 4-22. The InterfaceRect *Class*

```
Option Explicit On
Option Strict On

Imports System
Imports System.Windows.Forms
Imports System.Drawing
Imports System.Collections
Imports Microsoft.VisualBasic

Public Class InterfaceRect : Inherits Rect

  Public Sub New(ByVal startPoint As Point, ByVal endPoint As Point, _
    ByVal index As Integer)
    MyBase.New(startPoint, endPoint, index)
  End Sub

  Public Sub New(ByVal memento As InterfaceRectMemento)
    MyBase.New(memento.StartPoint, memento.EndPoint, memento.index)
    Me.Name = memento.name
    Me.operations = memento.operations
    Me.selected = memento.selected
  End Sub

  Protected Overrides Sub DrawName(ByRef g As Graphics)
    yPos = textTopMargin
    'draw prefix here
    Dim s As String = "<<Interface>>"
    Dim x As Integer = _
      CInt((Me.Width - g.MeasureString(s, Font).Width) / 2)
    If x > xpos Then
      g.DrawString(s, Font, textBrush, x, yPos)
    Else
      g.DrawString(s, Font, textBrush, xPos, yPos)
    End If
```

```vbnet
    yPos += fontHeight
    'draw name
    ' center text
    x = CInt((Me.Width - g.MeasureString(Me.Name, Font).Width) / 2)
    If x > xpos Then
      g.DrawString(Name, Font, textBrush, x, yPos)
    Else
      g.DrawString(Name, Font, textBrush, xPos, yPos)
    End If
    yPos += fontHeight
  End Sub


  Protected Overrides Sub DrawMembers(ByRef g As Graphics)
    'draw operations here
    'draw operations
    Dim opsEnum As IEnumerator = operations.GetEnumerator
    While opsEnum.MoveNext
      Dim operation As String = CType(opsEnum.Current, String)
      g.DrawString(operation, Font, textBrush, xpos, ypos)
      yPos += fontHeight
    End While
  End Sub


  Public Function GetMemento() As InterfaceRectMemento
    Dim memento As New InterfaceRectMemento()
    memento.index = Me.index
    memento.name = Me.Name
    memento.operations = Me.operations
    memento.StartPoint = Me.StartPoint
    memento.EndPoint = Me.EndPoint
    memento.selected = Me.selected
    Return memento
  End Function


End Class
```

319

The InterfaceRect Class's Constructors

The InterfaceRect class has two constructors. The first constructor is as follows:

```
Public Sub New(ByVal startPoint As Point, ByVal endPoint As Point, _
  ByVal index As Integer)
  MyBase.new(startPoint, endPoint, index)
End Sub
```

This constructor is called when the user has just drawn an interface structure. This constructor just calls the constructor in the base class (the Rect class).

The second constructor is called when the InterfaceRect object needs to be restored from the InterfaceRectMemento object. It accepts an InterfaceRectMemento object. This constructor calls the base class's constructor and restores any needed states from the RectMemento object:

```
MyBase.New(memento.StartPoint, memento.EndPoint, memento.index)
Me.Name = memento.name
Me.operations = memento.operations
Me.selected = memento.selected
```

The GetMemento Method

The GetMemento method returns an InterfaceRectMemento object for object serialization.

The DrawName Method

The DrawName method draws the name for this interface structure.

The DrawMembers Method

The DrawMembers method draws the list of operations in this interface structure.

The *InterfaceRectMemento* Class

The `InterfaceRectMemento` class represents the memento for the `InterfaceRect` object (see Listing 4-23). Note that this class is marked with the `<Serializable>` attribute to make it serializable.

Listing 4-23. The `InterfaceRectMemento` *Class*

```
Imports System
Imports System.Drawing
Imports System.Collections

<Serializable()> Public Class InterfaceRectMemento
  Public index As Integer
  Public name As String
  Public StartPoint As Point
  Public EndPoint As Point
  Public selected As Boolean = True
  Public operations As ArrayList
End Class
```

The *InputBox* Class

An `InputBox` object edits a class structure's name, list of attributes, and list of operations and edits a UML interface structure's name and list of operations. The `InputBox` object is represented by the `InputBox` class. The `InputBox` class derives from the `System.Windows.Forms.TextBox` class and is instantiated when the `DrawArea` control is constructed. The `InputBox` object is then added to the `Controls` collection of the `DrawArea` object. It is the first child control of the `DrawArea` object.

By default, the `InputBox` object is not visible. It is visible when the user right-clicks a class structure or an interface structure. When visible, the `InputBox` object is positioned on top of the clicked structure to give the impression that the `InputBox` is actually part of the structure. The `InputBox` object will become invisible again when it loses focus.

When it is shown, the `InputBox` object will receive a `Rect` object so that it will have access to the `Rect` object whose part is being edited. Listing 4-24 shows the `InputBox` class.

Listing 4-24. The InputBox *Class*

```
Option Explicit On
Option Strict On

Imports System
Imports System.Windows.Forms
Imports System.Collections

Public Class InputBox : Inherits TextBox
  'the interface or class that is being updated
  Public rect As Rect
  Public Property LineArrayList() As ArrayList
    Get
      Dim str() As String = Me.Lines
      Dim al As New ArrayList()
      Dim count As Integer = str.Length
      Dim i As Integer
      For i = 0 To count - 1
        al.Add(str(i))
      Next
      Return al
    End Get
    Set(ByVal al As ArrayList)
      Dim itemCount As Integer = al.Count
      If itemCount = 0 Then
        Me.Lines = Nothing
      Else
        Dim str(itemCount - 1) As String
        Dim i As Integer
        For i = 0 To itemCount - 1
          str(i) = CType(al.Item(i), String)
        Next
        Me.Lines = str
      End If
    End Set
  End Property

End Class
```

The InputBox class adds the LineArrayList property to the TextBox class. This property enables an ArrayList to populate the Lines property. Assigning an ArrayList object to the InputBox object will iterate the ArrayList and create an array of string that will then be fed to the Lines property:

```
Dim itemCount As Integer = al.Count
If itemCount = 0 Then
  Me.Lines = Nothing
Else
  Dim str(itemCount - 1) As String
  Dim i As Integer
  For i = 0 To itemCount - 1
    str(i) = CType(al.Item(i), String)
  Next
  Me.Lines = str
End If
```

This property returns an ArrayList object containing each element in the Lines array of strings:

```
Dim str() As String = Me.Lines
Dim al As New ArrayList()
Dim count As Integer = str.Length
Dim i As Integer
For i = 0 To count - 1
  al.Add(str(i))
Next
Return al
```

The Line Class

The Line class represents a relationship line. There are four types of lines in this application, and they differ only in the graphical appearance—in other words, the end cap and the line style.

There are two possible ways of implementing it. The first is to create a base Line class with four child classes, each representing a line type. The base Line class will have a virtual method for drawing itself and will depend on polymorphism to draw the correct type of line. This solution is elegant, but the number of extra classes adds to the maintenance burden.

The second way is to have a variable that holds the type of the line and then use a `Select Case` block to draw the correct type of line. This project uses the latter because the only difference among the four types of lines is the type of `Pen` object to draw those lines.

A line always has two structures at its ends. When one of its structures is moved, the line will follow. In other words, the line will adjust its own position based on the positions of its structures. When first created, the adjustment is automatic, meaning that the line can connect to a structure at any of the structure's sides.

The user can drag a line manually, causing the mode of adjustment to change to manual. In this case, the line will only connect to the structure at that particular side.

The `autoMove` variable in the `Line` class indicates a line's adjustment mode.

You can see the `Line` class in the `Line.vb` file in the project's directory. To save space, the `Line` class source code is not printed here.

The Line Class's Constructors

The `Line` class has two constructors. The first constructor is used when the user draws a `Line` object. Its signature is as follows:

```
Public Sub New(ByVal fromRect As Rect, ByVal toRect As Rect, _
    ByVal index As Integer, ByVal lineType As ShapeType)
```

Note that it accepts two `Rect` objects, `fromRect` and `toRect`. `fromRect` is the `Rect` object from which the line is drawn. `toRect` is the `Rect` object to which the line is drawn. It also accepts the index number and the line type. The line type is of type `ShapeType` enumeration.

This constructor first assigns the arguments to the class variables:

```
Me.lineType = lineType
Me.fromRect = fromRect
Me.toRect = toRect
Me.index = index
```

It then wires the `LocationChanged`, `HandleDestroyed`, and `Resize` events of both `Rect` objects.

```
AddHandler fromRect.LocationChanged, AddressOf rect_LocationChanged
AddHandler toRect.LocationChanged, AddressOf rect_LocationChanged
AddHandler fromRect.HandleDestroyed, AddressOf rect_HandleDestroyed
AddHandler toRect.HandleDestroyed, AddressOf rect_HandleDestroyed
AddHandler fromRect.Resize, AddressOf rect_Resize
AddHandler toRect.Resize, AddressOf rect_Resize
```

When one of its `Rect` objects is moved or resized, the `Line` object needs to readjust its position. Therefore, both the `rect_LocationChanged` and the `rect_Resize` event handlers call the `ReadjustPosition` method.

Next, the constructor constructs a `Pen` object used for drawing itself and readjusts its location by calling the `ConstructPen` and `ReadjustLocation` methods:

```
ConstructPen()
ReadjustLocation()
```

The second constructor reconstructs the `Line` object from a `LineMemento` object. Its signature is as follows:

```
Public Sub New(ByVal fromRect As Rect, ByVal toRect As Rect, _
    ByVal memento As LineMemento)
```

It calls the first constructor and then populates the `Line` object with the states from the `LineMemento` object.

The ConstructPen Method

This method constructs a `Pen` object based on the value of the `lineType` variable. The `ConstructPen` method is only called once—in other words, when the `Line` object is instantiated. The method contains a `Select Case` block such as the following:

```
Select Case Me.lineType
  Case ShapeType.Generalization
    ...
  Case ShapeType.Dependency
    ...
  Case ShapeType.Association
    ...
  Case ShapeType.Aggregation
    ...
End Select
```

The ReadjustLocation Method

The `ReadjustLocation` method changes the value of the `Line` object's `startPoint` and `endPoint`. There are two types of adjustments: automatic and manual, which are determined by the value of `autoMove`. When adjustment is automatic, the `ReadjustLocation` method takes into account the relative positions of `fromRect` and `toRect`.

When adjustment is manual, the Line object "remembers" which side of fromRect and toRect it connects to and at which points on those sides. The Line class uses a private enumeration whichSide that defines the four sides of a Rect object:

```
Private Enum whichSide As Integer
  Top = 0
  Bottom = 1
  Left = 2
  Right = 3
End Enum
```

As in the automatic adjustment, the manual adjustment aims at updating the value of the Line object's start point and end point of both fromRect and toRect. This is the skeleton of the part that deals with the manual adjustment:

```
'adjust the StartPoint
Select Case fromRectWhichSide
  Case whichSide.Bottom
    ...
  Case whichSide.Top
    ...
  Case whichSide.Left
    ...
  Case whichSide.Right
    ...
End Select

'adjust the EndPoint
Select Case toRectWhichSide
  Case whichSide.Bottom
    ...
  Case whichSide.Top
    ...
  Case whichSide.Left
    ...
  Case whichSide.Right
    ...
End Select
```

The Draw Method

The Draw method draws the following.

- The line connecting the start point and the end point

- The three labels at the left, center, and right side of the line

- The handles when the Line object is selected

Note that when the line type is ShapeType.Aggregation or ShapeType.Generalization, the Draw method needs to do the following extra work:

```
If lineType = ShapeType.Aggregation Or _
  lineType = ShapeType.Generalization Then

  'create a new GraphicsPath so the following transform won't affect the
  'arrow head
  Dim gp As GraphicsPath = CType(arrowHeadGraphicPath.Clone, GraphicsPath)
  Dim rotAngle As Single = GetRotationAngle()

  g.TranslateTransform(EndPoint.X, EndPoint.Y)
  g.RotateTransform(rotAngle + 270)
  g.FillPath(Brushes.White, gp)
  'FillPath will erase some of the graphics path
  'redraw the arrow head
  g.DrawPath(Pens.Black, gp)
  g.ResetTransform()
End If
```

To understand why it needs to do the extra work, look at the part near the end points of an aggregation line and a generalization line in Figure 4-25 if the Draw method does not do this.

Figure 4-25. Imperfect aggregation line and generalization line

See how the lines go through the arrow heads? The "extra work" patches the arrow heads with a GraphicsPath object filled with the background color (in this case, white):

```
g.FillPath(Brushes.White, gp)
```

Because the patching can override some points of the arrow head, the arrow head needs to be redrawn with the foreground color (in this case, black):

```
g.DrawPath(Pens.Black, gp)
```

The TranslateTransform method of the Graphics class is called to move the origin to the end point:

```
g.TranslateTransform(EndPoint.X, EndPoint.Y)
```

The RotateTransform method rotates the GraphicsPath object to the correct angle. The correct rotation angle is returned by the GetRotationAngle method.
Finally, you reset the transformation by calling the ResetTransform method:

```
g.ResetTransform()
```

The GetMemento Method

The GetMemento method returns a LineMemento object containing the states of the Line that need to be persisted.

The Removed Event

The Line class raises the Removed event when one of its structures is removed. The DrawArea control captures this event.

The LineMemento Class

The LineMemento class represents a memento for a Line object (see Listing 4-25). Note that this class is marked with the <Serializable> attribute to make the LineMemento object serializable.

Listing 4-25. The LineMemento *Class*

```
Imports System
Imports System.Drawing
<Serializable()> Public Class LineMemento
  Public index As Integer
  Public lineType As ShapeType
  Public fromRectIndex As Integer
  Public toRectIndex As Integer
  Public StartPoint As Point
  Public EndPoint As Point
  Public selected As Boolean
  Public leftText As String
  Public centerText As String
  Public rightText As String
  Public autoMove As Boolean
  Public fromRectXRelPos As Integer
  Public fromRectYRelPos As Integer
  Public toRectXRelPos As Integer
  Public toRectYRelPos As Integer
  Public fromRectWhichSide As Integer
  Public toRectWhichSide As Integer
End Class
```

The PropertyForm *Class*

A form edits the labels attached to a line. This form is called the *property form* and is represented by the PropertyForm class. You can find the PropertyForm class in the PropertyForm.vb file in the project's directory; it is not printed here to save space.

NOTE *The user can display the property form by pressing the F4 key or by clicking Property Form from the View menu.*

Figure 4-26 shows the property form.

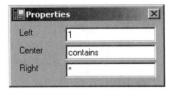

Figure 4-26. The property form

The `PropertyForm` class includes the `PropertyChanged` event, which is of type `PropertyEventHandler`. The `PropertyEventHandler` delegate is defined as follows:

```
Public Delegate Sub PropertyEventHandler(ByVal sender As Object, _
  ByVal e As EventArgs)
```

The `PropertyChanged` event triggers every time a property is updated.

The DrawArea Class

The `DrawArea` class represents the draw area of the application. It derives from the `System.Windows.Forms.Panel` class. You can find the `DrawArea` class in the `DrawArea.vb` file in the project's directory. It is not printed here to save space.

The Form

The form is represented by the `Form1` class, which is derived from the `System.Windows.Forms.Form` class. You can find it in the `Form1.vb` file in the project's directory. It is not printed here to save space.

Compiling and Running the Application

You can find all the classes used in the application in the `UMLClassDiagram.vb` file. To compile this application, follow these steps:

1. Create a working directory.

2. Copy all the .vb files to the working directory.

3. Run the `build.bat` file to build the project.

The content of the build.bat file is as follows:

```
vbc /t:library /r:System.dll Misc.vb
vbc /t:library /r:System.dll,System.Drawing.dll,mscorlib.dll MathUtil.vb
vbc /t:library /r:System.dll,System.Drawing.dll ClassRectMemento.vb
vbc /t:library /r:System.dll,System.Drawing.dll InterfaceRectMemento.vb
vbc /t:library /r:System.dll,System.Drawing.dll,↵
System.Windows.Forms.dll,Misc.dll,MathUtil.dll Rect.vb
vbc /t:library /r:System.dll,System.Drawing.dll,System.Windows.Forms.dll,↵
Misc.dll,MathUtil.dll,Rect.dll,ClassRectMemento.dll ClassRect.vb
vbc /t:library /r:System.dll,System.Drawing.dll,System.Windows.Forms.dll,↵
Misc.dll,MathUtil.dll,Rect.dll,InterfaceRectMemento.dll InterfaceRect.vb
vbc /t:library /r:System.dll,System.Drawing.dll,Misc.dll LineMemento.vb
vbc /t:library /r:System.dll,System.Drawing.dll,System.Windows.Forms.dll,↵
Misc.dll,MathUtil.dll,Rect.dll,LineMemento.dll Line.vb
vbc /t:library /r:System.dll,System.Drawing.dll,System.Windows.Forms.dll,↵
Line.dll PropertyForm.vb
vbc /t:library /r:System.dll,System.Drawing.dll,System.Windows.Forms.dll,↵
Rect.dll InputBox.vb
vbc /t:library /r:System.dll,System.Drawing.dll,System.Windows.Forms.dll,↵
Misc.dll,MathUtil.dll,Rect.dll,ClassRect.dll,InterfaceRect.dll,↵
ClassRectMemento.dll,InterfaceRectMemento.dll,Line.dll,↵
LineMemento.dll,InputBox.dll DrawArea.vb
vbc /t:winexe /r:System.dll,System.Drawing.dll,System.Windows.Forms.dll,↵
Misc.dll,MathUtil.dll,Rect.dll,ClassRect.dll,InterfaceRect.dll,↵
ClassRectMemento.dll,InterfaceRectMemento.dll,Line.dll,↵
LineMemento.dll,InputBox.dll,DrawArea.dll,PropertyForm.dll Form1.vb
```

To run the application, type form1.exe in the command prompt. Note that the images directory must be in the directory where the form1.exe file resides. You should see the screenshot as displayed in Figure 4-27.

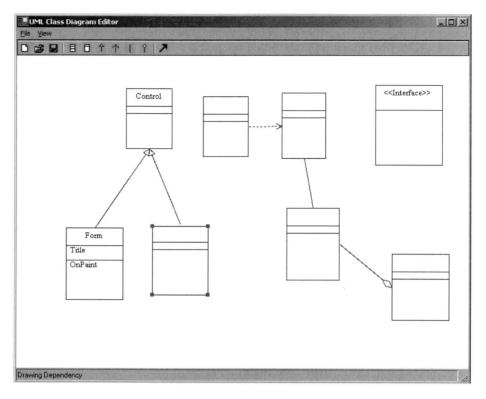

Figure 4-27. The UML class diagram editor

Summary

In this chapter you saw topics that you need to understand to build a GDI+ application that creates and edits a UML class diagram. You have also learned the following topics.

- GDI+ and drawing with .NET Framework

- Object serialization

- The Memento design pattern

CHAPTER 5

Developing an FTP Client Application

FILE TRANSFER IS an important networking task, and File Transfer Protocol (FTP) client applications are still in wide use despite the ever-increasing popularity of the Web. The FTP client application built for this chapter complies with the current standard as specified in RFC959 by the World Wide Web Consortium (www.w3.org); you can use it to connect to and engage in file transfer with standard FTP servers. The main purpose of developing this application is to show how to work with sockets in the .NET Framework.

Overview of the Chapter

This chapter starts by presenting a general overview of sockets and continues with FTP and the project itself. In this chapter, you will find the following sections:

- **"Working with Sockets"**: This section introduces sockets and explains how to use the System.Net.Sockets.Socket class and other related classes for network programming.

- **"Understanding FTP"**: This section discusses the protocol for file transfer as specified in RFC959.

- **"Creating an FTP Application Step by Step"**: This section covers a simple console application that is similar to the ftp.exe program included in the UNIX/Linux or Windows operating systems. This serves as an introduction to the chapter's FTP project.

- **"Implementing the Project"**: This section contains a detailed discussion on the FTP client application with a Graphical User Interface (GUI).

Working with Sockets

A *socket* is an end point of a connection. It is a descriptor that lets an application read from and write to the network. Using sockets, client applications and server applications can communicate by sending and receiving streams of bytes over connections. To send a message to another socket used in a software application, you need to know not only the machine's Internet Protocol (IP) address that hosts the software application but also the software's process identifier in that machine. A unique number, called a *port*, identifies a software process in a machine. Therefore, to send a message from a socket in one application to another socket in another connection, you need to know the machine's IP address and the application's port number.

In the .NET Framework, the System.Net.Sockets.Socket class represents a socket. This class is an implementation of the Sockets Application Programming Interface (API), which is also known as the *Berkeley sockets interface*. The Sockets API was developed in the early 80s at the University of California at Berkeley for the 4.1c release of Berkeley Software Distribution (BSD) Unix. This distribution contained an early version of the Internet protocols.

You can use the System.Net.Sockets.Socket class as a socket in a server application as well as in a client application. It also allows both synchronous and asynchronous operations. This chapter only covers using the Socket class in a client application. For more details on using this class in a server application, you should consult the .NET Framework documentation.

Instantiating a Socket Object

Instantiating a socket object requires you to pass three arguments to its constructor.

```
Public Sub New( _
  ByVal addressFamily As AddressFamily, _
  ByVal socketType As SocketType, _
  ByVal protocolType As ProtocolType _
)
```

AddressFamily, SocketType, and ProtocolType are enumerations that are part of the System.Net.Sockets namespace.

An AddressFamily member defines the addressing scheme that a Socket object uses to resolve an address. For socket applications that will work on the Internet, you use InterNetwork.

SocketType determines the type of socket. For this FTP client application, you will use the Stream type. This type of socket supports two-way, connection-based byte streams.

ProtocolType specifies the type of the low-level protocol that the socket uses to communicate. You must use a stream socket with the Transmission Control Protocol (TCP) type and the InterNetwork address family.

Therefore, instantiating a Socket object for your application requires the following code:

```
Dim mySocket As New Socket(AddressFamily.InterNetwork, _
  SocketType.Stream, ProtocolType.Tcp)
```

The arguments you pass to the constructor are available in the following read-only properties: AddressFamily, SocketType, and ProtocolType.

Connecting to a Remote Server

Once you have a socket instance, you can connect to a remote server using the Socket class's Connect method. The Connect method attempts to connect to a remote server synchronously. It waits until a connection attempt is successful or has failed before releasing control to the next line in the program. Even though this method is easy to use, there is some preliminary work before you can use this method to connect to a remote server. Consider the Connect method signature:

```
Public Sub Connect( ByVal remoteEP As EndPoint)
```

It accepts an argument: an instance of System.Net.EndPoint. The abstract EndPoint class represents a network address and has a subclass: System.Net.IPEndPoint. When using the Connect method, you typically pass an IPEndPoint object containing the IP address and port number of the remote server to which you want to connect. The question will then be, "How do you construct an IPEndPoint object for your socket to connect to a remote server?"

Now, look at the IPEndPoint class definition. It has two constructors:

```
Public Sub New( ByVal address As Long, ByVal port As Integer)
Public Sub New( ByVal address As IPAddress, ByVal port As Integer)
```

Of these two constructors, the second is usually used because IP addresses are dotted-quad notation such as 129.36.128.44 and, as you soon will see, in the .NET socket programming, it is easier to get an IP address in this notation than a Long. However, the two constructors are actually similar. It is just that the remote IP address in the first constructor is a Long, whereas in the second constructor it is a System.Net.IPAddress object. Whichever constructor you choose, you need to have an IP address and the port number of the remote server. The port number is usually not a problem because popular services are allocated default port numbers. For instance, HTTP uses port 80, Telnet uses port 25, and FTP uses port 21.

The IP address is not normally directly available because it is easier to remember domain names such as microsoft.com or amazon.com rather than the IP addresses mapped to them. With this in mind, you need to resolve a domain name to obtain the IP address of the remote server to which you would like to connect. In the event, to obtain an IPAddress instance that you can use to connect to a remote server, you need the following two other classes: System.Net.Dns and System.Net.IPHostEntry.

The Dns class is a final class that retrieves information about a specific host from the Internet Domain Name System (DNS)—hence the name Dns. It is mainly used for its Resolve method to obtain a set of IP addresses mapped to a domain name. The Resolve method returns an IPHostEntry object that contains an array of IP addresses. To obtain these IP addresses, you use the IPHostEntry class's AddressList property.

For example, the following code displays all IP addresses mapped to a DNS name:

```
Try
  Dim server As String = "microsoft.com"  'or any other domain name
  Dim hostEntry As IPHostEntry = Dns.Resolve(server)
  Dim ipAddresses As IPAddress() = hostEntry.AddressList

  Console.WriteLine(server & " is mapped to")
  Dim ipAddress As IPAddress
  For each ipAddress In ipAddresses
    Console.WriteLine(ipAddress.ToString())
  Next
Catch e As Exception
  Console.WriteLine(e.ToString())
End Try
```

When run, the code will display all IP addresses mapped to the DNS name microsoft.com.

If a DNS name is mapped to more than one IP address, you can use any of those addresses, even though people usually use the first one. The reason for choosing the first one is that a DNS name is often mapped to one IP address only. You can obtain the first IP address mapped to a DNS name using the following code:

```
HostEntry.AddressList(0)
```

What is more important, once you get an IPAddress object, is that you can construct an IPEndPoint object to connect to a remote server. If the connection is successful, the Socket instance will set its Connected property to True. A programmer often checks the value of this property before performing other operations on the socket instance because a server application can close a connection after a period of time lapses.

To close a connection explicitly when you are done with a socket, you use the Close method. Usually, you need to call the Shutdown method prior to invoking Close to flush all pending data.

Sending and Receiving Streams

After a socket is connected to a remote machine, you can use it to send and receive data. To send data in synchronous mode, you use the Send method. You must place the data you send in an array of bytes. There are four overloads of the Send method, all of which return an Integer indicating the number of bytes sent.

The first overload is the simplest and the easiest to use of the four. It has the following signature:

```
Overloads Public Function Send( ByVal buffer() As Byte ) As Integer
```

where *buffer* is an array of Byte containing the data you want to send. Using this overload, all data in the buffer will be sent.

The second overload allows you to send all data in the buffer and specify the bitwise combination of the System.Net.Sockets.SocketFlags enumeration members. It has the following signature:

```
Overloads Public Function Send( _
  ByVal buffer() As Byte, _
  ByVal socketFlags As SocketFlags _
  ) As Integer
```

The third overload allows you to send all or part of the data in the buffer and specify the bitwise combination of the SocketFlags enumeration:

```
Overloads Public Function Send( _
  ByVal buffer() As Byte, _
  ByVal size As Integer, _
  ByVal socketFlags As SocketFlags _
) As Integer
```

In this overload, *size* is the number of bytes to be sent.

The last overload is similar to the third overload, but it also allows you to specify an offset position in the buffer to begin sending data. Its signature is as follows:

```
Overloads Public Function Send( _
  ByVal buffer() As Byte, _
  ByVal offset As Integer, _
  ByVal size As Integer, _
  ByVal socketFlags As SocketFlags _
) As Integer
```

In this overload, *offset* is the offset position.

To receive data synchronously, you use the Receive method. This method also has four overloads that are similar to the Send method overloads. The signatures of the overloads are as follows:

```
Overloads Public Function Receive( ByVal buffer() As Byte ) As Integer

Overloads Public Function Receive( _
  ByVal buffer() As Byte, _
  ByVal socketFlags As SocketFlags _
 ) As Integer

Overloads Public Function Receive( _
  ByVal buffer() As Byte, _
  ByVal size As Integer, _
  ByVal socketFlags As SocketFlags _
) As Integer

Overloads Public Function Receive( _
  ByVal buffer() As Byte, _
  ByVal offset As Integer, _
  ByVal size As Integer, _
  ByVal socketFlags As SocketFlags _
) As Integer
```

When using the `Receive` method, you can use the `Socket` class's `Available` property, which specifies the number of bytes of data received and is available to be read.

Understanding FTP

RFC959 specifies the protocol for file transfer and is downloadable from `www.w3.org/Protocols/rfc959/A3_FTP_RFCs.html`. This protocol defines how an FTP client application and an FTP server must communicate.

Just like any client-server application, an FTP server should be available all the time and a server does not know anything about its clients. It is always the client that initiates a connection with the server. Before any file transfer can happen, a client needs to connect to the FTP server and log in with a username and a password. Some FTP servers allow anyone to access some or all of their content by requesting them to log in using an anonymous account—in other words, by using "anonymous" as the username and their email address as the password.

In FTP, two connections need to be established between a client and an FTP server. The first connection, the control connection, remains open during the whole session and acts as the communication channel the client uses to send requests to the server and for the server to send responses to those requests. The second connection is the data connection used to transfer files and other data. This connection opens just before some data need to be transferred. The data connection closes right after the data transfer.

Typically, the "conversation" on the control channel after a connection is established goes like this:

1. **Server**: OK, you are now connected. Tell me what you want.

2. **Client**: I would like to log in. Here is my username: "James."

3. **Server**: Username received. Now, send me your password.

4. **Client**: My password is "s3m1c0nduct0r."

By sending the username and password, the client tries to log in. If the login fails, the server asks the client to send the password again. If it is successful, an FTP session starts and file transfer can begin. The server terminates the session if it does not hear anything from the client within some period of time, usually 900 seconds.

The client can start transferring files between itself and the server. Again, the "conversation" goes like the following:

1. **Client**: Please send me `companySecret.doc`.

2. **Server**: Here you go. I am sending it from port *x*.

The client then uses another socket instance and tries to connect to the IP address and port specified by the server. Once connected at this port, the server starts sending the file. When all the data is sent, the server automatically closes the data connection. Then the server uses the control channel to send the client the following message:

Server: Connection complete.

A data connection also opens when the client needs to transfer a file or when the server needs to send the list of files and subdirectories in the specified directory. What really happens is of course more technical than the previous description. However, you should have the general idea.

Using FTP Commands

In a conversation between an FTP client application and an FTP server, the client sends a series of FTP commands and the server replies to each command sent by the client. The next client operation is determined by the previous server's reply.

Table 5-1 describes the FTP command that a client application can send to the server.

Table 5-1. FTP Commands

COMMAND	TYPE	DESCRIPTION
USER	Access control	Sends the username to the server to log in. This is normally the first command sent by the client after a control connection is established.
PASS	Access control	Sends the user password to the server to log in. This is normally the command that must be sent immediately after the USER command is sent.
ACCT	Access control	Sends the user's account information. Some FTP servers may require the user's account information to log in, and some may not. If required, this command must be sent right after the server sends the response to the client's PASS command. This response also determines whether the ACCT command needs to be sent. If the server sends a 332 cod to the client's PASS command, the ACCT command must be sent.

(Continued)

Table 5-1. FTP Commands (Continued)

COMMAND	TYPE	DESCRIPTION
CWD	Access control	Changes the server's working directory.
CDUP	Access control	Changes to the parent directory. This is a special case for the CWD command.
SMNT	Access control	Mounts a different file system data structure without altering the client's login or accounting information.
REIN	Access control	Terminates the client, flushing all input/output and account information. Upon receipt of this command, the server leaves the control connection open.
QUIT	Access control	Terminates the client and closes the control connection. If file transfer is in progress when this command is received, the connection remains open for the server to send the file transfer completion reply code. Afterward, the connection closes.
PORT	Transfer	Specifies the data port to be used in the data connection. This command is normally not necessary because there are defaults for both the user and server data ports.
PASV	Transfer	Asks the server to become passive—in other words, requests the server to listen on a data port and to wait for a connection rather than initiate one upon receipt of a file transfer command. The server replies by sending the host address and port number this server is listening on for the next file transfer.
TYPE	Transfer	Specifies the representation type—in other words, whether the representation is ASCII, EBCDIC, or Image (binary).
STRU	Transfer	Specifies the file structure.
MODE	Transfer	Specifies the transfer mode (Stream, Block, or Compressed). The default is Stream.
RETR	Service	Requests the transfer of the specified file from the server.
STOR	Service	Asks the server to accept a file from the client. If a file with the same name already exists in the working directory, the file will be overwritten.
STOU	Service	Similar to STOR, but the file is saved in a different name. The new filename is created in the current directory under a name unique to that directory.
APPE	Service	Asks the server to accept a file from the client. If a file with the same name already exists in the working directory, the transferred file will be appended to the existing file.

(Continued)

Table 5-1. FTP Commands (Continued)

COMMAND	TYPE	DESCRIPTION
ALLO	Service	Requests the server to reserve sufficient storage to accommodate the new file to be transferred.
REST	Service	Restarts a new file transfer.
RNFR	Service	Specifies the name of the file to be renamed. This command must be followed immediately by the RNTO command.
RNTO	Service	Specifies the new name for the file to be renamed.
ABOR	Service	Aborts the previous FTP service command.
DELE	Service	Deletes the specified file.
RMD	Service	Removes directory.
MKD	Service	Makes a new directory
PWD	Service	Prints the working directory.
LIST	Service	Requests the list of files/subdirectories in the specified directory and information on each individual file/subdirectory such as file size, modified date, and so on.
NLST	Service	Requests the list of files/subdirectories in the specified directory without information about each individual file/subdirectory.
SITE	Service	Asks the server to provide services specific to its system that are essential to file transfer but not sufficiently universal to be included a command in the protocol.
SYST	Service	Inquires about the server's operating system.
STAT	Service	Inquires about the status of a file transfer.
HELP	Service	Requests some helpful information regarding the server's implementation status over the control connection to the client.
NOOP	Service	No operation.

You terminate each FTP command with a carriage-return line feed. For example, the following code connects to ftp.microsoft.com and sends the USER command indicating the username James:

```
Private server As String = "ftp.microsoft.com"
Private port As Integer = 21
Private userName As String = "James"
Private controlSocket As Socket
Try
  controlSocket = New _
    Socket(AddressFamily.InterNetwork, SocketType.Stream, ProtocolType.Tcp)
  controlSocket.Connect(New IPEndPoint(Dns.Resolve(server).AddressList(0), port))
```

```
  If controlSocket.Connected Then
    Console.WriteLine("Connected. Waiting for reply...")
    Dim bytes(511) As Byte ' an array of 512 bytes
    Dim receivedByteCount As Integer
    ' receive the server's response on successful connect
    receivedByteCount = controlSocket.Receive(bytes)

    ' send the USER command
    Dim command As String
    command = "USER " & userName & ControlChars.CrLf
    controlSocket.Send(Encoding.ASCII.GetBytes(command), command.Length, 0)
  End If
Catch
End Try
```

An FTP connection carries a two-way dialogue between the FTP server and the client application. The FTP server sends a reply to any command sent by the client. To understand how the conversation takes place, it is important to understand the server's replies.

Sending FTP Replies

An FTP server replies to every FTP command from a client. These replies ensure that requests and actions are synchronized during the process of file transfer. They are also useful so that the client always know the state of the server.

An FTP command generates one or more replies. For example, a USER command makes the server send a reply requesting the client to send the PASS command. Some commands generate more replies. An example of multiple replies is when an FTP server is about to send a file to a client. First, the server sends a reply notifying the client that the file transfer process will commence. After the file transfer finishes and the data connection closes, the server sends the second reply telling the client that the file transfer has completed.

An FTP reply consists of a reply code followed by a space and some description. A reply code is always a three-digit number specified in RFC959, but the descriptions can be different from one server implementation to another. An FTP client should only rely on the reply code.

Each of the three digits in a reply code has special meaning. The first digit is the most important and indicates whether the FTP command is successful, has failed, or is incomplete. There are five possible values for the first digit in the reply code: 1, 2, 3, 4, and 5.

Table 5-2 describes the meaning of each possible value of the first digit in a reply code.

Table 5-2. The First Digit in an FTP Reply

VALUE	DESCRIPTION
1	Positive preliminary reply. The requested action is being initiated; expect another reply before proceeding with a new command. This type of reply indicates that the command was accepted and the client may now pay attention to the data connections for implementations where simultaneous monitoring is difficult.
2	Positive completion reply. The requested action has been successfully completed. A new request may be initiated.
3	Positive intermediate reply. The command has been accepted, but the requested action will not be active, pending receipt of further information. The user should send another command specifying this information.
4	Transient negative completion reply. The command was not accepted and the requested action did not take place, but the error condition is temporary and the action may be requested again. The user should return to the beginning of the command sequence, if any. Note that it is difficult to assign a meaning to *transient*, particularly when two distinct sites (server and client) have to agree on the interpretation.
5	Permanent negative completion reply. The command was not accepted and the requested action did not take place. The client is discouraged from repeating the exact request (in the same sequence).

Table 5-3 describes the meaning of each possible value of the second digit in a reply code.

Table 5-3. The Second Digit in an FTP Reply

VALUE	DESCRIPTION
0	These replies refer to syntax errors, syntactically correct commands that do not fit any functional category, and unimplemented or superfluous commands.
1	These are replies to requests for information, such as status or help.
2	These replies refer to the control and data connections.
3	Authentication and accounting. These are replies for the login process and accounting procedures.
4	Unspecified yet.
5	These replies indicate the status of the server file system *vis-à-vis* the requested transfer or other file system action.

The third digit of the reply code gives a finer gradation of the meaning indicated by the second digit. Table 5-4 should make it clearer.

Table 5-4. FTP Reply Codes in Numerical Order

VALUE	DESCRIPTION
110	Restart marker reply.
120	Service ready in *nnn* minutes.
125	Data connection already open; transfer starting.
150	File status OK; about to open data connection.
200	Command OK.
202	Command not implemented, superfluous at this site.
211	System status, or system help reply.
212	Directory status.
213	File status.
214	Help message.
215	NAME system type, where NAME is an official system name from the list in the Assigned Numbers document.
220	Service ready for new user.
221	Service closing control connection.
225	Data connection open; no transfer in progress.
226	Closing data connection. Request file action successful (for example, file transfer or file abort).
227	Entering Passive Mode (h1,h2,h3,h4,p1,p2).
230	User logged in; proceed.
250	Requested file action OK, completed.
257	"PATHNAME" created.
331	Username OK; need password.
332	Need account for login.
350	Requested file action pending further information.
421	Service not available, closing control connection. This may be a reply to any command if the service knows it must shut down.
425	Cannot open data connection.
426	Connection closed; transfer aborted.
450	Requested file action not taken. File unavailable (for example, file busy).
451	Requested action aborted: local error in processing.

(Continued)

Table 5-4. FTP Reply Codes in Numerical Order (Continued)

VALUE	DESCRIPTION
452	Requested action not taken. Insufficient storage space in system.
500	Syntax error, command unrecognized. This may include errors such as command line too long.
501	Syntax error in parameters or arguments.
502	Command not implemented.
503	Bad sequence of commands.
504	Command not implemented for that parameter.
530	Not logged in.
531	Need account for storing files.
550	Requested action not taken. File unavailable (for example, file not found, no access).
551	Requested action aborted: page type unknown.
552	Requested file action aborted. Exceeded storage allocation (for current directory or dataset).
553	Requested action not taken. Filename not allowed.

Usually, the description in a reply code is one line long. There are cases, however, where the text is longer than a single line. In these cases the complete text must be bracketed so the client application knows when it should stop reading the reply. This requires a special format on the first line to indicate that more than one line is coming, and another on the last line to designate it as the last. At least one of these lines must contain the appropriate reply code to indicate the state of the transaction. The RFC959 decides that both the first and last line codes should be the same in the case of multiline reply description.

For example, replying to a PASS command, an FTP server may send the single-line reply:

```
230 User logged in.
```

Another FTP server may send the following multiline reply:

```
230-User logged in. Welcome to the Atlantis Research Center.
Please note that access to this site is restricted to authorized people only.
This site is closely monitored 24 hours a day.
230 Please proceed.
```

Creating an FTP Application Step by Step

To test this application (and the project), you need an FTP server. If you are connected to the Internet, you can use a number of FTP servers that allow anonymous access. These servers normally allow you to download files but not upload files. Alternatively, you can use a local FTP server found in Windows 2000 Server. The following sections start with installing and configuring an FTP server and then continue with a simple FTP client application.

Installing and Configuring an FTP Server in Windows 2000 Server

If you have access to Windows 2000 Server, you are in luck. One of the programs you can install is an FTP server. If it is already installed, you can configure it through the Internet Service Manager whose applet can be found in Administrative Tools in the Control Panel. If it is not yet installed, it is now time to do so.

To install the FTP Server in Windows 2000 Server, follow these steps:

1. Double-click Add/Remove Programs from Control Panel.

2. Click the Add/Remove Windows Components button on the left side of the page. The Windows Components Wizard will display. One of the items displayed in the Components list is Internet Information Services (IIS). Click this item.

3. Click the Details button. The Internet Information Services dialog box shows.

4. Check the File Transfer Protocol (FTP) Server subcomponent.

5. Click the OK button and follow the instructions to install. You will be asked to insert the Windows 2000 Server installation CD.

The main task in the configuration is to map the directory that will become the root of the FTP server. In addition, you can also set the session timeout and the directory list style. Any user who has access to the Windows 2000 server will have the same access to the FTP server.

To configure the FTP server, follow these steps:

1. Double-click Administrative Tools from Control Panel.

2. Double-click the Internet Service Manager icon. You should be able to see the Default FTP Site icon under the machine name.

3. Right-click the Default FTP Site icon and click Properties. The Default FTP Site Properties dialog box will display.

4. Click the Home Directory tab, as shown in Figure 5-1.

5. In the FTP Site Directory section, browse to the directory that you want to be the root of the FTP server.

6. In the FTP Site Directory section, make sure that the Read and Write check boxes are selected.

7. Select UNIX in the Directory Listing Style section.

8. Click the Apply button and then the OK button.

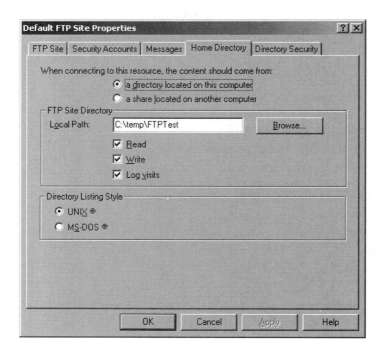

Figure 5-1. The Home Directory tab of the Default FTP Site Properties dialog box

Using the NETFTP Application

The NETFTP console application is a simple FTP client application that is similar to the `ftp.exe` program you can find in Unix/Linux or Windows. It consists of a class, NETFTP, that you can find in the `Listings/Ch05/Other/NETFTP.vb` file. The main purpose of this small application is to show how to use the `System.Net.Sockets.Socket` class to connect to an FTP server and do file transfer; it does not worry too much about error handling. After understanding this application, you can understand the project more easily.

To compile this program, type the following command in the command prompt:

```
vbc -r:System.dll FTPNET.vb
```

The result is an executable called `FTPNET.exe`.

The first thing to do to use this program is connect to an FTP server by typing the following:

```
NETFTP <server> <user name> <password>
```

If the connection attempt was successful, a message such as the following will display in the console.

```
Connected. Waiting for reply...

220 bulbul Microsoft FTP Service (Version 5.0).
USER Administrator

331 Password required for Administrator.
PASS
230 User Administrator logged in.

215 Windows_NT version 5.0

200 Type set to A.
```

If the connection failed, an error message will display.

Once connected, you will see the `NETFTP>` prompt. You can type one of the following commands in this prompt: CWD, DELE, LIST, PWD, QUIT, RETR, STOR. Upon execution, the server sends a reply that will display on the console. Other than that, the program outputs the "Command Invalid" message.

Upon successful execution of a command, the program displays the NETFTP> prompt again, indicating it is ready to accept a new command.

The valid commands are explained in the following sections.

CWD

This command causes the program to send a CWD command to the FTP server. This command changes the remote working directory. The syntax of this command is as follows:

CWD *directory*

where *directory* is the name of the directory to which you want to change. For example, to change the working directory to the /files/program directory, type the following:

CWD /files/program

You can also pass a relative path as the argument. To change to the parent directory of the current directory, type the following:

CWD ..

If the command successfully executes, the server sends the following message, which displays on the console:

250 CWD command successful.

If it cannot find the destination directory, the server sends the following message:

550 /prog/images: The system cannot find the file specified.

DELE

This command causes the application to send a DELE command to the connected FTP server. The DELE command deletes a file in the server. The syntax of this command is as follows:

DELE *pathToFileToDelete*

LIST

This command does not take an argument. It causes the application to send a LIST command to the server. The LIST command displays the content of the current directory. For example, the following is the output of the LIST directory:

```
227 Entering Passive Mode (127,0,0,1,6,77).

125 Data connection already open; Transfer starting.
226 Transfer complete.
drwxrwxrwx   1 owner    group                0 Jul 28 21:30 April2001
-rwxrwxrwx   1 owner    group           344064 Jul 29 13:25 Chapter5.doc
-rwxrwxrwx   1 owner    group            12118 Jul 29 13:25 complete.wav
-rwxrwxrwx   1 owner    group            12118 Jul 30 10:05 complete2.wav
-rwxrwxrwx   1 owner    group             1050 Jul 29 13:25 Folder.gif
-rwxrwxrwx   1 owner    group            53248 Jul 28 20:08 FTPClient.exe
drwxrwxrwx   1 owner    group                0 Jul 28 20:21 June 2002
-rwxrwxrwx   1 owner    group             9216 Jul 30 10:02 NETFTP.exe
-rwxrwxrwx   1 owner    group            12077 Jul 30 10:02 NETFTP.vb
drwxrwxrwx   1 owner    group                0 Jul 30 10:05 New Folder
drwxrwxrwx   1 owner    group                0 Jul 26 20:09 New Folder (2)
-rwxrwxrwx   1 owner    group           132717 Jul 29 13:24 rfc959.txt
```

Note that this directory listing is in the Unix style. An FTP server can choose to use another style.

PWD

The PWD command causes the application to send a PWD command to the FTP server. The PWD command displays the current directory. This command does not take an argument. On successful execution, this is an example of what the server may send:

```
257 "/" is current directory.
```

QUIT

The QUIT command causes the application to send a QUIT command to the FTP server. The QUIT command causes the connection to be closed. This command does not take an argument.

RETR

The RETR command causes the application to send a RETR command to the FTP server. The RETR command downloads a file from the server. The syntax of this command is as follows:

```
RETR pathToFileToDownload
```

STOR

The STOR command causes the application to send a STOR command to the FTP server. The STOR command uploads a file in the local directory. The syntax of this command is as follows:

```
STOR pathToFileToUpload
```

How the NETFTP Program Works

The NETFTP program comprises one class: NETFTP. The following sections describe the NETFTP class.

Declarations

The following is the declarations part of the NETFTP class:

```
Private port As Integer = 21
Private controlSocket As _
  New Socket(AddressFamily.InterNetwork, SocketType.Stream, ProtocolType.Tcp)
Private dataSocket As Socket
Private serverAddress As String

Public replyMessage As String
Public replyCode As String
```

Note that there are two Socket object references used in this class: control-Socket and dataSocket.

Methods

The following are the methods in the NETFTP class.

Connect

The Connect method connects to an FTP server (see Listing 5-1).

Listing 5-1. The Connect *Method*

```
Public Sub Connect(ByVal server As String)
  Try
    controlSocket.Connect(New↵
    IPEndPoint(Dns.Resolve(server).AddressList(0), port))
  Catch e As Exception
    Console.WriteLine(e.ToString())
    Return
  End Try
  If controlSocket.Connected Then
    Console.WriteLine("Connected. Waiting for reply...")
    GetResponse()
  Else
    Console.WriteLine("Couldn't connect.")
  End If
End Sub
```

The Connect method uses the controlSocket's Connect method to connect to an FTP server:

```
Try
  controlSocket.Connect(New IPEndPoint(Dns.Resolve(server).AddressList(0), port))
Catch e As Exception
  Console.WriteLine(e.ToString())
  Return
End Try
```

If the connection attempt is successful, the controlSocket's Connected property will be set to True. In this case, a message prints on the console and the GetResponse method is invoked:

```
If controlSocket.Connected Then
  Console.WriteLine("Connected. Waiting for reply...")
  GetResponse()
```

Otherwise, a "Couldn't connect" message displays on the console:

```
Else
  Console.WriteLine("Couldn't connect.")
End If
```

PassiveData

The PassiveData method sends the PASV command to the connected FTP server to make the server become passive (see Listing 5-2).

Listing 5-2. The PassiveData *Method*

```
Private Sub PassiveDataConnection()
  SendCommand("PASV" & ControlChars.CrLf)
  GetResponse()
  Dim addr As String = replyMessage

  addr = addr.Substring(addr.IndexOf("("c) + 1, _
    addr.IndexOf(")"c) - addr.IndexOf("("c) - 1)
  Dim address As String() = addr.Split(","c)

  Dim ip As String = address(0) & "." & address(1) & "." & address(2) & "." & _
    address(3)
  Dim port As Integer = Convert.ToInt32(address(4)) * 256 + _
    Convert.ToInt32(address(5))

  dataSocket = New Socket(AddressFamily.InterNetwork, SocketType.Stream, _
    ProtocolType.Tcp)
  dataSocket.Connect(New IPEndPoint(IPAddress.Parse(ip), port))
End Sub
```

If the PASV command successfully executes at the server, the server sends the address and port number of the data connection for the client to connect. Therefore, on a successful execution of PASV, the server replies by sending a string of the following format:

```
227 Entering Passive Mode (a1,a2,a3,a4,p1,p2).
```

where a1, a2, a3, and a4 are parts of an IP address in dotted-quad notation, and p1 and p2 signify the port number. Consequently, you can obtain the IP address using the following lines:

```
Dim addr As String = replyMessage
addr = addr.Substring(addr.IndexOf("("c) + 1, _
addr.IndexOf(")"c) - addr.IndexOf("("c) - 1)
Dim address As String() = addr.Split(","c)
Dim ip As String = address(0) & "." & address(1) & "." _
& address(2) & "." & address(3)
```

You obtain the port number by multiplying p1 with 256 and adding the result to p2:

```
Dim port As Integer = Convert.ToInt32(address(4)) * _
256 + Convert.ToInt32(address(5))
```

Then, you instantiate a data socket and invoke its Connect method:

```
dataSocket = New Socket(AddressFamily.InterNetwork, SocketType.Stream, _
  ProtocolType.Tcp)
dataSocket.Connect(New IPEndPoint(IPAddress.Parse(ip), port))
```

After the Connect method is called, the data socket is readily available to the method that invokes the PassiveData method.

GetResponse

The GetResponse method receives the byte stream from the connected FTP server. This method is invoked immediately after an FTP command is sent to the server (see Listing 5-3).

Listing 5-3. The GetResponse *Method*

```vb
Private Sub GetResponse()
  ' this method listens for the server response and receives all bytes
  ' sent by the server
  ' A server response can be single line or multiline.
  ' If the fourth byte of the first line is a hyphen, then it is
  ' multiline. If multiline, waits until the line that starts with the
  ' response code (the first three bytes of the first line).

  Dim bytes(511) As Byte ' an array of 512 bytes
  Dim receivedByteCount As Integer
  Dim response As String = ""

  ' get the first line
  receivedByteCount = controlSocket.Receive(bytes)
  response = Encoding.ASCII.GetString(bytes, 0, receivedByteCount)
  Dim multiline As Boolean = (response.Chars(3) = "-"c)

  If multiline Then
    If response.Length > 3 Then
      replyCode = response.Substring(0, 3)
    End If
    Dim line As String = ""
    Dim lastLineReached As Boolean = False
    While Not lastLineReached
      receivedByteCount = controlSocket.Receive(bytes)
      line = Encoding.ASCII.GetString(bytes, 0, receivedByteCount)
      response += line

      If line.IndexOf(ControlChars.CrLf & replyCode & " ") <> -1 Then
        lastLineReached = True
      End If
      If lastLineReached Then
        'just wait until CRLF is reached
        While Not line.EndsWith(ControlChars.CrLf)
          receivedByteCount = controlSocket.Receive(bytes)
          line = Encoding.ASCII.GetString(bytes, 0, receivedByteCount)
          response += line
        End While
      End If
    End While
  Else
```

```
    While receivedByteCount = bytes.Length And _
      Not response.EndsWith(ControlChars.CrLf)
      receivedByteCount = controlSocket.Receive(bytes)
      response += Encoding.ASCII.GetString(bytes, 0, receivedByteCount)
    End While
  End If

  Console.WriteLine()
  Console.Write(response)

  If response.Length > 3 Then
    replyCode = response.Substring(0, 3)
    replyMessage = response.Substring(3, response.Length - 3)
  Else
    replyCode = ""
    replyMessage = "Unexpected Error has occurred."
  End If

End Sub
```

The first thing this method does is to check the fourth byte of the reply to determine whether the server reply is a single-line or a multiline response. The fourth byte in a single-line response is a space, whereas it will be a hyphen in a multiline response:

```
Dim bytes(511) As Byte ' an array of 512 bytes
Dim receivedByteCount As Integer
Dim response As String = ""

' get the first line
receivedByteCount = controlSocket.Receive(bytes)
response = Encoding.ASCII.GetString(bytes, 0, receivedByteCount)
Dim multiline As Boolean = (response.Chars(3) = "-"c)
```

If the response is multilined, the GetResponse method reads the reply code (the first three digits of the first line) and keeps reading the response in a While loop until the last line is reached. The last line is a line that starts with a reply code:

```
If multiline Then
  If response.Length > 3 Then
    replyCode = response.Substring(0, 3)
  End If
  Dim line As String = ""
```

```
Dim lastLineReached As Boolean = False
While Not lastLineReached
  receivedByteCount = controlSocket.Receive(bytes)
  line = Encoding.ASCII.GetString(bytes, 0, receivedByteCount)
  response += line

  If line.IndexOf(ControlChars.CrLf & replyCode & " ") <> -1 Then
    lastLineReached = True
  End If
```

When the last line is reached, it continues reading until the last byte is received:

```
If lastLineReached Then
  'just wait until CRLF is reached
  While Not line.EndsWith(ControlChars.CrLf)
    receivedByteCount = controlSocket.Receive(bytes)
    line = Encoding.ASCII.GetString(bytes, 0, receivedByteCount)
    response += line
  End While
```

If it is a single-line response, it just continues reading until the last byte in the stream is received:

```
Else
  While receivedByteCount = bytes.Length And _
    Not response.EndsWith(ControlChars.CrLf)
    receivedByteCount = controlSocket.Receive(bytes)
    response += Encoding.ASCII.GetString(bytes, 0, receivedByteCount)
  End While
```

The response will then be sent to the console:

```
Console.WriteLine()
Console.Write(response)
```

Next, `replyCode` and `replyMessage` are assigned the reply code and message of the server response, respectively:

```
replyCode = response.Substring(0, 3)
replyMessage = response.Substring(3, response.Length - 3)
```

Login

The `Login` method accepts a username and a password that will be sent as the user's credential to log in to the connected FTP server (see Listing 5-4).

Listing 5-4. The `Login` *Method*

```
Public Function Login(ByVal userName As String, ByVal password As String) As String
  If controlSocket.Connected Then

    ' Sending user name
    Dim command As String
    command = "USER " & userName & ControlChars.CrLf
    Console.WriteLine(command)
    SendCommand(command)
    GetResponse()

    ' Sending password
    command = "PASS " & password & ControlChars.CrLf
    Console.Write("PASS")  'do not display password
    SendCommand(command)
    GetResponse()
    Return replyCode
  Else
    Console.Write("Login failed because no connection is available")
  End If
  Return ""
End Function
```

The `Login` method sends the USER and PASS commands in sequence. It returns the three-digit reply code. Login is successful only if the three-digit code is 230.

SendCommand

The SendCommand method sends a command to the connected FTP server (see Listing 5-5).

Listing 5-5. The SendCommand *Method*

```
Private Sub SendCommand(ByVal command As String)
  Try
    controlSocket.Send(Encoding.ASCII.GetBytes(command), command.Length, 0)
  Catch
  End Try
End Sub
```

SendCWDCommand

The SendCWDCommand method uses the SendCommand method to send a CWD command to the connected FTP server (see Listing 5-6).

Listing 5-6. The SendCWDCommand *Method*

```
Public Sub SendCWDCommand(ByVal path As String)
  SendCommand("CWD " & path & ControlChars.CrLf)
  GetResponse()
End Sub
```

SendDELECommand

The SendDELECommand method sends a DELE command to the connected FTP server using the SendCommand method (see Listing 5-7).

Listing 5-7. The SendDELECommand *Method*

```
Public Sub SendDELECommand(ByVal filename As String)
  SendCommand("DELE " & filename & ControlChars.CrLf)
  GetResponse()
End Sub
```

SendLISTCommand

The SendLISTCommand method sends a LIST command to the connected FTP server and displays the returned directory list (see Listing 5-8).

Listing 5-8. The SendLISTCommand *Method*

```
Public Sub SendLISTCommand()

  PassiveDataConnection()
  SendCommand("LIST" & ControlChars.CrLf)
  GetResponse()

  Dim byteReceivedCount As Integer
  Dim msg As New StringBuilder(2048)
  Dim bytes(511) As Byte
  Do
    byteReceivedCount = _
      dataSocket.Receive(bytes, bytes.Length, SocketFlags.None)
    msg.Append(Encoding.ASCII.GetString(bytes, 0, byteReceivedCount))
  Loop Until byteReceivedCount = 0

  Console.WriteLine(msg.ToString())

  'because the 226 response might be sent
  'before the data connection finishes, only try to get "completion message"
  'if it's not yet sent
  If replyMessage.IndexOf("226 ") = -1 Then
    GetResponse()
  End If
End Sub
```

The SendLISTCommand method starts by calling the PassiveDataConnection and sends the LIST command:

```
PassiveDataConnection()
SendCommand("LIST" & ControlChars.CrLf)
    GetResponse()
```

The data socket instantiated in the `PassiveDataConnection` method then reads the data from the server:

```
Dim byteReceivedCount As Integer
Dim msg As New StringBuilder(2048)
Dim bytes(511) As Byte
Do
  byteReceivedCount = _
    dataSocket.Receive(bytes, bytes.Length, SocketFlags.None)
  msg.Append(Encoding.ASCII.GetString(bytes, 0, byteReceivedCount))
Loop Until byteReceivedCount = 0
```

The data then displays on the console:

```
Console.WriteLine(msg.ToString())
```

Upon sending the directory list, the server should send the 226 reply code indicating the transfer completion. However, in my testing, the 226 reply code might be sent *before* the data is received. Therefore, you call the GetResponse method only if the 226 reply code has not been sent:

```
If replyMessage.IndexOf("226 ") = -1 Then
  GetResponse()
End If
```

SendMKDCommand

The `SendMKCommand` method sends an MKD command to the connected FTP server (see Listing 5-9).

Listing 5-9. The SendMKDCommand *Method*

```
Public Sub SendMKDCommand(ByVal dir As String)
  SendCommand("MKD " & dir & ControlChars.CrLf)
  GetResponse()
End Sub
```

SendPWDCommand

The `SendPWDCommand` method sends a PWD command to the connected FTP server (see Listing 5-10).

Listing 5-10. The SendPWDCommand *Method*

```
Public Sub SendPWDCommand()
  SendCommand("PWD" & ControlChars.CrLf)
  GetResponse()
End Sub
```

SendRMDCommand

The SendRMDCommand method sends a RMD command to the connected FTP server (see Listing 5-11).

Listing 5-11. The SendRMDCommand *Method*

```
Public Sub SendRMDCommand(ByVal dir As String)
  SendCommand("RMD " & dir & ControlChars.CrLf)
  GetResponse()
End Sub
```

SendQUITCommand

The SendQUITCommand method sends a QUIT command to the connected FTP server (see Listing 5-12). After the response is received, it calls the Shutdown and Close methods of the control socket.

Listing 5-12. The SendQUITCommand *Method*

```
Public Sub SendQUITCommand()
  SendCommand("QUIT" & ControlChars.CrLf)
  GetResponse()
  controlSocket.Shutdown(SocketShutdown.Both)
  controlSocket.Close()
End Sub
```

SendRETRCommand

The SendRETRCommand method downloads a file in the connected FTP server (see Listing 5-13).

Listing 5-13. The SendRETRCommand *Method*

```
Public Sub SendRETRCommand(ByVal filename As String)

  Dim f As FileStream = File.Create(filename)

  SendTYPECommand("I")
  PassiveDataConnection()

  SendCommand("RETR " & filename & ControlChars.CrLf)
  GetResponse()

  Dim byteReceivedCount As Integer
  Dim totalByteReceived As Integer = 0
  Dim bytes(511) As Byte
  Do
    byteReceivedCount = _
      dataSocket.Receive(bytes, bytes.Length, SocketFlags.None)
    totalByteReceived += byteReceivedCount
    f.Write(bytes, 0, byteReceivedCount)
  Loop Until byteReceivedCount = 0

  f.Close()

  'because the 226 response might be sent
  'before the data connection finishes, only try to get "completion message"
  'if it's not yet sent
  If replyMessage.IndexOf("226 ") = -1 Then
    GetResponse()
  End If

  SendTYPECommand("A")
End Sub
```

The method starts by creating a file in the current local directory:

```
Dim f As FileStream = File.Create(filename)
```

It then changes the transmission mode to image (binary) by calling the Send-
TYPECommand method, passing "I" to the method:

```
SendTYPECommand("I")
```

Next, it calls the `PassiveDataConnection` method to get a data socket for the data transmission and sends a RETR command to the server:

```
PassiveDataConnection()
SendCommand("RETR " & filename & ControlChars.CrLf)
GetResponse()
```

The data socket created in the `PassiveDataConnection` method is then used to read the data stream. The incoming stream is written to the file created at the beginning of this method:

```
Dim byteReceivedCount As Integer
Dim totalByteReceived As Integer = 0
Dim bytes(511) As Byte
Do
  byteReceivedCount = _
    dataSocket.Receive(bytes, bytes.Length, SocketFlags.None)
  totalByteReceived += byteReceivedCount
  f.Write(bytes, 0, byteReceivedCount)
Loop Until byteReceivedCount = 0
```

Next, the file closes:

```
f.Close()
```

After the data transmission completes, the server closes the data connection and sends a 226 transfer completion code through the control connection. However, the 226 reply code might be sent *before* all the data is received. Therefore, you call the `GetResponse` method only if the 226 reply code has not been sent:

```
If replyMessage.IndexOf("226 ") = -1 Then
  GetResponse()
End If
```

Finally, it changes the mode back to ASCII:

```
SendTYPECommand("A")
```

SendSTORCommand

The SendSTORCommand method uploads a file in the connected FTP server (see Listing 5-14).

Listing 5-14. The SendSTORCommand *Method*

```
Public Sub SendSTORCommand(ByVal filename As String)

  Dim f As FileStream = File.Open(filename, FileMode.Open)
  SendTYPECommand("I")
  PassiveDataConnection()

  SendCommand("STOR " & filename & ControlChars.CrLf)
  GetResponse()

  Dim byteReadCount As Integer
  Dim totalByteSent As Integer
  Dim bytes(511) As Byte

  Do
    byteReadCount = f.Read(bytes, 0, bytes.Length)
    If byteReadCount <> 0 Then
      dataSocket.Send(bytes, byteReadCount, SocketFlags.None)
      totalByteSent += byteReadCount
    End If
  Loop Until byteReadCount = 0

  dataSocket.Shutdown(SocketShutdown.Both)
  dataSocket.Close()

  f.Close()
  GetResponse()

  SendTYPECommand("A")
End Sub
```

The method starts by opening the file to upload to the connected FTP server:

```
Dim f As FileStream = File.Open(filename, FileMode.Open)
```

It then changes the transmission mode to image (binary) and calls the `PassiveDataConnection` to obtain a data socket for the file transmission:

```
SendTYPECommand("I")
PassiveDataConnection()
```

Then it sends a STOR command to indicate to the server that it is going to send a file to that server:

```
SendCommand("STOR " & filename & ControlChars.CrLf)
GetResponse()
```

The data socket created by the `PassiveDataConnection` transfers the file.

```
Dim byteReadCount As Integer
Dim totalByteSent As Integer
Dim bytes(511) As Byte

Do
  byteReadCount = f.Read(bytes, 0, bytes.Length)
  If byteReadCount <> 0 Then
    dataSocket.Send(bytes, byteReadCount, SocketFlags.None)
    totalByteSent += byteReadCount
  End If
Loop Until byteReadCount = 0
```

After the file transfer completes, the data socket closes:

```
dataSocket.Shutdown(SocketShutdown.Both)
dataSocket.Close()
```

Then, the file closes and the mode switches back to ASCII:

```
f.Close()
GetResponse()
SendTYPECommand("A")
```

SendSYSTCommand

The `SendSYSTCommand` method sends a SYST method to the connected FTP server (see Listing 5-15).

Listing 5-15. The SendSYSTCommand *Method*

```
Public Sub SendSYSTCommand()
  SendCommand("SYST" & ControlChars.CrLf)
  GetResponse()
End Sub
```

SendTYPECommand

You use the SendTYPECommand method to change the transmission mode from the client to the server (see Listing 5-16).

Listing 5-16. The SendTYPECommand *Method*

```
Public Sub SendTYPECommand(ByVal type As String)
  SendCommand("TYPE " & type & ControlChars.CrLf)
  GetResponse()
End Sub
```

Main

The Main static method is the entry point of the program. It does the following:

- Ensures that the program is invoked using the correct number of arguments.

- Controls the program flow with a While loop so that the user can enter one FTP command after the execution of another.

- Invokes the correct method upon receiving a valid user input.

- Displays an error message on receiving an invalid user input.

  Listing 5-17 shows the Main method.

Listing 5-17. The Main *Method*

```
Public Shared Sub Main(ByVal args As String())
  If args.Length <> 3 Then
    Console.WriteLine("usage: NETFTP server username password")
  Else
    Dim ftp As New NETFTP()
```

```vbnet
        ftp.Connect(args(0))
        Dim replyCode As String = ftp.Login(args(1), args(2))

        If replyCode.Equals("230") Then
          'login successful, allow user to type in commands
          ftp.SendSYSTCommand()
          ftp.SendTYPECommand("A")

          Dim command As String = ""
          Try
            While Not command.ToUpper.Equals("QUIT")
              Console.Write("NETFTP>")
              command = Console.ReadLine().Trim()
              If command.ToUpper.Equals("PWD") Then
                ftp.SendPWDCommand()
              ElseIf command.ToUpper.StartsWith("CWD") Then
                If command.Length > 3 Then
                  Dim path As String = command.Substring(4).Trim()
                  If path.Equals("") Then
                    Console.WriteLine("Please specify the directory to change to")
                  Else
                    ftp.SendCWDCommand(path)
                  End If
                End If
              ElseIf command.ToUpper.StartsWith("DELE") Then
                If command.Length > 4 Then
                  Dim path As String = command.Substring(5).Trim()
                  If path.Equals("") Then
                    Console.WriteLine("Please specify the file to delete")
                  Else
                    ftp.SendDELECommand(path)
                  End If
                End If
              ElseIf command.ToUpper.Equals("LIST") Then
                ftp.SendLISTCommand()
              ElseIf command.ToUpper.StartsWith("MKD") Then
                If command.Length > 3 Then
                  Dim dir As String = command.Substring(4).Trim()
                    If dir.Equals("") Then
                      Console.WriteLine("Please specify the name↵
of the directory to create")
                  Else
                    ftp.SendMKDCommand(dir)
                  End If
                End If
```

```vbnet
                    ElseIf command.ToUpper.Equals("QUIT") Then
                    ElseIf command.ToUpper.StartsWith("RMD") Then
                      If command.Length > 3 Then
                        Dim dir As String = command.Substring(4).Trim()
                        If dir.Equals("") Then
                          Console.WriteLine("Please specify the name↵
of the directory to delete")
                        Else
                          ftp.SendRMDCommand(dir)
                        End If
                      End If
                    ElseIf command.ToUpper.StartsWith("RETR") Then
                      If command.Length > 4 Then
                        Dim filename As String = command.Substring(5).Trim()
                        If filename.Equals("") Then
                          Console.WriteLine("Please specify a file to retrieve")
                        Else
                          ftp.SendRETRCommand(filename)
                        End If
                      End If
                    ElseIf command.ToUpper.StartsWith("STOR") Then
                      If command.Length > 4 Then
                        Dim filename As String = command.Substring(5).Trim()
                        If filename.Equals("") Then
                          Console.WriteLine("Please specify a file to store")
                        Else
                          ftp.SendSTORCommand(filename)
                        End If
                      End If
                    Else
                      Console.WriteLine("Invalid command.")
                    End If
                  End While
                  ftp.SendQUITCommand()
                Catch e As Exception
                  Console.WriteLine(e.ToString())
                End Try
                Console.WriteLine("Thank you for using NETFTP.")
              Else
                ftp.SendQUITCommand()
                Console.WriteLine("Login failed. Please try again.")
              End If
            End If
          End Sub
```

The `Main` method starts by checking that the user passes three arguments: server, username, and password. If the number of arguments is not three, it prints the following message on the console:

```
usage: NETFTP server username password
```

If the number of arguments is correct, the `Main` method instantiates a NETFTP object and uses the first argument (server) to connect to the remote server by calling the `Connect` method:

```
ftp.Connect(args(0))
```

Once connected, the `Main` method uses the second and third argument to log in by calling the `Login` method:

```
Dim replyCode As String = ftp.Login(args(1), args(2))
```

The remote server returning a reply code of 230 indicates a successful login. If login was successful, it calls the `SendSYSTCommand` and `SendTYPECommand` methods. The `SendSYSTCommand` method prints the server's operating system information, and the `SendTYPECommand` method is called by passing "A" as the argument. This in effect changes the transfer mode to ASCII:

```
If replyCode.Equals("230") Then
  'login successful, allow user to type in commands
  ftp.SendSYSTCommand()
  ftp.SendTYPECommand("A")
```

After the user is successfully logged in, the program enters a `While` loop. Inside the `While` loop is the code that gets the user's input and sends the corresponding FTP command. Control exits the `While` loop when the user types *QUIT*:

```
Dim command As String = ""
Try
  While Not command.ToUpper.Equals("QUIT")
```

Inside the `While` loop, the `Main` method first displays the `NETFTP>` prompt and uses the `Console` class's `ReadLine` to read the user input:

```
Console.Write("NETFTP>")
command = Console.ReadLine().Trim()
```

Then, it goes through a series of `If` commands to execute code based on the command entered by the user. Valid commands are PWD, CWD, DELE, LIST, MKD, QUIT, RMD, RETR, and STOR.

If the command equals PWD, the `SendPWDCommand` method is called:

```
If command.ToUpper.Equals("PWD") Then
  ftp.SendPWDCommand()
```

If the command is CWD, it ensures that there is a parameter, a path, after the CWD command and that the parameter does not consist of spaces only. If the path looks valid, it calls the `SendCWDCommand` method. Otherwise, it prints a warning on the console:

```
ElseIf command.ToUpper.StartsWith("CWD") Then
  If command.Length > 3 Then
    Dim path As String = command.Substring(4).Trim()
    If path.Equals("") Then
      Console.WriteLine("Please specify the directory to change to")
    Else
      ftp.SendCWDCommand(path)
    End If
  End If
```

If the command is DELE, it makes sure there is a valid parameter, a filename. If the command has a valid parameter, it invokes the `SendDELECommand` method. Otherwise, it prints a warning to the user:

```
ElseIf command.ToUpper.StartsWith("DELE") Then
  If command.Length > 4 Then
    Dim path As String = command.Substring(5).Trim()
    If path.Equals("") Then
      Console.WriteLine("Please specify the file to delete")
    Else
      ftp.SendDELECommand(path)
    End If
  End If
```

If the command equals LIST, it invokes the `SendLISTCommand` method:

```
ElseIf command.ToUpper.Equals("LIST") Then
  ftp.SendLISTCommand()
```

If the command starts with MKD and there is a valid parameter (a directory name), it calls the SendMKDCommand method. Otherwise, a warning displays on the console:

```
ElseIf command.ToUpper.StartsWith("MKD") Then
  If command.Length > 3 Then
    Dim dir As String = command.Substring(4).Trim()
    If dir.Equals("") Then
      Console.WriteLine("Please specify the name of the directory to create")
    Else
      ftp.SendMKDCommand(dir)
    End If
  End If
```

If the command equals QUIT, it does not do anything as this will be captured by the conditional statement in the While loop:

```
ElseIf command.ToUpper.Equals("QUIT") Then
```

If the command starts with RMD and there is a valid parameter (a directory name to remove), it invokes the SendRMDCommand method. Otherwise, a warning displays on the console:

```
ElseIf command.ToUpper.StartsWith("RMD") Then
  If command.Length > 3 Then
    Dim dir As String = command.Substring(4).Trim()
    If dir.Equals("") Then
      Console.WriteLine("Please specify the name of the directory to delete")
    Else
      ftp.SendRMDCommand(dir)
    End If
  End If
```

If the command starts with RETR and there is a parameter (a filename), the SendRETRCommand method is invoked. Otherwise, it prints a warning on the console:

```
ElseIf command.ToUpper.StartsWith("RETR") Then
  If command.Length > 4 Then
    Dim filename As String = command.Substring(5).Trim()
    If filename.Equals("") Then
      Console.WriteLine("Please specify a file to retrieve")
    Else
      ftp.SendRETRCommand(filename)
    End If
  End If
```

If the command starts with STOR and there is a parameter (a filename), it invokes the SendSTORCommand method. Otherwise, it prints a warning on the console:

```
ElseIf command.ToUpper.StartsWith("STOR") Then
  If command.Length > 4 Then
    Dim filename As String = command.Substring(5).Trim()
    If filename.Equals("") Then
      Console.WriteLine("Please specify a file to store")
    Else
      ftp.SendSTORCommand(filename)
    End If
  End If
```

Finally, if the command is none of the valid commands, it simply prints "Invalid command" on the console:

```
Else
  Console.WriteLine("Invalid command.")
End If
```

When the user types QUIT, the control exits the While loop, and the SendQUITCommand method is invoked:

```
ftp.SendQUITCommand()
```

Before closing itself, the program prints a thank you message.

```
Console.WriteLine("Thank you for using NETFTP.")
```

Implementing the Project

The project for this chapter is an FTP client application with a graphical user interface, as shown in Figure 5-2. This section starts with a general overview of the application. It then describes each class in detail.

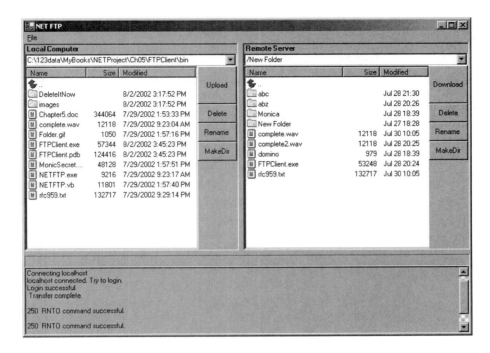

Figure 5-2. The FTP client application

To get a feel for the application, you are encouraged to try this application by double-clicking the Form1.exe file in the listings/Ch05/Project directory.

When the application activates, it retrieves the content of the local current directory and displays it on the left panel of the form.

Before you can do a file transfer, you need to connect to an FTP server. You can connect and log in at the same time by pressing F3 or selecting File ➤ Connect. To log in, you type your login details in the Login Form window, as shown in Figure 5-3.

Login Form	
Server	ftp.brainysoftware.com
User Name	Administrator
Password	××××××××
	OK Cancel

Figure 5-3. The Login Form window

You need to enter the server, the username, and the password into the Login Form window and then click the OK button.

If the connection is successful, the content of the remote home directory displays in the right panel of the form. If the login fails, the Login Form window remains open until you enter the correct login details or until you click the Cancel button.

The four buttons to the right of the left panel are for manipulating local files and directories, and the buttons to the right of the right panel are for manipulating remote files and directories. You can change the local or remote directory by double-clicking the directory icon on both panels.

To upload a file, you can select a file from the local computer and click the Upload button. Alternatively, you can simply double-click the file icon on the left panel.

To download a file, select a file from the remote computer and then click the Download button. Or, you can double-click the file icon.

Creating the Class Diagram

Figure 5-4 shows the class diagram for this application.

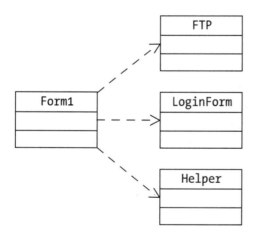

Figure 5-4. The class diagram

The application is comprised of the following classes:

- **FTP**: Contains properties and methods to send FTP commands to an FTP server.

- **Form1**: The main form of the application.

- **Helper**: Contains static methods used by the Form1 class

- **LoginForm**: Represents a form for the user to log in.

- **Three EventArgs subclasses**: EndDownloadEventArgs, EndUploadEventArgs, and TransferProgressChangedEventArgs. These are event argument classes used in several delegates in the FTP class.

You will now learn about the classes starting with the easiest.

Creating the Helper Class

You can find the Helper class in the Helper.vb file under the project's directory. It provides two static methods used by the Form1 class: IsDirectory and IsDirectoryItem.

The Helper Class's Methods

The following sections describe the two methods of the Helper class.

IsDirectory

The IsDirectory method accepts a string argument and returns True if the specified string is a path to a directory.

The method definition is as follows:

```
Public Shared Function IsDirectory(ByVal path As String) As Boolean
  If File.Exists(path) Or Directory.Exists(path) Then
    ' it is a file or a directory
    Dim attr As FileAttributes = File.GetAttributes(path)
    If (attr And FileAttributes.Directory) = FileAttributes.Directory Then
      Return True
    End If
  End If
End Function
```

IsDirectoryItem

The `IsDirectoryItem` method accepts a `System.Windows.Form.ListViewItem` and returns `True` if the item's `ImageIndex` is 1, the image index of the folder icon. Its definition is as follows:

```
Public Shared Function IsDirectoryItem(ByVal item As ListViewItem) As Boolean
  If item.ImageIndex = 1 Then
    Return True
  Else
    Return False
  End If
End Function
```

Creating the LoginForm Class

You can find the `LoginForm` class in the `LoginForm.vb` file in the project's directory. It represents the login form for the user to login. This form displays as a modal dialog box from the `Form1` class when the user attempts to connect to a remote server.

The class contains three `Label` controls (`label1`, `label2`, and `label3`), three `TextBox` controls (`serverTextBox`, `userTextBox`, and `passwordTextBox`), and two `Button` controls (`okButton` and `cnlButton`).

The `passwordTextBox` control accepts the user's password, and the characters entered are masked by setting its `PasswordChar` property as follows:

```
Me.passwordTextBox.PasswordChar = Microsoft.VisualBasic.ChrW(42)
```

You set the `okButton` control's `DialogResult` property to `System.Windows.Forms.DialogResult.OK` so that when the form is shown as a modal dialog box, it returns `DialogResult.OK` when the `okButton` control is clicked:

```
Me.okButton.DialogResult = System.Windows.Forms.DialogResult.OK
```

On the other hand, you set the `cnlButton.DialogResult` property to `System.Windows.Forms.DialogResult.Cancel`. When the form displays as a modal dialog box, clicking the `cnlButton` control results in the form returning `Dialog.Cancel`:

```
Me.cnlButton.DialogResult = System.Windows.Forms.DialogResult.Cancel
```

The okButton control's Click event is wired with the okButton_Click event handler. This event handler populates three private fields with the values entered by the user into the serverTextBox, userTextBox, and passwordTextBox controls:

```
Private Sub okButton_Click(ByVal sender As System.Object, _
  ByVal e As System.EventArgs) Handles okButton.Click
  userNameField = userTextBox.Text
  passwordField = passwordTextBox.Text
  serverField = serverTextBox.Text
  Me.Close()
End Sub
```

The last line of this event handler also closes the form.

After the form returns—in other words, when either okButton or cnlButton is clicked—you can obtain the values of serverField, userNameField, and passwordField from the three read-only properties: Server, UserName, and Password:

```
Public ReadOnly Property Server() As String
  Get
    Return serverField
  End Get
End Property

Public ReadOnly Property UserName() As String
  Get
    Return userNameField
  End Get
End Property

Public ReadOnly Property Password() As String
  Get
    Return passwordField
  End Get
End Property
```

Creating the FTP Class

You can find the FTP class in the FTP.vb file in the project's directory. This class encapsulates functions to communicate with an FTP server. Using this class, you can connect to a remote FTP server, log in, print the working directory, change the directory, delete and rename a remote file, and download and upload a file.

Some of the functions in the FTP class are similar to those in the NETFTP class discussed previously. However, you use a separate thread for downloading and uploading a file to improve the perceived performance. For synchronization, a Boolean called transferring prevents multiple upload/download at the same time. The Upload and Download methods return immediately if the value of transferring is True.

Finally, the FTP class has five public events as described in "The FTP Class's Events" section.

The FTP Class's Declaration

The FTP class contains the following variable declaration:

```
Private port As Integer = 21
Private controlSocket, dataSocket As Socket
Private serverAddress As String
Private directoryListField As String
'the thread used for uploading and downloading files
Private dataTransferThread As Thread
'indicates whether dataTransferThread is being used
'if it is, do not allow another operation
Private transferring As Boolean

'for transferring filename and localDir when calling DoUpload and
'DoDownload
Private filename, localDir As String

Public replyMessage As String
Public replyCode As String
```

The FTP Class's Properties

The FTP class has two read-only properties.

Connected

The Connected property indicates whether the control socket is connected:

```
Public ReadOnly Property Connected() As Boolean
  Get
    If Not controlSocket Is Nothing Then
```

```
      Return controlSocket.Connected
    Else
      Return False
    End If
  End Get
End Property
```

DirectoryList

The DirectoryList property returns the directory list obtained from the GetDirList method in raw form:

```
Public ReadOnly Property DirectoryList() As String
  Get
    Return directoryListField
  End Get
End Property
```

The FTP Class's Methods

The following sections describe the methods in the FTP class.

ChangeDir

The ChangeDir method changes the current remote directory by sending the CWD command:

```
Public Sub ChangeDir(ByVal path As String)
  SendCommand("CWD " & path & ControlChars.CrLf)
  GetResponse()
End Sub
```

ChangeToAsciiMode

The ChangeToAsciiMode method changes the transfer mode to ASCII:

```
Public Sub ChangeToAsciiMode()
  SendTYPECommand("A")
End Sub
```

Connect

This method connects to a remote server:

```
Public Sub Connect(ByVal server As String)
  Try
    controlSocket = New _
      Socket(AddressFamily.InterNetwork, SocketType.Stream, ProtocolType.Tcp)
    controlSocket.Connect(New _
      IPEndPoint(Dns.Resolve(server).AddressList(0), port))
  Catch e As Exception
    Console.WriteLine(e.ToString())
    Return
  End Try
  If controlSocket.Connected Then
    Console.WriteLine("Connected. Waiting for reply...")
    GetResponse()
  Else
    Console.WriteLine("Couldn't connect.")
  End If
End Sub
```

DeleteDir

The DeleteDir method deletes a directory on the connected server by sending an RMD command. A 2xx reply code indicates a successful RMD command. The method definition is as follows:

```
Public Function DeleteDir(ByVal dir As String) As Boolean
  SendCommand("RMD " & dir & ControlChars.CrLf)
  GetResponse()
  If replyCode.StartsWith("2") Then
    Return True
  Else
    Return False
  End If
End Function
```

DeleteFile

The DeleteFile method deletes a file on the connected server by sending a DELE command. A 2xx reply code indicates a successful DELE command. The method definition is as follows:

```vb
Public Function DeleteFile(ByVal filename As String) As Boolean
  SendCommand("DELE " & filename & ControlChars.CrLf)
  GetResponse()
  If replyCode.StartsWith("2") Then
    Return True
  Else
    Return False
  End If
End Function
```

Disconnect

The Disconnect method disconnects from the remote server:

```vb
Public Sub Disconnect()
  If controlSocket.Connected Then
    SendCommand("QUIT" & ControlChars.CrLf)
    GetResponse()
    controlSocket.Shutdown(SocketShutdown.Both)
    controlSocket.Close()
  End If
End Sub
```

DoDownload

The DoDownload method does the actual file download. This method is called from the Download method. The following is the DoDownload method:

```vb
Public Sub DoDownload()
  OnBeginDownload(New EventArgs())
  Dim completePath As String = Path.Combine(localDir, filename)
  Try

    Dim f As FileStream = File.Create(completePath)
    SendTYPECommand("I")
    PassiveDataConnection()
    SendCommand("RETR " & filename & ControlChars.CrLf)
    GetResponse()
    Dim byteReceivedCount As Integer
    Dim totalByteReceived As Integer = 0
    Dim bytes(511) As Byte
    Do
      byteReceivedCount = _
```

```
      dataSocket.Receive(bytes, bytes.Length, SocketFlags.None)
    totalByteReceived += byteReceivedCount

    f.Write(bytes, 0, byteReceivedCount)
    OnTransferProgressChanged(New _
      TransferProgressChangedEventArgs(totalByteReceived))
  Loop Until byteReceivedCount = 0

  f.Close()
  'because the 226 response might be sent
  'before the data connection finishes, only try to get "completion message"
  'if it's not yet sent
  If replyMessage.IndexOf("226 ") = -1 Then
    GetResponse()
  End If

  SendTYPECommand("A")
  Catch
  End Try
  Dim e As New EndDownloadEventArgs()
  e.Message = "Finished downloading " & filename
  OnEndDownload(e)
  transferring = False
End Sub
```

The DoDownload method starts by raising the BeginDownload event:

```
OnBeginDownload(New EventArgs())
```

The DoDownload method is the method assigned to a new thread created in the Download method. Prior to starting the new thread, the Download method sets the localDir and filename variables. The localDir is the current local directory to which the downloaded file will be saved. The filename variable contains the name of the file to be downloaded.

The next thing the DoDownload method does after raising the BeginDownload event is combine localDir and filename:

```
Dim completePath As String = Path.Combine(localDir, filename)
```

Next, it creates a file on the local machine using the combined string of
localDir and filename:

```
Dim f As FileStream = File.Create(completePath)
```

Then, it changes the transfer mode to image (binary) and calls the
PassiveDataConnection method. The latter constructs a data socket to be
used for the file transfer:

```
SendTYPECommand("I")
PassiveDataConnection()
```

The actual file download starts when a RETR command is sent:

```
SendCommand("RETR " & filename & ControlChars.CrLf)
GetResponse()
```

Then, the data socket resulted from the PassiveDataConnection method
receives the data stream:

```
Dim byteReceivedCount As Integer
Dim totalByteReceived As Integer = 0
Dim bytes(511) As Byte
Do
  byteReceivedCount = _
    dataSocket.Receive(bytes, bytes.Length, SocketFlags.None)
  totalByteReceived += byteReceivedCount

  f.Write(bytes, 0, byteReceivedCount)
  OnTransferProgressChanged(New _
    TransferProgressChangedEventArgs(totalByteReceived))
Loop Until byteReceivedCount = 0
```

Note from the previous Do loop that the TransferProgressChanged event raises
after each invocation of the data socket's Received method, passing the total number
of bytes received so far. The user of the FTP class can use this event to notify the user
of the progress of the file transfer, for example, by using a progress bar.

Afterward, the file closes:

```
f.Close()
```

After the file transfer completes, the server sends the 226 reply code. However, sometimes this reply code is received even before the whole data transferred is received. Therefore, you check to see that a 226 reply code has not been received prior to calling the GetResponse method:

```
If replyMessage.IndexOf("226 ") = -1 Then
  GetResponse()
End If
```

It then changes the mode to ASCII:

```
  SendTYPECommand("A")
Catch
End Try
```

Finally, the EndDownload event triggers, passing the "Finished downloading *filename*" message, where *filename* is the name of the file downloaded and the transferring Boolean resets to allow a future file transfer:

```
Dim e As New EndDownloadEventArgs()
e.Message = "Finished downloading " & filename
OnEndDownload(e)
transferring = False
```

DoUpload

The DoUpload method does the actual file upload. This method is called from the Upload method. The DoUpload method starts by raising the BeginUpload event:

```
OnBeginUpload(New EventArgs())
```

The DoUpload method is the method assigned to a new thread created in the Upload method. Prior to starting the new thread, the Upload method sets the localDir and filename variables. The localDir is the current local directory to which the downloaded file will be saved. The filename variable contains the name of the file to be downloaded.

The next thing the DoUpload method does after raising the BeginUpload event is combine localDir and filename:

```
Dim completePath As String = Path.Combine(localDir, filename)
```

Then it opens the file to upload, changes the mode to ASCII, and calls the
PassiveDataConnection method. The PassiveDataConnection method constructs a
data socket to be used for the file transfer:

```
Dim f As FileStream = _
  File.Open(completePath, FileMode.Open, FileAccess.Read)
SendTYPECommand("I")
PassiveDataConnection()
```

The actual file upload starts when a STOR command is sent:

```
SendCommand("STOR " & filename & ControlChars.CrLf)
GetResponse()
```

Then, the data socket resulted from the PassiveDataConnection method
receives the data stream:

```
Dim byteReadCount As Integer
Dim totalByteSent As Integer
Dim bytes(511) As Byte

Do
  byteReadCount = f.Read(bytes, 0, bytes.Length)
  If byteReadCount <> 0 Then
    dataSocket.Send(bytes, byteReadCount, SocketFlags.None)
    totalByteSent += byteReadCount
    OnTransferProgressChanged( _
      New TransferProgressChangedEventArgs(totalByteSent))
  End If
Loop Until byteReadCount = 0
```

Note from the previous Do loop that the TransferProgressChanged event raises
after each invocation of the data socket's Send method, passing the total number
of bytes sent so far. The user of the FTP class can use this event to notify the user of
the progress of the file transfer, for example, by using a progress bar.

Afterward, the data socket and the file close:

```
dataSocket.Shutdown(SocketShutdown.Both)
dataSocket.Close()
f.Close()
```

When the data socket closes, the server knows that the file transfer is completed and sends a reply code that you receive using the GetResponse method:

```
GetResponse()
```

Then, it changes the mode back to ASCII:

```
SendTYPECommand("A")
```

Finally, the EndUpload event triggers, passing the "Finished uploading *filename*" message, where *filename* is the name of the file uploaded and the transferring Boolean resets to allow a future file transfer:

```
Dim ev As New EndUploadEventArgs()
ev.Message = "Finished uploading " & filename
OnEndUpload(ev)
transferring = False
```

Download

The Download method checks if file transfer is allowed and, if it is, creates a new thread to download a file:

```
Public Sub Download(ByVal filename As String, ByVal localdir As String)
  If Not transferring Then
    transferring = True
    Me.filename = filename
    Me.localDir = localdir
    dataTransferThread = _
      New Thread(New ThreadStart(AddressOf DoDownload))
    dataTransferThread.Start()
  End If
End Sub
```

GetRemoteDirectory

GetRemoteDirectory is a helper method used to obtain the directory name at the remote server. The argument passed to this function is a string that is the server reply after a PWD command is sent. Therefore, the argument has the following format:

```
"path" is current directory
```

This method returns the "*path*" portion of the argument. The definition for this method is as follows:

```
Private Function GetRemoteDirectory(ByVal message As String) As String
  'message is the server response upon sending the "PWD" command
  'its format is something like: "path" is current directory
  'this function obtains the string between the double quotes
  Dim path As String = ""
  Dim index As Integer = message.IndexOf("""")
  If index <> -1 Then
    Dim index2 As Integer = message.IndexOf("""", index + 1)
    If index2 <> -1 Then
      path = message.Substring(index + 1, index2 - index - 1)
    End If
  End If
  Return path
End Function
```

GetResponse

The GetResponse method receives the server reply and is the same as the GetResponse method in the NETFTP class.

Login

The Login method logs in to a connected FTP server and is similar to the Login method in the NETFTP class. The difference is that this method returns a Boolean because the server's reply is tested at the end of the method, as follows:

```
If replyCode.Equals("230") Then
  Return True
Else
  Return False
End If
```

MakeDir

The MakeDir method creates a new directory in the remote server by sending an MKD command:

```
Public Sub MakeDir(ByVal dir As String)
  SendCommand("MKD " & dir & ControlChars.CrLf)
  GetResponse()
End Sub
```

PassiveDataConnection

The `PassiveDataConnection` method is the same as the `PassiveDataConnection` method in the `NETFTP` class.

Rename

The `Rename` method changes the name of a remote file. It does so by sending the RNFR command and the RNTO command in sequence. Its definition is as follows:

```
Public Sub Rename(ByVal renameFrom As String, ByVal renameTo As String)
  SendCommand("RNFR " & renameFrom & ControlChars.CrLf)
  GetResponse()
  Console.WriteLine(replyCode & " " & replyMessage)
  SendCommand("RNTO " & renameTo & ControlChars.CrLf)
  GetResponse()
  Console.WriteLine(replyCode & " " & replyMessage)
End Sub
```

SendCommand

The `SendCommand` method sends a specified command to the connected server. Its definition is as follows:

```
Private Sub SendCommand(ByVal command As String)
  Try
    controlSocket.Send(Encoding.ASCII.GetBytes(command), command.Length, 0)
  Catch
  End Try
End Sub
```

SendTYPECommand

The `SendTYPECommand` method is the same as the `SendTYPECommand` method in the `NETFTP` class.

Upload

The Upload method checks if file transfer is allowed by checking the value of transferring. If the value is False, file transfer is allowed. It then creates a new thread for
the file transfer and starts the DoUpload method:

```
Public Sub Upload(ByVal filename As String, ByVal localDir As String)
  If Not transferring Then
    transferring = True
    Me.filename = filename
    Me.localDir = localDir
    dataTransferThread = New Thread(New ThreadStart(AddressOf DoUpload))
    dataTransferThread.Start()
  End If
End Sub
```

The FTP Class's Events

The FTP class can raise the following events: BeginDownload, EndDownload,
BeginUpload, EndUpload, and TransferProgressChanged. The first four are self-
explanatory. The TransferProgressChanged event raises several times during the
download and upload processes. The user of the FTP class can capture this event
to obtain the number of bytes of data transfer so far.

The definitions of public delegates are as follows:

```
Public Delegate Sub BeginDownloadEventHandler(ByVal sender As Object, _
  ByVal e As EventArgs)

Public Delegate Sub EndDownloadEventHandler(ByVal sender As Object, _
  ByVal e As EndDownloadEventArgs)

Public Delegate Sub BeginUploadEventHandler(ByVal sender As Object, _
  ByVal e As EventArgs)

Public Delegate Sub EndUploadEventHandler(ByVal sender As Object, _
  ByVal e As EndUploadEventArgs)

Public Delegate Sub TransferProgressChangedEventHandler(ByVal sender As Object, _
  ByVal e As TransferProgressChangedEventArgs)
```

Creating the EventArgs Subclasses

The following are the three subclasses of EventArgs class:

```
Public Class EndDownloadEventArgs : Inherits EventArgs
  Public Message As String
End Class

Public Class EndUploadEventArgs : Inherits EventArgs
  Public Message As String
End Class

Public Class TransferProgressChangedEventArgs : Inherits EventArgs
  Public TransferredByteCount As Integer

  Public Sub New()
  End Sub

  Public Sub New(ByVal size As Integer)
    TransferredByteCount = size
  End Sub
End Class
```

Creating the Form1 Class

You can find the Form1 class in the Form1.vb file in the project's directory. It represents the main form in the application. This section starts by showing various controls used in the form. It then describes how those controls connect together. The description makes frequent references to the class's members, each of which is given in detail at the end of the section.

To understand how the form works, let's start with its visual description. Figure 5-5 shows various controls on Form1.

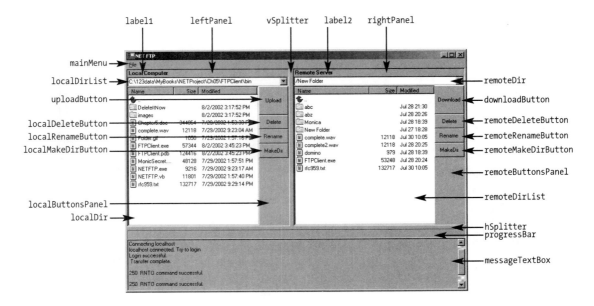

Figure 5-5. Control names on Form1

You can find the declaration of the controls in the Form1 class body:

```
Private hSplitter As System.Windows.Forms.Splitter
Private vSplitter As System.Windows.Forms.Splitter
Private leftPanel As System.Windows.Forms.Panel
Private rightPanel As System.Windows.Forms.Panel
Private localButtonsPanel As System.Windows.Forms.Panel
Private remoteButtonsPanel As System.Windows.Forms.Panel
Private progressBar As System.Windows.Forms.ProgressBar
Private label1 As System.Windows.Forms.Label
Private label2 As System.Windows.Forms.Label
Private localDir As System.Windows.Forms.ComboBox
Private localDeleteButton As System.Windows.Forms.Button
Private localRenameButton As System.Windows.Forms.Button
Private localMakeDirButton As System.Windows.Forms.Button
Private localDirList As System.Windows.Forms.ListView
Private uploadButton As System.Windows.Forms.Button
Private remoteDir As System.Windows.Forms.ComboBox
Private remoteDirList As System.Windows.Forms.ListView
Private remoteDeleteButton As System.Windows.Forms.Button
Private downloadButton As System.Windows.Forms.Button
Private remoteRenameButton As System.Windows.Forms.Button
```

```
Private remoteMakeDirButton As System.Windows.Forms.Button
Private messageTextBox As System.Windows.Forms.TextBox
Private mainMenu As System.Windows.Forms.MainMenu
Private fileMenuItem As System.Windows.Forms.MenuItem
Private connectFileMenuItem As System.Windows.Forms.MenuItem
Private exitFileMenuItem As System.Windows.Forms.MenuItem
Private imageList As System.Windows.Forms.ImageList
```

When first instantiated, the class's constructor calls the InitializeComponent method that instantiated the controls used in the form. At the last line, the InitializeComponent method calls the InitializeControls method, which wires events with event handlers, loads images, and so on.

The form has an ImageList control with three images used to represent a parent directory, a folder, and a file. The image files (Up.gif, Folder.gif, and File.gif) are located in the images directory under the project's directory. You add the images to imageList in the InitializeControls method:

```
imageList.Images.Add(Bitmap.FromFile("./images/Up.gif"))
imageList.Images.Add(Bitmap.FromFile("./images/Folder.gif"))
imageList.Images.Add(Bitmap.FromFile("./images/File.gif"))
```

At the end of its body, the InitializeControls method calls the following two methods:

```
SelectLocalDirectory(localCurrentDir)
Log("Welcome. Press F3 for quick login.")
```

The SelectLocalDirectory method populates the localDirList control with the list of subdirectories/files in the current directory, and the Log method displays a message in the messageTextBox control. The current local directory displays in the localDir ComboBox control.

Without being connected to a remote server, you can browse through your local directory by double-clicking the parent directory icon and any subdirectory in the current directory.

You can even do some simple file/directory manipulations such as the following:

- Create a new directory by clicking the localMakeDirButton control. The Click event of the localMakeDirButton control is handled by localMakeDirButton_Click, which calls the MakeLocalDir method.

- Delete a file/subdirectory by selecting a file/directory in the localDirList control and clicking the localDeleteButton control. The Click event of the localDirList control is wired with the localDeleteButton_Click event handler. This event handler calls the DeleteLocalFile method.

- Rename a file/directory by selecting a file/directory in the localDirList control and clicking the localRenameButton control. This button's Click event is wired to the localRenameButton_Click event handler, which calls the RenameLocalFile method.

However, using an FTP client application, you will want to connect to a remote server. You do this by pressing F3 or by selecting File ➤ Connect. Both the F3 shortcut and the Connect menu item activates the Connect method. The Connect method has two functions. When no FTP server is connected, it connects to the server. When there is an FTP server connected, it disconnects the connection.

Connecting to a remote server requires you to enter the server name, username, and password into the Login Form window. The Login Form window is called from the Connect method and is shown as a modal dialog box.

If you click the OK button in the Login Form window, the Connect method tries to connect you to the remote server. If the connection is successful, it also logs you in. Whether login was successful, it calls the Log method. This method appends the specified message to the messageTextBox control.

If login is successful, the Connect method displays the remote server's home directory content on the remoteDirList control.

The Form1 Class's Declaration

The Form1 class has the following declarations part:

```
Private localCurrentDir As String = Directory.GetCurrentDirectory()
Private remoteCurrentDir As String
Private server, userName, password As String
Private ftp As New ftp()
'the size of the file being downloaded/uploaded
Private fileSize As Integer

Private Structure DirectoryItem
  Public name As String
  Public modifiedDate As String
  Public size As String
End Structure
```

Note that the DirectoryItem structure represents either a directory or a file.

The Form1 Class's Methods

The following sections describe the Form1 class's methods.

ChangeLocalDir

The ChangeLocalDir method changes the local directory. This method is called when the user double-clicks an item in the localDirList control. The action taken by this method depends on the item activated. It changes directory if the activated item is either the parent directory icon or a folder. If the item is a file, the ChangeLocalDir method calls the UploadFile method.

This is the ChangeLocalDir method:

```
Private Sub ChangeLocalDir()
  'get activated item (the items that was double-clicked
  Dim item As ListViewItem = localDirList.SelectedItems(0)
  If item.Text.Equals("..") Then
    Dim parentDir As DirectoryInfo = Directory.GetParent(localCurrentDir)
    If Not parentDir Is Nothing Then
      localCurrentDir = parentDir.FullName
      SelectLocalDirectory(localCurrentDir)
    End If
  Else
    Directory.SetCurrentDirectory(localCurrentDir)
    Dim fullPath As String = Path.GetFullPath(item.Text)
    If Helper.IsDirectory(fullPath) Then
      localCurrentDir = fullPath
      SelectLocalDirectory(localCurrentDir)
    Else
      UploadFile()
    End If
  End If
End Sub
```

This method begins by obtaining the selected item from localDirList:

```
'get activated item (the items that was double-clicked
Dim item As ListViewItem = localDirList.SelectedItems(0)
```

It then checks whether the item is a parent directory icon. If it is, it constructs a `DirectoryInfo` object for the parent directory of the current directory using the `GetParent` method of the `System.IO.Directory` class:

```
If item.Text.Equals("..") Then
  Dim parentDir As DirectoryInfo = Directory.GetParent(localCurrentDir)
```

If the `GetParent` method returns a non-null value, it sets `localCurrentDir` to the parent directory's full name and calls the `SelectLocalDirectory` method to repopulate the `localDirList` control:

```
If Not parentDir Is Nothing Then
  localCurrentDir = parentDir.FullName
  SelectLocalDirectory(localCurrentDir)
End If
```

If the activated item is not a parent directory icon, it sets the application current directory to the value of `localCurrentDir` so that it can get the full path to the currently activated item:

```
Else
  Directory.SetCurrentDirectory(localCurrentDir)
  Dim fullPath As String = Path.GetFullPath(item.Text)
```

Now, it has to determine whether the activated item is a file or a directory using the `Helper` class's `IsDirectory` method. If it is a directory, it sets `localCurrentDir` to the full path obtained from the `GetFullPath` method in the previous line and then calls the `SelectLocalDirectory` to repopulate the `localDirList` control:

```
If Helper.IsDirectory(fullPath) Then
  localCurrentDir = fullPath
  SelectLocalDirectory(localCurrentDir)
```

If the activated item is a file, the `ChangeLocalDir` method simply calls the `UploadFile` method:

```
UploadFile()
```

ChangeRemoteDir

The ChangeRemoteDir method changes the directory in the connected server:

```
Private Sub ChangeRemoteDir()
  If ftp.Connected Then

    'get activated item (the item that was double-clicked)
    Dim item As ListViewItem = remoteDirList.SelectedItems(0)

    If item.Text.Equals("..") Then
      Dim index As Integer 'get the last index of "/"
      index = remoteCurrentDir.LastIndexOf("/")
      If index = 0 Then
        remoteCurrentDir = "/"
      Else
        remoteCurrentDir = remoteCurrentDir.Substring(0, index)
      End If
      ftp.ChangeDir(remoteCurrentDir)
      If ftp.replyCode.StartsWith("2") Then 'successful
        SelectRemoteDirectory(remoteCurrentDir)
      End If
      Log(ftp.replyMessage)
    ElseIf Helper.IsDirectoryItem(remoteDirList.SelectedItems(0)) Then
      If remoteCurrentDir.Equals("/") Then
        remoteCurrentDir += item.Text
      Else
        remoteCurrentDir += "/" & item.Text
      End If
      ftp.ChangeDir(remoteCurrentDir)
      If ftp.replyCode.StartsWith("2") Then 'successful
        SelectRemoteDirectory(remoteCurrentDir)
      End If
      Log(ftp.replyMessage)
    Else
      DownloadFile()
    End If

  Else
    NotConnected()
  End If
End Sub
```

First, the method only executes the code in its body if a remote server is connected. Checking a connection is through the FTP class's Connected property:

```
If ftp.Connected Then
    ...
Else
  NotConnected()
End If
```

After making sure that a remote server is connected, it obtains the activated item from the remoteDirList control:

```
'get activated item (the item that was double-clicked)
Dim item As ListViewItem = remoteDirList.SelectedItems(0)
```

The action taken by this method depends on the activated item. If the item is a parent directory icon or a folder, it calls the FTP class's ChangeDir method. If the activated item is a file, it calls the FTP class's Download method.

Note that because you are dealing with a remote server, you do not have access to the directory system. Instead, you work with paths.

If the activated item is the parent directory icon, the method tries to obtain the parent directory of the remote current directory. The remoteCurrentDir variable holds the remote current directory. Obtaining the parent directory is by trimming the characters after the last / (assuming that the remote server uses a Unix directory listing):

```
If item.Text.Equals("..") Then
  Dim index As Integer 'get the last index of "/"
  index = remoteCurrentDir.LastIndexOf("/")
  If index = 0 Then
    ' we are already in the root
    remoteCurrentDir = "/"
  Else
    remoteCurrentDir = remoteCurrentDir.Substring(0, index)
  End If
```

This gives you a new remote current directory. You just need to call the FTP class's ChangeDir method and pass the new directory name:

```
ftp.ChangeDir(remoteCurrentDir)
```

Now, if the `ChangeDir` method returns a successful reply message, you call the `SelectRemoteDirectory` to repopulate the `remoteDirList` control. You also log the reply message from the server:

```
If ftp.replyCode.StartsWith("2") Then 'successful
  SelectRemoteDirectory(remoteCurrentDir)
End If
Log(ftp.replyMessage)
```

If the activated item is a folder, the user clicks a subdirectory in the current remote directory. You can obtain the new current directory by appending the item's text to the current directory. Note, however, if you are currently in the root, you do not append a / before appending the directory name:

```
ElseIf Helper.IsDirectoryItem(remoteDirList.SelectedItems(0)) Then
  If remoteCurrentDir.Equals("/") Then
    remoteCurrentDir += item.Text
  Else
    remoteCurrentDir += "/" & item.Text
  End If
```

Having a new directory, you call the FTP class's `ChangeDir`, passing the destination directory:

```
ftp.ChangeDir(remoteCurrentDir)
```

If the `ChangeDir` method returns a server's successful message, you call the `SelectRemoteDirectory` to repopulate the `remoteDirList` control. You also log the server's reply message:

```
If ftp.replyCode.StartsWith("2") Then 'successful
  SelectRemoteDirectory(remoteCurrentDir)
End If
Log(ftp.replyMessage)
```

If the activated item is a file, you call the `DownloadFile` method:

```
DownloadFile()
```

Connect

The Connect method connects to and disconnects from a remote server. If the connectFileMenuItem's Text displays *Disconnect*, the application may be connected to a remote server. Because the remote server can disconnect a client if the client is idle for a given period of time, it is possible that the application is not connected to any server even though the client thinks it is still connected. Either way, the Connect method handles the situation well. The definition of the Connect method is as follows:

```
Private Sub Connect()
  'connect and disconnect
  If connectFileMenuItem.Text.Equals("&Disconnect") Then
    'disconnect
    If MessageBox.Show("Disconnect from remote server?", "Disconnect", _
      MessageBoxButtons.OKCancel, MessageBoxIcon.Question) = _
      DialogResult.OK Then
      If ftp.Connected Then
        ftp.Disconnect()
        Log("Disconnected.")
        connectFileMenuItem.Text = "&Connect"
        'clearing the ListView
        'don't use the remoteDirList.Clear because it removes the columns too,
        'instead use remoteDirList.Items.Clear()
        remoteDirList.Items.Clear()
        'clearing the combo box
        remoteDir.Items.Clear()
        remoteDir.Text = ""
      End If
    End If
  Else
    'connect
    Dim loginForm As New LoginForm()
    Dim loggedIn As Boolean = False
    While Not loggedIn AndAlso loginForm.ShowDialog() = DialogResult.OK
      server = loginForm.Server
      userName = loginForm.UserName
      password = loginForm.Password
      Log("Connecting " & server)
      Try
        ftp.Connect(server)
        If ftp.Connected Then
          Log(server & " connected. Try to login.")
```

```
        If ftp.Login(userName, password) Then
          connectFileMenuItem.Text = "&Disconnect"
          Log("Login successful.")
          loggedIn = True
          ' try to get the remote list
          ftp.ChangeToAsciiMode()
          remoteCurrentDir = ftp.GetCurrentRemoteDir()
          If Not remoteCurrentDir Is Nothing Then
            SelectRemoteDirectory(remoteCurrentDir)
          End If
        Else
          Log("Login failed.")
        End If
      Else
        Log("Connection failed")
      End If
    Catch e As Exception
      Log(e.ToString())
    End Try
  End While
  If Not loggedIn AndAlso _
    Not ftp Is Nothing AndAlso _
    ftp.Connected Then
    ftp.Disconnect()
  End If
  End If
End Sub
```

The `Connect` method first checks the `connectFileMenuItem`'s `Text` property. If it is `&Disconnect`, it tries to disconnect from the connected remote server:

```
If connectFileMenuItem.Text.Equals("&Disconnect") Then
  'disconnect
```

Before disconnecting, it asks for the user's confirmation:

```
If MessageBox.Show("Disconnect from remote server?", "Disconnect", _
  MessageBoxButtons.OKCancel, MessageBoxIcon.Question) = _
  DialogResult.OK Then
```

If the user says OK, it checks if the application is really connected to a remote server. If it is, it calls the FTP class's Disconnect method, logs a message, changes the connectFileMenuItem's Text to &Connect, and clears the remoteDirList and remoteDir controls:

```
If ftp.Connected Then
  ftp.Disconnect()
  Log("Disconnected.")
  connectFileMenuItem.Text = "&Connect"
  'clearing the ListView
  'don't use the remoteDirList.Clear because it removes the columns too,
  'instead use remoteDirList.Items.Clear()
  remoteDirList.Items.Clear()
  'clearing the combo box
  remoteDir.Items.Clear()
  remoteDir.Text = ""
End If
```

If no server is connected, the Connect method tries to connect. It starts by defining a Boolean called loggedIn and showing the Login Form window as a modal dialog box. It then does a While loop that loops until one of the following conditions is satisfied:

- The user clicks the Cancel button on the Login Form window.

- The user clicks the OK button on the Login Form window and logs in successfully. This is the code that does that:

  ```
  'connect
  Dim loginForm As New LoginForm()
  Dim loggedIn As Boolean = False
  While Not loggedIn AndAlso loginForm.ShowDialog() = DialogResult.OK
  ```

When the user clicks the OK button, it takes the values of the Login Form window's Server, UserName, and Password properties and logs a message:

```
server = loginForm.Server
userName = loginForm.UserName
password = loginForm.Password
Log("Connecting " & server)
```

It then tries to connect to the specified server using the FTP class's Connect method:

```
Try
  ftp.Connect(server)
```

If the connection is successful, it logs a message and tries to log in using the FTP class's Login method, passing the username and password:

```
If ftp.Connected Then
  Log(server & " connected. Try to login.")
  If ftp.Login(userName, password) Then
```

The Login method returns True if the user logs in successfully and False otherwise. For a successful login, you change the connectFileMenuItem's Text property to Disconnect, log a successful login message, and change the transfer mode by calling the ChangeToAsciiMode of the FTP class:

```
connectFileMenuItem.Text = "&Disconnect"
Log("Login successful.")
loggedIn = True
' try to get the remote list
ftp.ChangeToAsciiMode()
```

Next, it tries to obtain the remote current directory by calling the GetCurrentRemoteDir method of the FTP class:

```
remoteCurrentDir = ftp.GetCurrentRemoteDir()
```

If this method executes successfully on the remote server, it should return a non-null value, the remote current directory. You then use it as an argument to the SelectRemoteDirectory that displays the content of the remote current directory:

```
If Not remoteCurrentDir Is Nothing Then
  SelectRemoteDirectory(remoteCurrentDir)
End If
```

If the FTP class's Login method you called returns False, you log a "Login failed" message:

```
Log("Login failed.")
```

DeleteLocalFile

The DeleteLocalFile method deletes a local file and is called when the user selects an item in the localDirList control and clicks the localDeleteButton control. The definition of this method is as follows:

```
Private Sub DeleteLocalFile()
  Dim selectedItemCount As Integer = localDirList.SelectedItems.Count
  If selectedItemCount = 0 Then
    MessageBox.Show("Please select a file/directory to delete.", _
      "Warning", MessageBoxButtons.OK, MessageBoxIcon.Warning)
  Else
    If MessageBox.Show("Delete the selected file/directory?", _
      "Delete Confirmation", _
      MessageBoxButtons.OKCancel, MessageBoxIcon.Question) _
      = DialogResult.OK Then
      Dim completePath As String = _
        Path.Combine(localCurrentDir, localDirList.SelectedItems(0).Text)
      Try
        If Helper.IsDirectory(completePath) Then
          Directory.Delete(completePath)
        Else
          File.Delete(completePath)
        End If
        LoadLocalDirList()
      Catch ex As Exception
        MessageBox.Show(ex.ToString(), "Error", MessageBoxButtons.OK, _
          MessageBoxIcon.Error)
      End Try
    End If
  End If

End Sub
```

The DeleteLocalFile starts by checking if an item is selected in the localDirList control. If not, it displays a message box:

```
Dim selectedItemCount As Integer = localDirList.SelectedItems.Count
If selectedItemCount = 0 Then
  MessageBox.Show("Please select a file/directory to delete.", _
    "Warning", MessageBoxButtons.OK, MessageBoxIcon.Warning)
```

If an item is selected, the DeleteLocalFile method asks for the user confirmation that the user intends to delete the item to make sure that the user did not click the localDeleteButton control by accident:

```
If MessageBox.Show("Delete the selected file/directory?", _
  "Delete Confirmation", _
  MessageBoxButtons.OKCancel, MessageBoxIcon.Question) _
  = DialogResult.OK Then
```

If deletion is confirmed, it tries to obtain the complete path to the item by combining the local current directory and the item's text:

```
Dim completePath As String = _
  Path.Combine(localCurrentDir, localDirList.SelectedItems(0).Text)
```

Then, it checks whether it is a directory or a file. If it is a directory, it calls the Delete method of the System.IO.Directory class. If it is a file, the Delete method of the System.IO.File class is invoked:

```
If Helper.IsDirectory(completePath) Then
  Directory.Delete(completePath)
Else
  File.Delete(completePath)
End If
```

After deletion, the localDirList is refreshed by calling the LoadLocalDirList method:

```
LoadLocalDirList()
```

DeleteRemoteFile

The DeleteRemoteFile method deletes a file on the connected remote server:

```
Private Sub DeleteRemoteFile()
  If ftp.Connected Then
    Dim selectedItemCount As Integer = remoteDirList.SelectedItems.Count
    If selectedItemCount = 0 Then
      MessageBox.Show("Please select a file/directory to delete.", _
        "Warning", MessageBoxButtons.OK, MessageBoxIcon.Warning)
```

```
      Else
        If MessageBox.Show("Delete the selected file/directory?", _
          "Delete Confirmation", _
          MessageBoxButtons.OKCancel, MessageBoxIcon.Question) _
          = DialogResult.OK Then
          Try
            Dim selectedItem As ListViewItem = remoteDirList.SelectedItems(0)
            If Helper.IsDirectoryItem(selectedItem) Then
              If ftp.DeleteDir(selectedItem.Text) Then
                LoadRemoteDirList()
              Else
                Log(ftp.replyMessage)
              End If
            Else
              If ftp.DeleteFile(selectedItem.Text) Then
                LoadRemoteDirList()
              Else
                Log(ftp.replyMessage)
              End If
            End If
          Catch ex As Exception
            MessageBox.Show(ex.ToString, "Error", MessageBoxButtons.OK, _
              MessageBoxIcon.Error)
          End Try
        End If
      End If
    Else
      NotConnected()
    End If
End Sub
```

Note that the method only executes its body if the application is connected to a remote FTP server:

```
If ftp.Connected Then
    ...
Else
  NotConnected()
End If
```

After making sure that a remote server is connected, it checks that an item is selected in the remoteDirList control. If no item is selected, a warning displays in a message box:

```
Dim selectedItemCount As Integer = remoteDirList.SelectedItems.Count
If selectedItemCount = 0 Then
  MessageBox.Show("Please select a file/directory to delete.", _
    "Warning", MessageBoxButtons.OK, MessageBoxIcon.Warning)
```

If an item is selected, it asks for the user's confirmation to make sure that the remoteDeleteButton control was not clicked by accident:

```
Else
  If MessageBox.Show("Delete the selected file/directory?", _
    "Delete Confirmation", _
    MessageBoxButtons.OKCancel, MessageBoxIcon.Question) _
    = DialogResult.OK Then
```

If deletion is confirmed, the method obtains the selected item and sends it to the Helper class's IsDirectoryItem to determine if the selected item is a directory or a file:

```
Try
  Dim selectedItem As ListViewItem = remoteDirList.SelectedItems(0)
  If Helper.IsDirectoryItem(selectedItem) Then
```

If the selected item is a directory, it calls the FTP class's DeleteDir method and, upon successful completion of this method, calls the LoadRemoteDirList to repopulate the remoteDirList control. If the DeleteDir method returns False to indicate that the deletion failed, it logs the message:

```
If ftp.DeleteDir(selectedItem.Text) Then
  LoadRemoteDirList()
Else
  Log(ftp.replyMessage)
End If
```

If the selected item is a file, it calls the FTP class's DeleteFile method and, upon successful completion of this method, calls the LoadRemoteDirList to repopulate the remoteDirList control. If the DeleteFile method failed, it logs the message:

```
If ftp.DeleteFile(selectedItem.Text) Then
  LoadRemoteDirList()
```

```
Else
  Log(ftp.replyMessage)
End If
```

DownloadFile

The DownloadFile method downloads a file from the connected remote server:

```
Private Sub DownloadFile()
  If ftp.Connected Then
    Dim selectedItemCount As Integer = remoteDirList.SelectedItems.Count

    If selectedItemCount = 0 Then
      MessageBox.Show("Please select a file to download.", _
        "Warning", MessageBoxButtons.OK, MessageBoxIcon.Warning)
    Else
      Dim item As ListViewItem = remoteDirList.SelectedItems(0)
      If Helper.IsDirectoryItem(item) Then
        MessageBox.Show("You cannot download a directory.", _
          "Error downloading file", MessageBoxButtons.OK, _
          MessageBoxIcon.Error)
      Else
        Try
          fileSize = Convert.ToInt32(item.SubItems(1).Text)
        Catch
        End Try
        ftp.Download(item.Text, localCurrentDir)
      End If
    End If
  Else
    NotConnected()
  End If
End Sub
```

Note that the method only executes its body if the application is connected to a remote FTP server:

```
If ftp.Connected Then
  ...
Else
  NotConnected()
End If
```

After making sure that a remote server is connected, it checks that an item is selected in the remoteDirList control. If no item is selected, a warning displays:

```
Dim selectedItemCount As Integer = remoteDirList.SelectedItems.Count
If selectedItemCount = 0 Then
  MessageBox.Show("Please select a file to download.", _
    "Warning", MessageBoxButtons.OK, MessageBoxIcon.Warning)
```

If an item is selected, it gets the selected item from the remoteDirList control and sends the item to the Helper class's IsDirectoryItem method to determine whether the selected item is a directory or a file:

```
Dim item As ListViewItem = remoteDirList.SelectedItems(0)
```

If the item is a directory, the method shows an error message, warning the user that they cannot download a directory:

```
If Helper.IsDirectoryItem(item) Then
  MessageBox.Show("You cannot download a directory.", _
    "Error downloading file", MessageBoxButtons.OK, _
    MessageBoxIcon.Error)
```

If the selected item is a file, it gets the file size from the item and assigns it to the fileSize variable. The FTP class's BeginDownload event handler uses this value to calculate the transfer progress:

```
Try
  fileSize = Convert.ToInt32(item.SubItems(1).Text)
Catch
End Try
```

It then calls the FTP class's Download method, passing the filename and the local current directory. These two arguments determine where to save the downloaded file:

```
ftp.Download(item.Text, localCurrentDir)
```

GetDirectoryItem

This FTP client application only works properly if the remote server returns a directory listing in Unix style. If this is the case, the list contains lines of data that include the directory/filename and each directory/file's meta information. The

GetDirectoryItem method processes the line that contains a directory/file information and returns it as a DirectoryItem object. The resulting DirectoryItem object can contain information about a directory or a file.

The raw data passed to this method has the following format:

```
-rwxrwxrwx   1 owner     group                11801 Jul 23 10:52 NETFTP.vb
```

or this format:

```
drwxrwxrwx   1 owner     group                    0 Jul 26 20:11 New Folder
```

The method definition is as follows:

```vb
Private Function GetDirectoryItem(ByVal s As String) As DirectoryItem
  's is in the following format
  '-rwxrwxrwx   1 owner    group                11801 Jul 23 10:52 NETFTP.vb
  '
  'or
  '
  'drwxrwxrwx   1 owner    group                    0 Jul 26 20:11 New Folder

  Dim dirItem As New DirectoryItem()
  If Not s Is Nothing Then
    Dim index As Integer
    index = s.IndexOf(" "c)
    If index <> -1 Then
      s = s.Substring(index).TrimStart() 'removing "drwxrwxrwx" part
      'now s is in the following format
      '1 owner     group               11801 Jul 23 10:52 NETFTP.vb
      '
      'or
      '
      '1 owner     group                   0 Jul 26 20:11 New Folder
      index = s.IndexOf(" "c)
      If index <> -1 Then
        s = s.Substring(index).TrimStart() 'removing the '1' part
        'now s is in the following format
        'owner     group               11801 Jul 23 10:52 NETFTP.vb
        '
        'or
        '
        'owner     group                   0 Jul 26 20:11 New Folder
        index = s.IndexOf(" "c)
```

```
If index <> -1 Then
  s = s.Substring(index).TrimStart() 'removing the 'owner' part
  'now s is in the following format
  'group          11801 Jul 23 10:52 NETFTP.vb
  '
  'or
  '
  'group              0 Jul 26 20:11 New Folder
  index = s.IndexOf(" "c)
  If index <> -1 Then
    s = s.Substring(index).TrimStart() 'removing the 'group' part
    'now s is in the following format
    '11801 Jul 23 10:52 NETFTP.vb
    '
    'or
    '
    '0 Jul 26 20:11 New Folder
    'now get the size.
    index = s.IndexOf(" "c)
    If index > 0 Then
      dirItem.size = s.Substring(0, index)
      s = s.Substring(index).TrimStart() 'removing the size
      'now s is in the following format
      'Jul 23 10:52 NETFTP.vb
      '
      'or
      '
      'Jul 26 20:11 New Folder
      'now, get the 3 elements of the date part
      Dim date1, date2, date3 As String
      index = s.IndexOf(" "c)
      If index <> -1 Then
        date1 = s.Substring(0, index)
        s = s.Substring(index).TrimStart()
        index = s.IndexOf(" "c)
        If index <> -1 Then
          date2 = s.Substring(0, index)
          s = s.Substring(index).TrimStart()
          index = s.IndexOf(" "c)
          If index <> -1 Then
            date3 = s.Substring(0, index)
            dirItem.modifiedDate = date1 & " " & date2 & " " & date3
            ' get the name
```

```
                    dirItem.name = s.Substring(index).Trim()
                  End If
                End If
              End If
            End If
          End If
        End If
      End If
    End If
  End If
  Return dirItem
End Function
```

The method starts by constructing a DirectoryItem object. This object will be populated and returned to the function's caller:

```
Dim dirItem As New DirectoryItem()
```

First the method checks that s (the argument passed to this method) is not null:

```
If Not s Is Nothing Then
```

If s is not null, then the method finds the first space in s, modifies s so that s does not include the string before the space, and left-trims s until the next non-space character:

```
Dim index As Integer
index = s.IndexOf(" "c)
    If index <> -1 Then
  s = s.Substring(index).TrimStart() 'removing "drwxrwxrwx" part
```

s now has the following format:

```
1 owner     group          11801 Jul 23 10:52 NETFTP.vb
```

or this format:

```
1 owner     group              0 Jul 26 20:11 New Folder
```

Then, you do the same thing as you did just now:

```
index = s.IndexOf(" "c)
If index <> -1 Then
  s = s.Substring(index).TrimStart() 'removing the '1' part
```

to get s in the following format:

```
owner    group          11801 Jul 23 10:52 NETFTP.vb
```

or this format:

```
owner    group              0 Jul 26 20:11 New Folder
```

And again:

```
index = s.IndexOf(" "c)
If index <> -1 Then
  s = s.Substring(index).TrimStart() 'removing the 'owner' part
```

to get s in the following format:

```
group          11801 Jul 23 10:52 NETFTP.vb
```

or this format:

```
group              0 Jul 26 20:11 New Folder
```

And yet another one:

```
index = s.IndexOf(" "c)
If index <> -1 Then
  s = s.Substring(index).TrimStart() 'removing the 'group' part
```

Now, s has the following format:

```
11801 Jul 23 10:52 NETFTP.vb
```

or this format:

```
0 Jul 26 20:11 New Folder
```

Now, you can get the size and do the same operation:

```
index = s.IndexOf(" "c)
If index > 0 Then
  dirItem.size = s.Substring(0, index)
  s = s.Substring(index).TrimStart() 'removing the size
```

Afterward, s has the following format:

```
Jul 23 10:52 NETFTP.vb
```

or this one:

```
Jul 26 20:11 New Folder
```

Now, get the three elements of the date part:

```
Dim date1, date2, date3 As String
index = s.IndexOf(" "c)
If index <> -1 Then
  date1 = s.Substring(0, index)
  s = s.Substring(index).TrimStart()
  index = s.IndexOf(" "c)
  If index <> -1 Then
    date2 = s.Substring(0, index)
    s = s.Substring(index).TrimStart()
    index = s.IndexOf(" "c)
    If index <> -1 Then
      date3 = s.Substring(0, index)
      dirItem.modifiedDate = date1 & " " & date2 & " " & date3
      ' get the name
      dirItem.name = s.Substring(index).Trim()
```

Finally, return the DirectoryItem object:

```
Return dirItem
```

InitializeProgressBar

The `InitializeProgressBar` method initializes the progress bar prior to file transfer:

```
Private Sub InitializeProgressBar()
  progressBar.Value = 0
  progressBar.Maximum = fileSize
End Sub
```

The `InitializeProgressBar` method sets the `Value` property to 0 and the `Maximum` property to `fileSize`. `fileSize` contains the number of bytes to transfer:

```
progressBar.Value = 0
progressBar.Maximum = fileSize
```

LoadLocalDirList

The `LoadLocalDirList` method populates the `localDirList` control with the content of the current directory. If the current directory is not the root, an icon representing a parent directory is also added. The method definition is as follows:

```
Private Sub LoadLocalDirList()
  localDirList.Items.Clear()
  Dim item As ListViewItem

  ' if current directory is not root, add pointer to parent dir
  If Not Directory.GetParent(localCurrentDir) Is Nothing Then
    item = New ListViewItem("..", 1)
    item.ImageIndex = 0
    localDirList.Items.Add(item)
  End If

  ' list of directories
  Dim directories As String() = Directory.GetDirectories(localCurrentDir)
  Dim length As Integer = directories.Length
  Dim dirName As String
  For Each dirName In directories
    item = New ListViewItem(Path.GetFileName(dirName), 1)
    item.SubItems.Add("")
    item.SubItems.Add(Directory.GetLastAccessTime(dirName).ToString())
    item.ImageIndex = 1
    localDirList.Items.Add(item)
```

```
  Next
  'list of files
  Dim files As String() = Directory.GetFiles(localCurrentDir)
  length = files.Length
  Dim fileName As String
  For Each fileName In files
    item = New ListViewItem(Path.GetFileName(fileName), 1)
    Dim fi As New FileInfo(fileName)
    item.SubItems.Add(Convert.ToString(fi.Length))
    item.SubItems.Add(File.GetLastWriteTime(fileName).ToString())
    item.ImageIndex = 2
    localDirList.Items.Add(item)
  Next

End Sub
```

The method starts by clearing the localDirList control and defining a ListViewItem called item:

```
localDirList.Items.Clear()
Dim item As ListViewItem
```

If the current directory is not root, it adds a parent directory icon:

```
If Not Directory.GetParent(localCurrentDir) Is Nothing Then
  item = New ListViewItem("..", 1)
  item.ImageIndex = 0
  localDirList.Items.Add(item)
End If
```

Next, it adds all subdirectories in the current directory. You obtain the list of directories from the GetDirectories method of the System.IO.Directory class:

```
Dim directories As String() = Directory.GetDirectories(localCurrentDir)
Dim length As Integer = directories.Length
Dim dirName As String
For Each dirName In directories
  item = New ListViewItem(Path.GetFileName(dirName), 1)
  item.SubItems.Add("")
  item.SubItems.Add(Directory.GetLastAccessTime(dirName).ToString())
  item.ImageIndex = 1
  localDirList.Items.Add(item)
Next
```

Finally, it adds all files in the current directory. You obtain the list of files from the GetFiles method of the Directory class:

```
Dim files As String() = Directory.GetFiles(localCurrentDir)
length = files.Length
Dim fileName As String
For Each fileName In files
  item = New ListViewItem(Path.GetFileName(fileName), 1)
  Dim fi As New FileInfo(fileName)
  item.SubItems.Add(Convert.ToString(fi.Length))
  item.SubItems.Add(File.GetLastWriteTime(fileName).ToString())
  item.ImageIndex = 2
  localDirList.Items.Add(item)
Next
```

LoadRemoteDirList

The LoadRemoteDirList method populates the remoteDirList control with the content of the remote current directory. If the remote current directory is not the root, an icon representing a parent directory is also added. The definition of the LoadRemoteDirList is as follows:

```
Private Sub LoadRemoteDirList()
  If ftp.Connected Then
    remoteDirList.Items.Clear()
    Dim item As ListViewItem

    If Not remoteCurrentDir.Equals("/") Then
      item = New ListViewItem("..", 1)
      item.ImageIndex = 0
      remoteDirList.Items.Add(item)
    End If

    Try
      ftp.ChangeDir(remoteCurrentDir)
      ftp.GetDirList()
      Dim lines As String() = _
        ftp.DirectoryList.Split(Convert.ToChar(ControlChars.Cr))
      Dim line As String
      Dim fileList As New ArrayList()
      Dim dirList As New ArrayList()
      For Each line In lines
        If line.Trim().StartsWith("-") Then ' a file
```

```
        fileList.Add(line)
      ElseIf line.Trim().StartsWith("d") Then ' a directory
        dirList.Add(line)
      End If
    Next


    ' now load subdirectories to DirListView
    Dim enumerator As IEnumerator = dirList.GetEnumerator
    While enumerator.MoveNext
      Dim dirItem As DirectoryItem = _
        GetDirectoryItem(CType(enumerator.Current, String))
      If Not dirItem.name Is Nothing Then
        item = New ListViewItem(dirItem.name, 1)
        item.SubItems.Add("")
        item.SubItems.Add(dirItem.modifiedDate)
        remoteDirList.Items.Add(item)
      End If
    End While


    enumerator = fileList.GetEnumerator
    While enumerator.MoveNext
      Dim dirItem As DirectoryItem = _
        GetDirectoryItem(CType(enumerator.Current, String))
      If Not dirItem.name Is Nothing Then
        item = New ListViewItem(dirItem.name, 2)
        item.SubItems.Add(diritem.size)
        item.SubItems.Add(dirItem.modifiedDate)
        remoteDirList.Items.Add(item)
      End If
    End While
  Catch e As Exception
    Debug.WriteLine(e.ToString())
  End Try
Else
  NotConnected()
End If
End Sub
```

The method starts by checking if the application is connected to a remote server. It only executes the rest of the code in its body if the application is connected:

```
If ftp.Connected Then
   ...
Else
  NotConnected()
End If
```

If the application is connected, the remoteDirList control is cleared and a ListViewItem variable called item is defined:

```
remoteDirList.Items.Clear()
Dim item As ListViewItem
```

If the remote current directory is not root, the method adds the icon representing the parent directory:

```
If Not remoteCurrentDir.Equals("/") Then
  item = New ListViewItem("..", 1)
  item.ImageIndex = 0
  remoteDirList.Items.Add(item)
End If
```

Next, it changes directory to the remote current directory and calls the FTP class's GetDirList to obtain the directory listing:

```
Try
  ftp.ChangeDir(remoteCurrentDir)
  ftp.GetDirList()
```

The directory listing returns in a long string containing file and directory information in the remote current directory. The string then splits into lines:

```
Dim lines As String() = _
  ftp.DirectoryList.Split(Convert.ToChar(ControlChars.Cr))
```

The subdirectories and files returned are not grouped by type, but you want to display subdirectories in one group and files in another. Therefore, you construct an ArrayList called fileList that will hold the list of files and an ArrayList named dirList to hold the list of directories:

```
Dim line As String
Dim fileList As New ArrayList()
Dim dirList As New ArrayList()
```

Then, each line that starts with a hyphen in a file is added to `fileList` and lines starting with *d* are added to `dirList`:

```
For Each line In lines
  If line.Trim().StartsWith("-") Then ' a file
    fileList.Add(line)
  ElseIf line.Trim().StartsWith("d") Then ' a directory
    dirList.Add(line)
  End If
Next
```

Now, you can add all subdirectories to the `remoteDirList` control. Note that you use the `GetDirectoryItem` to convert the raw text to a `DirectoryItem` object:

```
Dim enumerator As IEnumerator = dirList.GetEnumerator
While enumerator.MoveNext
  Dim dirItem As DirectoryItem = _
    GetDirectoryItem(CType(enumerator.Current, String))
  If Not dirItem.name Is Nothing Then
    item = New ListViewItem(dirItem.name, 1)
    item.SubItems.Add("")
    item.SubItems.Add(dirItem.modifiedDate)
    remoteDirList.Items.Add(item)
  End If
End While
```

Next, you add all files to the `remoteDirList` control, again using the `GetDirectoryItem` method to get `DirectoryItem` objects:

```
enumerator = fileList.GetEnumerator
While enumerator.MoveNext
  Dim dirItem As DirectoryItem = _
    GetDirectoryItem(CType(enumerator.Current, String))
  If Not dirItem.name Is Nothing Then
    item = New ListViewItem(dirItem.name, 2)
    item.SubItems.Add(diritem.size)
    item.SubItems.Add(dirItem.modifiedDate)
    remoteDirList.Items.Add(item)
  End If
End While
```

Log

The Log method appends the text passed to it to the messageTextBox control's Text property and forces the messageTextBox control to scroll to the end of the text:

```
Private Sub Log(ByVal message As String)
  messageTextBox.Text += message & ControlChars.CrLf
  'forces the TextBox to scroll
  messageTextBox.SelectionStart = messageTextBox.Text.Length
  messageTextBox.ScrollToCaret()
End Sub
```

MakeLocalDir

The MakeLocalDir method creates a new directory under the local current directory:

```
Private Sub MakeLocalDir()
  Dim dirName As String = InputBox( _
    "Enter the name of the directory to create in the local computer", _
    "Make New Directory").Trim()
  If Not dirName.Equals("") Then
    Dim fullPath As String = Path.Combine(localCurrentDir, dirName)
    If Directory.Exists(fullPath) Then
      MessageBox.Show("Directory already exists.", _
        "Error creating directory", MessageBoxButtons.OK, _
        MessageBoxIcon.Error)
    Else
      If File.Exists(fullPath) Then
        MessageBox.Show("Directory name is the same as the name of a file.", _
          "Error creating directory", MessageBoxButtons.OK, _
          MessageBoxIcon.Error)
      Else
        Try
          Directory.CreateDirectory(fullPath)
          LoadLocalDirList()
        Catch e As Exception
          MessageBox.Show(e.ToString, _
            "Error creating directory", MessageBoxButtons.OK, _
            MessageBoxIcon.Error)
        End Try
      End If
    End If
  End If
End Sub
```

It begins by prompting the user to enter a name for the new directory:

```
Dim dirName As String = InputBox( _
  "Enter the name of the directory to create in the local computer", _
  "Make New Directory").Trim()
```

If the user enters a valid name, it gets the full path by combining the local current directory and the entered name:

```
If Not dirName.Equals("") Then
  Dim fullPath As String = Path.Combine(localCurrentDir, dirName)
```

Next, it checks if the directory already exists:

```
If Directory.Exists(fullPath) Then
  MessageBox.Show("Directory already exists.", _
    "Error creating directory", MessageBoxButtons.OK, _
    MessageBoxIcon.Error)
```

It also checks if the directory name resembles a file in the same directory:

```
If File.Exists(fullPath) Then
  MessageBox.Show("Directory name is the same as the name of a file.", _
    "Error creating directory", MessageBoxButtons.OK, _
    MessageBoxIcon.Error)
```

If the name is unique in the directory, it uses the CreateDirectory method of the System.IO.Directory class to create a new directory:

```
Directory.CreateDirectory(fullPath)
```

Upon a successful create operation, it refreshes the content of the localDirList control by calling the LoadLocalDirList method:

```
LoadLocalDirList()
```

MakeRemoteDir

The MakeRemoteDir method creates a new directory in the remote current directory. If the application is connected to a remote server, it prompts the user for a directory name. The MakeRemoteDir method definition is as follows:

```
Private Sub MakeRemoteDir()
  If ftp.Connected Then
    Dim dirName As String = InputBox( _
      "Enter the name of the directory to create in the remote server", _
      "Make New Directory").Trim()
    If Not dirName.Equals("") Then
      ftp.MakeDir(dirName)
      Log(ftp.replyMessage)
      If ftp.replyCode.StartsWith("2") Then
        LoadRemoteDirList()
        'Dim item As New ListViewItem(dirName, 1)
        'If remoteCurrentDir.Equals("/") Then
        ' remoteDirList.Items.Insert(1, item)
        'Else
        ' remoteDirList.Items.Insert(0, item)
        'End If
      End If
    End If
  Else
    NotConnected()
  End If
End Sub
```

It starts by prompting the user to enter a directory name into an InputBox:

```
If ftp.Connected Then
  Dim dirName As String = InputBox( _
    "Enter the name of the directory to create in the remote server", _
    "Make New Directory").Trim()
```

If the name is not blank, it calls the FTP class's MakeDir method and logs the message:

```
If Not dirName.Equals("") Then
  ftp.MakeDir(dirName)
  Log(ftp.replyMessage)
```

If the `MakeDir` method is successful (indicated by a reply code starting with 2), it calls the `LoadRemoteDirList` method:

```
If ftp.replyCode.StartsWith("2") Then
  LoadRemoteDirList()
End If
```

NotConnected

The `NotConnected` method is called every time another method finds out that the application is not connected to a remote server. It logs a message and then changes the `connectFileMenuItem`'s Text property to &Connect. The method definition is as follows:

```
Private Sub NotConnected()
  Log("Not connected")
  connectFileMenuItem.Text = "&Connect"
  'clearing the ListView
  'don't use the remoteDirList.Clear because it removes the columns too,
  'instead use remoteDirList.Items.Clear()
  remoteDirList.Items.Clear()
  'clearing the combo box
  remoteDir.Items.Clear()
  remoteDir.Text = ""
End Sub
```

The first thing it does is to log the "Not connected" message and change the `connectFileMenuItem`'s Text property:

```
Log("Not connected")
connectFileMenuItem.Text = "&Connect"
```

It then clears the `remoteDirList` and `remoteDir` controls:

```
remoteDirList.Items.Clear()
'clearing the combo box
remoteDir.Items.Clear()
remoteDir.Text = ""
```

RenameLocalFile

The RenameLocalFile method renames a file in the local computer. This method is invoked when the user clicks the localRenameButton control. The method definition is as follows:

```
Private Sub RenameLocalFile()
  Dim selectedItemCount As Integer = localDirList.SelectedItems.Count
  If selectedItemCount = 0 Then
    MessageBox.Show("Please select a file/directory to rename.", _
      "Warning", MessageBoxButtons.OK, MessageBoxIcon.Warning)
  Else
    Dim newName As String = InputBox("Enter the new name", "Rename").Trim()
    If Not newName.Equals("") Then
      Dim item As ListViewItem = localDirList.SelectedItems(0)
      If newName.Equals(item.Text) Then
        MessageBox.Show("Please enter a different name from the " & _
          "file/directory you are trying to rename.", _
          "Error renaming file/directory", MessageBoxButtons.OK, _
          MessageBoxIcon.Error)
      Else
        Dim fullPath As String = Path.Combine(localCurrentDir, item.Text)
        If Helper.IsDirectory(fullPath) Then
          Directory.Move(fullPath, Path.Combine(localCurrentDir, newName))
        Else
          Dim fi As New FileInfo(fullPath)
          fi.MoveTo(Path.Combine(localCurrentDir, newName))
        End If
        LoadLocalDirList()
      End If
    End If
  End If
End Sub
```

It first checks if an item is selected in the localDirList control. If not, it shows a warning:

```
Dim selectedItemCount As Integer = localDirList.SelectedItems.Count
If selectedItemCount = 0 Then
  MessageBox.Show("Please select a file/directory to rename.", _
    "Warning", MessageBoxButtons.OK, MessageBoxIcon.Warning)
```

If an item is selected in the localDirList control, it prompts for a new name:

```
Dim newName As String = InputBox("Enter the new name", "Rename").Trim()
```

If the new name does not consist only of spaces, it gets the selected item from the localDirList control and checks the old name. If the old name is the same as the new name, it displays an error message:

```
If Not newName.Equals("") Then
  Dim item As ListViewItem = localDirList.SelectedItems(0)
  If newName.Equals(item.Text) Then
    MessageBox.Show("Please enter a different name from the " & _
      "file/directory you are trying to rename.", _
      "Error renaming file/directory", MessageBoxButtons.OK, _
      MessageBoxIcon.Error)
```

If the new name does not conflict with the old one, it composes the full path using the static Combine method of the System.IO.Path class:

```
Dim fullPath As String = Path.Combine(localCurrentDir, item.Text)
```

Then it checks whether the selected item is a directory or a file. If it is a file, the method calls the Move method of the System.IO.Directory class to change the name:

```
If Helper.IsDirectory(fullPath) Then
  Directory.Move(fullPath, Path.Combine(localCurrentDir, newName))
```

If the selected item is a file, the method constructs a FileInfo object and calls its MoveTo method to change the filename:

```
Dim fi As New FileInfo(fullPath)
fi.MoveTo(Path.Combine(localCurrentDir, newName))
```

Finally, it invokes the LoadLocalDirList to refresh the content of the localDirList control:

```
LoadLocalDirList()
```

RenameRemoteFile

The RenameRemoteFile method renames a file on the connected remote server. It only runs the code in its body if the application is connected to a remote server. The method definition is as follows:

```
Private Sub RenameRemoteFile()
  If ftp.Connected Then
    Dim selectedItemCount As Integer = remoteDirList.SelectedItems.Count
    If selectedItemCount = 0 Then
      MessageBox.Show("Please select a file/directory to rename.", _
        "Warning", MessageBoxButtons.OK, MessageBoxIcon.Warning)
    Else
      Dim dirName As String = InputBox( _
        "Enter the new name", "Rename").Trim()
      If Not dirName.Equals("") Then
        Dim item As ListViewItem = remoteDirList.SelectedItems(0)
        If dirName.Equals(item.Text) Then
          MessageBox.Show("Please enter a different name from the " & _
            "file/directory you are trying to rename.", _
            "Error renaming file/directory", MessageBoxButtons.OK, _
            MessageBoxIcon.Error)
        Else
          ftp.Rename(item.Text, dirName)
          If ftp.replyCode.StartsWith("2") Then
            item.Text = dirName
          End If
          Log(ftp.replyCode & " " & ftp.replyMessage)
        End If
      End If
    End If
  Else
    NotConnected()
  End If
End Sub
```

It starts by checking if there is a selected item in the remoteDirList control. If there is not, an error message displays:

```
If ftp.Connected Then
  Dim selectedItemCount As Integer = remoteDirList.SelectedItems.Count
  If selectedItemCount = 0 Then
    MessageBox.Show("Please select a file/directory to rename.", _
      "Warning", MessageBoxButtons.OK, MessageBoxIcon.Warning)
```

If there is a selected item, the method prompts the user for a new name:

```
Dim dirName As String = InputBox( _
  "Enter the new name", "Rename").Trim()
```

If the new name does not consists of spaces only, it gets the selected item and gets the old name in the item's Text property. It then compares the new name with the old name:

```
If Not dirName.Equals("") Then
  Dim item As ListViewItem = remoteDirList.SelectedItems(0)
```

If the new name equals the old name, it displays an error message:

```
If dirName.Equals(item.Text) Then
  MessageBox.Show("Please enter a different name from the " & _
    "file/directory you are trying to rename.", _
    "Error renaming file/directory", MessageBoxButtons.OK, _
    MessageBoxIcon.Error)
```

Otherwise, it calls the FTP class's Rename method, passing both the old name and the new name:

```
ftp.Rename(item.Text, dirName)
```

If the Rename method successfully executes (indicated by a server reply code starting with 2), the method updates the item's Text property in the remoteDirList control:

```
If ftp.replyCode.StartsWith("2") Then
  item.Text = dirName
End If
```

Finally, it logs the reply message from the server:

```
Log(ftp.replyCode & " " & ftp.replyMessage)
```

SelectLocalDirectory

The SelectLocalDirectory method inserts the local current directory into the localDir combo box:

```
Private Sub SelectLocalDirectory(ByVal path As String)
  ' add current dir to the list
  localDir.Items.Remove(path)
  localDir.Items.Insert(0, path)
  'this will trigger the localDir ComboBox's SelectedIndexChanged event
  localDir.SelectedIndex = 0
End Sub
```

Prior to insertion, it removes the same item to avoid duplication:

```
' add current dir to the list
localDir.Items.Remove(path)
localDir.Items.Insert(0, path)
```

The method then sets the SelectedIndex property of the localDir combo box to 0 to make the new item selected. This also triggers the combo box's SelectedIndexChanged event:

```
localDir.SelectedIndex = 0
```

SelectRemoteDirectory

If the application is connected to a remote server, this method inserts a remote directory name at the first position in the remoteDir combo box. The method definition is as follows:

```
Private Sub SelectRemoteDirectory(ByVal path As String)
  If ftp.Connected Then
    ' add current dir to thel ist
    remoteDir.Items.Remove(path)
    remoteDir.Items.Insert(0, path)
    'this will trigger the remoteDir ComboBox's SelectedIndexChanged event
    remoteDir.SelectedIndex = 0
  Else
    NotConnected()
  End If
End Sub
```

The first thing the method does is to remove the same item to avoid duplication:

```
If ftp.Connected Then
  ' add current dir to thel ist
  remoteDir.Items.Remove(path)
  remoteDir.Items.Insert(0, path)
```

It then sets the SelectedIndex property to 0. This triggers the SelectedIndexChanged event of the remoteDir combo box:

```
remoteDir.SelectedIndex = 0
```

UpdateLocalDir

The UpdateLocalDir method is invoked when the localDir control's SelectedIndexChanged event is triggered. This event is raised when the user manually selects a directory from the localDir control or the index is changed programmatically. Then, this method refreshes the content of the localDirList control. The method definition is as follows:

```
Private Sub UpdateLocalDir()
  Dim selectedIndex As Integer = localDir.SelectedIndex
  If localDir.SelectedIndex <> -1 Then
    localCurrentDir = CType(localDir.Items(selectedIndex), String)
    LoadLocalDirList()
  End If
End Sub
```

UpdateProgressBar

The UpdateProgressBar method is called repeatedly by the event handler that handles the TransferProgressChanged event. This method updates the value of the progress bar. The method definition is as follows:

```
Private Sub UpdateProgressBar(ByVal count As Integer)
  progressBar.Value = count
End Sub
```

UpdateRemoteDir

The UpdateRemoteDir method is invoked when the remoteDir control's
SelectedIndexChanged event triggers. This event is raised when the user
manually selects a directory from the remoteDir control or the index is
changed programmatically. This is the UpdateRemoteDir method:

```
Private Sub UpdateRemoteDir()
  If ftp.Connected Then
    Dim selectedIndex As Integer = remoteDir.SelectedIndex
    If remoteDir.SelectedIndex <> -1 Then
      remoteCurrentDir = CType(remoteDir.Items(selectedIndex), String)
      LoadRemoteDirList()
    End If
  Else
    NotConnected()
  End If
End Sub
```

When the application is connected to a remote server, this method refreshes
the content of the remoteDirList control.

UploadFile

The UploadFile method uploads a file to the connected remote server if the
application is connected to a remote server. This is the method definition:

```
Private Sub UploadFile()
  If ftp.Connected Then
    Dim selectedItemCount As Integer = localDirList.SelectedItems.Count
    If selectedItemCount = 0 Then
      MessageBox.Show("Please select a file to upload.", _
        "Warning", MessageBoxButtons.OK, MessageBoxIcon.Warning)
    Else
      Dim item As ListViewItem = localDirList.SelectedItems(0)
      If Helper.IsDirectoryItem(item) Then
        MessageBox.Show("You cannot upload a directory.", _
          "Error uploading file", MessageBoxButtons.OK, _
          MessageBoxIcon.Error)
      Else
        Try
          fileSize = Convert.ToInt32(item.SubItems(1).Text)
        Catch
```

```
      End Try
      ftp.Upload(item.Text, localCurrentDir)
    End If
  End If
Else
  NotConnected()
End If
End Sub
```

It first checks if the application is connected to a remote server:

```
If ftp.Connected Then
```

If the application is connected, the method checks if there is a selected item in the localDirList control. If there is no item selected, it displays an error message:

```
Dim selectedItemCount As Integer = localDirList.SelectedItems.Count
If selectedItemCount = 0 Then
  MessageBox.Show("Please select a file to upload.", _
    "Warning", MessageBoxButtons.OK, MessageBoxIcon.Warning)
```

If there is an item selected, it gets the selected item from the localDirList control:

```
Dim item As ListViewItem = localDirList.SelectedItems(0)
```

It then checks if the item is a directory item. If it is, the method displays an error message:

```
If Helper.IsDirectoryItem(item) Then
  MessageBox.Show("You cannot upload a directory.", _
    "Error uploading file", MessageBoxButtons.OK, _
    MessageBoxIcon.Error)
```

If the selected item is a file item, it assigns the file size to fileSize and calls the FTP class's Upload method:

```
Try
  fileSize = Convert.ToInt32(item.SubItems(1).Text)
Catch
End Try
ftp.Upload(item.Text, localCurrentDir)
```

Compiling and Running the Application

You can find the source files for the application in the chapter's project directory. To compile the application, run the `Build.bat` file. The content of the `Build.bat` file is as follows:

```
vbc /t:library /r:System.Windows.Forms.dll Helper.vb
vbc /t:library /r:System.dll,System.Windows.Forms.dll,System.Drawing.dll
LoginForm.vb
vbc /t:library /r:System.dll FTP.vb
vbc /t:winexe /r:System.dll,System.Windows.Forms.dll, ↵
System.Drawing.dll,Helper.dll,LoginForm.dll, ↵
FTP.dll Form1.vb
```

Summary

In this chapter you learned how to use sockets to connect to a remote server. You also saw the code to resolve a DNS name into an IP address. You also learned about the RFC959 specification and saw how it is implemented in an FTP client application.

CHAPTER 6

Building an Online Store

THIS CHAPTER SHOWS you how to develop BuyDirect, an ASP.NET online store for selling electronic goods. The application developed in this chapter serves as a template that you can easily extend and modify. To build the application, you should be familiar with the basics of ASP.NET programming, even though some theory will be given. The ASP.NET programming topics covered in this chapter include Web forms, server components, authorization methods, session management, user input validation, application configuration, and so on. In addition, it also focuses on how to work with data processing using ActiveX Data Objects for the .NET Framework (ADO.NET), which is a set of classes that exposes data access services for creating distributed, data-sharing applications. It is assumed you are familiar with the Structured Query Language (SQL).

It should not be hard for you to imagine what kind of application BuyDirect is. There are countless such applications, and you have probably developed one yourself in classic ASP.

Overview of the Chapter

The chapter starts by presenting some introductory topics that will help you understand each piece of the software. It then concludes by discussing a project. The main sections in this chapter are as follows:

- **"Understanding ADO.NET"**: This section explains what ADO.NET is and how to use it to connect to a relational database and manipulate the data in it. In addition, it discusses working with Extensible Markup Language (XML) documents with ADO.NET. This section focuses on the types in the System.Data namespace as well as providing discussion on the supported data providers: OLE DB, SQL Server, ODBC, Oracle, and SQL Server CE.

- **"Data Binding"**: Data binding enables server controls to automatically obtain values or data from an expression or a data source. It is a feature that gives you more control over your data and helps you shorten development time. This section provides the basics of data binding.

- **"Configuring ASP.NET Applications"**: This section discusses ASP.NET application configuration using the `web.config` and `global.aspx` files. It also covers application deployment.

- **"Securing ASP.NET Applications"**: This section covers the methods for securing ASP.NET applications.

- **"Implementing the Project"**: This section provides a complete discussion of the application built for this chapter. It explains the database structure, page design, each page in the application, plus all the classes used in the application.

Understanding ADO.NET

Connecting to a database and manipulating the data in a relational database are important tasks performed in many applications. The .NET Framework programmers use ADO.NET to do database programming. ADO.NET is an integral part of the .NET Framework. It is a set of classes that exposes data access services to the .NET programmer, and it provides a rich set of components for creating distributed, data-sharing applications. With ADO.NET you can create a database; select, insert, and delete data in a table; execute a stored procedure; change the structure of a table; and so on. In addition to working with the structure and data in a relational database, you can use ADO.NET to manipulate XML documents.

ADO.NET is a broad topic. A complete discussion of ADO.NET requires a book of its own and therefore cannot be presented in this chapter alone. This chapter discusses the architecture of ADO.NET and the basic features you can use to access and manipulate data. You will find a discussion of the object models as well as examples you can use to do various database tasks.

After the overview of the ADO.NET architecture, the following sections specifically focus on the two main components in ADO.NET: the .NET data providers (in "Introducing the .NET Data Providers") and the `DataSet` and accompanying objects (in "Working with DataSets").

Introducing ADO.NET Architecture

There are two central components in ADO.NET: the data providers and the `System.Data.DataSet` object. The object model for the .NET data providers is similar to those in ActiveX Data Objects (ADO) that you use to access and manipulate data in relational databases in classic ASP. The .NET data providers connect to and query a data source. Basically, you can send any SQL statement to the data source using a .NET data provider, which means in many cases working with .NET data providers alone is sufficient.

However, in ADO.NET you can also use the DataSet object to work with a disconnected set of data. The DataSet object gives you more flexibility and the capability to bind data to Web server controls. It is not equivalent to the recordset object in ADO. In fact, it is more like a disconnected data container that resembles a database that can hold data tables and maintain relationships between any two tables.

Figure 6-1 shows the architecture of ADO.NET.

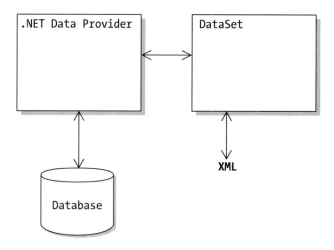

Figure 6-1. ADO.NET architecture

The .NET Framework 1.1 class library provides eight namespaces that contain types for ADO.NET:

- System.Data

- System.Data.Common

- System.Data.OleDb

- System.Data.SqlClient

- `System.Data.SqlTypes`

- `System.Data.Odbc`

- `System.Data.OracleClient`

- `System.Data.SqlCe`

NOTE *The* `System.Data.Odbc, System.Data.OracleClient,` *and* `System.Data.SqlCe` *namespaces were not available in the .NET Framework 1.0.*

The most important members of these namespaces are discussed in detail throughout the following sections. The two main components of ADO.NET are discussed in the sections "Introducing the .NET Data Providers" and "Working with DataSets."

Introducing the .NET Data Providers

There are five data providers in ADO.NET:

OLE DB .NET data provider: This is the data provider for OLE DB data sources, including Microsoft SQL Server version 6.5 and earlier. Types you can use to access and manipulate data in OLE DB data sources are located in the `System.Data.OleDb` namespace.

SQL Server .NET data provider: This is the data provider for Microsoft SQL Server version 7.0 and later. This data provider is described by the collection of types in the `System.Data.SqlClient` namespace. This provider uses its own protocol to communicate with SQL Server and does not support the use of an ODBC Data Source Name (DSN).

ODBC .NET data provider: This is the data provider for ODBC databases. You can find types that you use to access and manipulate data in ODBC data sources in the `System.Data.Odbc` namespace.

Oracle .NET data provider: This is the data provider for Oracle databases. You can find types to help you access and manipulate data in Oracle databases in the `System.Data.OracleClient` namespace.

SQL Server CE .NET data provider: This is the data provider for SQL Server CE. The types for accessing and manipulating data in SQL Server CE databases are available in the System.Data.SqlServerCe namespace.

All the five data provider namespaces contain equivalent classes that provide similar functionality.

The four most important objects in a .NET data provider are the connection object, the command object, the data adapter object, and the data reader object. All the data provider namespaces have classes that represent those objects.

A type name in the System.Data.SqlClient namespace starts with *Sql*, and in the System.Data.OleDb namespace, type names start with *OleDb*. In the Oracle data provider they start with *Oracle*, in SQL Server CE with *SqlCe*, and in the ODBC data provider with *Odbc*. For example, the connection object in the System.Data.SqlClient namespace is represented by the SqlConnection class, whereas in the System.Data.OleDb namespace the same object is represented by the OleDbConnection class. These classes are similar and share most properties and methods.

Table 6-1 lists the important members of the data provider namespaces. The following sections discuss in detail the connection, command, data adapter, and data reader classes. For other classes you should refer to the .NET Framework reference.

Table 6-1. Important Members of the Data Provider Namespaces

SQL SERVER	OLE DB	ODBC	ORACLE	SQL SERVER CE	OBJECT REPRESENTED
SqlCommand	OleDbCommand	OdbcCommand	OracleCommand	SqlCeCommand	Command object
SqlConnection	OleDbConnection	OdbcConnection	OracleConnection	SqlCeConnection	Connection object
SqlDataAdapter	OleDbDataAdapter	OdbcDataAdapter	OracleDataAdapter	SqlCeDataAdapter	Data adapter object
SqlDataReader	OleDbDataReader	OdbcDataReader	OracleDataReader	SqlCeDataReader	Data reader object

The Connection Object

The connection object in ADO.NET represents a connection to a data source and supports the notion of transactions. You will first learn about the connection object model—in other words, the properties, methods, and events of the connection object. Then, you will see how you can build connection strings to access data sources in the five .NET data providers.

The Connection Object's Properties

The following are the common properties of the connection classes:

- **ConnectionString**: The string used to connect and open a data source.

- **ConnectionTimeout**: The number of seconds to wait when attempting to establish a connection before terminating the effort and throwing an exception. This property is not available in the `System.Data.OracleClient.OracleConnection` class.

- **Database**: The current database or the database to which to connect. This property is not available in the `System.Data.OracleClient.OracleConnection` class.

- **DataSource**: In the `OleDbConnection` class, this property represents the path and filename of the data source. In the `SqlConnection` and `OracleConnection` classes, this is the name of the instance of database server to which to connect.

- **ServerVersion**: The version of the server to which the client is connected. This property is not available in the `System.Data.SqlServerCe.SqlCeConnection` class.

- **State**: The state of the connection. Its value is a bitwise combination of the members of the `System.Data.ConnectionState` enumeration: `Broken`, `Closed`, `Connecting`, `Executing`, `Fetching`, and `Open`.

The `OleDbConnection` class has one property not available in other connection classes: `Provider`. This property is a string containing the name of the OLE DB provider.

The Connection Object's Methods

The following are the common methods of the connection classes:

- **BeginTransaction**: Begins a transaction. This method returns a transaction object.

- **ChangeDatabase**: Changes the current database for the open connection. This property is not available in the `System.Data.OracleClient.OracleConnection` class.

- **Close**: Closes the connection. If connection pooling is enabled, the connection object is returned to the pool. Closing a connection rolls back any pending transaction.

- **CreateCommand**: Creates and returns a command object associated with the connection.

- **Dispose**: Destroys the connection object.

- **Open**: Opens a database connection.

Of these methods, Open and Close are the most frequently used when working with the connection object. You will also use the BeginTransaction method to begin a transaction. However, there are no methods for committing and rolling back a transaction. For more information on how to commit or roll back a transaction, see "Working with Transactions" later in this chapter.

The Connection Object's Events

The connection classes have two common events:

- **InfoMessage**: This event is triggered when an information message is added.
- **StateChange**: This event is raised when the connection state changes.

Building OLE DB Connection Strings

Building a connection string is sometimes the trickiest part of working with the connection object. Oftentimes a connection object failure is simply caused by an incorrect piece of information in the connection string.

A connection string for a .NET OLE DB data provider must match the format of an OLE DB connection string. The Provider value must not be "MSDASQL" because the OLE DB .NET data provider does not support the OLE DB Provider for ODBC (MSDASQL).

The following are two examples of valid OLE DB connection strings:

```
Provider=SQLOLEDB;Data Source=localhost;Initial Catalog=MyDb;
Provider=Microsoft.Jet.OLEDB.4.0;Data Source=C:\Data\MyDb.mdb
```

Building SQL Server Connection Strings

An SQL Server connection string comprises a set of name-value pairs specifying details on the SQL Server instance and the user credential. Table 6-2 describes the list of names that you can use in an SQL Server .NET data provider connection string.

Table 6-2. Valid Names for Values Within an SQL Server Connection String

NAME	DEFAULT VALUE	DESCRIPTION
Application Name		The name of the application.
AttachDBFilename *or* Extended Properties *or* Initial File Name		The full primary filename of an attachable database. The database name must be specified with the keyword *database*.
Connect Timeout *or* Connection Timeout	15	The number of seconds to wait for a connection to the server before terminating the effort and throwing an exception.
Connection Lifetime	0	This name-value pair is used in a clustered configuration to force load balancing between a running server and a server just started. The connection lifetime specifies the maximum number of seconds the creation time of a connection can differ from the time the connection is returned to the pool. The connection will be destroyed if the difference between the time it is returned to the pool and the creation time exceeds the value of the connection lifetime.
Connection Reset	True	If the value is True, the connection is reset when being removed from the pool. Setting this name to False avoids an additional server round-trip when obtaining a connection.
Current Language		The SQL Server Language record name.
Data Source *or* Server *or* Address *or* Addr *or* Network Address		The name or address of the SQL Server instance to connect.
Enlist	True	Setting this name to True enlists the connection in the creation thread's current transaction context automatically.
Initial Catalog *or* Database		The database name.

Table 6-2. Valid Names for Values Within an SQL Server Connection String (Cont.)

NAME	DEFAULT VALUE	DESCRIPTION
Integrated Security *or* Trusted_Connection	False	Indicates whether the connection is a secure connection. In addition to False and True, you can also use sspi, which has the same effect as True.
Max Pool Size	100	The maximum number of connections permitted in the pool when connection pooling is enabled.
Network Library *or* Net	dbmssocn	The network library for establishing a connection to an SQL Server instance. The default value specifies TCP/IP.
Packet Size	8192	The size (in bytes) of the network packet used to communicate with an SQL Server instance.
Password *or* Pwd		The user's password used to connect to the SQL Server.
Persist Security Info	False	If the value is False, sensitive information is not returned as part of the connection is open or has ever been in an open state.
Pooling	True	Indicates whether connection pooling is true.
User ID		The login account to get access to the SQL Server instance.
Workstation ID	The local machine name	The name of the machine connecting to the SQL Server instance.

The following is an example of a valid connection string for the SQL Server .NET data provider:

```
User ID=udin;Password=17Agt45;Initial Catalog=MySQLDb Data
Source=localhost;Connection Timeout=20
```

Constructing a Connection Object

All the connection classes have two constructors: a no-argument constructor and a constructor that accepts a connection string. The signatures of both constructors are as follows:

```
Public Sub New()


Public Sub New(ByVal connectionString As String)
```

The no-argument constructor is easier to use. However, using this constructor requires you to set the ConnectionString property of the connection object at a later stage. The following code constructs an SqlConnection object using the no-argument constructor:

```
Dim connectionString As String = "User ID=udin;" & _
  "Password=17Agt45;Initial Catalog=MySQLDb;" & _
  "Data Source=localhost;Connection Timeout=20
' Use the no-argument constructor
Dim connection As New SqlConnection()
connection.ConnectionString = connectionString
```

The following code uses the alternative constructor to create an instance of the SqlConnection class, resulting in more compact code:

```
Dim connectionString As String = "User ID=udin;" & _
  "Password=17Agt45;Initial Catalog=MySQLDb;" & _
  "Data Source=localhost;Connection Timeout=20
' Use the alternative constructor
Dim connection As New SqlConnection(connectionString)
```

Unless you have a valid reason to construct a connection object using the no-argument constructor, using the alternative constructor is preferable.

The Command Object

The command object represents an SQL statement or stored procedure that can be executed on the server. All command classes share most of the properties and methods.

The Command Object's Properties

The following are the common properties of the command classes:

- **CommandText**: The SQL statement or the name of the stored procedure to execute at the database server.

- **CommandTimeout**: The number of seconds the command object will wait before terminating an attempt to execute a command and throwing an exception. This property is not available in the System.Data.OracleClient.OracleCommand class.

- **CommandType**: The type of the command. The value of this property determines how the value of the CommandText property is interpreted. The value of the CommandType property can be one of the members of the System.Data.CommandType enumeration: StoredProcedure, TableDirect, and Text.

- **Connection**: The connection object used by the command object. The type of the property value is either System.Data.OleDb.OleDbConnection or System.Data.SqlClient.SqlConnection.

- **DesignTimeVisible**: A value indicating whether the command object should be visible in a customized Windows Forms Designer control. This property is not available in the System.Data.SqlServerCe.SqlCeCommand class.

- **Parameters**: Represents the collection of parameters of this command object.

- **Transaction**: The transaction in which the command object executes.

- **UpdatedRowSource**: This property determines how the results from executing the command text are applied to the DataRow when used by the Update method of the data adapter object.

The Command Object's Methods

The following are the common methods of the command classes:

- **Cancel**: Cancels the execution of the command object.

- **CreateParameter**: Creates a parameter object.

- **ExecuteNonQuery**: Executes an update, insert, or delete SQL statement and returns the number of records affected by the execution.

- **ExecuteReader**: Executes a select SQL statement and returns the result as a DataReader object.

- **ExecuteScalar**: Executes the command object's query that returns a single value. This is more efficient than the ExecuteReader method.

- **Prepare**: Compiles the command on the data source.

- **ResetCommandTimeout**: Assigns the CommandTimeout property
  with its original value. This property is not available in the
  System.Data.OracleClient.OracleCommand and
  System.Data.SqlServerCe.SqlCeCommand classes.

Constructing the Command Object

All the command classes have four constructors whose signatures are as follows:

```
Public Sub New()

Public Sub New(ByVal commandText As String)

Public Sub New( _
  ByVal commandText As String, _
  ByVal connection As xxxConnection _
)

Public Sub New( _
  ByVal commandText As String, _
  ByVal connection As xxxConnection, _
  ByVal transaction As xxxTransaction _
)
```

where *xxx* is Sql, OleDb, Odbc, Oracle, or SqlCe.

The code that shows how to construct an OleDbCommand object is as follows:

```
Dim sql As String = "SELECT * FROM Products"
' Instantiate a new connection object
' by passing the connection string
Dim connection As New OleDbConnection()
' connectionString is a valid connection string
connection.ConnectionString = connectionString
connection.Open()

' Create a Command object
Dim command As New OleDbCommand()
command.Connection = connection
command.CommandText = sql
```

To construct an SqlCommand object, replace OleDbConnection with SqlConnection
and OleDbCommand with SqlCommand, as demonstrated in the following code:

```
Dim sql As String = "SELECT * FROM Products"
' Instantiate a new connection object
' by passing the connection string
Dim connection As New SqlConnection()
' connectionString is a valid connection string
connection.ConnectionString = connectionString
connection.Open()

' Create a Command object
Dim command As New SqlCommand()
command.Connection = connection
command.CommandText = sql
```

A more compact way to construct a command object is to use the constructor that accepts an SQL statement and an open connection object. You can rewrite the previous code as follows to produce an OleDbCommand object:

```
Dim sql As String = "SELECT * FROM Products"
' Instantiate a new connection object
' by passing the connection string
Dim connection As New OleDbConnection()
' connectionString is a valid connection string
connection.ConnectionString = connectionString
connection.Open()

' Create a Command object
Dim command As New OleDbCommand(sql, connection)
```

And the following is the equivalent to instantiate the SqlCommand class by using the constructor that accepts an SQL statement and an open connection object:

```
Dim sql As String = "SELECT * FROM Products"
' Instantiate a new connection object
' by passing the connection string
Dim connection As New SqlConnection()
' connectionString is a valid connection string
connection.ConnectionString = connectionString
connection.Open()

' Create a Command object
Dim command As New SqlCommand(sql, connection)
```

Modifying Data Using the Command Object

You can modify data in a database using a connection object and a command object. The following three sections show how to insert a new record, update records, and delete records in a database table. Even though the examples use an OLE DB .NET data provider, you can use them to modify data in other .NET data providers by changing the connection string and the types of the connection and command objects.

Inserting a New Record

The following example inserts a new record into a Products table. The SQL statement passes values for the ProductName column and the Price column:

```
Dim connectionString As String = _
  "Provider=Microsoft.Jet.OLEDB.4.0;" & _
  "Data Source=C:\db\MyDB.mdb"

Dim sql As String = "INSERT INTO Products " & _
  "(ProductName, Price) VALUES ('groggrog', 123)"
' Instantiate a new connection object
' by passing the connection string
Dim connection As New OleDbConnection(connectionString)

connection.Open()
' Create a Command object
Dim command As New OleDbCommand(sql, connection)
' Execute the SQL statement
Dim recordsAffected As Integer = command.ExecuteNonQuery()
```

The ExecuteNonQuery method in the last line of the code should return 1 as the number of records affected.

Updating Records

The following is an example of how to update records in a Products table. All prices in the table are increased by 10 percent by multiplying the old prices with 1.1:

```
Dim connectionString As String = _
  "Provider=Microsoft.Jet.OLEDB.4.0;" & _
  "Data Source=C:\db\MyDB.mdb"
```

```
Dim sql As String = "UPDATE Products" & _
  " SET Price=Price * 1.1"
' Instantiate a new connection object
' by passing the connection string
Dim connection As New OleDbConnection(connectionString)

connection.Open()
' Create a Command object
Dim command As New OleDbCommand(sql, connection)
' Execute the SQL statement
Dim recordsAffected As Integer = command.ExecuteNonQuery()
```

Deleting Records

The following is an example of how to delete records in a products table:

```
Dim connectionString As String = _
  "Provider=Microsoft.Jet.OLEDB.4.0;" & _
  "Data Source=C:\db\MyDB.mdb"

Dim sql As String = "DELETE FROM Products" & _
  " WHERE ProductId = 19"
' Instantiate a new connection object
' by passing the connection string
Dim connection As New OleDbConnection(connectionString)

connection.Open()
' Create a Command object
Dim command As New OleDbCommand(sql, connection)
' Execute the SQL statement
Dim recordsAffected As Integer = command.ExecuteNonQuery()
```

The Data Reader Object

The data reader object represents a stream of data rows from a data source. The stream can only be read in a forward direction. You can get a data reader object from the ExecuteReader method of the command object.

The Data Reader Object's Properties

The following are the common properties of the data reader classes:

- **Depth**: Returns the depth of nesting for the current row.

- **FieldCount**: Returns the current row's number of columns.

- **IsClosed**: Indicates whether the data reader object is closed.

- **Item**: Returns the value of a column in the current row in its native format. You can either pass the column position or the column name.

- **RecordsAffected**: Returns the number of columns affected by the execution of the SQL statement. For a select SQL statement, this property returns –1.

The Data Reader Object's Methods

The following are the methods of the data reader classes:

- **Close**: Closes the data reader object.

- **GetXXX**: Returns the value of the specified column. *XXX* represents the data type returned by this method. For example, the GetByte method returns the value of the specified column as a byte. Other methods include GetBoolean, GetDouble, GetFloat, GetInt32, GetInt64, GetString, and so on.

- **GetDataTypeName**: Returns the name of the data type of the column specified by a zero-based ordinal.

- **GetFieldType**: Returns a System.Type object representing the type of the column specified by a zero-based ordinal.

- **GetName**: Returns the name of the column specified by a zero-based ordinal.

- **GetOrdinal**: Returns the ordinal of the column whose name is passed as the method argument.

- **GetSchemaTable**: Returns a System.Data.DataTable object representing the column metadata of the data reader object.

- **GetValue**: Returns the value of the specified column in its native format. This method returns an object of type System.Object.

- **GetValues**: Retrieves all the columns in the current row. The method accepts an array of System.Object objects as its argument and populates the array with all the values in the current row. This method returns an integer specifying the size of the array.

- **IsDBNull**: Indicates whether the column contains nonexistent or missing values.

- **NextResult**: This method is used only when reading the results of batch SQL statements. It advances the data reader object to the next result.

- **Read**: Moves to the next record and returns True if there are more rows. Otherwise, it returns False. As an example of how to use a data reader object, consider the code in Listing 6-1.

However, note that Listings 6-1 to 6-19 use the Access database MyDb.mdb that is included in the downloadable file for this chapter. You must save this file in the parent directory of the virtual directory of your ASP.NET testing application. You access the database using the following connection string:

```
Dim connectionString As String = _
  "Provider=Microsoft.Jet.OLEDB.4.0;" & _
  "Data Source=" & Request.PhysicalApplicationPath & _
  "..\MyDb.mdb"
```

where Request.PhysicalApplicationPath returns the physical application path.

Listing 6-1. Using a Data Reader Object

```
<%@ Import Namespace="System.Data" %>
<%@ Import Namespace="System.Data.OleDb" %>

<html>
<head>
<title>Search Result</title>

<script language="VB" runat="server">
```

```
Sub Page_Load(sender As Object, e As EventArgs)
  Dim s As New StringBuilder(2048)

  Dim connectionString As String = _
    "Provider=Microsoft.Jet.OLEDB.4.0;" & _
    "Data Source=" & Request.PhysicalApplicationPath & _
    "..\MyDb.mdb"

  ' Instantiate a new connection object
  ' by passing the connection string
  Dim connection As New OleDbConnection(connectionString)

  connection.Open()
  ' Create a Command object
  Dim command As New OleDbCommand(sql, connection)

  ' Instantiate a DataReader object
  ' using the OleDbCommand class's ExecuteReader method
  Dim dataReader As OleDbDataReader = command.ExecuteReader()

  ' Loop through the DataReader
  Do While dataReader.Read()
    s.Append("<br>").Append(dataReader.GetString(2))
  Loop

  message.Text = s.ToString()
End Sub

</script>
</head>

<body>
<asp:Label id="message" runat="server"/>
</body>
</html>
```

The Page_Load method first constructs a connection object to connect to an OLE DB data provider whose data source is an Access database in MyDb.mdb, located in the parent directory of the application's virtual root. The command text used to retrieve data is assigned the following SQL statement:

```
SELECT * FROM Products
```

After the connection and command objects are constructed, it calls the ExecuteReader method of the command object:

```
Dim dataReader As OleDbDataReader = command.ExecuteReader()
```

Then, you can loop through the data reader object by using its Read method. This method returns True if there are more rows in the data reader:

```
Do While dataReader.Read()
  s.Append("<br>").Append(dataReader.GetString(2))
Loop
```

For each record, it appends the value of the third column to the System.Text.StringBuilder s, assuming that the third column is a string.

Working with Transactions

Looking at the list of methods of the connection object, you will probably wonder why there is a method to begin a transaction (BeginTransaction), but there is no method to commit or roll back a transaction. In ADO.NET, committing and rolling back are methods of a transaction object, which is represented by the System.Data.SqlClient.SqlTransaction class, the System.Data.OleDb.OleDbTransaction class, the System.Data.Odbc.OdbcTransaction class, the System.Data.OracleClient.OracleTransaction class, or the System.Data.SqlServerCe.SqlCeTransaction class, depending on which .NET data provider you are using.

You get an instance of one of the transaction classes when you call the BeginTransaction method of a connection class. You can then call the transaction object's Commit method to commit the transaction or the Rollback method to roll back the transaction.

As an example, the following code begins a transaction and either commits it or rolls it back:

```
' Assuming connection is an active OleDbConnection object,
' and command is an OleDbCommand object
' you can call its BeginTransaction method.
Dim transaction As OleDbTransaction = connection.BeginTransaction()
command.Transaction = transaction
Try
  ' Do something with the command object here
  ' .
```

```
  ' .
  ' .
  ' Ready to commit the transaction
  transaction.Commit()
Catch e As Exception
  ' oops? something bad happened
  transaction.Rollback()
End Try
```

The Data Adapter Object

You have seen how you can access a database and manipulate its data using the connection object, the command object, and the data reader object. ADO.NET lets you manipulate data in a disconnected way using a DataSet object. However, the DataSet object cannot connect to the data source directly. It still needs a data provider to retrieve data from the database and push it back to the data source if there are changes to the data. The data adapter object is the object in the data provider that populates a DataSet object. It serves as a bridge between the data source and the DataSet object. Because this object works closely with the DataSet object, you will see examples after the discussion of the DataSet object in the "Working with DataSets" section.

The DataAdapter Object's Properties

The following are the properties of the data adapter object:

- **DeleteCommand**: The SQL statement used to delete records from the data source

- **InsertCommand**: The SQL statement used to insert records into the data source

- **SelectCommand**: The SQL statement used to select records from the data source

- **UpdateCommand**: The SQL statement used to update records in the data source

The DataAdapter Object's Methods

For methods in other data adapter classes, refer to the .NET Framework documentation.

Working with DataSets

Although you can access a data source and manipulate data using the objects in a .NET data provider, DataSet provides functionality to work with disconnected data and let you bind Web server controls with the data. You achieve this using the DataSet object and its corresponding objects.

The DataSet object is a data container that resembles a relational database. It can contain zero or more tables, and each table lets you access its columns and rows individually. Once populated, a DataSet object is disconnected from the data source. Therefore, each DataSet object holds a copy of the data. You can manipulate the data in the DataSet object independently. If you want this change to be reflected in the originating data source, you must use data providers to send the change back to the data source.

In addition to obtaining data from a data source, the DataSet object can be populated programmatically, as discussed in the section "Populating a DataSet Object Programmatically."

The System.Data namespace provides types that allow you to work with the DataSet object and its supporting objects. The following classes are discussed next:

- DataSet

- DataTableCollection

- DataTable

- DataColumn

- DataRow

- DataView

The System.Data.DataSet Class

The DataSet class represents a DataSet object and provides properties and methods for data manipulation. A DataSet object contains zero or more tables that can be accessed through its table collection.

In addition, methods for converting data to and from an XML document are also available. However, manipulating XML documents is not discussed in this chapter.

The DataSet Properties

The following are the properties of the DataSet class:

- **CaseSensitive**: Indicates whether case sensitivity applies to string comparisons within the DataSet's DataTable objects.

- **DataSetName**: The name of the DataSet object.

- **DefaultViewManager**: Returns a System.Data.DataViewManager object that allows you to create custom settings for each DataTable object in the DataSet.

- **EnforceConstraints**: Indicates whether constraints are enforced in update operations.

- **ExtendedProperties**: Returns a System.Data.PropertyCollection object containing custom user information.

- **HasErrors**: Indicates whether there are errors in any row in any of the tables.

- **Locale**: A System.Globalization.CultureInfo object that represents the locale information used to compare strings within the table.

- **Namespace**: The namespace of the DataSet.

- **Prefix**: The XML prefix used as an alias for the namespace of the DataSet.

- **Relations**: Returns a System.Data.DataRelationCollection containing a collection of all DataRelation objects in the DataSet.

- **Site**: A System.ComponentModel.ISite object for the DataSet.

- **Tables**: Represents the collection of all DataTable objects in the DataSet.

The DataSet Methods

The following are the more important methods of the DataSet class:

- **AcceptChanges**: Accepts all the changes to the DataSet object since it was loaded or the last time this method was invoked.

- **BeginInit**: Begins the initialization of a DataSet that is used on a form or used by another component.

- **Clear**: Removes all rows in all tables, thus clearing the DataSet of any data.

- **Clone**: Copies the DataSet structure.

- **Copy**: Copies both the DataSet's data and structure.

- **EndInit**: Ends the initialization of a DataSet.

- **GetChanges**: Returns a copy of the DataSet object containing all changes made since it was last loaded or since the AcceptChanges method was invoked.

- **HasChanges**: Indicates whether the DataSet has changes.

- **HasSchemaChanged**: Indicates whether the schema has changed.

- **Merge**: Merges this DataSet with a specified DataSet.

- **RejectChanges**: Cancels the changes made to the DataSet object since it was created or since the AcceptChanges method was last invoked.

For a complete list of methods in the DataSet class, refer to the .NET Framework class library.

The System.Data.DataTableCollection Class

The DataTableCollection class represents the collection of tables in a DataSet object. The most important properties and methods of the DataTableCollection class are discussed next.

The DataTableCollection Properties

The following are the properties of the DataTableCollection class:

- **Item**: Returns the specified DataTable.

- **List**: Returns a System.Collections.ArrayList object containing all the tables.

The DataTableCollection Properties

The following are some of the methods in the DataTableCollection class:

- **Add**: Adds a DataTable object to the collection.

- **Clear**: Clears the collection of all tables.

- **Contains**: Tests if a table whose name is specified as the argument exists in the collection.

- **Remove**: Removes a DataTable object from the collection.

- **RemoveAt**: Removes the table at the specified index.

The System.Data.DataTable Class

The DataTable class represents a database table. A DataTable object exposes its individual column and row that you can access using its Columns and Rows properties. The following are the more important properties and methods in this class.

The DataTable Properties

The following are some of the properties of the DataTable class:

- **CaseSensitive**: Indicates whether case sensitivity applies to string comparisons in the table.

- **Columns**: Returns the DataColumn collection of the table.

- **Constraints**: Returns the collection of constraints in the table.

- **DataSet**: Returns the owner DataSet of this table.

- **MinimumCapacity**: The initial size of the table.

- **PrimaryKey**: An array of DataColumn objects representing all primary key fields in the table.

- **Rows**: Returns the DataRow collection of the table.

- **TableName**: The name of the table.

Of the properties, you will use the Columns and Rows properties most often.

The DataTable Methods

The following are the more important methods of the DataTable class:

- **AcceptChanges**: Accepts all changes to this table since the AcceptChanges method was last invoked.

- **Clear**: Clears the table of any row.

- **Clone**: Copies the DataTable's structure.

- **Copy**: Copies both the DataTable's structure and data.

- **NewRow**: Returns a DataRow object with the same structure as the rows in the table.

- **RejectChanges**: Rejects changes to this table since the AcceptChanges method was last invoked.

- **Select**: Selects DataRow objects that match certain filter criteria.

The NewRow method is an important method you use to create a DataRow object whose structure is the same as the rows in the DataTable object. Constructing a DataRow object using the NewRow method guarantees that the DataRow is compatible with the DataTable object and can be added to the DataTable object later. Also, using the NewRow method saves you from having to set each column in the DataRow individually.

The System.Data.DataColumn Class

The DataColumn class represents a table column in a DataTable object. This class has properties that reflect those of a column of a database table. For example, it allows you to specify its data type, whether a DataColumn object can accept null values, whether a column is auto-incremented, or whether the column is read-only.

The following are the more important properties of the DataColumn class:

- **AllowDBNull**: Indicates whether this column can accept a null value.

- **AutoIncrement**: Indicates whether the value of this column is generated automatically when a row is added.

- **AutoIncrementSeed**: The starting value of this column if the AutoIncrement property is set to True.

- **AutoIncrementStep**: The increment used by a column whose AutoIncrement property is set to True.

- **ColumnName**: The name of this column

- **DataType**: The System.Type object representing the data type of this column.

- **DefaultValue**: The default value of this column for a new row.

- **MaxLength**: The maximum length of text column.

- **Ordinal**: The position of this column in the collection.

- **ReadOnly**: Indicates whether the column is read only.

- **Table**: The table to which the column belongs.

- **Unique**: Indicates whether the values in each row of this column must be unique.

The System.Data.DataRow Class

The DataRow class represents a record in a DataTable object. You will see it's more important properties and methods next.

The DataRow Properties

The following are the more important properties in the DataRow class:

- **HasErrors**: Indicates whether there are errors in the column collection.

- **Item**: Returns value in the specified column.

- **RowState**: The row state indicated by one of the members of the
  System.Data.DataRowState enumeration: Added, Deleted, Detached, Modified,
  and Unchanged.

The DataRow Methods

The following are the more important methods in the DataRow class:

- **AcceptChanges**: Accepts changes to the row since the AcceptChanges method
  was last invoked.

- **BeginEdit**: Begins an edit operation on a DataRow object.

- **CancelEdit**: Cancels the edit on the row.

- **Delete**: Deletes this row.

- **EndEdit**: Ends the edit on the row.

- **GetChildRows**: Returns the child rows of a row.

- **GetParentRow**: Returns the parent row of a row.

- **IsNull**: Indicates whether the specified column contains a null.

- **RejectChanges**: Rejects changes to the row since the AcceptChanges method
  was last invoked.

The System.Data.DataView Class

The DataView class represents a view to a DataTable object. You can use a DataView
object to sort, filter, edit, and navigate data in a DataTable object. More important,
however, you can bind a DataView with a server control to provide a view to the
data. You will see the most important properties and methods next.

The DataView Properties

The following are the more important properties of the DataView class:

- **AllowDelete**: Indicates whether delete operations are allowed.

- **AllowEdit**: Indicates whether edit operations are allowed.

- **AllowNew**: Indicates whether new rows can be added using the AddNew methods.

- **Count**: Returns the number of rows in the DataView object after applying RowFilter and RowStateFilter.

- **Item**: Returns a row of data from a specified table.

- **Sort**: The sort column(s) and the sort order of the table.

- **Table**: The source data table.

The DataView Methods

The following offers some of the more important methods in the DataView class:

- **AddNew**: Adds a new row to the DataView.

- **Close**: Closes the DataView object.

- **Delete**: Deletes the row at the given index position.

- **Find**: Locates a row in the DataView by the specified primary key value.

- **GetEnumerator**: Returns a System.Collections.IEnumerator object for this DataView object.

- **Open**: Opens this DataView object.

- **Reset**: Resets this DataView object.

Populating a DataSet Object Programmatically

You normally use a DataSet object as a temporary data container for data from a database. However, this is not always the case. Sometimes you need to populate your DataSet programmatically. For example, you may have an algorithm that you use to populate a table, or you may have data stored in a text file.

Listing 6-2 shows how you can populate a DataSet programmatically by performing the following steps:

1. Create a DataSet object.

2. Create a DataTable object representing a table.

3. Create several DataColumn objects and add them to the DataTable object.

4. Create a DataRow object using the NewRow method of the DataTable class.

5. Assign values to the DataRow object's cells.

6. Add the DataRow object to the DataTable object.

7. Add the DataTable object to the DataSet.

Listing 6-2. Populating a DataSet *Object Programmatically*

```
<%@ Import Namespace="System.Data" %>
<html>
<head>
<title>Populating DataSet</title>

<script language="VB" runat="server">

Sub Page_Load(sender As Object, e As EventArgs)

  ' Create a DataSet object called "Warehouse"
  Dim dataSet As New DataSet("Warehouse")
  ' Create a DataTable object called "Products"
  Dim dataTable As New DataTable("Products")
  ' Create four columns called Id(Integer),
  ' ProductName(String),
  ' CategoryId(Integer),
  ' Price(Decimal)
```

```
Dim column1 As New DataColumn("Id", _
  Type.GetType("System.Int32"))
Dim column2 As New DataColumn("ProductName", _
  Type.GetType("System.String"))
Dim column3 As New DataColumn("CategoryId", _
  Type.GetType("System.Int32"))
Dim column4 As New DataColumn("Price", _
  Type.GetType("System.Decimal"))
' Add all columns to the table's Columns collection
' All columns must be added before creating a new row
dataTable.Columns.Add(column1)
dataTable.Columns.Add(column2)
dataTable.Columns.Add(column3)
dataTable.Columns.Add(column4)

' Create a new DataRow object using the NewRow
' method of the DataTable class
' The resulting DataRow object will have the same
' structure as the table row
Dim row As DataRow = dataTable.NewRow()
' Populating the four cells
row(0) = "14"
row(1) = "Pelesonic Digital Camera"
row(2) = "2"
row(3) = "429.95"
' Add the populated row to the table's Rows collection
dataTable.Rows.Add(row)
' Add the table to the DataSet object
dataSet.Tables.Add(dataTable)

' Now display the data
Dim s As New StringBuilder(512)
Dim row2 As DataRow = dataSet.Tables("Products").Rows(0)

s.Append("Id:").Append(row2("Id"))
' Another way is to reference the row cell by using the format
' Rows(row index)(column name)
s.Append("<br>ProductName:")
s.Append(dataSet.Tables("Products").Rows(0)("ProductName"). _
  ToString())

s.Append("<br>CateogryId:").Append(row2("CategoryId"))
s.Append("<br>Price:").Append(row2("Price"))
```

```
    message.Text = s.ToString()

End Sub

</script>
</head>

<body>
<asp:Label id="message" runat="server"/>
</body>
</html>
```

The only method in Listing 6-2 is the Page_Load method, which gets invoked when the page is loaded. The first thing the method does is to create a DataSet object called Warehouse, containing a DataTable object named Products:

```
' Create a DataSet object called "Warehouse"
Dim dataSet As New DataSet("Warehouse")
' Create a DataTable object called "Products"
Dim dataTable As New DataTable("Products")
```

Then, you construct four DataColumn objects to be added to the Products DataTable. The DataColumn objects have the following names and data types: Id (Integer), ProductName (String), CategoryId (Integer), and Price (Decimal).

You construct a DataColumn object by using its constructor that accepts a column name and a data type. A data type has the type of System.Type and can be constructed using the GetType method of the System.Type class by passing the type name. For example, you instantiate a DataColumn object named Id with an integer data type using the following code:

```
Dim column1 As New DataColumn("Id", _
  Type.GetType("System.Int32"))
```

The following code creates four DataColumn objects for the Products table:

```
' Create four columns called Id(Integer),
' ProductName(String),
' CategoryId(Integer),
' Price(Decimal)
Dim column1 As New DataColumn("Id", _
  Type.GetType("System.Int32"))
Dim column2 As New DataColumn("ProductName", _
  Type.GetType("System.String"))
```

```
Dim column3 As New DataColumn("CategoryId", _
  Type.GetType("System.Int32"))
Dim column4 As New DataColumn("Price", _
  Type.GetType("System.Decimal"))
' Add all columns to the table's Columns collection
' All columns must be added before creating a new row
```

Once you have the DataColumn objects, you can add them to the DataTable by calling the Add method of the Columns collection, as in the following code:

```
dataTable.Columns.Add(column1)
dataTable.Columns.Add(column2)
dataTable.Columns.Add(column3)
dataTable.Columns.Add(column4)
```

The next step is to create a DataRow object for each row you want to add to the DataTable object. You can easily create a DataRow object with the same structure as the rows in the Products table by calling the NewRow method of the DataTable class:

```
' Create a new DataRow object using the NewRow
' method of the DataTable class
' The resulting DataRow object will have the same
' structure as the table row
Dim row As DataRow = dataTable.NewRow()
```

Once you have a DataRow object, you can populate data by referring to each data cell using an index number. Index number 0 represents the first column in the row. Therefore, the following code assigns values to all the four columns in the row:

```
' Populating the four cells
row(0) = "14"
row(1) = "Pelesonic Digital Camera"
row(2) = "2"
row(3) = "429.95"
```

Next, you can add the DataRow object to the Products table using the Add method of the Rows collection, and add the table to the DataSet object using the Add method of the Tables collection:

```
' Add the populated row to the table's Rows collection
dataTable.Rows.Add(row)
' Add the table to the DataSet object
dataSet.Tables.Add(dataTable)
```

The next lines of the `Page_Load` method display the data in the browser. A `StringBuilder` object composes the HTML tags and assigns the string to the `Text` property of the `Label` control named `message`:

```
' Now display the data
Dim s As New StringBuilder(512)
Dim row2 As DataRow = dataSet.Tables("Products").Rows(0)

s.Append("Id:").Append(row2("Id"))
' Another way is to reference the row cell by using the format
' Rows(row index)(column name)
s.Append("<br>ProductName:")
s.Append(dataSet.Tables("Products").Rows(0)("ProductName"). _
  ToString())

s.Append("<br>CateogryId:").Append(row2("CategoryId"))
s.Append("<br>Price:").Append(row2("Price"))

message.Text = s.ToString()
```

If you run the code in a Web browser, you should see the following result:

```
Id:14
ProductName:Tomtom Chocolate
CateogryId:2
Price:4.95
```

Populating DataSet with Data from a Database

Listing 6-3 grabs data from the Products table in an Access database and displays the data using a `Label` control.

Listing 6-3. Populating a DataSet *with Data from a Database*

```
<%@ Import Namespace="System.Data" %>
<%@ Import Namespace="System.Data.OleDb" %>
<html>
<head>
<title>Populating DataSet</title>

<script language="VB" runat="server">
```

```
Sub Page_Load(sender As Object, e As EventArgs)

    ' --------   Populate DataSet -----------
    Dim connectionString As String = _
      "Provider=Microsoft.Jet.OLEDB.4.0;" & _
      "Data Source=" & Request.PhysicalApplicationPath & _
      "..\MyDb.mdb"

    Dim sql As String = "SELECT * FROM Products WHERE ProductId<10"

    ' Instantiate a new connection object
    ' by passing the connection string
    Dim connection As New OleDbConnection(connectionString)

    Dim dataAdapter As New OleDbDataAdapter(sql, connection)

    Dim dataSet As New DataSet()
    dataAdapter.Fill(dataSet, "Products")

    ' --------   Now display the data  -----------
    Dim s As New StringBuilder(1024)
    Dim i, j As Integer 'counters

    Dim dataTable As DataTable = dataSet.Tables("Products")
    Dim dataRowCollection As DataRowCollection = dataTable.Rows
    Dim rowCount As Integer = dataRowCollection.Count

    s.Append("<table border=1><tr>")

    Dim dataColumnCollection As DataColumnCollection = dataTable.Columns
    Dim columnCount As Integer = dataColumnCollection.Count
    For i = 0 To columnCount - 1
      Dim column As DataCOlumn = dataColumnCollection(i)
      Dim columnName As String = column.ColumnName
      s.Append("<td>").Append(columnName)
      s.Append(" (")
      s.Append(column.DataType.ToString())
      s.Append(")")
      s.Append("</td>")
    Next i
    s.Append("</tr>")

    For i = 0 To rowCount - 1
```

```
    Dim row As DataRow = dataRowCollection(i)
    s.Append("<tr>")
    For j = 0 To columnCount - 1
      Dim cell As Object = row.Item(j)
      s.Append("<td>").Append(cell.ToString()).Append("</td>")
    Next j
    s.Append("</tr>")
  Next i

  message.Text = s.ToString()

End Sub

</script>
</head>

<body>
<asp:Label id="message" runat="server"/>
</body>
</html>
```

To populate a DataSet with data from a database, you use a data adapter object's Fill method. However, first you need to create an instance of a data adapter. In this example, you use an OleDbDataAdapter object that you construct by passing an SQL statement and a connection object:

```
Dim connectionString As String = _
  "Provider=Microsoft.Jet.OLEDB.4.0;" & _
  "Data Source=" & Request.PhysicalApplicationPath & _
  "..\MyDb.mdb"

Dim sql As String = "SELECT * FROM Products WHERE ProductId<10"

' Instantiate a new connection object
' by passing the connection string
Dim connection As New OleDbConnection(connectionString)

Dim dataAdapter As New OleDbDataAdapter(sql, connection)

Dim dataSet As New DataSet()
dataAdapter.Fill(dataSet, "Products")
```

The `Fill` method populates the `DataSet` object called `dataSet` with the content of the Products table. Now, displaying the data is no different from the previous code. First, you need to obtain the Products table and assign it to a `DataTable` object variable called `dataTable`:

```
Dim dataTable As DataTable = dataSet.Tables("Products")
```

Next, you can obtain the row collection of the table from the `Rows` property and the number of rows from the `Count` property:

```
Dim dataRowCollection As DataRowCollection = dataTable.Rows
Dim rowCount As Integer = dataRowCollection.Count
```

The number of rows is important when you iterate the row collection to display the values in each row.

The next lines of code display the table in an HTML table. The data displayed includes the column information. The column collection is obtained from the `Columns` property of the `DataTable` object, and the number of columns from the `Count` property of the column collection:

```
Dim dataColumnCollection As DataColumnCollection = dataTable.Columns
Dim columnCount As Integer = dataColumnCollection.Count
```

Having the column count, you can then retrieve the name and data type of each column. Each column is assigned to a `DataColumn` object reference column. The column name of each column comes from the `ColumnName` of the `DataColumn` object. The following code fragment iterates the column collection in a `For` loop:

```
For i = 0 To columnCount - 1
  Dim column As DataColumn = dataColumnCollection(i)
  Dim columnName As String = column.ColumnName
  s.Append("<td>").Append(columnName)
  s.Append(" (")
  s.Append(column.DataType.ToString())
  s.Append(")")
  s.Append("</td>")
Next i
```

Each column is presented in the following format:

```
column name (data type)
```

Next, you use two For loops to iterate each cell in the table. You obtain a data cell using the Item property of the DataRow object:

```
For i = 0 To rowCount - 1
  Dim row As DataRow = dataRowCollection(i)
  s.Append("<tr>")
  For j = 0 To columnCount - 1
    Dim cell As Object = row.Item(j)
    s.Append("<td>").Append(cell.ToString()).Append("</td>")
  Next j
  s.Append("</tr>")
Next I
```

Invoking the page from a Web browser gives you Figure 6-2.

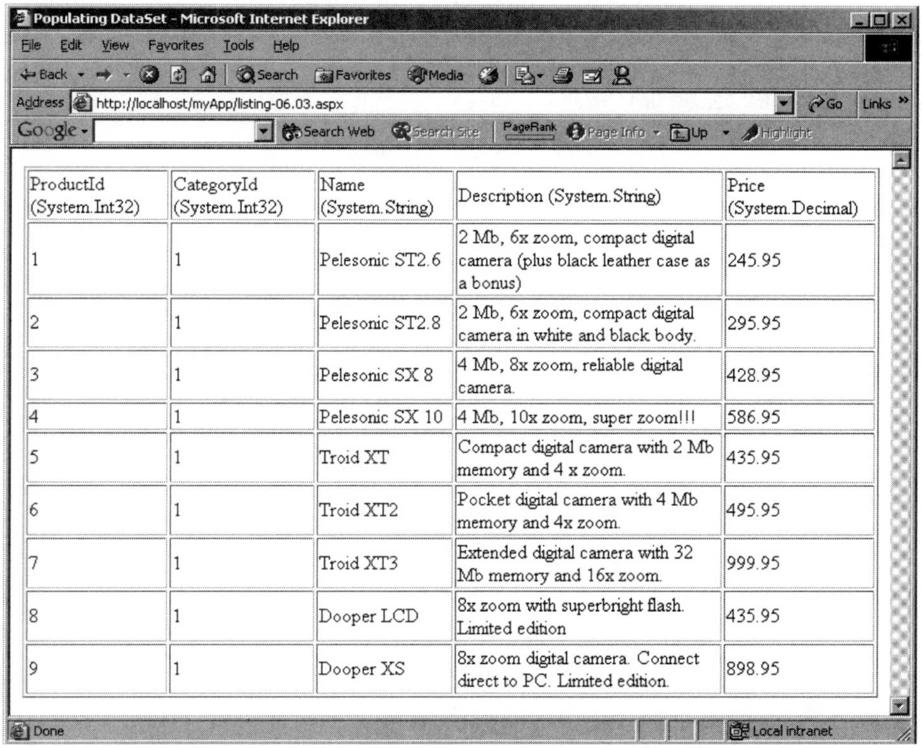

ProductId (System.Int32)	CategoryId (System.Int32)	Name (System.String)	Description (System.String)	Price (System.Decimal)
1	1	Pelesonic ST2.6	2 Mb, 6x zoom, compact digital camera (plus black leather case as a bonus)	245.95
2	1	Pelesonic ST2.8	2 Mb, 6x zoom, compact digital camera in white and black body.	295.95
3	1	Pelesonic SX 8	4 Mb, 8x zoom, reliable digital camera.	428.95
4	1	Pelesonic SX 10	4 Mb, 10x zoom, super zoom!!!	586.95
5	1	Troid XT	Compact digital camera with 2 Mb memory and 4 x zoom.	435.95
6	1	Troid XT2	Pocket digital camera with 4 Mb memory and 4x zoom.	495.95
7	1	Troid XT3	Extended digital camera with 32 Mb memory and 16x zoom.	999.95
8	1	Dooper LCD	8x zoom with superbright flash. Limited edition	435.95
9	1	Dooper XS	8x zoom digital camera. Connect direct to PC. Limited edition.	898.95

Figure 6-2. Populating a DataSet

Modifying Data in a DataSet

Modifying data in a DataSet object is an involved process because the DataSet object is disconnected from its data source and the changes to the DataSet object must be sent back to the data source. You send changes back to the data source through a data adapter object. As the following examples show, inserting rows or updating and deleting them requires you to do the following steps:

1. Populate a DataSet object using the Fill method of the data adapter class.

2. Build an insert, an update, or a delete command for a corresponding action. Inserting a record requires you to build an insert command for the data adapter object, and you need to build an update command if you want to update record(s) in the data source. By the same token, you need a delete command for the data adapter if you want to delete a record or a number of records in the data source. These commands are merely the correct SQL statements for the intended operations.

3. Manipulate the data in the DataSet object.

4. Call the Update method of the data adapter passing the modified data.

As you can see, data changes must be reflected in the command in step 2 as well as in the DataSet itself in step 3. Therefore, data modification that needs to be passed back to the data source can really be a pain. However, the next sections show how you can alleviate this a bit.

The following are three examples of how to insert a record, update a record, and delete a record.

Adding a Record

Listing 6-4 offers code that inserts a record into the Products table. The record contains the product name and the price for the new record.

Listing 6-4. Adding a Record into a Table

```
<%@ Import Namespace="System.Data" %>
<%@ Import Namespace="System.Data.OleDb" %>
<html>
<head>
<title>Adding a new record</title>
```

```vb
<script language="VB" runat="server">

Sub Page_Load(sender As Object, e As EventArgs)

  ' --------   Populate DataSet -----------
  Dim connectionString As String = _
    "Provider=Microsoft.Jet.OLEDB.4.0;" & _
    "Data Source=" & Request.PhysicalApplicationPath & _
    "..\MyDb.mdb"

  Dim sql As String = "SELECT * FROM Products"

  ' Instantiate a new connection object
  Dim connection As New OleDbConnection(connectionString)
  Dim dataAdapter As New OleDbDataAdapter(sql, connection)


  ' Add a new row, setting two fields: ProductName and Price
  Dim productName As String = "Pelesonic T3X "
  Dim price As Decimal = 512.95

  ' Build the insert command
  Dim insertCommand = "INSERT INTO Products (Name, Price)" & _
    " VALUES ('" & productName & "'," & price.ToString() & ")"

  dataAdapter.InsertCommand = New OleDbCommand(insertCommand, connection)

  connection.Open()
  Dim dataSet As New DataSet()
  dataAdapter.Fill(dataSet, "Products")
  connection.Close()

  ' Construct a new DataRow object for the new row
  Dim row As DataRow = dataSet.Tables("Products").NewRow()
  ' Assign values for the ProductName and Price fields
  row("Name") = productName
  row("Price") = price
  ' Add a new row to the table
  dataSet.Tables("Products").Rows.Add(row)
  connection.Open()

  ' Get the added row(s)
  Dim addedRows As DataRow() = dataSet.Tables("Products"). _
```

```
    Select(Nothing, Nothing, DataViewRowState.Added)
  dataAdapter.Update(addedRows)

  connection.Close()


End Sub
</script>
</head>

<body>
<asp:Label id="message" runat="server"/>
</body>
</html>
```

You start the process in the Page_Load method by constructing an OleDbConnection object and building an insert command for the data adapter:

```
' --------  Populate DataSet -----------
Dim connectionString As String = _
  "Provider=Microsoft.Jet.OLEDB.4.0;" & _
  "Data Source=C:\db\MyDb.mdb"

Dim sql As String = "SELECT * FROM Products"

' Instantiate a new connection object
Dim connection As New OleDbConnection(connectionString)
Dim dataAdapter As New OleDbDataAdapter(sql, connection)


' Add a new row, setting two fields: ProductName and Price
Dim productName As String = "Vegemite Crackers"
Dim price As Decimal = 12.95

' Build the insert command
Dim insertCommand = "INSERT INTO Products (ProductName, Price)" & _
  " VALUES ('" & productName & "'," & price.ToString() & ")"

dataAdapter.InsertCommand = New OleDbCommand(insertCommand, connection)
connection.Open()
```

The next step is to populate the `DataSet` object using the `Fill` method of the data adapter object:

```
Dim dataSet As New DataSet()
dataAdapter.Fill(dataSet, "Products")
connection.Close()
```

Afterward, you construct a `DataRow` object using the `NewRow` method of the `DataTable` class, guaranteeing that the resulting `DataRow` object has the same structure as any other row in the table:

```
' Construct a new DataRow object for the new row
Dim row As DataRow = dataSet.Tables("Products").NewRow()
```

You can then populate the cells in the `DataRow` object and add the row to the table:

```
' Assign values for the ProductName and Price fields
row("ProductName") = productName
row("Price") = price
' Add a new row to the table
dataSet.Tables("Products").Rows.Add(row)
connection.Open()
```

And now, this is the important part: You use the `Select` method of the `DataTable` class to retrieve all the newly added rows. Note how the `DataViewRowState` enumeration supplies the record state as the third argument. The enumeration member `Added` indicates you are only interested in the records that were added to the table:

```
' Get the added row(s)
Dim addedRows As DataRow() = dataSet.Tables("Products"). _
  Select(Nothing, Nothing, DataViewRowState.Added)
```

Finally, you use the `Update` method of the data adapter to update the changes to the `DataSet` object in the data source:

```
dataAdapter.Update(addedRows)
```

Updating Records

Listing 6-5 is similar to the code in Listing 6-4. This time, instead of inserting a record into a table, you change the values of the rows in the Products table.

Listing 6-5. Updating Records

```
<%@ Import Namespace="System.Data" %>
<%@ Import Namespace="System.Data.OleDb" %>
<html>
<head>
<title>Updating Records in DataSet</title>

<script language="VB" runat="server">

Sub Page_Load(sender As Object, e As EventArgs)

    ' --------  Populate DataSet -----------
    Dim connectionString As String = _
      "Provider=Microsoft.Jet.OLEDB.4.0;" & _
      "Data Source=" & Request.PhysicalApplicationPath & _
      "..\MyDb.mdb"

    Dim sql As String = "SELECT * FROM Products"

    ' Instantiate a new connection object
    Dim connection As New OleDbConnection(connectionString)
    Dim dataAdapter As New OleDbDataAdapter(sql, connection)

    ' Change the record with ProductId = 1, set ProductName="Pelesonic XP"
    Dim productName As String = "Pelesonic XP"
    Dim productId As Integer = 1

    Dim updateCommand = "UPDATE Products SET Name='" & productName & _
      "' WHERE ProductId=" & productId.ToString()

    dataAdapter.UpdateCommand = New OleDbCommand(updateCommand, connection)

    connection.Open()
    Dim dataSet As New DataSet()
    dataAdapter.Fill(dataSet, "Products")
    connection.Close()
```

```
' Change the data
Dim row As DataRow = dataSet.Tables("Products").Rows(0)
row("Name") = productName
connection.Open()

' Get the modified row(s)
Dim modifiedRows As DataRow() = dataSet.Tables("Products"). _
   Select(Nothing, Nothing, DataViewRowState.ModifiedCurrent)
dataAdapter.Update(modifiedRows)

connection.Close()

End Sub

</script>
</head>

<body>
<asp:Label id="message" runat="server"/>
</body>
</html>
```

The difference from the code in Listing 6-4 is that you do not call the NewRow method to construct a new row. Instead, you assign the first row in the table to the row object reference and change the value of the Name column:

```
' Change the data
Dim row As DataRow = dataSet.Tables("Products").Rows(0)
row("Name") = productName
connection.Open()
```

Then, you obtain an array of DataRow objects using the Select method. This time the third argument to this method is the ModifiedCurrent member of the DataViewRowState enumeration:

```
' Get the modified row(s)
Dim modifiedRows As DataRow() = dataSet.Tables("Products"). _
   Select(Nothing, Nothing, DataViewRowState.ModifiedCurrent)
```

Like the previous example, you can then update the change in the data source by calling the Update method of the data adapter:

```
dataAdapter.Update(modifiedRows)
```

Deleting Records

You also delete records using similar code. Listing 6-6 presents the code that deletes a record from the Products table.

Listing 6-6. Deleting Records

```
<%@ Import Namespace="System.Data" %>
<%@ Import Namespace="System.Data.OleDb" %>
<html>
<head>
<title>Deleting Records in DataSet</title>

<script language="VB" runat="server">

Sub Page_Load(sender As Object, e As EventArgs)

  Dim connectionString As String = _
    "Provider=Microsoft.Jet.OLEDB.4.0;" & _
    "Data Source=" & Request.PhysicalApplicationPath & _
    "..\MyDb.mdb"

  Dim sql As String = "SELECT * FROM Products"

   ' Instantiate a new connection object
  Dim connection As New OleDbConnection(connectionString)
  Dim dataAdapter As New OleDbDataAdapter(sql, connection)


   ' Delete the record with ProductId = 3
  Dim productId As Integer = 3

  Dim deleteCommand = "DELETE FROM Products WHERE ProductId=" & _
    productId.ToString()

  dataAdapter.DeleteCommand = New OleDbCommand(deleteCommand, connection)

  connection.Open()
  Dim dataSet As New DataSet()
  dataAdapter.Fill(dataSet, "Products")
  connection.Close()

   ' Change the data
```

```
      Dim row As DataRow = dataSet.Tables("Products").Rows(0)
      row.Delete()
      connection.Open()

      ' Get the deleted row(s)
      Dim deletedRows As DataRow() = dataSet.Tables("Products"). _
        Select(Nothing, Nothing, DataViewRowState.Deleted)
      dataAdapter.Update(deletedRows)

      connection.Close()

End Sub

</script>
</head>

<body>
<asp:Label id="message" runat="server"/>
</body>
</html>
```

Once you reference the first row in the Products table, you call the Delete method to delete the row:

```
' Change the data
Dim row As DataRow = dataSet.Tables("Products").Rows(0)
row.Delete()
connection.Open()
```

As in the previous examples, you filter the DataTable to obtain all deleted records. This time you use the DataViewRowState enumeration member Deleted to indicate you want all the deleted records:

```
' Get the deleted row(s)
Dim deletedRows As DataRow() = dataSet.Tables("Products"). _
  Select(Nothing, Nothing, DataViewRowState.Deleted)
```

Finally, the Update method updates the change in the data source:

```
dataAdapter.Update(deletedRows)
```

Modifying Data in a DataSet Using Parameters

You have seen that you can only modify data after constructing an insert/update/ delete command and modifying the DataSet object itself. Every change requires you to construct a different command for the data adapter. Using parameters can ease the process involved.

Listing 6-7 uses parameters to construct a generic update command and uses it to modify two rows.

Listing 6-7. Using Parameters to Modify Data

```vb
<%@ Import Namespace="System.Data" %>
<%@ Import Namespace="System.Data.OleDb" %>
<html>
<head>
<title>Updating Records with Parameters</title>

<script language="VB" runat="server">

Sub Page_Load(sender As Object, e As EventArgs)

  ' --------  Populate DataSet -----------
  Dim connectionString As String = _
    "Provider=Microsoft.Jet.OLEDB.4.0;" & _
    "Data Source=" & Request.PhysicalApplicationPath & _
    "..\MyDb.mdb"

  Dim sql As String = "SELECT * FROM Products"

  ' Instantiate a new connection object
  Dim connection As New OleDbConnection(connectionString)

  Dim updateCommand As String = "UPDATE Products SET Name=?" & _
    " WHERE ProductId=?"
  Dim dataAdapter As New OleDbDataAdapter(sql, connection)
  dataAdapter.UpdateCommand = New OleDbCommand(updateCommand, connection)

  dataAdapter.UpdateCommand.Parameters.Add( _
    "@ProductName", OleDbType.VarChar, 15, "Name")

  Dim param As OleDbParameter = _
    dataAdapter.UpdateCommand.Parameters.Add("@ProductId", OleDbType.Integer)
```

```
    param.SourceColumn = "ProductId"
    param.SourceVersion = DataRowVersion.Original

    connection.Open()
    Dim dataSet As New DataSet()
    dataAdapter.Fill(dataSet, "Products")
    connection.Close()

    ' Change the data
    Dim row1 As DataRow = dataSet.Tables("Products").Rows(0)
    row1("Name") = "Product 1"
    Dim row2 As DataRow = dataSet.Tables("Products").Rows(1)
    row2("Name") = "Product 2"
    connection.Open()

    ' Get the modified row(s)
    Dim modifiedRows As DataRow() = dataSet.Tables("Products"). _
      Select(Nothing, Nothing, DataViewRowState.ModifiedCurrent)
    dataAdapter.Update(modifiedRows)

    connection.Close()

End Sub

</script>
</head>

<body>
<asp:Label id="message" runat="server"/>
</body>
</html>
```

Updating Data with the CommandBuilder Object

Using parameters in data modification code can make the process less involved. However, there is an even easier way to modify data: using the CommandBuilder object. With this approach, there is no need for you to construct an insert/update/delete command for the data adapter. The CommandBuilder object does this for you. The catch is you have to have a primary key for the table to be modified.

Listing 6-8 shows how to use a CommandBuilder object to modify data.

Listing 6-8. Using the CommandBuilder *Object*

```vb
<%@ Import Namespace="System.Data" %>
<%@ Import Namespace="System.Data.OleDb" %>
<html>
<head>
<title>Using Command Builder</title>

<script language="VB" runat="server">

Sub Page_Load(sender As Object, e As EventArgs)

  ' --------   Populate DataSet -----------
  Dim connectionString As String = _
    "Provider=Microsoft.Jet.OLEDB.4.0;" & _
    "Data Source=" & Request.PhysicalApplicationPath & _
    "..\MyDb.mdb"

  Dim sql As String = "SELECT * FROM Products"

  ' Instantiate a new connection object
  Dim connection As New OleDbConnection(connectionString)

  Dim dataAdapter As New OleDbDataAdapter()
  dataAdapter.SelectCommand = New OleDbCommand(sql, connection)
  Dim commandBuilder As OleDbCommandBuilder = _
    New OleDbCommandBuilder(dataAdapter)
  connection.Open()

  Dim dataSet As New DataSet()
  dataAdapter.Fill(dataSet, "Products")

  Dim row As DataRow = dataSet.Tables("Products").Rows(0)
  row("Name") = "Toroid"

  'Without the CommandBuilder, the following line would fail
  dataAdapter.Update(dataSet, "Products")
  connection.Close()

End Sub

</script>
</head>

<body>
<asp:Label id="message" runat="server"/>
</body>
</html>
```

Data Binding

Put simply, data binding enables server controls to automatically get values or data from an expression or a data source. Data binding gives you more control over your data and helps you shorten development time of your ASP.NET projects. You can bind almost any type of data to any server control in your Web forms, even though the power of data binding is much more obvious when you are using the three data-binding controls: `Repeater`, `DataList`, and `DataGrid`.

The following section introduces data binding, shows an example of simple data binding with a server control, and explains a data-binding expression. Then, you will see techniques you can use to display and update data using the data-binding technique with the three Web server controls: `Repeater`, `DataList`, and `DataGrid`.

Introducing Data Binding

You bind data to a control using a data-binding expression of the following syntax:

```
<%# expression %>
```

Consider having a `Label` control whose `Text` property is bound to a variable. Whatever value you assign to the variable, the `Label` control adjusts its `Text` automatically. For example, Listing 6-9 binds the variable `myString` to a `Label` control named `label` using the following expression in the body of the `Label` control:

```
Text="<%# myString %>"
```

Alternatively, you can assign the `DataSource` property of a control to a data source or a collection, such as the following:

```
control.DataSource = dataSource
```

or as the following:

```
control.DataSource = anArray
```

However, for the actual data-binding operation to happen, you need to call the `DataBind` method of the control or the page. The `DataBind` method inherits from the `System.Web.UI.Control` class. It binds a data source to the invoked server control and all of its child controls. Therefore, in an ASP.NET page, for each control that needs to be bound, you can call the `DataBind` method of each control or the `DataBind` method of the `Page` class to bind all controls in the page (see Listing 6-9).

Listing 6-9. Simple Data Binding

```
<html>
<head>
<title>Data Binding</title>
<script language="VB" runat="server">

Dim myString As String = "Hello ASP.NET"

Sub Page_Load(sender As Object, e As EventArgs)
  ' calling the DataBind() method of the Page class
  ' Alternatively, you can call the DataBind method of
  ' the Label control.
  DataBind()
End Sub

</script>
</head>
<body>
  <asp:Label id="label"
    runat="server"
    Text="<%# myString %>"
  />
</body>
</html>
```

If you run the Web form in Listing 6-9, you will see something similar to Figure 6-3.

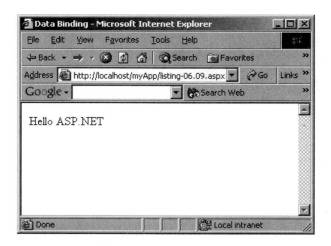

Figure 6-3. Simple data binding

Listing 6-9 illustrates the use of data binding; however, the power of data binding itself is not that apparent. This is because you can simply assign the label's Text property with the value of myString, such as the following:

```
<asp:Label id="label"
    runat="server"
    Text="Hello ASP.NET"
  />
```

The example in Listing 6-10 gives more reason to use data binding. In this code snippet, an array of strings is bound to a ListBox control.

Listing 6-10. Data Binding an Array to a ListBox *Control*

```
<html>
<head>
<title>Data Binding</title>
<script language="VB" runat="server">

Dim colorArray() As String = _
  {"Blue", "Pink", "Red", "Orange", "Yellow"}

Sub Page_Load(sender As Object, e As EventArgs)

  colorListBox.DataSource = colorArray
  DataBind()

End Sub

</script>
</head>
<body>
<form runat="server">
  <asp:ListBox id="colorListBox" runat="server"/>
</form>
</body>
</html>
```

Figure 6-4 displays the result from Listing 6-10.

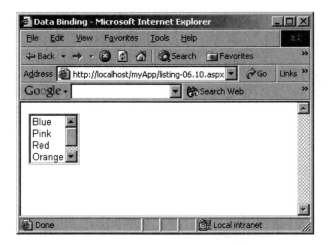

Figure 6-4. Data binding with a ListBox *control*

Without data binding, the code in Listing 6-10 must be rewritten as that in Listing 6-11 to add some programming to populate the ListBox control.

Listing 6-11. Populating a Control Programmatically

```
<html>
<head>
<title>Populating ListBox control programmatically </title>
<script language="VB" runat="server">

Dim colorArray() As String = _
  {"Blue", "Pink", "Red", "Orange", "Yellow"}

Sub Page_Load(sender As Object, e As EventArgs)

  ' Populating the ListBox
  Dim itemCollection As ListItemCollection = colorListBox.Items
  Dim item As Object
  For Each item In colorArray
    itemCollection.Add(item)
  Next

End Sub
```

```
</script>
</head>
<body>
<form runat="server">
  <asp:ListBox id="colorListBox" runat="server"/>
</form>
</body>
</html>
```

Compare the amount of work you do in the Page_Load event handler of both Listing 6-10 and Listing 6-11.

Listing 6-12 shows another example. This example expands on the code in Listing 6-11. Here, the ListBox control's AutoPostBack property is set to True to immediately update the label's value.

Listing 6-12. Using AutoPostBack *to Update Values*

```
<html>
<head>
<title>ListBox programming</title>
<script language="VB" runat="server">

Dim colorArray() As String = _
  {"Blue", "Pink", "Red", "Orange", "Yellow"}

Sub Page_Load(sender As Object, e As EventArgs)

  If Not IsPostBack Then
    Dim itemCollection As ListItemCollection = _
      colorListBox.Items

    Dim item As Object
    For Each item In colorArray
      itemCollection.Add(item)
    Next
  End If

End Sub

Sub colorListBox_SelectedIndexChanged(sender As Object, _
  e As EventArgs)
  message.Text = colorListBox.SelectedItem.Text
End Sub
```

```
</script>
</head>
<body>
<center>
<form runat="server">
  <asp:ListBox id="colorListBox"
    runat="server"
    AutoPostBack="True"
    OnSelectedIndexChanged="colorListBox_SelectedIndexChanged"
  />

  <p>
  <asp:Label id="message" runat="server"/>
</form>
</center>
</body>
</html>
```

Listing 6-12 first populates the ListBox control using the following snippet. Note that you only need to do this once, when the page is first loaded. For subsequent requests, the state management mechanism provides the ListBox control with its previous values:

```
If Not IsPostBack Then
  Dim itemCollection As ListItemCollection = _
    colorListBox.Items

  Dim item As Object
  For Each item In colorArray
    itemCollection.Add(item)
  Next
End If
```

Note that the ListBox has its SelectedIndexChanged event connected to the colorListBox_SelectedIndexChanged event handler:

```
OnSelectedIndexChanged="colorListBox_SelectedIndexChanged"
```

The colorListBox_SelectedIndexChanged event handler updates the Text property of the Label control named message, as in the following code:

```
Sub colorListBox_SelectedIndexChanged(sender As Object, _
  e As EventArgs)
  message.Text = colorListBox.SelectedItem.Text
End Sub
```

Running the Web form in Listing 6-12 gives you the same result as Figure 6-5.

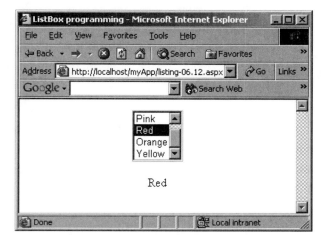

Figure 6-5. Using the SelectedIndexChanged *event of the* ListBox *control*

You can obtain the same result using data binding, as demonstrated in
Listing 6-13.

Listing 6-13. Data Binding to a ListBox *Control*

```
<html>
<head>
<title>ListBox Data Binding</title>
<script language="VB" runat="server">

Dim colorArray() As String = _
  {"Blue", "Pink", "Red", "Orange", "Yellow"}

Sub Page_Load(sender As Object, e As EventArgs)

  If Not IsPostBack Then
    colorListBox.DataSource = colorArray
    colorListBox.SelectedIndex = 0
    DataBind()
  End If

End Sub
```

```
Sub colorListBox_SelectedIndexChanged(sender As Object, e As EventArgs)
  DataBind()
End Sub


</script>
</head>
<body>
<center>
<form runat="server">
  <asp:ListBox id="colorListBox"
    runat="server"
    AutoPostBack="True"
    OnSelectedIndexChanged="colorListBox_SelectedIndexChanged"
  />

  <p>
  <asp:Label id="message" runat="server"
    Text='<%# colorListBox.SelectedItem.Text %>'
  />

</form>
</center>
</body>
</html>
```

Now, there is no more programming to populate the ListBox control or update the Label control's Text property. You just need to call the DataBind method of the Page class.

Binding Data to the DataGrid Control

In ASP.NET the DataGrid control is the ultimate data-binding control. In addition to formatting data in a data grid, this control allows you to update data in the way that reminds you of working with a Graphical User Interface (GUI) program of a database application such as Microsoft Access. Using the DataGrid control, you can present the data in a row/column format as well as let each cell be edited. Also, a nice additional feature is the easy-to-use automatic paging.

The following two sections present two examples of how to use the DataGrid control. The first demonstrates how to do data editing. The second example demonstrates easy data paging using the DataGrid control.

Data Editing

Listing 6-14 shows how to do data editing.

Listing 6-14. Data Editing with a DataGrid *Control*

```
<%@ Import Namespace="System.Data" %>
<%@ Import Namespace="System.Data.OleDb" %>
<html>
<head>
<title>DataGrid control</title>
<script language="VB" runat="server">

Dim dataView As DataView
Dim sql As String = "SELECT * FROM Products"
Dim connectionString As String
Sub Page_Load(sender As Object, e As EventArgs)

  connectionString = _
  "Provider=Microsoft.Jet.OLEDB.4.0;" & _
  "Data Source=" & Request.PhysicalApplicationPath & _
  "..\MyDb.mdb"

  ' Instantiate a new connection object
  Dim connection As New OleDbConnection(connectionString)

  Dim dataAdapter As New OleDbDataAdapter(sql, connection)
  connection.Open()

  Dim dataSet As New DataSet()
  dataAdapter.Fill(dataSet, "Products")

  dataView = dataSet.Tables(0).DefaultView
  If Not IsPostBack Then
    BindGrid()
  End If
End Sub

Sub BindGrid()
  myDataGrid.DataSource = dataView
  myDataGrid.DataBind()
End Sub
```

```
Sub myDataGrid_EditCommand(sender As Object, e As DataGridCommandEventArgs)
  myDataGrid.EditItemIndex = CInt(e.Item.ItemIndex)
  BindGrid()
End Sub


Sub myDataGrid_CancelCommand(sender As Object, e As DataGridCommandEventArgs)
  myDataGrid.EditItemIndex = -1
  BindGrid()
End Sub


Sub myDataGrid_DeleteCommand(sender As Object, e As DataGridCommandEventArgs)
  Dim editItem As DataGridItem = e.Item
  Dim editItemIndex = CInt(editItem.ItemIndex)

  ' Instantiate a new connection object
  Dim connection As New OleDbConnection(connectionString)

  Dim dataAdapter As New OleDbDataAdapter()
  dataAdapter.SelectCommand = New OleDbCommand(sql, connection)
  Dim commandBuilder As OleDbCommandBuilder = _
    New OleDbCommandBuilder(dataAdapter)
  connection.Open()

  Dim dataSet As New DataSet()
  dataAdapter.Fill(dataSet, "Products")

  Dim row As DataRow = dataSet.Tables("Products").Rows(editItemIndex)
  row.Delete()
  dataAdapter.Update(dataSet, "Products")
  connection.Close()
  'Refresh dataView
  dataView = dataSet.Tables("Products").DefaultView
  myDataGrid.EditItemIndex = -1
  BindGrid()
End Sub


Sub myDataGrid_UpdateCommand(sender As Object, e As DataGridCommandEventArgs)

  Dim editItem As DataGridItem = e.Item
  Dim editItemIndex = CInt(editItem.ItemIndex)

  ' Instantiate a new connection object
  Dim connection As New OleDbConnection(connectionString)
```

```
Dim dataAdapter As New OleDbDataAdapter()
dataAdapter.SelectCommand = New OleDbCommand(sql, connection)
Dim commandBuilder As OleDbCommandBuilder = _
  New OleDbCommandBuilder(dataAdapter)
connection.Open()

Dim dataSet As New DataSet()
dataAdapter.Fill(dataSet, "Products")

Dim row As DataRow = dataSet.Tables("Products").Rows(editItemIndex)
Dim priceTextBox As TextBox = CType(e.Item.Cells(1).Controls(0), TextBox)

Try
  Dim newPrice As Decimal = CDec(priceTextBox.Text)
  row("Price") = newPrice
  dataAdapter.Update(dataSet, "Products")
Catch ex As Exception
End Try
connection.Close()
'Refresh dataView
dataView = dataSet.Tables("Products").DefaultView
myDataGrid.EditItemIndex = -1
BindGrid()
End Sub

</script>
</head>
<body>
<center>
<form runat="server">

  <asp:DataGrid id="myDataGrid" runat="server"
    BorderColor="black"
    BorderWidth="1"
    CellPadding="3"
    Font-Name="Verdana"
    Font-Size="8pt"
    OnEditCommand="myDataGrid_EditCommand"
    OnCancelCommand="myDataGrid_CancelCommand"
    OnUpdateCommand="myDataGrid_UpdateCommand"
    OnDeleteCommand="myDataGrid_DeleteCommand"
    AllowSorting="True"
    AutoGenerateColumns="false">
```

```
        <HeaderStyle BackColor="#aaaadd" ForeColor="white"/>

        <EditItemStyle BackColor="yellow"/>

        <Columns>

          <asp:BoundColumn HeaderText="Product Name"
            ReadOnly="True"
            DataField="Name"
          />

          <asp:BoundColumn HeaderText="Price"
            ReadOnly="False"
            DataField="Price">
            <ItemStyle HorizontalAlign="Right"/>
          </asp:BoundColumn>

          <asp:EditCommandColumn
            EditText="Edit"
            CancelText="Cancel"
            UpdateText="Update"
            HeaderText="Edit Price">
            <ItemStyle Wrap="false"/>
            <HeaderStyle Wrap="false"/>
          </asp:EditCommandColumn>
          <asp:ButtonColumn
            HeaderText="Delete Item"
            ButtonType="LinkButton"
            Text="Delete"
            CommandName="Delete"
          />
        </Columns>

    </asp:DataGrid>

  </form>
  </center>
  </body>
  </html>
```

The DataGrid control in Listing 6-14 contains four columns. The first two columns are bound columns, the first of which is bound to the Name column of the Products table and the second to the Price column of the Products table. The third column contains an EditCommandColumn, and the fourth contains a ButtonColumn, which acts as a Delete button. Each bound column that cannot be changed is marked by its ReadOnly property set to True:

```
ReadOnly="True"
```

Figure 6-6 shows the DataGrid control. Note especially the EditCommandColumn.

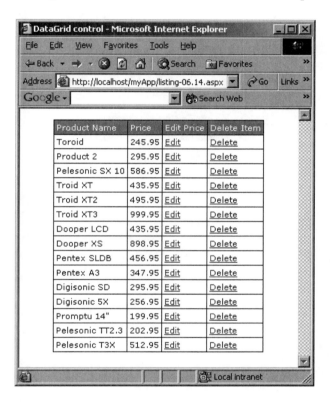

Figure 6-6. The DataGrid *control*

When a user clicks the Edit command button, the command is automatically replaced by two buttons: an Update button and a Cancel button, as shown in Figure 6-7. Therefore, you have four types of button: Edit, Delete, Cancel, and Update. You click the Edit button when you want to edit an item. Then, after you edit an item, you can either click the Cancel or Update button to cancel the change or make it permanent. The Delete button deletes an item.

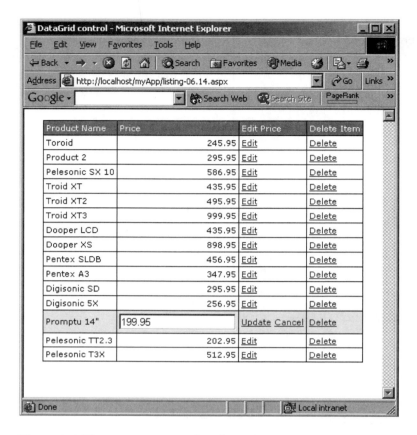

Figure 6-7. The DataGrid *control with Update and Cancel buttons*

These four buttons invoke the four event handlers as defined in the DataGrid control:

```
OnEditCommand="myDataGrid_EditCommand"
OnCancelCommand="myDataGrid_CancelCommand"
OnUpdateCommand="myDataGrid_UpdateCommand"
OnDeleteCommand="myDataGrid_DeleteCommand"
```

The myDataGrid_EditCommand event handler sets the EditItemIndex property. A value of –1 specifies that no item is selected. Specifying a zero or a positive integer to this property makes the item selected. The Edit button for that item will be replaced by the Cancel and Update buttons:

```
Sub myDataGrid_EditCommand(sender As Object, e As DataGridCommandEventArgs)
  myDataGrid.EditItemIndex = CInt(e.Item.ItemIndex)
  BindGrid()
End Sub
```

Clicking the Cancel button cancels the selection by setting the EditItemIndex property to –1:

```
Sub myDataGrid_CancelCommand(sender As Object, e As DataGridCommandEventArgs)
  myDataGrid.EditItemIndex = -1
  BindGrid()
End Sub
```

The myDataGrid_DeleteCommand and myDataGrid_UpdateCommand event handlers delete an item and update the change to the data source.

Data Paging Using the DataGrid Control

This section illustrates how to use automatic paging with a DataGrid control. To use automatic paging, you need to do two things:

1. Set the AllowPaging property of the DataGrid control to True, and optionally specify the PageSize property:

    ```
    AllowPaging="True"
    PageSize="8"
    ```

    The PageSize property specifies the number of items in one page. If the PageSize property is not set, the default size of 10 is used.

2. Write an event handler for the PageIndexChanged event of the DataGrid control. The purpose of having this event handler is to set the CurrentPageIndex so that the DataGrid control displays the selected page. In this example, the PageIndexChanged is connected to the myDataGrid_PageIndexChanged event handler as follows:

    ```
    Sub myDataGrid_PageIndexChanged(sender As Object, _
      e As DataGridPageChangedEventArgs)
      myDataGrid.CurrentPageIndex = e.NewPageIndex
      BindGrid()
    End Sub
    ```

Listing 6-15 gives the code for such a DataGrid control.

Listing 6-15. Data Paging with a DataGrid *Control*

```vb
<%@ Import Namespace="System.Data" %>
<%@ Import Namespace="System.Data.OleDb" %>
<html>
<head>
<title>DataGrid control</title>
<script language="VB" runat="server">

Dim dataView As DataView

Sub Page_Load(sender As Object, e As EventArgs)

  Dim connectionString As String = _
    "Provider=Microsoft.Jet.OLEDB.4.0;" & _
    "Data Source=" & Request.PhysicalApplicationPath & _
    "..\MyDb.mdb"

  Dim sql As String = "SELECT * FROM Products"

  ' Instantiate a new connection object
  Dim connection As New OleDbConnection(connectionString)

  Dim dataAdapter As New OleDbDataAdapter(sql, connection)
  connection.Open()

  Dim dataSet As New DataSet()
  dataAdapter.Fill(dataSet, "Products")

  dataView = dataSet.Tables(0).DefaultView
  If Not IsPostBack Then
    BindGrid()
  End If
End Sub

Sub BindGrid()
  myDataGrid.DataSource = dataView
  myDataGrid.DataBind()
End Sub

Sub myDataGrid_EditCommand(sender As Object, e As DataGridCommandEventArgs)
  myDataGrid.EditItemIndex = CInt(e.Item.ItemIndex)
  BindGrid()
End Sub
```

```
Sub MyDataGrid_PageIndexChanged(sender As Object, _
  e As DataGridPageChangedEventArgs)
  myDataGrid.CurrentPageIndex = e.NewPageIndex
  BindGrid()
End Sub



</script>
</head>
<body>
<center>
<form runat="server">

  <asp:DataGrid id="myDataGrid" runat="server"
    BorderColor="black"
    BorderWidth="1"
    CellPadding="3"
    Font-Name="Verdana"
    Font-Size="8pt"
    AllowSorting="True"
    AllowPaging="True"
    PageSize="8"
    OnPageIndexChanged="myDataGrid_PageIndexChanged"
    AutoGenerateColumns="false">

    <HeaderStyle BackColor="#aaaadd" ForeColor="white"/>
    <PagerStyle Mode="NumericPages" HorizontalAlign="Right"/>

    <EditItemStyle BackColor="yellow"/>

    <Columns>
      <asp:BoundColumn HeaderText="Product Name"
        ReadOnly="True"
        DataField="Name"
      />

      <asp:BoundColumn HeaderText="Price"
        ReadOnly="False"
        DataField="Price">
        <ItemStyle HorizontalAlign="Right"/>
      </asp:BoundColumn>

    </Columns>
```

```
    </asp:DataGrid>

    <asp:Label id="message" runat="server"/>
  </form>
  </center>
  </body>
  </html>
```

Figure 6-8 shows the result of the code in Listing 6-15.

Figure 6-8. Automatic paging with a DataGrid *control*

Note that the DataGrid control defines a PagerStyle property for the pager. Its Mode attribute can have one of the two possible values: NumericPages and NextPrev (default). With the first, a pager with numbered buttons accesses pages directly. With NextPrev, a pager with Previous and Next buttons accesses the next and previous pages.

Configuring ASP.NET Applications

You can control any type of .NET applications, including ASP.NET applications, by changing various settings in the configuration files. There are three types of configuration files in the .NET, all of which are XML files:

- The machine configuration file

- The application configuration file

- The security configuration file

In addition to these files, an ASP.NET can also have a `global.asax` file that is similar to the `global.asa` file in classic ASP. The following sections discuss the machine configuration file, the application file, and the `global.asax` file. The security configuration file is related to the security aspect of an ASP.NET application and is discussed in the "Working with the Machine and Application Configuration Files" section.

Working with the Machine and Application Configuration Files

A computer has one machine configuration file that includes settings that apply to all .NET applications in that computer. This file is located in `%runtime install path%\Config\Machine.config`.

The application configuration file is named differently for different types of .NET applications. For ASP.NET applications, the application configuration file is `web.config`. Usually, there is one `web.config` file, which is located in the application directory. However, a subdirectory of the application directory can have its own `web.config` file, and any subdirectory or the application directory's subdirectory can also have its own `web.config` file.e

When there is more than one application configuration file in an ASP.NET application, the `web.config` file in a directory located higher in the hierarchy is the parent of any `web.config` file in any directory below it. A child `web.config` file inherits all settings in the parent configuration file and overwrites the settings that are similar. The `web.config` file in the application directory itself is the child of the machine configuration file.

For example, if the root directory of an ASP.NET application is C:\Inetpub\ wwwroot\myApp and there is a web.config file in that directory, this web.config file is the main application configuration file of that ASP.NET application and is the child of the machine configuration file. If there is a directory called shopping under C:\Inetpub\wwwroot\myApp and there is a web.config file in the C:\Inetpub\wwwroot\myApp\shopping directory, this web.config file is the child of the web.config file in the C:\Inetpub\wwwroot\myApp directory.

The root element of a configuration file is always <configuration>. There are two main areas in a configuration file:

Configuration section declaration area: Contains all configuration section declarations in the <configSections> container tags. The <configSections> tags can contain <section> tags and <sectionGroup> tags.

You use a <section> tag for each class that must access information in the configuration file. This tag contains two attributes:

- **type**: The name of the class that reads the information.

- **name**: The name of the tag containing the information that will be read by the section handler.

Because a child configuration file inherits all settings from its parent, you can declare settings in the machine configuration file and write the settings themselves in the application configuration file.

You use a <sectionGroup> tag as a container tag to group related sections. Therefore, a <sectionGroup> tag contains zero or more <section> tags. Using a <sectionGroup> tag is also a good way to avoid naming conflicts between the section you declare and sections declared by someone else.

Configuration section settings area: Contains the settings of each section declared in the configuration section's declaration area.

The skeleton of a configuration file is as follows:

```
<?xml version="1.0" encoding="utf-8" ?>
<configuration>
  <!-- the configuration section declaration area -->
  <configSections>

    <!-- declarations of <section> and <sectionGroup>
         tags go here -->
```

```
    </configSections>
    <!-- end of the configuration section declaration area -->

    <!-- settings go here -->

</configuration>
```

The following is an example of a configuration file. The configuration section's declaration area has a `<section>` tag and a `<sectionGroup>` tag. The `<section>` tag's name is `customSection` and the `<sectionGroup>` tag's name is `customGroup`:

```
<?xml version="1.0" encoding="utf-8" ?>
<configuration>
  <!-- the configuration section declaration area -->
  <configSections>
    <section name="customSection"
      type="System.Configuration.SingleTagSectionHandler" />
    <sectionGroup name="customGroup">
      <section name="groupCustomSection"
        type="System.Configuration.NameValueSectionHandler,System" />
    </sectionGroup>
    <!-- declarations of <section> and <sectionGroup>
        tags go here -->

  </configSections>
  <!-- end of the configuration section declaration area -->

  <!-- settings go here -->
  <customSection setting1="value1" setting2="value2"/>
  <customGroup>
    <groupCustomSection setting1="value1" setting2="value2"/>
  </customGroup>
</configuration>
```

The default machine configuration file comes with a predefined configuration section named `appSettings`. You use this setting to define custom settings for your ASP.NET application. The syntax for this setting is as follows:

```
<appSettings>
  <add key="key" value="value"/>
</appSettings>
```

For example, Listing 6-16 offers an application configuration file that defines two keys in the <appSettings> element: author and company.

Listing 6-16. Defining Two Keys in the <appSettings> *Element*

```
<?xml version="1.0" encoding="utf-8" ?>
<configuration>
  <appSettings>
    <add key="author" value="Budi Kurniawan"/>
    <add key="company" value="BrainySoftware"/>
  </appSettings>
</configuration>
```

You can access the custom application settings you define in the configuration file. For example, the code in Listing 6-17 prints the author and company values defined in the application configuration file given in Listing 6-16.

Listing 6-17. Accessing the Custom Application Settings

```
<html>
<head>
<title>Accessing the configuration settings</title>
<script language="VB" runat="server">
Sub Page_Load(sender As Object, e As EventArgs)
  message.Text = "Author: " & _
    ConfigurationSettings.AppSettings("author") & _
    "<br>Company: " & _
    ConfigurationSettings.AppSettings("company")

End Sub
</script>
</head>
<body>
<form runat="server">
  <asp:Label id="message" runat="server"/>
</form>
</body>
</html>
```

Of special interest for ASP.NET application developers and system administrators is the `<system.web>` section. This section contains subsections that have specific meanings to the ASP.NET application. Table 6-3 describes all subsections contained in the `<system.web>` section.

Table 6-3. Configuration Sections in the `<system.web>` Section

CONFIGURATION SECTION	DESCRIPTION
`<authentication>`	The setting for ASP.NET authentication
`<authorization>`	The setting for ASP.NET authorization
`<browserCaps>`	The setting for the browser capabilities component
`<compilation>`	The setting for ASP.NET compilation options
`<customErrors>`	The setting that controls the custom error messages for the application
`<globalization>`	The globalization setting
`<httpHandlers>`	The setting that maps HTTP requests' Uniform Resource Locators (URLs) to IHttpHandler classes
`<httpModules>`	The setting used for adding, removing, or clearing HTTP modules within an application
`<httpRuntime>`	The setting responsible for the ASP.NET HTTP runtime configuration
`<identity>`	The setting for the application identity
`<machineKey>`	The setting that determines the key used in the encryption and decryption of forms authentication cookie data
`<pages>`	Contains page-specific configuration settings
`<processModel>`	The setting that controls the process model of ASP.NET on the Internet Information Services (IIS)
`<securityPolicy>`	The setting that defines valid mappings of named security levels to policy files
`<sessionState>`	The setting that manages the session management scheme for that application
`<trace>`	The setting used for the ASP.NET trace service
`<trust>`	Configures the code access security permission used to run a particular application
`<webServices>`	The setting that controls the ASP.NET Web services

The following sections describe the often-used subsections from Table 6-3.

<authentication>

You use the <authentication> setting to configure ASP.NET authentication:

```
<authentication mode="Windows|Forms|Passport|None">
  <forms name="name" loginUrl="url"
    protection="All|None|Encryption|Validation"
    timeout="30" path="/">
    <credentials passwordFormat="Clear|SHA1|MD5">
      <user name="username" password="password" />
    </credentials>
  </form>
  <passport redirectUrl="internal"/>
</authentication>
```

(You can find more information about this setting in the "Securing ASP.NET Applications" section.)

<authorization>

You use the <authorization> setting to configure ASP.NET authorization:

```
<authorization>
  <allow users="comma-separated list of users"
    roles="comma-separated list of roles"
    verbs="comma-separated list of verbs" />

  <deny users="comma-separated list of users"
    roles="comma-separated list of roles"
    verbs="comma-separated list of verbs" />
</authorization>
```

(You can find more information about this setting in the "Securing ASP.NET Applications" section.)

<browserCaps>

The <browserCaps> setting configures the browser capabilities component. For example, the application configuration file in Listing 6-18 contains a <browserCaps> element.

Listing 6-18. Using the <browserCaps> *Setting*

```
<?xml version="1.0" encoding="utf-8" ?>
<configuration>
  <system.web>
    <browserCaps>
      <result type="System.Web.HttpBrowserCapabilities" />
      <use var="HTTP_USER_AGENT" />
      browser=Unknown
      version=0.0
      majorversion=0
      minorversion=0
      frames=false
      tables=false
      cookies=false
      backgroundsounds=false
      vbscript=false
      javascript=false
      javaapplets=false
      activexcontrols=false
      win16=false
      win32=false
      beta=false
      ak=false
      sk=false
      aol=false
      crawler=false
      cdf=false
      gold=false
      authenticodeupdate=false
      tagwriter=System.Web.UI.Html32TextWriter
      ecmascriptversion=0.0
      msdomversion=0.0
      w3cdomversion=0.0
      platform=Unknown
      clrVersion=0.0
      css1=false
      css2=false
      xml=false
    </browserCaps>
  </system.web>
</configuration>
```

<customErrors>

You use the <customErrors> setting to control the custom error messages for your ASP.NET application:

```
<customErrors
  defaultRedirect="url"
  mode="On|Off|RemoteOnly">
  <error statusCode="statusCode"
    redirect="url"/>
</customErrors>
```

For example, the application configuration file in Listing 6-19 causes the user to be redirected to the www.brainysoftware.com/ErrorPage.html if there is an uncaught exception in any ASP.NET page in the application.

Listing 6-19. Using the <customErrors> *Setting*

```
<?xml version="1.0" encoding="utf-8" ?>
<configuration>
  <system.web>
    <customErrors
defaultRedirect="http://www.brainysoftware.com/ErrorPage.html"
      mode="On">
    </customErrors>
  </system.web>
</configuration>
```

<globalization>

You use the <globalization> setting to configure globalization options of your ASP.NET application:

```
<globalization
  requestEncoding="a valid encoding string"
  responseEncoding="a valid encoding string"
  fileEncoding="a valid encoding string"
  culture="a valid culture string"
  uiCulture="a valid culture string"/>
```

The default value for the requestEncoding and responseEncoding attributes is "iso-8859-1".

‹httpRuntime›

The ‹httpRuntime› setting configures ASP.NET runtime options:

```
<httpRuntime useFullyQualifiedRedirectUrl="true|false"
  maxRequestLength="size in kilobytes"
  executionTimeout="number of seconds"/>
```

The useFullyQualifiedRedirectUrl attribute specifies whether client-side redirects must be fully qualified URLs. Setting this attribute to false sends relative redirection URLs to the clients.

The maxRequestLength attribute specifies the maximum size of the HTTP request in kilobytes (KB). You can use this setting to restrict the maximum number of bytes of uploaded files or to prevent denial of service attacks.

The executionTimeout attribute specifies the number of seconds an ASP.NET page can be executed before it is terminated by ASP.NET.

Listing 6-20 presents a typical application configuration file that uses the ‹httpRuntime› setting.

Listing 6-20. Using the ‹httpRuntime› *Setting*

```
<?xml version="1.0" encoding="utf-8" ?>
<configuration>
  <system.web>
    <httpRuntime
      maxRequestLength="1024"
      executionTimeout="120"
    />
  </system.web>
</configuration>
```

‹identity›

You use the ‹identity› setting to determine the identity of your ASP.NET application:

```
<identity
  impersonate="true|false"
  userName="username"
  password="password"/>
```

(You can find more information about this setting in the "Applying Settings to Certain Resources" section.)

<pages>

The <pages> setting enables you to control specific options related to the ASP.NET pages in the application. For instance, you can determine whether page output buffering is enabled, whether state management is on, and so on. The syntax for this setting is as follows:

```
<pages
  buffer="true|false"
  enableSessionState="true|false|ReadOnly"
  enableViewState="true|false"
  enableViewStateMac="true|false"
  autoEventWireup="true|false"
  pageBaseType="typename, assembly"
  userControlBaseType="typename"/>
```

The following describes the attributes:

- **buffer**: Indicates whether response buffering is enabled.

- **enabledSessionState**: Indicates whether the pages in the application participate in the ASP.NET session management. Assigning ReadOnly to this setting causes the application to be able to read but not modify session state variables.

- **enableViewState**: Indicates whether state management is enabled.

- **enableViewStateMac**: Indicates whether ASP.NET should run a machine authentication check (MAC) on the page's view state when the page is posted back from the client.

- **autoEventWireup**: Indicates whether page events are enabled automatically.

- **pageBaseType**: Forces the page class to inherit the specified code-behind class.

- **userControlBaseType**: Forces user controls to inherit the specified code-behind class.

For example, the application configuration file in Listing 6-21 causes the application's response to be buffered, makes the application's pages not participate in the session management, and disables the state management.

Listing 6-21. Using the <pages> *Setting*

```xml
<?xml version="1.0" encoding="utf-8" ?>
<configuration>
  <system.web>
    <pages
      buffer="true"
      enableSessionState="false"
      enableViewState="false"
    />
  </system.web>
</configuration>
```

<processModel>

The <processModel> setting controls the ASP.NET process model options on IIS:

```
<processModel
  enabled="true|false"
  timeout="minutes"
  idleTimeout="minutes"
  shutdownTimeout="hours:minutes:seconds"
  requestLimit="num"
  requestQueueLimit="num"
  memoryLimit="percent"
  cpuMask="num"
  webGarden="true|false"
  userName="username"
  password="password" />
```

The following describes each attribute:

- **enabled**: Indicates whether the process model is enabled.

- **timeout**: The number of minutes ASP.NET will wait before starting a new worker process to take over processing from the current one. The default is infinite.

- **idleTimeout**: The number of minutes of continuous inactivity that causes ASP.NET to shut down the worker process. The default is infinite.

- **shutdownTimeout**: The number of minutes given to the worker process to shut itself down. When the time expires, ASP.NET shuts down the worker process. The time is expressed in hr:min:sec format, so 0:00:05 is 5 seconds. The default is 5 seconds.

- **requestLimit**: The maximum number of requests that must be reached before ASP.NET automatically starts a new worker process to take over from the current one. The default is infinite.

- **requestQueueLimit**: The maximum number of requests allowed in the queue. ASP.NET will begin returning the "503—Server Too Busy" error to the new requests once this number is exceeded. The default is 5000.

- **memoryLimit**: The maximum size in percentage of the total system memory that the worker process can use before ASP.NET starts a new process and reassigns existing requests. The default is 40 percent.

- **cpuMask**: Specifies which processors on a multiprocessor server are eligible to run ASP.NET process. The cpuMask value specifies a bit pattern that indicates the CPUs eligible to run ASP.NET threads.

- **webGarden**: Determines the CPU affinity when used in conjunction with the cpuMask attribute.

- **userName**: When present, represents the user name of the account running the worker process.

- **password**: When present, causes the worker process to run with the configured Windows identity.

`<sessionState>`

The `<sessionState>` setting controls ASP.NET session management for the application.

`<trace>`

The `<trace>` setting determines whether the application trace functionality is enabled:

```
<trace
  enabled="true|false"
  requestLimit="number"
  pageOutput="true|false"
  traceMode="SortByTime|SortByCategory"
  localOnly="true|false"/>
```

The following describes each attribute:

- **enabled**: Indicates whether tracing is enabled. The default is `false`.

- **requestLimit**: The number of trace requests to store on the server. The default is 10.

- **pageOutput**: Indicates whether trace output is rendered at the end of each page. The default is `false`.

- **traceMode**: Specifies whether the trace information is displayed in the order it is processed or alphabetically by user-defined category. The default is `SortByTime`.

- **localOnly**: Indicates whether the trace viewer (`trace.axd`) is available only on the host Web server. The default is `true`.

As an example, the application configuration file in Listing 6-22 presents an ASP.NET configuration that uses a `<trace>` setting.

Listing 6-22. Using the `<trace>` Setting

```
<?xml version="1.0" encoding="utf-8" ?>
<configuration>
  <system.web>
    <trace
      enabled="true"
      requestLimit="20"
      pageOutput="true"
      traceMode="SortByCategory"
      localOnly="false"
    />
  </system.web>
</configuration>
```

Applying Settings to Certain Resources

The settings in an application configuration file located in a directory apply to all ASP.NET pages in that directory and pages in the subdirectories of that directory. Therefore, it is not possible to have two or more configuration files in a directory to apply specific settings to some pages and other settings to other pages in the same directory. To achieve this, you can use the <location> element on top of the <system.web> setting to define options that only apply to specific resources.

In addition to specifying a resource in the current directory, the <location> setting can also define settings for all resources in a subdirectory under the current directory. To use the <location> setting, you specify the resource name or the subdirectory name in the path attribute of this element.

For example, the configuration file in Listing 6-23 defines settings for the following resources:

- All resources in the current directory

- The Special.aspx file in the current directory

- All resources in the subdir1 subdirectory

- All resources in the subdir2 subdirectory

Listing 6-23. Using the <location> *Setting*

```
<?xml version="1.0" encoding="utf-8" ?>
<configuration>
  <system.web>
    <!-- configuration that applies to the current
         directory and all subdirectories under it -->
  </system.web>

  <location path="Special.aspx">
    <system.web>
      <!-- configuration that applies only
           to the Special.aspx
           file in the current directory -->
    </system.web>
  </location>
```

```
<location path="subdir1">
  <system.web>
    <!-- configuration that applies only to all pages
         under the subdir1 subdirectory -->
  </system.web>
</location>

<location path="subdir2">
  <system.web>
    <!-- configuration that applies only to all pages
         under the subdir2 subdirectory -->
  </system.web>
</location>

</configuration>
```

NOTE *You can add an* `allowOverride="false"` *attribute to a* `<location>` *setting to disallow the setting defined for a subdirectory to be overridden in the application configuration file in that subdirectory.*

Working with the Global.asax File

You can also configure the ASP.NET application using the `global.asax` file. This file must reside in the root directory of your application and will be compiled into a class that extends the `System.Web.HttpApplication` class. Any change to the `global.asax` file will automatically take effect at the next HTTP request for any resource in the application. There can only be one `global.asax` file per application.

NOTE *The* `global.asax` *file is the replacement for the* `global.asa` *file in classic ASP. Fortunately, ASP.NET supports backward compatibility for the ASP* `global.asa` *file. Therefore, you can copy your old* `global.asa` *file into a* `global.asax` *file when migrating to ASP.NET.*

Compared to the global.asa file in an ASP application, the global.asax file can be much more complex. Four elements can appear in a global.asax file:

- Application directives

- Code declaration blocks

- Server-side object tags

- Server-side include directives

Application Directives

Application directives for an ASP.NET application appear on the top of the global.asax file and specify settings for the page compiler. These directives are similar to the directives for an ASP.NET page, and there are three directives you can use in a global.asax file: @ Application, @ Import, and @ Assembly.

The @ Application Directive

The @ Application directive gives instructions to the ASP.NET compiler. The syntax for the @ Application directive is as follows:

```
<%@ Application [attribute="value"]+ %>
```

where the plus (+) sign indicates that there is one or more repetition of the content in the bracket.

The attribute for the @ Application directive is either Inherits or Description. The Inherits attribute specifies the name of the class to extend, and the Description attribute is assigned the description of the application. For instance, the following is an @ Application directive that instructs the compiler that the application class must extend the MyParentApp class:

```
<%@ Application Inherits="MyParentApp"
  Description="E-commerce app"%>
```

NOTE *The class you specify for the* Inherits *attribute must inherit the* System.Web.HttpApplication *class.*

The @ Import Directive

The @ Import directive imports a namespace into an application so that you can use the types in that namespace in your `global.asax` file. The @ Import directive has the following syntax:

```
<%@ Import Namespace="namespace" %>
```

For instance, the following imports the `System.Data` namespace into your `global.asax` file:

```
<%@ Import Namespace="System.Data" %>
```

NOTE *If you want to import more than one namespace, you use one @ Import directive for each namespace.*

The @ Assembly Directive

You use the @ Assembly directive to link an assembly to the application at parse-time. The syntax for the @ Assembly directive is as follows:

```
<%@ Assembly Name="assembly" %>
```

For example, the following @ Assembly directive links the `BuyDirect.dll` assembly:

```
<%@ Assembly Name="BuyDirect.dll" %>
```

Code Declaration Blocks

A code declaration block in the `global.asax` file contains application member variables, methods, and event handlers. Its syntax is as follows:

```
<script runat="server" language="language" src="externalfile">
  ' the code goes here
</script>
```

The `language` attribute is an optional attribute that specifies the language used in the current code declaration block and can be any .NET-compliant language. The `src` attribute is also optional and is assigned the name of the file that contains the code that is loaded and used in the current code declaration block.

For example, the following code declaration block contains the `Application_OnStart` event handler and a method called `WriteToFile`:

```
<script runat="server">
  Sub Application_OnStart()
    ' write code here
  End Sub

  Sub WriteToFile()
    ' write code here
  End Sub
</script>
```

Server-Side Object Tags

A server-side object tag declares and creates new application and session variables. Its syntax is one of the following:

```
<object id="id" runat="server"
  scope="application|session|pipeline" class="class name"/>
<object id="id" runat="server"
  scope="application|session|pipeline" progid="COM ProgID"/>
<object id="id" runat="server"
  scope="application|session|pipeline" classid="COM ClassID"/>
```

The attributes are as follows:

- **id**: A unique identifier for an object.

- **scope**: The scope at which the object is declared. "Pipeline" (the default) means that the object is available only to the `HttpPipeline` instance defined by the containing ASP.NET application file. "Application" causes the object to be stored in the `HttpApplicationState` object. "Session" causes the object to be stored in the user's session object.

- **class**: Identifies the type of the object that will be instantiated.

- **progid**: The COM component to be instantiated.

- **classid**: The COM component to be instantiated.

NOTE *The class attribute must not be assigned an interface or an abstract class.*

As an example, Listing 6-24 is a global.asax file that instantiates a Hashtable object and assigns it to an identifier called myHashtable. Some entries are added to the Hashtable object in the Application_OnStart event handler. Listing 6-25 is an ASP.NET page showing that the object is available in any page in that application.

Listing 6-24. The global.asax *File Containing a Server-Side Object Tag*

```
<object id="myHashtable" runat="server"
  scope="application" class="System.Collections.Hashtable"/>

<script runat="server">
  Sub Application_OnStart()
    myHashtable.Add("name1", "value1")
    myHashtable.Add("name2", "value2")
  End Sub

</script>
```

Listing 6-25. Using the Static Object in an ASP.NET Page

```
<html>
<head>
<title>Using Server-side Object Tag</title>
<script language="VB" runat="server">
Sub Page_Load(sender As Object, e As EventArgs)

  Dim sb As New StringBuilder(1024)
  Dim entry As DictionaryEntry
  For Each entry in myHashtable
    sb.Append(entry.Value).Append("<br>")
  Next
  message.Text = sb.ToString()

End Sub
</script>
</head>
```

```
<body>
<form runat="server">
  <asp:Label id="message" runat="server"/>
</form>
</body>
</html>
```

Server-Side Include Directives

You can use a server-side include directive to include the content of a file. Its syntax is either one of these two:

```
<!-- #include File="filename" -->
<!-- #include Virtual="filename" -->
```

The included file is processed before any dynamic content is executed.

Event Handlers

There are four events that can be present in a global.asa file: Application_OnStart, Application_OnEnd, Session_OnStart, and Session_OnEnd. These events are still available in the global.asax file. However, because a global.asax file is compiled into a class derived from the System.Web.HttpApplication class, all events in that class are also available.

You can view the complete list of events in the .NET Framework Software Development Kit (SDK) reference. Some useful events are BeginRequest, EndRequest, Error, PreSendRequestContent, PostRequestHandlerExecute, and so on. All of these events are self-explanatory.

As an example, the global.asax file in Listing 6-26 uses some events to write to a file when that event fires.

Listing 6-26. Utilizing the Event Handlers in a global.asax *File*

```
<%@ Import Namespace="System.IO" %>
<script runat="server" language="VB">
  Sub Application_OnStart()
    WriteToFile("Application_OnStart")
  End Sub
```

```
Sub Application_OnEnd()
  WriteToFile("Application_OnEnd")
End Sub

Sub Session_OnStart()
  WriteToFile("Session_OnStart")
End Sub

Sub Session_OnEnd()
  WriteToFile("Session_OnEnd")
End Sub

Sub Application_BeginRequest(source As Object, e As EventArgs)
  WriteToFile("Application_BeginRequest")
End Sub

Sub WriteToFile(s As String)
  Dim sw AS StreamWriter = File.AppendText("C:\log.txt")
  sw.WriteLine(s)
  sw.Close()
End Sub
</script>
```

Deploying ASP.NET Applications

Compared to classic ASP, application deployment in ASP.NET is extremely easy. There is no more DLL problem when deploying an ASP application. There is no more using regsvr32.exe program to register your COM component, and there are no more headaches with the versioning of your DLL files.

In fact, this section is short because ASP.NET application deployment is straightforward. Basically, you need to perform the following steps in the deployment stage:

1. Create a directory and all needed subdirectories for your application.

2. Use the Internet Information Services Manager to create an ASP.NET application, just as you would create an ASP application.

3. Copy all ASP.NET pages into the application directory and subdirectories.

4. Copy any .dll files containing user controls or other custom controls to the bin directory under the application directory.

5. Make sure the debugging mode is false—in other words, that the debug attribute of the compilation element under `<system.web>` is assigned the value `false`:

```
<system.web>
  <compilation debug="false"/>
</system.web>
```

By default, the machine configuration file disables debugging. However, if you enabled debugging in the application configuration file when developing the project, it is now time to turn it off. Enabling debugging will incur a memory/performance penalty.

6. Deploy assemblies into the Global Assembly Cache, if necessary.

The assemblies containing components you deploy into the `bin` directory of your application directory can only be used from that particular application. ASP.NET, however, allows you to deploy global components that can be used by all applications in that machine. To do this, you have to deploy the global component into the Global Assembly Cache. However, assemblies that are to be shared by multiple applications must be signed with strong names using standard public key cryptography.

Deploying assemblies into the Global Assembly Cache therefore involves the following steps:

1. Creating a public and private cryptographic key pair using the Strong Name tool (`sn.exe`)

2. Compiling the code file using the `/keyfile` option.

3. Installing the assembly using the Global Assembly Cache tool (`gacutil.exe`)

As an example of creating an assembly that is deployed into the Global Assembly Cache, consider a class named `MyFirstClass` in the `MyNamespace` namespace, as shown in Listing 6-27. This class is written to the `MyFirstClass.vb` file.

Listing 6-27. The MyFirstClass *Class (*MyFirstClass.vb)

```
NamespaceMyNamespace
  Public Class MyFirstClass
    Public Const MyConstant As String = "secret"
  End Class
End Namespace
```

Compiling this class and deploying it into the Global Assembly Cache requires the following steps:

1. Open a command prompt window.

2. Create a public key for it by typing:

    ```
    sn -k MyKeyPair.snk
    ```

    A file called MyKeyPair.snk will be created. For easier deployment, copy this file to the directory where MyFirstClass.vb is located.

3. Change directory to where MyFirstClass.vb is located.

4. Compile the MyFirstClass.vb file using the key pair by typing the following:

    ```
    vbc /t:library /out:MyAssembly.dll /keyfile:MyKeyPair.snk↵
    MyFirstClass.vb
    ```

5. Install the assembly into the global cache using the gacutil program. Type the following:

    ```
    gacutil -i MyAssembly.dll
    ```

6. Test the assembly by creating an ASP.NET file in Listing 6-28.

7. To uninstall MyAssembly.dll, type gacutil -u MyAssembly.

Listing 6-28. Testing the Assembly in the Global Assembly Cache

```
<%@ Import Namespace="MyNamespace" %>
<html>
<head>
<title>Deploying assembly into global cache</title>
<script language="VB" runat="server">
Sub Page_Load(sender As Object, e As EventArgs)
  Response.Write(MyFirstClass.MyConstant)
End Sub
</script>
</head>
</html>
```

Running the ASP.NET page in Listing 6-28 should display the word *secret* on the browser.

Securing ASP.NET Applications

In a Web application, there are normally resources that are restricted to certain users. For instance, in an online store application, there are usually two parts of the application. The first part, which allows people to select shopping items and purchase them, is available to anyone with Internet access. The second part, which consists of administration pages where store managers or store owners can manage the products, categories, orders and so on, is accessible to the manager or owner of that online store. In these cases, you need to protect those restricted resources so that they are only viewable by and accessible to the people who are supposed to see them. In other words, you need to secure your ASP.NET application.

Securing an ASP.NET application basically comes down to the following three techniques that can be applied separately or in conjunction with each other:

- **Authentication**: The process of verifying that a user is really who he claims to be. Authentication is the most common type of security method. An application checks a user's credential by prompting him to supply the correct username and password.

- **Authorization**: The technique to determine whether an authenticated user should be granted or denied access to a resource.

- **Impersonation**: This process enables the application to operate on behalf of an authenticated user or an anonymous user who is currently accessing the application. This is to say that the application impersonates the user. Therefore, access to certain resources will depend on whether the user has access to those resources.

Securing a Web application using one or more of the aforementioned techniques is a serious business that requires careful planning. However, ASP.NET provides features that make it easy to accomplish these, either through configuration files or by coding.

Before you start devising a plan to secure your ASP.NET application, you should first understand the ASP.NET infrastructure in relation to its surrounding subsystems: the .NET Framework and IIS. Because ASP.NET is part of the .NET Framework, ASP.NET applications can utilize the low-level security features of the .NET Framework. Also, because all traffic from the user to the application and vice versa must go through IIS, understanding how you can use IIS to secure your application is also critical. Figure 6-9 depicts the relationship of the ASP.NET applications, the .NET Framework, and IIS.

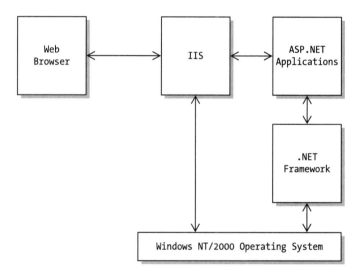

Figure 6-9. The ASP.NET infrastructure for security

One other important aspect to consider is that securing ASP.NET applications requires you to modify settings in the machine and application configuration files. Therefore, it is mandatory to understand how various configuration settings affect your applications, as discussed previously.

In this section you will find various methods for ASP.NET authentication, authorization, and impersonation. If the meanings of the three are not clear right now, do not worry. Each method comes with examples that should make them easier to comprehend.

Using Authentication

Put simply, authentication is the security technique that is commonly used. In authentication, a user must prove to the application that she is one of the users registered in the system's database or other data sources. A user must enter a username and password before she is granted access to a resource she requested. For authentication, ASP.NET works hand in hand with IIS using one of the following methods:

- Windows authentication

- Forms-based authentication

- Microsoft Passport authentication

To enable authentication, you use the `<authentication>` element in the configuration file:

```
<configuration>
  <system.web>
    <authentication mode="Windows|Forms|Passport|None">
    </authentication>
  </system.web.
</configuration>
```

where the `mode` attribute is assigned one of the authentication modes: Windows (the default), Forms, Passport, or None. Setting the mode attribute to None causes no authentication to be performed.

NOTE *The* <authentication> *element can only appear at the application configuration file on the root directory of the application, but not in the application configuration file on the subdirectories.*

The following sections explain each of these authentication methods.

Windows Authentication

Windows authentication is called so because it relies on the Windows operating system user accounts. Windows authentication is something with which any ASP programmer should be familiar. In this section I briefly describe this type of authentication to refresh your memory.

In Windows authentication, IIS conducts the authentication process using one of the following three methods:

- Basic authentication

- Digest authentication

- Integrated Windows authentication

The Basic authentication is the simplest of the three methods. This is widely used because it is an industry standard that works with most browsers. This is what happens when a user requests a resource from a restricted area on the server when the Basic authentication is enforced:

1. IIS sends an HTTP "401 Unauthorized" header.

2. The Web browser receives the message and displays a Login dialog box, prompting the user to enter her credentials.

3. The Web browser passes the credentials to IIS.

4. If the credentials are valid, IIS sends the requested page. Otherwise, it repeats step 1.

NOTE *In Basic authentication, the username and password sent to the server are not encrypted, making it possible for malicious hackers to steal them.*

Digest authentication is similar to Basic authentication. However, the username and password are encrypted before being sent over the network. This authentication method only works in Internet Explorer browsers.

With Integrated Windows authentication, which is also known as *NTLM* or *Kerberos*, authentication happens automatically in the background. When you use Integrated Windows authentication, the browser sends the encrypted version of the user's Windows username and password to the server. Not surprisingly, this authentication method only works if the client is using a Windows operating system and an Internet Explorer browser.

Basically, no coding is necessary to apply Windows authentication. All you need to do is change the security setting for your ASP.NET application directory or any subdirectory below your application directory. Securing a directory forces the user to log in before they can access any resource in that directory or a directory below the directory you secure.

To secure a directory, do the following:

1. From the Control Panel, select Administrative Tools and then double-click the Internet Service Manager icon.

2. Select a directory to secure, right-click it, and select Properties.

3. On the Properties dialog box for that directory, click the Directory Security tab.

4. In the Anonymous Access and Authentication Control panel, click the Edit button. You should see the Authentication Methods dialog box like the one in Figure 6-10.

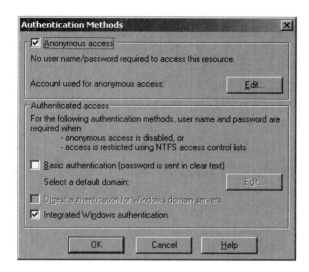

Figure 6-10. Securing a directory using Windows authentication

The Authentication Methods dialog box shows the Windows security setting for the selected directory. There are two panels in that dialog box: the Anonymous Access panel and the Authenticated Access panel. The Anonymous Access check box in the first panel specifies whether anonymous access is allowed to the selected directory. If this check box is checked, the options selected in the Authenticated Access panel are ignored. The Authenticated Access panel allows you to select one of the three Windows authentication methods: Basic, Digest, or Integrated Windows authentication.

By default, as shown in Figure 6-10, the Anonymous Access check box is selected, indicating that no username and password is required for a user to access the resources in that directory. To apply authentication, uncheck the Anonymous Access check box and check one of the options in the Authenticated Access panel or a combination of the three options. Clicking the OK button on the Authentication Methods dialog box and then clicking OK on the Properties dialog box for that directory applies the authentication.

When a directory is secured, every time a user tries to access a resource in that directory, IIS tries to authenticate that user. For example, if Basic authentication is used, the user will be prompted to enter a username and password in the dialog box shown in Figure 6-11.

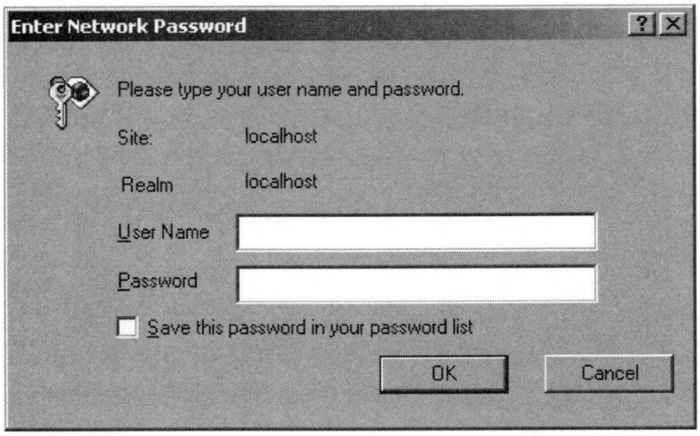

![Enter Network Password dialog box showing Site: localhost, Realm: localhost, with User Name and Password fields, a "Save this password in your password list" checkbox, and OK and Cancel buttons]

Figure 6-11. Basic authentication

Once a username and a password are typed into the login window, the credentials will be matched to those in the Windows operating system. The user is only required to enter the correct username and password once. Subsequent requests carry an authentication token so that the user will not be asked to enter their credentials anymore. If the user enters incorrect credentials three times, a HTTP 401.2 header will be sent to the browser, notifying the user that they are not authorized to view the requested page.

NOTE *When using Windows authentication, you do not need to edit the configuration file.*

Forms-Based Authentication

In this method of authentication, ASP.NET redirects HTTP requests that come without an authentication token to the specified login form. The user then must enter his credential (username and password) and submit the form. If the credential is authenticated by the application, the application adds an authentication cookie to the response and this cookie guarantees that the next request from the same user is not redirected to the login form again. On the other hand, the user will be denied access if he cannot supply the correct username and password.

In this method of authentication, IIS authentication is not used by the application. HTTP requests are passed to ASP.NET. Each request then follows the path depicted in Figure 6-12.

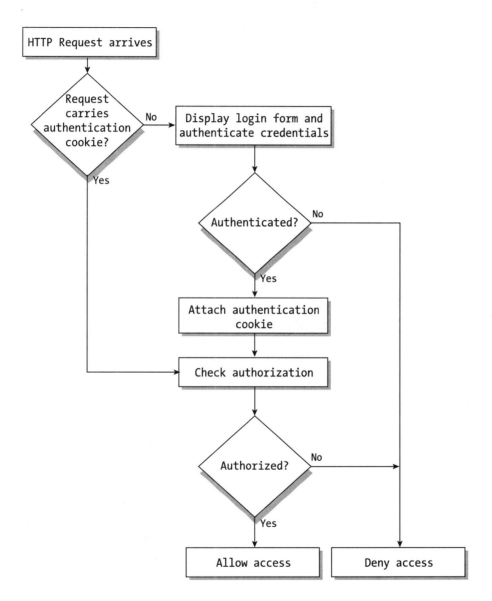

Figure 6-12. Forms-based authentication

Even though IIS authentication is not used by the application, the method requires that the IIS Anonymous Access setting be enabled. Otherwise, all requests that do not meet the criteria for the enabled method of IIS authentication will be rejected and will never reach the ASP.NET application.

Using forms-based authentication requires you to set the `<authentication>` and `<authorization>` elements of the configuration file. The `<authentication>` element has the following format:

```
<authentication mode="Windows|Forms|Passport|None">
  <forms name="name" loginUrl="url"
    protection="All|None|Encryption|Validation"
    timeout="30" path="/">
    <credentials passwordFormat="Clear|SHA1|MD5>
      <user name="username" password="password" />
    </credentials>
  </form>
  <passport redirectUrl="internal"/>
</authentication>
```

When using the forms-based authentication method, you will also be working with the `System.Web.Security.FormsAuthentication` class. The `System.Web.Security` namespace is implicitly imported, so you do not need to import it to use the `FormsAuthentication` class from your ASP.NET page.

The `FormsAuthentication` class has two properties:

- **FormsCookieName**: The name of the cookie configured for the current application

- **FormsCookiePath**: The path of the cookie configured for the current application

And, the following are some important methods of the `FormsAuthentication` class:

- **Authenticate**: Authenticates the supplied user credentials against the configured credential store. This method accepts the username and password.

- **GetAuthCookie**: Returns an authentication cookie for a given username. The return value type is `System.Web.HttpCookie`.

- **GetRedirectUrl**: Returns the original URL requested by the user before the user is redirected to the login form.

- **RedirectFromLoginPage**: Redirects the user to the original requested URL.

- **SignOut**: Logs the user out.

Looking at a Form-Based Authentication Example

As an illustration of how you can use the forms-based authentication method, the following is an example. There are two files you need to create or modify. The first file, shown in Listing 6-29, is the application configuration file (web.config) that should be placed in the root directory of this application.

The second file is a file called Login.aspx file, shown in Listing 6-30, which is the Login form that each user must submit to send their credentials to the server.

Listing 6-29. The web.config *File*

```
<?xml version="1.0" encoding="utf-8" ?>
<configuration>
  <system.web>
    <authentication mode="Forms">
      <forms name="formAuth" loginUrl="Login.aspx"/>
    </authentication>
    <authorization>
      <deny users="?"/>
    </authorization>
  </system.web>
</configuration>
```

The important point to note from the web.config file in Listing 6-29 is the <authorization> element, which basically says that anonymous users should be denied access:

```
<authorization>
  <deny users="?"/>
</authorization>
```

This will be explained further in the "Using Authorization" section.

The <authentication> element indicates that the authentication mode for this ASP.NET application is forms-based, and the login form for user login is the Login.aspx page:

```
<authentication mode="Forms">
  <forms name="formAuth" loginUrl="Login.aspx"/>
</authentication>
```

Listing 6-30. The Login.aspx *File*

```
<html>
<head>
<title>Login Form</title>
<script language="VB" runat="server">
Sub Login(sender As Object, e As EventArgs)
  If userName.Text.Equals("mfranks") And _
    password.Text.Equals("theLadyWantsToKnow") Then

    FormsAuthentication.RedirectFromLoginPage( _
      userName.Text, False)

  Else
    message.Text = "Login failed. Please try again."
  End If
End Sub

</script>
</head>
<body>
<form runat="server">
<asp:Label runat="server"
  id="message"
/>

<hr>

<h2>Login Form</h2>
<table>
<tr>
  <td>Username:</td>
  <td><asp:TextBox runat="server" id="userName"/></td>
</tr>
<tr>
  <td>Password:</td>
  <td>
    <asp:TextBox runat="server"
      TextMode="password" id="password"
    />
  </td>
</tr>
<tr>
```

```
  <td align="right" colspan="2">
    <asp:Button runat="server"
      Text="Login"
      OnClick="Login"
    />
  </td>
</tr>
</table>
</form>
</body>
</html>
```

The Login.aspx file is a normal Web form with a username TextBox control, a password TextBox control, and a Button control. This button is connected to the Login event handler.

The Login event handler checks the value entered into the userName and the password TextBox controls. If the userName and password are equal to the specified username and password, the FormsAuthentication class's RedirectFromLoginpage method is called, passing the username and False. In effect, this redirects the user to the original page he requested and sets the authentication cookie to the response:

```
FormsAuthentication.RedirectFromLoginPage( _
  userName.Text, False)
```

The Login form in Listing 6-30 looks similar to Figure 6-13. Note that the original URL is added as the value of the ReturnUrl parameter in the query string.

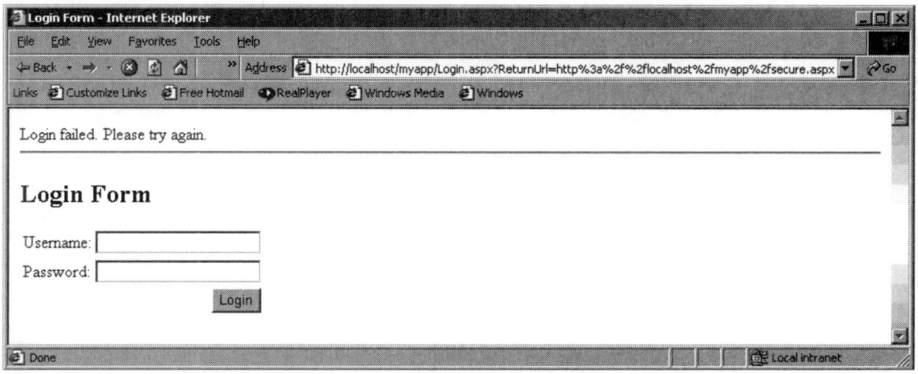

Figure 6-13. The Login form

Putting the Credentials in the Configuration File

The previous example showed how you can use forms-based authentication methods for one user whose username and password is hard-coded in the Login event handler. Although this is an easy-to-write page, sometimes it is not practical to hard-code the user's credentials. Also, sometimes you want more than one user to be able to log in to the application.

ASP.NET allows you to specify multiple users that should have access to your application in the application configuration file. Using this method, you do not need to hard-code the user credentials in your code.

The following example is the modification of the previous example. Listing 6-31 shows the web.config file, and Listing 6-32 shows the login page.

Listing 6-31. The web.config *File*

```
<?xml version="1.0" encoding="utf-8" ?>
<configuration>
  <system.web>
    <authentication mode="Forms">
      <forms name="formAuth" loginUrl="Login.aspx" >
        <credentials passwordFormat="Clear">
          <user name="mfranks" password="theLadyWantsToKnow"/>
          <user name="ken" password="vancouver"/>
        </credentials>
      </forms>
    </authentication>
    <authorization>
      <deny users="?"/>
    </authorization>
  </system.web>
</configuration>
```

The difference between the web.config file in Listing 6-29 and the one in Listing 6-31 is that in the latter the <forms> element contains the <credentials> element. The <credentials> element is where you put all users' credentials. Theoretically, you can write as many <user> elements as you want. In the application configuration file in Listing 6-31, there are two users:

```
<credentials passwordFormat="Clear">
  <user name="mfranks" password="theLadyWantsToKnow"/>
  <user name="ken" password="vancouver"/>
</credentials>
```

NOTE *Assigning* "Clear" *to the* passwordFormat *attribute of the* <credentials> *element causes the credentials to be sent to the server without using any encryption. Other possible values for this attribute are MD5 or SHA1, which make the credentials encrypted using the MD5 and SHA1 encryption algorithms (respectively) before the credentials are sent to the server.*

Listing 6-32. The Login.aspx *File*

```
<html>
<head>
<title>Login Form</title>
<script language="VB" runat="server">
Sub Login(sender As Object, e As EventArgs)
  If FormsAuthentication.Authenticate( _
    userName.Text, password.Text) Then

    FormsAuthentication.RedirectFromLoginPage( _
      userName.Text, False)
  Else
    message.Text = "Login failed. Please try again."
  End If
End Sub

</script>
</head>
<body>
<form runat="server">
<asp:Label runat="server"
  id="message"
/>

<hr>

<h2>Login Form</h2>
<table>
<tr>
  <td>Username:</td>
  <td><asp:TextBox runat="server" id="userName"/></td>
</tr>
<tr>
```

```
    <td>Password:</td>
    <td>
      <asp:TextBox runat="server"
        TextMode="password" id="password"
      />
    </td>
  </tr>
  <tr>
    <td align="right" colspan="2">
      <asp:Button runat="server"
        Text="Login"
        OnClick="Login"
      />
    </td>
  </tr>
  </table>
  </form>
  </body>
</html>
```

The login page in Listing 6-32 is different from the one in Listing 6-30 in that the username and password are not hard-coded. Instead, you call the `Authenticate` method of the `FormsAuthentication` class to authenticate the username and password supplied by the user:

```
If FormsAuthentication.Authenticate( _
  userName.Text, password.Text) Then
```

Passport Authentication

Passport authentication is Microsoft's initiative that offers a centralized authentication service that is basically a forms-based authentication service (see www.passport.com). To provide Passport authentication in a Web site, the owner must download, install, and configure the Passport SDK from www.passport.com/business. This does not come free, though. You must pay a fee to obtain the SDK.

To use Passport authentication in your ASP.NET application, you must specify "Passport" as the value for the mode attribute of the `<authentication>` element:

```
<authentication mode="Passport">
</authentication>
```

The following illustrates how Passport authentication works:

1. A client requests a protected resource from your Web site.

2. For the first request, the request does not contain a valid Passport ticket, so your Web server redirects the client to the Passport Logon service. The redirection URL contains the original requested resource, just like the one in forms-based authentication.

3. The user logs in to the Login form presented by the Passport logon server. The username and password are submitted using Secure Sockets Layer (SSL).

4. The logon server authenticates the user and, if the authentication is successful, redirects the user to the original URL in your Web site with the authentication ticket encrypted in the query string.

5. Your Web server detects the presence of the authentication ticket this time and grants access to the requested resource.

From the user's point of view, it can be beneficial because each user only has one username and password to access multiple Web sites.

Using Authorization

Authorization means checking if an authenticated user has access to a resource. Imagine an office where each employee has a card to go into the office building as well as to enter each room in the office. To enter the building, an employee must swipe their card into a machine. The machine authenticates them. However, once in the building, not all employees have access to all rooms. For example, a deliveryman may not have access to the boardroom. When he swipes his card to enter the room, he will be rejected access to it. The director, on the other hand, has access to the boardroom, and she can use her card to open the boardroom door. It is said that the director is authorized to enter the boardroom but not the deliveryman.

Similarly, authenticated users may have different access to different resources in a Web application. ASP.NET allows you to determine who can access which resource by editing the configuration file for an application.

There are two types of authorization in ASP.NET:

- **File authorization**: This type of authorization relies on the Windows operating system's Access Control List (ACL) to decide whether a user should have access to a resource. To view the ACL of a file or directory, right-click a file or directory in Windows Explorer, select Properties, and click the Security tab. You should see a dialog box like the one in Figure 6-14. File authorization is active when you use Windows authentication (see the section "Using Impersonation").

- **URL authorization**: This type of authorization maps user identities to the directories specified in the requested URLs. To establish the URL authorization for a directory, you create an application configuration file that contains an <authorization> element in that directory. Thanks to the inheritance nature of a configuration file as explained in the previous section, the <authorization> element specified in a directory applies to all its subdirectories. However, you can apply different URL authorizations by placing a different application configuration file in a subdirectory.

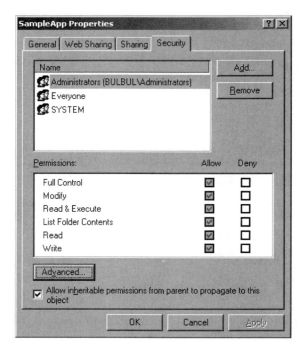

Figure 6-14. A file's/directory's ACL

You configure URL authorization in ASP.NET using the `<authorization>` setting under the `<system.web>` element. The syntax for the `<authorization>` setting is as follows:

```
<authorization>
  <allow users="comma-separated list of users"
    roles="comma-separated list of roles"
    verbs="comma-separated list of verbs" />

  <deny users="comma-separated list of users"
    roles="comma-separated list of roles"
    verbs="comma-separated list of verbs" />
</authorization>
```

The `<authorization>` element can have two subelements, `<allow>` and `<deny>`, both of which are optional. The `<allow>` element specifies the users/roles allowed access to a resource. The `<deny>` element specifies the users/roles that must be revoked access to a resource.

Both `<allow>` and `<deny>` elements can contain three optional attributes: `users`, `roles`, and `verbs`.

> **NOTE** *For more information on role-based security, see*
> `http://msdn.microsoft.com/library/default.asp?url=/library/en-us/`
> `cpguidnt/html/cpconcodeaccesssecurity.asp`.

In addition to names, the `users` attribute can accept two special identities:

- **?**: Represents the anonymous identity

- *****: Represents all identities

The section "Using Authentication" demonstrated how to use the ? character. For instance, the following `<authorization>` element instructs ASP.NET to reject the anonymous user access to all resources in the directory where the application configuration that contains the `<authorization>` element resides:

```
<authorization>
  <deny users="?"/>
</authorization>
```

The following `<authorization>` element allows ken and denies rob:

```
<authorization>
  <allow users="ken"/>
  <deny users="rob"/>
</authorization>
```

The following code snippet denies all users except ken:

```
<authorization>
  <allow users="ken"/>
  <deny users="*"/>
</authorization>
```

You can add the verbs attribute to the `<allow>` and `<deny>` elements to specify the HTTP methods (such as POST, GET, HEAD) that apply to that element. For instance, the following `<authorization>` element allows all users to request a resource using the GET method, but not the POST method.

```
<authorization>
  <allow verb="GET" users="*"/>
  <deny verb="POST" users="*"/>
</authorization>
```

The following code snippet allows all users to request a resource using the GET method, but only ken can use the POST method:

```
<authorization>
  <allow verb="GET" users="*"/>
  <allow verb="POST" users="ken"/>
  <deny verb="POST" users="*"/>
</authorization>
```

Using Impersonation

Impersonation enables the application to operate on behalf of an authenticated user or an anonymous user who is currently accessing the application. Therefore, access to certain resources depends on whether the user has access to those resources. By default, impersonation is disabled for backward compatibility with classic ASP and is used only to avoid dealing with authentication and authorization issues in the ASP.NET application code.

With impersonation, you rely on IIS to authenticate the user and continue with one of the following:

- If authentication was successful, IIS passes an authenticated token to the ASP.NET application. The ASP.NET application then impersonates this user.

- If authentication failed, IIS passes an unauthenticated token to the ASP.NET application. The ASP.NET application will then impersonate the anonymous user, which is IUSR_*MachineName*.

The ASP.NET application then impersonates the user and relies on the settings in the Windows operating system ACL to either allow or revoke the user access to the requested resource.

Impersonation can be a convenient way of securing your ASP.NET applications if you already have an extensive list of Windows accounts.

To use impersonation, you use the `<identity>` element under the `<system.web>` element in the configuration file of the ASP.NET application you would like to secure. The syntax for this element is as follows:

```
<identity
  impersonate="true|false"
  userName="username"
  password="password"/>
```

To enable impersonation, set the impersonate attribute to `true`. The `userName` and `password` attributes are optional.

As an example, the following application configuration file will impersonate the user Administrator:

```
<?xml version="1.0" encoding="utf-8" ?>
<configuration>
  <system.web>
    <identity
      impersonate="true"
      userName="Administrator"
      password="popsicleToes"
    />
  </system.web>
</configuration>
```

Implementing the Project

The online store application in this chapter consists of two parts. The first part is available for everyone on the Internet and allows users to do the following things:

- Search for certain products based on product names or descriptions

- Browse the list of products by category

- View a product's details

- Put a product into the shopping cart

- View and edit the shopping cart

- Check out and place an order

The second part of the application is the administration section that is password-protected and restricted to the administrator of the application, normally the store manager. This part allows the administrator to add, modify, and delete categories and products.

This section has the following subsections:

- **The database**: Discusses the data structure and the tables used in this application as well as the script to create the database

- **The directory structure**: Shows the application directory structure as well as explains all the files used in the application

- **The page design**: Explains the common design used in every page

- **The ShoppingItem class**: Discusses the class that represents a shopping item

- **Accessing the database**: Discusses the DbObject class, the class that encapsulates the functionality to access and manipulate data in the database regardless the database server used

- **The user controls**: Covers the three user controls used in the application

- **The ASP.NET pages**: Discusses all the ASP.NET pages used in the first part of the application

- **The Admin section**: Explains all the pages and code-behind files used by the administration section

The Database

A relational database stores data in the application. You can use a database server from any vendor for which a data provider is available. This includes Microsoft SQL Server, Oracle, Sybase, Access, and so on. The downloadable file accompanying this chapter contains an Access database and a script file to generate the database tables and populate them with data. You can use the Access database to quickly test the application. However, for deployment, you are encouraged to use an SQL Server or another scalable and powerful database engine. For this, you need to run the script file to create the database and tables. The script also populates some of the tables with data so that you can work with it instantly. You can find both the Access database file and the script file in the project's db directory.

There are four tables used: Categories, Products, Orders, and OrderDetails. The following sections give the structure of each table.

The Categories Table

The Categories table stores product categories (see Table 6-4).

Table 6-4. The Categories Table

COLUMN NAME	DATA TYPE
CategoryId	AutoNumber
Category	Text

The Products Table

The Products table stores the details of every product (see Table 6-5). Note that the table has a CategoryId column used to categorize the products.

Table 6-5. The Products Table

COLUMN NAME	DATA TYPE
ProductId	AutoNumber
CategoryId	Number
Name	Text
Description	Text
Price	Number

The Orders Table

The Orders table holds order information, including delivery addresses, credit card details, and contact names (see Table 6-6). There is a unique identifier for each order to link all shopping items in that order. These shopping items are stored in the OrderDetails table.

Table 6-6. The Orders Table

COLUMN NAME	DATA TYPE
OrderId	Number
ContactName	Text
DeliveryAddress	Text
CCName	Text
CCNumber	Text
CCExpiryDate	Text

The OrderDetails Table

The OrderDetails table stores all shopping items for each order (see Table 6-7).

Table 6-7. The OrderDetails Table

COLUMN NAME	DATA TYPE
Id	AutoNumber
OrderId	Number
ProductId	Number
Quantity	Number
Price	Number

Directory Structure

Figure 6-15 shows the directory structure. Note that the root, App, represents the application directory.

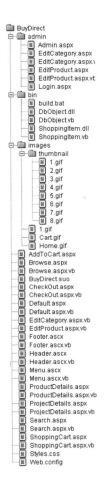

Figure 6-15. The directory structure

The following are the types of files in the directory structure:

- The .aspx files under the application directory are the ASP.NET pages for the first part of the application. The .vb files are code-behind files.

- The Styles.css file in the application directory is the Cascading Style Sheets (CSS) file that determines the look of all ASP.NET pages in the application directory.

- The web.config file is the application configuration file.

- The four .aspx files under App/Admin are the ASP.NET pages for the Admin section of the application.

- The `bin` directory contains supporting classes (in DLL files) for the first part of the application.

- The `images` directory contains the image files used by the first part of the application.

- The `images/thumbnail` directory contains small images for the products.

Page Design

For consistency in the look and feel of the application, each ASP.NET page uses the same design. There is a header on top of each page and a menu on the left, as shown in Figure 6-16.

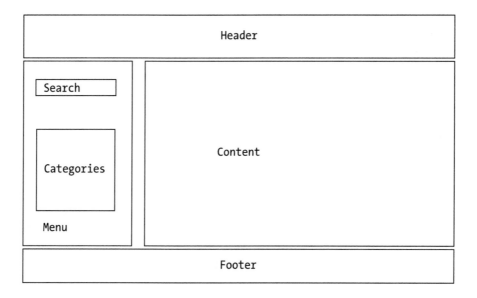

Figure 6-16. The page design

You achieve this look using the following HTML page template:

```
<html>
<head>
<title><!-- The title --></title>
</head>
<body>
```

```
<table>
<tr>
  <td colspan="2">
    <!-- The header -->
  </td>
</tr>
<tr>
  <td valign="top">
    <!-- The menu -->
  </td>
  <td valign="top">
    <!-- Content -->
  </td>
</tr>
<tr>
  <td colspan="2">
    <!-- The footer -->
  </td>
</tr>
</table>
</body>
</html>
```

NOTE *A cascading style sheets file (*style.css*) residing in the application directory, gives each ASP.NET page its look. It is linked from each page using the following tag:*
`<link rel=stylesheet type="text/css" href=style.css>`.

The ShoppingItem Class

The small ShoppingItem class represents a shopping item. You can find it in the ShoppingItem.vb file in the bin directory (see Listing 6-33).

Listing 6-33. The ShoppingItem *Class*

```
Namespace BuyDirect
Public Class ShoppingItem
  Public ProductId As String
```

```
    Public Name As String ' the name of the product
    Public Description As String
    Public Price As String
    Public Quantity As String
End Class
End Namespace
```

A shopping item has a product identifier, a product name, a description, a price, and a quantity.

Accessing the Database

As discussed in the earlier "Understanding ADO.NET" section, .NET applications can access a relational database and manipulate data using ADO.NET. As shown, ADO.NET makes these tasks easy to achieve. However, note that there are various database servers on the market, including Oracle, Microsoft SQL Server, Sybase SQL Server, IBM DB2, and so on.

When developing an application that uses a database, sometimes you want to make sure your application is flexible enough to access different databases. This is because you cannot guarantee your client will use a certain brand. There are cases where one client has invested in a certain database and another client has bought a different database. Wanting to cater to these clients without having to create many different variants of your applications requires you to use a certain strategy.

This ASP.NET application is designed to use many different types of databases without requiring too many changes. In fact, there is only one class, DbObject, which handles all database connections and manipulations. The DbObject is an abstract class that defines all the abstract methods that will be used by the ASP.NET application. You support a certain database server by creating a subclass of DbObject that provides implementation of the abstract methods. Adding a support for a new database server does not change the application or affect the support for the existing databases.

DbObject acts as an interface between the ASP.NET application and the implementation for connecting to and manipulating the database. It has a shared method, GetDbObject, which returns an instance of the correct subclass. At the moment, two subclasses are provided: AccessDbObject and MsSqlDbObject. Figure 6-17 shows the class diagram.

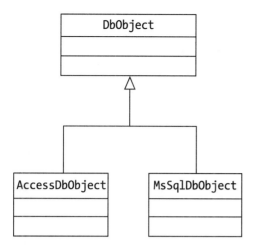

Figure 6-17. The DbObject *class and its subclasses*

NOTE *You can find the* DbObject *class and its subclasses in the* DbObject.vb *file under the* bin *directory.*

Therefore, if the application uses an Access database, the DbObject class's GetDbObject method returns an instance of AccessDbObject. If Microsoft SQL Server 7 or later is used, the same method returns an instance of MsSqlDbObject. The information about the database server used is stored as an application setting in the web.config file. If the key db has a value of MsSQL, MS SQL Server 7 or later is used. If the key db is Access, a Microsoft Access database is used. Another key, connectionString, defines the connection string. The following is the fragment of the web.config file that holds the database information:

```
<appSettings>
  <add key="db" value="MsSQL"/>
  <add key="connectionString"
    value="Integrated Security=False;Data Source=localhost;↵
Initial Catalog=BuyDirect;User ID=sa;Password=password"/>
</appSettings>
```

The db value is read from the configuration file when the application starts:

```
Private Shared db As String = ConfigurationSettings.AppSettings("db")
```

And the connectionString value is read when an instance of DbObject is created:

```
Protected connectionString As String = _
  ConfigurationSettings.AppSettings("connectionString")
```

Note that the connectionString variable has a Protected access modifier so that it is accessible from subclasses.

The GetDbObject method is as follows:

```
Public Shared Function GetDbObject() As DbObject
  If db.ToUpper().Equals("ACCESS") Then
    Return (New AccessDbObject())
  ElseIf db.ToUpper().Equals("MSSQL") Then
    Return (New MsSqlDbObject())
  End If
End Function
```

If you want to add support for a different database, you just add another ElseIf statement to the If block in the GetDbObject method.

The DbObject class also has a utility method called FixFieldValue that accepts a string and adds a single quote character for each occurrence of single quote character in the given string. This method is used to "fix" a value used as part of an SQL statement that may contain a single quote character. The FixFieldValue method is as follows:

```
Public Shared Function FixFieldValue(ByVal value As String) As String
  If value Is Nothing Then
    Return Nothing
  Else
    Return value.Replace("'", "''")
  End If
End Function
```

The abstract methods that must be implemented in subclasses are as follows:

```
Public MustOverride Function GetCategories() As DataSet
```

```
Public MustOverride Function GetSearchResult(ByVal searchKey As String) As DataSet
```

```
Public MustOverride Function GetBrowseResult(ByVal categoryId As String) As DataSet

' pass a product id, return a ShoppingItem object populated
' with the product details
Public MustOverride Function GetShoppingItem(ByVal productId As String) As _
  ShoppingItem

Public MustOverride Function ProcessPurchase( _
  ByVal contactName As String, _
  ByVal deliveryAddress As String, _
  ByVal ccName As String, _
  ByVal ccNumber As String, _
  ByVal ccExpiryDate As String, _
  ByVal cart As HashTable) As Boolean

Public MustOverride Function GetAllProducts() As DataSet

Public MustOverride Function GetAllCategoriesAsString() As String

Public MustOverride Sub InsertProduct( _
  ByVal categoryId As String, _
  ByVal newProductName As String, _
  ByVal newProductDescription As String, _
  ByVal newProductPrice As String)

Public MustOverride Sub EditProduct( _
  ByVal productId As String, _
  ByVal productName As String, _
  ByVal productDescription As String, _
  ByVal productPrice As String)

Public MustOverride Sub DeleteProduct(ByVal productId As String)

Public MustOverride Function GetAllCategories() As DataSet

Public MustOverride Sub InsertCategory(ByVal category As String)

Public MustOverride Sub EditCategory( _
  ByVal categoryId As String, _
  ByVal category As String)

Public MustOverride Sub DeleteCategory(ByVal categoryId As String)
```

User Controls

Three user controls are used: the Header, the Footer, and Menu user controls. These user controls are given in Listings 6-34, 6-35, and 6-36, respectively. The header is saved as the Header.ascx file, the footer as the Footer.ascx file, and the menu as the Menu.ascx file. These files reside in the application directory.

Listing 6-34. The Header *User Control*

```
<%@ Control Language="VB" %>
<table border="0" width="100%" cellpadding="5" cellspacing="0" class="Header">
<tr>
  <td align="left">
    <div class="HeaderText1">Buy Direct</div>
    <br>
    <div class="HeaderText2">Lowest prices today!!!</div>
  </td>
  <td align="right">
    <a href=Default.aspx><img border="0" src="images/Home.gif" width="30"
      alt="Home"></a> <a href=ShoppingCart.aspx>↵
<img border="0" src="images/Cart.gif"
      alt="Shopping Cart">
    </a>
  </td>
</table>
```

The Header user control cannot be simpler. It consists of a table with two cells, one displaying some text and the other containing the home and shopping cart image files.

Listing 6-35. The Footer *User Control*

```
<%@ Control Language="VB" %>
<center>
<div class="Footer">&copy;2003 Buy Direct</div>
</center>
```

The footer simply contains a copyright logo.

Listing 6-36. The Menu *User Control*

```
<%@ Control Language="vb" AutoEventWireup="false" Src="Menu.ascx.vb"
  Inherits="BuyDirect.Menu" %>
<%@ OutputCache Duration="86400" VaryByParam="None" %>

<!-- the main table containing two other tables: Search table and Browse table -->
<table border="0" cellpadding="0" cellspacing="0"
  width="<%=ConfigurationSettings.AppSettings("menuWidth")%>">
<tr>
<td>

<!-- the Search table -->
<table cellspacing="0" cellpadding="1"
  width="100%"
  border="0" class="OuterTable"
>
<tr>
  <td>
    <table cellspacing="0" cellpadding="5"
      width="100%" border="0"
      class="InnerTable">
    <tr>
      <td class="MenuHeader">Search</td>
    </tr>
    <tr valign="middle">
      <td rowspan="2">
        <form method="post" action="Search.aspx">
        <input type="text" name="searchKey" size="13">
        <input type="submit" value="Go">
        </form>
      </td>
    </tr>
    </table>
  </td>
</tr>
</table>

</td>
</tr>

<!-- space between the Search table and Browse table -->
<tr>
```

```
<td height="7"></td>
</tr>

<!-- the Browse table -->
<tr>
<td>
<table cellspacing="0" cellpadding="1"
  width="100%" border="0"
  class="OuterTable">
<tr>
  <td>

    <table cellspacing="0" cellpadding="5" width="100%"↩
border="0" class="InnerTable">
    <tr>
      <td class="MenuHeader">Browse</td>
    </tr>
    <tr valign="top">
      <td>
        <asp:DataList id="categoryList" runat="server"
          cellpadding="3" cellspacing="0" width="145"
          SelectedItemStyle-BackColor="dimgray"
          EnableViewState="false">
        <ItemTemplate>
          <asp:HyperLink runat="server"
            Font-Name="Verdana"
            CssClass="MenuItem"
            Text='<%# DataBinder.Eval(Container.DataItem, "Category") %>'
            NavigateUrl='<%# "Browse.aspx?CategoryId=" & _
            DataBinder.Eval(Container.DataItem, "CategoryID") %>'
          />
        </ItemTemplate>
        </asp:DataList>
      </td>
    </tr>
    </table>
  </td>
</tr>
</table>

</td>
</tr>
</table>
```

Note that the Menu.ascx file uses a code-behind file called Menu.ascx.vb. This file contains the Menu class that extends the System.Web.UI.UserControl class. Listing 6-37 gives the Menu class.

Listing 6-37. The Menu *Class*

```
Imports System
Imports System.Web
Imports System.Web.UI
Imports System.Web.UI.WebControls
Imports System.Data

Namespace BuyDirect
Public Class Menu : Inherits UserControl

Public CategoryList As DataList

Sub Page_Load(ByVal sender As Object, ByVal e As EventArgs)

  Dim dbo As DbObject = DbObject.GetDbObject()
  Dim ds As DataSet = dbo.GetCategories
  categoryList.DataSource = ds.Tables("Categories").DefaultView
  categoryList.DataBind()

End Sub

End Class
End Namespace
```

The Menu user control pulls all records from the Categories table and binds the data to a DataList control. The control's <ItemTemplate> contains a Hyperlink control that displays a clickable link with the following navigate URL:

```
Browse.aspx?CategoryID=categoryID
```

where *categoryID* comes from the CategoryID column of the Categories table.

The text for a hyperlink is the name of the category itself, coming from the Category column in the Categories table.

The ASP.NET Pages

Now it is time to present all the ASP.NET pages in the first part of the application. There are seven pages in total in the first part of the application, but one (AddToCart.aspx) does not have a user interface.

Each page links to a code-behind file located in the application directory having the same name plus the .vb extension. The following sections discuss the ASP.NET pages. To save space, none of the pages' code is printed here.

The Default Page

The Default page is the main page the user will see when they first visit the Web site (see Figure 6-18). In essence, it embeds the Header, Footer, and Menu user controls and displays a welcome message.

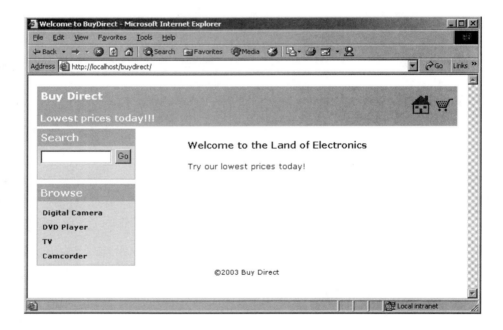

Figure 6-18. The Default page

From this page, the user can use the search form in the Menu user control to search for a product or browse the category by clicking one of the categories on the menu. If the user uses the search form, the search will be handled by the Search page. Clicking a category will bring them to the Browse page.

The Search Page

The Search page handles user searches for a product and supports automatic paging, as discussed in the section "Data Binding" earlier in this chapter (see Figure 6-19). This page can receive requests from either the Search form on the menu in other pages or from the Search page itself when the user moves to another page of records.

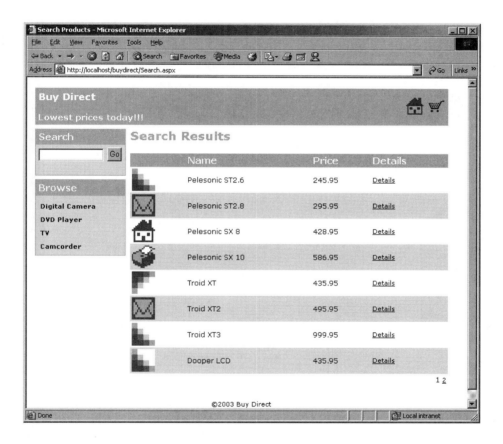

Figure 6-19. The Search page

Also, requests from the Search form must be checked to determine whether or not the requests contain a keyword. A search is only performed when a keyword exists. Otherwise, the user could click the Go button in the Search form without typing in any keyword and make the Search page display everything in the Products table.

Therefore, three types of cases need to be handled separately:

- When the request comes from the Search form and carries a keyword

- When the request comes from the Search form without a keyword

- When the request comes from the SearchResults page itself as a result of the user navigating to another page

To process each type of request accordingly, the Page_Load event handler contains the following code snippet:

```
Sub Page_Load(sender As Object, e As EventArgs)
  If Not IsPostBack Then
    searchKey = Request.Params("searchKey")
    If Not searchKey Is Nothing Then
      ' request coming from the Search form
      If searchKey.Trim().Equals("") Then
        message.Text = "Please enter a search key."
        SearchResultGrid.DataSource = Nothing
      Else
        ' search key is not empty
        ViewState.Add("searchKey", searchKey)
        BindGrid()
      End If
    Else
      ' request did not come from the Search form
      Server.Transfer("Default.aspx")
    End If
  End If
End Sub
```

The Page_Load event handler first retrieves the search key using the Request object's Params property, passing the string searchKey. If it finds the searchKey parameter in the Request object, the request must come from the Search form. In this case, it tests the value of the search key. If the search key is empty, then it displays the message *Please enter a search key* and assigns nothing to the DataSource property of the DataGrid.

If the search key is not empty, the Page_Load handler does the following:

1. It saves the search key in the ViewState object so that different pages in the DataGrid can be displayed correctly.

2. It calls the `BindGrid` subroutine to prepare the data display in the `DataGrid`. You will examine the `BindGrid` subroutine shortly.

When the user navigates to a different page, the `DataGrid` control's `PageIndexChanged` event triggers. As a result, its event handler, `SearchResultDataGrid_PageIndexChanged`, executes:

```
Sub SearchResultGrid_PageIndexChanged(sender As Object, _
  e As DataGridPageChangedEventArgs)
  searchKey = ViewState("searchKey").ToString()
  SearchResultGrid.CurrentPageIndex = e.NewPageIndex
  BindGrid()
End Sub
```

The `SearchResultGrid_PageIndexChanged` event handler first retrieves the search key from the `StateBag` and assigns the value to the `searchKey` variable. Then it assigns the value of the `DataGrid` control's `CurrentPageIndex` property with the `NewPageIndex` property of the `DataGridPageChangedEventArgs` object and calls the `BindGrid` method.

The `BindGrid` method is responsible for binding the data to the `DataGrid` control:

```
Sub BindGrid()
  Dim dbo As DbObject = DbObject.GetDbObject()
  Dim ds As DataSet = dbo.GetSearchResult(searchKey)
  SearchResultGrid.DataSource = ds.Tables("Products").DefaultView
  SearchResultGrid.DataBind()
End Sub
```

The `BindGrid` method does the following:

1. It obtains a `DbObject` object.

2. It calls the `DbObject` class's `GetSearchResult` method to retrieve all the records that match the search key and packages them in a `DataSet` object.

3. It assigns the `Products` table in the `DataSet` object to the `DataSource` property of the `DataGrid` control.

4. It calls the `DataGrid` control's `DataBind` method to bind the data.

If you look at the SQL statement used in the GetSearchResult methods in both the AccessDbObject class and the MsSqlDbObject class method, you will find that instead of a simple SELECT statement, the code uses a much more complicated one. In the AccessDbObject class, the following code composes the SQL statement in the GetSearchResult method:

```
sql.Append("SELECT '<img src=images/thumbnail/' & ProductId")
sql.Append(" & '.gif width=40 height=40>' As [ ],")
sql.Append(" Name, Price,")
sql.Append(" '<a href=ProductDetails.aspx?productId=' " & _
  "& ProductId & '>Details</a>' As Details")
sql.Append(" FROM Products")
sql.Append(" WHERE Name LIKE '%" & searchKey & "%'")
sql.Append(" OR Description LIKE '%" & searchKey & "%'")
```

And the following code composes the SQL statement in the same method in the MsSqlDbObject class:

```
sql.Append("SELECT '<img src=images/thumbnail/' + CONVERT(varchar(5), ProductId)")
sql.Append(" + '.gif width=40 height=40>' As [ ],")
sql.Append(" Name, Price,")
sql.Append(" '<a href=ProductDetails.aspx?productId=' " & _
  "+ CONVERT(varchar(5), ProductId) + '>Details</a>' As Details")
sql.Append(" FROM Products")
sql.Append(" WHERE Name LIKE '%" & searchKey & "%'")
sql.Append(" OR Description LIKE '%" & searchKey & "%'")
```

This has to do with the fact that you use automatic column generation of the DataGrid by setting its AutoGenerateColumns property to True. In other words, by enabling the automatic column generation in a DataGrid control, you do not need to specify each individual column for the DataGrid manually. In fact, you do not use the DataGrid control's Columns property at all. With automatic column generation, a DataGrid control displays the headers and rows of a bound data source as they are.

Even though automatic column generation simplifies the user interface of the DataGrid control, this also means that the source table must contain the exact headers and data. In most cases, this is fine. However, in your case, because you want to include a thumbnail image for each product, you have to tweak the SQL statement to produce a column that contains a hyperlink to the image.

The Browse Page

The Browse page is invoked when the user clicks one of the categories on the menu (see Figure 6-20). The way this page works is similar to the Search page. Instead of a search key, the Browse page receives a category identifier. Therefore, you save a category identifier in the StateBag, not a search key.

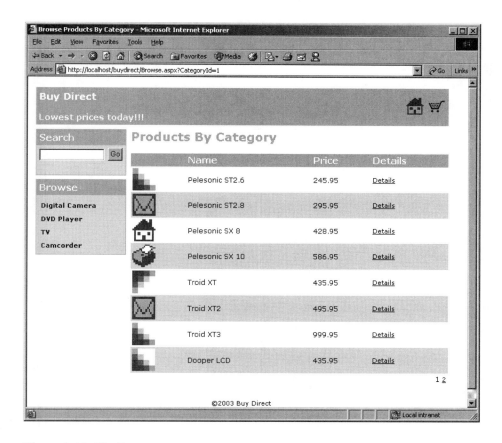

Figure 6-20. The Browse page

The ProductDetails Page

The ProductDetails page displays the details of a product (see Figure 6-21).

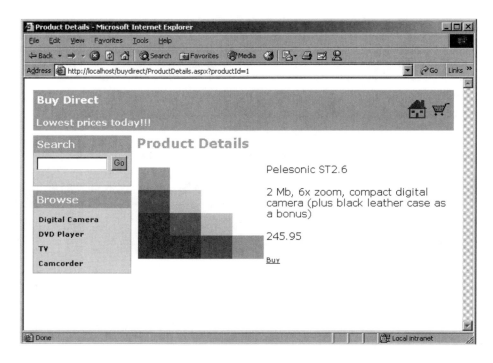

Figure 6-21. The ProductDetails page

This page is invoked from either the Search page or the Browse page. Each call to this page should carry the identifier of the product whose details are to be displayed. This is the Page_Load event handler of the ProductDetails page:

```
productId = Request.Params("productId")
  If productId Is Nothing Then
    Response.Redirect("Default.aspx")
  Else
    DisplayDetails()
    addToCart.NavigateUrl = "AddToCart.aspx?ProductID=" & productId
  End If
```

It first checks if there is a product identifier. If a product identifier is not found, the user is redirected to the Default page. If a product identifier is found, the Page_Load event handler calls the DisplayDetails method and populates the addToCart hyperlink's NavigateUrl property with the following:

```
AddToCart.aspx?ProductId=productId
```

This is the `DisplayDetails` method:

```
Sub DisplayDetails()
  Dim dbo As DbObject = DbObject.GetDbObject()
  Dim item As ShoppingItem = dbo.GetShoppingItem(productId)
  productImage.ImageUrl = "images/" & productId & ".gif"
  name.Text = item.name
  description.Text = item.description
  price.Text = item.price
End Sub
```

The `DisplayDetails` method obtains an instance of a `DbObject` object and calls its `GetShoppingItem` method. From the `ShoppingItem` object it received, the `DisplayDetails` method populates the properties of these controls: `productImage`, `name`, `description`, `price`.

The AddToCart Page

From the ProductDetails page, the user can add a product into the shopping cart by calling the AddToCart page. This page does not have a user interface, and upon performing its task redirects the user to the ShoppingCart page.

In a nutshell, the AddToCart page has one event handler, `Page_Load`:

```
Sub Page_Load(ByVal sender As Object, ByVal e As EventArgs)
  Dim productId As String = Request.Params("productId")
  If productId Is Nothing Then
    Server.Transfer("Default.aspx")
  Else
    Dim dbo As DbObject = DbObject.GetDbObject()
    Dim shoppingItem As ShoppingItem = dbo.GetShoppingItem(productId)
    Dim cart As Hashtable = CType(Session("cart"), Hashtable)
    If cart Is Nothing Then
      cart = new Hashtable()
    End If
    ' Before adding an item, check if the key (productId) exists
    Dim obj As Object = cart.Item(productId)
    If Not obj Is Nothing Then
      cart.Remove(productId)
    End If
    cart.Add(productId, shoppingItem)
    Session.Add("cart", cart)
    Server.Transfer("ShoppingCart.aspx")
  End If
End Sub
```

The `Page_Load` event handler transfers the user to the Default page if no product identifier is found in the `Request` object. If a product identifier is found, it does the following:

1. It gets an instance of the `DbObject` object and calls its `GetShoppingItem`. This method returns a `ShoppingItem` object.

2. It attempts to obtain a `Hashtable` object identified with the key "cart" from the `Session` object. If `Nothing` is returned, it creates a new `Hashtable` object and assigns it to the `cart` variable.

3. It removes the `ShoppingItem` object identified with the same product identifier from the cart, if one exists.

4. It adds the `ShoppingItem` object to the cart. This `ShoppingItem` object is linked to the product identifier.

5. It inserts the cart to the `Session` object.

6. It transfers the user to the ShoppingCart page.

The ShoppingCart Page

The user can view the ShoppingCart page after adding an item into the shopping cart or by clicking the cart logo on the header of every page (see Figure 6-22). Either way, the ShoppingCart page will be displayed.

Let's start the discussion of this page by examining the `DataGrid` control in the user interface. Of particular interest are the four following events in the control:

```
OnEditCommand="MyDataGrid_Edit"
OnCancelCommand="MyDataGrid_Cancel"
OnUpdateCommand="MyDataGrid_Update"
OnDeleteCommand="MyDataGrid_Delete"
```

These events trigger when an item in the `DataGrid` control is edited (`MyDataGrid_Edit`), when the change is updated (`MyDataGrid_Update`) or cancelled (`MyDataGrid_Cancel`), or when a row is deleted (`MyDataGrid_Delete`).

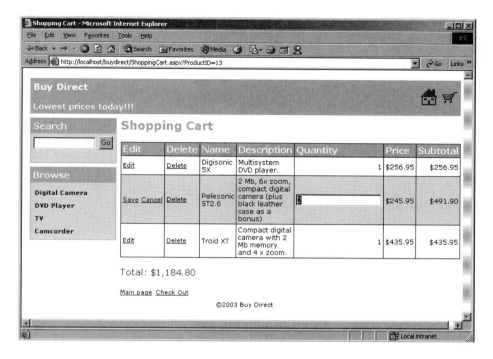

Figure 6-22. The ShoppingCart page

The construction of the columns in the `DataGrid` is not automatic; you construct the columns by declaring each individual column as follows:

```
<Columns>
  <asp:EditCommandColumn
    EditText="Edit"
    CancelText="Cancel"
    UpdateText="Save"
    HeaderText="Edit">
    <ItemStyle Wrap="false"/>
    <HeaderStyle Wrap="false"/>
  </asp:EditCommandColumn>

  <asp:ButtonColumn
    HeaderText="Delete"
    ButtonType="LinkButton"
    Text="Delete"
    CommandName="Delete"
  />
  <asp:BoundColumn HeaderText="Name"
```

```
        ReadOnly="True"
        DataField="Name"/>
      <asp:BoundColumn HeaderText="Description"
        ReadOnly="True"
        DataField="Description"/>

      <asp:BoundColumn HeaderText="Quantity"
        DataField="Quantity">
        <ItemStyle HorizontalAlign="Right"/>
      </asp:BoundColumn>

      <asp:BoundColumn HeaderText="Price"
        ReadOnly="True"
        DataField="Price">
        <ItemStyle HorizontalAlign="Right"/>
      </asp:BoundColumn>

      <asp:BoundColumn HeaderText="Subtotal"
        ReadOnly="True"
        DataField="Subtotal">
        <ItemStyle HorizontalAlign="Right"/>
      </asp:BoundColumn>

      <asp:BoundColumn HeaderText="ProductId"
        ReadOnly="True"
        Visible="False"
        DataField="ProductId"/>

    </Columns>
```

Now, let's move on to the code in the `ShoppingCart.aspx.vb` file.

For starters, you define and instantiate a `DataTable` and a `DataView` object. The `DataTable` object stores all the shopping items from the shopping cart, and the `DataView` object is a view to the data:

```
Public dataTable As New DataTable
Public cartView As DataView
```

Now, look at the `Page_Load` event handler:

```
Sub Page_Load(sender As Object, e As EventArgs)
  If Not Session("cart") Is Nothing Then
    Dim cart As Hashtable = CType(Session("cart"), Hashtable)
```

```
        dataTable.Columns.Add( _
          New DataColumn("Name", GetType(String)))
        dataTable.Columns.Add( _
          New DataColumn("Description", GetType(String)))
        dataTable.Columns.Add( _
          New DataColumn("Quantity", GetType(String)))
        dataTable.Columns.Add( _
          New DataColumn("Price", GetType(String)))
        dataTable.Columns.Add( _
          New DataColumn("Subtotal", GetType(String)))
        dataTable.Columns.Add( _
          New DataColumn("ProductId", GetType(String)))


        ' Make some rows and put some sample data in
        Dim enumerator As IEnumerator = cart.GetEnumerator()
        While (enumerator.MoveNext())

          'enumerator.Current returns a DictionaryEntry object, so use
          'its Value property to obtain the ShoppingItem
          Dim shoppingItem As ShoppingItem = _
            CType(enumerator.Current.Value, ShoppingItem)
          Dim dr As DataRow = CreateNewDataRow(shoppingItem)
          dataTable.Rows.Add(dr)

        End While

      CartView = New DataView(dataTable)
      CartView.Sort = "Name"
      If Not IsPostBack Then
        BindGrid()
      End If
    End If
    UpdateTotal()
End Sub 'Page_Load
```

The first thing the Page_Load event handler does is retrieve the shopping cart from the Session object and add six columns to the DataTable object:

```
Dim cart As Hashtable = CType(Session("cart"), Hashtable)

dataTable.Columns.Add( _
  New DataColumn("Name", GetType(String)))
```

```
dataTable.Columns.Add( _
  New DataColumn("Description", GetType(String)))
dataTable.Columns.Add( _
  New DataColumn("Quantity", GetType(String)))
dataTable.Columns.Add( _
  New DataColumn("Price", GetType(String)))
dataTable.Columns.Add( _
  New DataColumn("Subtotal", GetType(String)))
dataTable.Columns.Add( _
  New DataColumn("ProductId", GetType(String)))
```

And then, the Page_Load event handler iterates the shopping items in the shopping cart Hashtable object and populates the data table with its content inside a While loop:

```
' Make some rows and put some sample data in
Dim enumerator As IEnumerator = cart.GetEnumerator()
While (enumerator.MoveNext())
  'enumerator.Current returns a DictionaryEntry object, so use
  'its Value property to obtain the ShoppingItem
  Dim shoppingItem As ShoppingItem = _
    CType(enumerator.Current.Value, ShoppingItem)
  Dim dr As DataRow = CreateNewDataRow(shoppingItem)
  dataTable.Rows.Add(dr)
End While
```

Afterward, it instantiates a DataView object, passing the data table as the argument:

```
CartView = New DataView(dataTable)
```

The DataView is a view to the shopping cart. The records are sorted by the name of the product:

```
CartView.Sort = "Name"
```

For the first call to the ShoppingCart page, the Page_Load event handler calls the BindGrid method (you will examine the BindGrid method shortly):

```
If Not IsPostBack Then
  BindGrid()
End If
```

Finally, it calls the UpdateTotal method that in turn calls the GetTotal function and displays it in the totalLabel Label control:

```
Sub UpdateTotal()
  totalLabel.Text = "Total: " & GetTotal().ToString("C")
End Sub
```

The GetTotal function itself returns a Decimal as a result of the total of the purchase in the shopping cart. It does so by iterating the shopping cart Hashtable object obtained from the Session object and keeps adding the Price field of each ShoppingItem object.

The BindGrid method is simple enough, consisting only of two lines of code. It assigns the DataView object to the DataSource property of the DataGrid control and calls its DataBind method:

```
MyDataGrid.DataSource = CartView
MyDataGrid.DataBind()
```

The four event handlers are more complex than the DataBind method. The MyDataGrid_Edit is the simplest, consisting of two lines of code:

```
Sub MyDataGrid_Edit(sender As Object,  e As DataGridCommandEventArgs)
  MyDataGrid.EditItemIndex = e.Item.ItemIndex
  BindGrid()
End Sub 'MyDataGrid_Edit
```

This event handler receives a DataGridCommandEventArgs as the second argument from which the index of the edited item can be retrieved and set to the EditItemIndex property of the DataGrid control. As a result, the edited item is displayed in a different color.

An edited item can either be cancelled or updated. If it is cancelled, the MyDataGrid_Cancel event handler is invoked. If it is updated, the MyDataGrid_Update event handler is called.

The MyDataGrid_Cancel event handler sets the EditItemIndex property of the DataGrid control to −1, effectively unselecting the previously edited item:

```
Sub MyDataGrid_Cancel(sender As Object, _
  e As DataGridCommandEventArgs)
  MyDataGrid.EditItemIndex = - 1
  BindGrid()
End Sub 'MyDataGrid_Cancel
```

The `MyDataGrid_Update` event handler is more complex than the previous two. First, it retrieves the corresponding `ShoppingItem` object from the `Session` object whose key matches the product identifier of the item being updated and updates the quantity of the shopping item:

```
shoppingItem = CType(cart.Item(productId), ShoppingItem)
If Not shoppingItem Is Nothing Then
  shoppingItem.Quantity = quantity
End If
```

Then, it updates the `DataTable` object by removing an old row and adds a new one:

```
' Now update the DataTable
' We'll delete the old row and replace it with a new one.
If Not shoppingItem Is Nothing Then
  ' Remove old entry.
  CartView.RowFilter = "ProductId='" & _
    shoppingItem.ProductId & "'"
  If CartView.Count > 0 Then
    CartView.Delete(0)
  End If
  CartView.RowFilter = ""

  ' Add new entry.
  Dim dr As DataRow = CreateNewDataRow(shoppingItem)
  dataTable.Rows.Add(dr)
End If
```

Note that you create a new row by calling the `CreateNewDataRow` method, passing the shopping item. The `CreateNewDataRow` method creates a new `DataRow` object by calling the `NewRow` method of the `DataTable` class and populates its column with the field values of the shopping item:

```
Function CreateNewDataRow(ByVal ShoppingItem As ShoppingItem) As DataRow
  Dim dr As DataRow = dataTable.NewRow()
  dr(0) = shoppingItem.Name
  dr(1) = shoppingItem.Description
  dr(2) = shoppingItem.Quantity
  dr(3) = CDec(shoppingItem.Price).ToString("C")
```

```
  'Calculating subtotal
  dim subtotal As Decimal
  Try
    subtotal = CInt(shoppingItem.quantity) * _
      CDec(shoppingItem.price)
  Catch ex As InvalidCastException
    ' do nothing, but subtotal will be 0
  End Try
  dr(4) = subtotal.ToString("C")
  dr(5) = shoppingItem.ProductId
  Return dr
End Function
```

The last event handler, MyDataGrid_Delete, removes the deleted item from the DataTable object as well as from the shopping cart object:

```
Sub MyDataGrid_Delete(sender As Object, _
  e As DataGridCommandEventArgs)
  Dim productId As String = e.Item.Cells(7).Text
  ' Update the shopping item in the Session object
  Dim cart As Hashtable = CType(Session("cart"), Hashtable)

  If Not cart Is Nothing Then
    cart.Remove(productId)
  End If
  ' Now delete the row from DataTable
  CartView.RowFilter = "ProductId='" & productId & "'"
  If CartView.Count > 0 Then
    CartView.Delete(0)
  End If
  CartView.RowFilter = ""
  MyDataGrid.EditItemIndex = - 1
  BindGrid()
  UpdateTotal()
End Sub 'MyDataGrid_Delete
```

The CheckOut Page

When shopping is completed, the user can check out using the CheckOut page (see Figure 6-23).

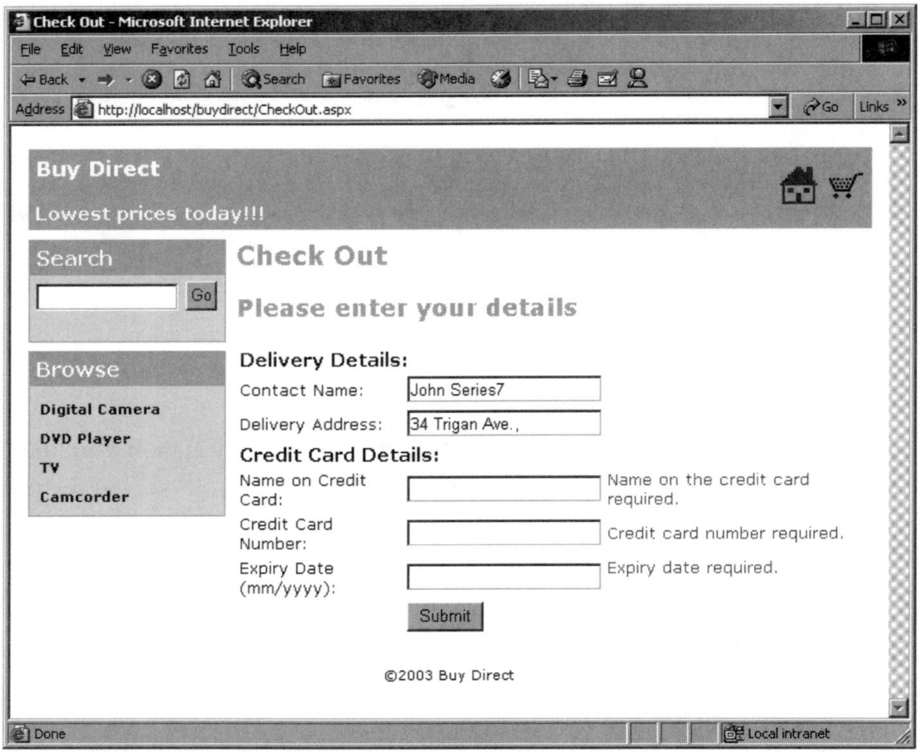

Figure 6-23. The CheckOut page

This page contains a form that accepts the user details (contact name and delivery address) and credit card details (name on the credit card, credit card number, and expiry date). Each entry box is a TextBox control that is "watched" by a validator. The validators make sure that all TextBox controls are filled in and the input is valid. The Button control in the form is wired to the following ProcessPurchase event handler, which is invoked when the user submits the form:

```
Sub ProcessPurchase(sender As Object, e As EventArgs)
  'Check input
  If contactNameValidator.IsValid() AndAlso _
    deliveryAddressValidator.IsValid() AndAlso _
    ccNameValidator.IsValid() AndAlso _
    ccNumberValidator.IsValid() AndAlso _
    ccExpiryDateValidator1.IsValid() AndAlso _
    ccExpiryDateValidator2.IsValid() Then
```

```
    myTable.Visible = False
    ' process purchase
    header2.Text = ""
    If ProcessPurchase() Then
      ' Empty shopping cart
      Session("cart") = Nothing
      header1.Text = "Transaction completed successfully."
    Else
      header1.Text = "Transaction failed."
    End If
  End If
End Sub
```

The `ProcessPurchase` event handler first checks the validity of each `TextBox` control, and if all are OK, it calls the `ProcessPurchase` function that does the processing. The latter returns `True` if the processing is successful, and `False` otherwise. The event handler then prints a message notifying the user of the purchase process result.

The `ProcessPurchase` function is as follows:

```
Public Function ProcessPurchase As Boolean
  Dim dbo As DbObject = DbObject.GetDbObject()
  Return dbo.ProcessPurchase(contactName.Text, _
    deliveryAddress.Text, _
    ccName.Text, _
    ccNumber.Text, _
    ccExpiryDate.Text, _
    CType(Session("cart"), Hashtable))

End Function
```

The function creates an instance of the `DbObject` class and calls its `ProcessPurchase` method.

The Admin Section

The Admin section comprises the second part of the BuyDirect application. This part is only accessible to authorized users, and it administers the Categories and Products tables. However, based on the example in the following sections, it is easy to extend the application to cover other administration tasks. The following sections discuss the four pages in the Admin section.

You can access the Admin section using the following link:

```
http://domain/buydirect/admin/Admin.aspx
```

The user will then be redirected to the Login page. Upon a successful login, the user will be brought to the main menu, from which they can choose one of the two links. The first link brings the user to the EditCategory page, and the second to the EditProduct page.

The Login Page

Only authorized users registered in the Users table can access the Admin section. Therefore, the first page of this part is a Login form. Upon successful login, the user will be presented with two hyperlinks: one to the EditCategory page and the other to the EditProduct page. Figure 6-24 shows the Login page.

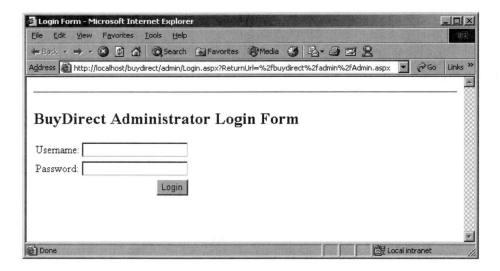

Figure 6-24. The Admin Login page

The Login page's user interface has a form with two TextBox controls, userName and password, and a Button control whose Click event is wired to the Login event handler. The earlier section "Securing ASP.NET Applications" explains how this Login event handler works.

The Main Menu Page

Upon a successful login, the user is redirected to the main menu (the `Admin.aspx` file), as shown in Figure 6-25.

Figure 6-25. The Admin main menu page

The EditCategory Page

The EditCategory page allows you to manipulate the data in the Categories table. The form in this page has a `TextBox` control and a `Button` control to add a new category and a `DataGrid` control that displays all the categories and edits and deletes existing categories.

The `Button` control's `Click` event is wired with the `AddCategory` event handler:

```
Sub AddCategory(source As Object, e As EventArgs)
  Dim newCat As String = newCategory.Text.Trim()
  If Not newCat.Equals("") Then

    Dim dbo As DbObject = DbObject.GetDbObject()
    dbo.InsertCategory(newCat)

    newCategory.Text = ""
    PopulateDataSet()
    BindGrid()
  End If
```

The `AddCategory` event handler creates an instance of the `DbObject` class and calls its `InsertCategory` method, passing the new category supplied by the user. It then assigns a blank string to the `newCategory` TextBox control and calls the `PopulateDataSet` and `BindGrid` methods.

The `PopulateDataSet` method consists of four lines of code:

```
Sub PopulateDataSet()
  Dim dbo As DbObject = DbObject.GetDbObject()
  Dim ds As DataSet = dbo.GetCategories()
  dataTable = ds.Tables("Categories")
  dataView = New DataView(dataTable)
End Sub
```

It instantiates the `DbObject` class and calls its `GetCategories` method to obtain all the records in the Categories table. The `DataSet` returned by the `GetCategories` method, `ds`, creates a `DataTable` object that then can be used to construct a `DataView` object. This `DataView` object is assigned to the `DataSource` property of the `DataGrid` in the `BindGrid` method:

```
Sub BindGrid()
  MyDataGrid.DataSource = dataView
  MyDataGrid.DataBind()
End Sub 'BindGrid
```

The event handlers that handle the events of the `DataGrid` control work similarly to the `DataGrid`'s event handlers discussed in the ShoppingCart page. You should refer to "The ShoppingCart Page" section if you find difficulty in understanding how they work.

Figure 6-26 shows the EditCategory page.

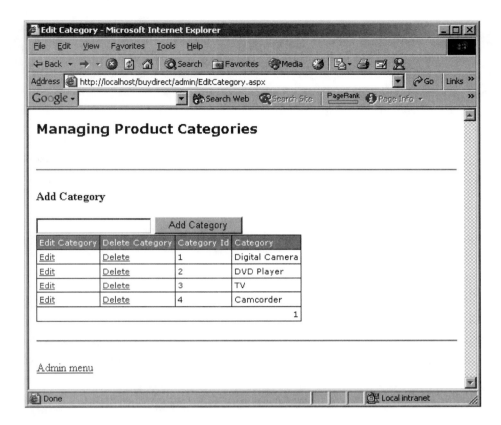

Figure 6-26. The EditCategory page

The EditProduct Page

The EditProduct page allows the user to administer the Products table by adding a new product, editing a product, and deleting an existing product. The way it works is similar to the EditCategory page. There are two forms in the EditProduct page. The first form adds a product and is handled by the Page_Load event handler. The second form contains a DataGrid that displays all the available products and lets the user edit and delete an existing product.

Figure 6-27 shows the EditProduct page.

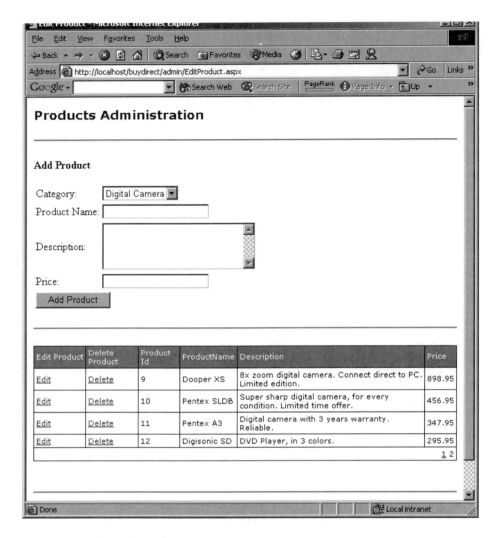

Figure 6-27. The EditProduct page

Summary

In this chapter you learned about how to work with data in the .NET Framework using ADO.NET and data binding. You also learned about application configuration and how to secure ASP.NET applications. You have used that knowledge to develop a fully functional online store called BuyDirect. This application has two parts. The first part is for users to search and browse products and purchase. The second part is the administration section for managing the categories and products.

Index

Numbers and Symbols

" (quotation marks) in XML documents, meaning of, 101–102

$ (dollar sign) in Doggie computer game, meaning of, 214

% (percent) sign used with MoveCat method, meaning of, 249

& (ampersand), using with entities in DTDs, 107

' (single quotes) in XML documents, meaning of, 101

(i), (ii), (iii), and (iv), 305–306

* (asterisk)
  in Doggie computer game, 213
  as operator for child elements in XML documents, 105
  using with users attribute, 541

+ (plus sign)
  as operator for child elements in XML documents, 105
  using with @ Application directive in Global.asax file, 516
  using with public external DTDs, 106

, (comma) operator, using with child elements in XML documents, 105

- (hyphen), using as menu separator, 126

– (minus sign), using with public external DTDs, 106

// (double forward slashes), using with FPIs, 106

; (semicolon) using with entities in DTDs, 107

<!-- and --> symbols in XML documents, meaning of, 100

< ... > notation in XML, meaning of, 96

</ and > in XML documents, meaning of, 101

< and > in XML documents, meaning of, 101

<!ELEMENT> XML tag, meaning of, 103–104

? (question mark)
  as operator for child elements in XML documents, 105
  using with users attribute, 541

[] (brackets), meaning of, 215

\ (backslash), meaning of, 225

| (pipe) operator, using with child elements in XML documents, 105

0 default value in SQL Server connection strings, description of, 442

0–5 values in second-digit FTP replies, explanations of, 344

1–5 values in first-digit FTP replies, explanations of, 344

2D vector graphics service in GDI+, explanation of, 256

15 default value in SQL Server connection strings, description of, 442

32-bit color, specifying, 260

100 default value in SQL Server connection strings, description of, 443

110-553 values in third-digit FTP replies, explanations of, 345–346

180-degree turns in Doggie computer game
  explanation of, 231, 237
  implementing, 247

226 FTP reply code, example of, 362, 365, 386

230 FTP reply code, example of, 371

8192 default value in SQL Server connection strings, description of, 443

A

ABOR FTP command, description of, 342

Aborted member of System.Threading.ThreadState enumeration, description of, 191

AbortRequested member of System.Threading.ThreadState enumeration, description of, 191

abstract coupling, introducing to subjects, 15

AcceptChanges method
  of DataRow class, 461
  of DataSet class, explanation of, 457
  of DataTable class, 459

ACCT FTP command, description of, 340

ACLs (access control lists), viewing, 540

F

T

About Apress

Apress, located in Berkeley, CA, is a fast-growing, innovative publishing company devoted to meeting the needs of existing and potential programming professionals. Simply put, the "A" in Apress stands for *The Author's Press™*. Apress' unique approach to publishing grew out of conversations between its founders, Gary Cornell and Dan Appleman, authors of numerous best-selling, highly regarded books for programming professionals. In 1998 they set out to create a publishing company that emphasized quality above all else. Gary and Dan's vision has resulted in the publication of over 70 titles by leading software professionals, all of which have *The Expert's Voice™*.

Do You Have What It Takes to Write for Apress?

Apress is rapidly expanding its publishing program. If you can write and you refuse to compromise on the quality of your work, if you believe in doing more than rehashing existing documentation, and if you're looking for opportunities and rewards that go far beyond those offered by traditional publishing houses, we want to hear from you!

Consider these innovations that we offer all of our authors:

- **Top royalties with *no* hidden switch statements**
  Authors typically receive only half of their normal royalty rate on foreign sales. In contrast, Apress' royalty rate remains the same for both foreign and domestic sales.

- **Sharing the wealth**
  Most publishers keep authors on the same pay scale even after costs have been met. At Apress author royalties dramatically increase the more books are sold.

- **Serious treatment of the technical review process**
  Each Apress book is reviewed by a technical expert(s) whose remuneration depends in part on the success of the book since he or she too receives royalties.

Moreover, through a partnership with Springer-Verlag, New York, Inc., one of the world's major publishing houses, Apress has significant venture capital and distribution power behind it. Thus, we have the resources to produce the highest quality books *and* market them aggressively.

If you fit the model of the Apress author who can write a book that provides *What The Professional Needs To Know™*, then please contact us for more information:

editorial@apress.com